# Race on Screen

What did audiences want when it came to 'race' on screen in twentieth-century Britain? This was the question that drove producers and makers of film and television as they competed for viewers, and organisations such as the BBC and ITV developed a new field of 'audience research' to address it. Christine Grandy examines how film and television producers, censors and researchers sought to locate audience preferences when it came to presentations of 'race'. Through empire films, home movies and television classics such as *Love Thy Neighbour* and *The Cosby Show*, this study explores what was at stake for white British audiences as they consumed material featuring problematic and positive presentations of Black and south Asian people. *Race on Screen* further uncovers the efforts of Black and south Asian audiences to draw attention to their own roles as overlooked audiences and to name film and television content as racist.

Christine Grandy is Associate Professor of Modern British History at the University of Lincoln. Her work examines the social and cultural history of Britain and its media in the twentieth and twenty-first centuries. She is the author of *Heroes and Happy Endings: Class, Gender, and Nation in Popular Film and Fiction in Interwar Britain* (2014).

# Race on Screen
*Audience Racism in Twentieth-Century Britain*

Christine Grandy
*University of Lincoln*

Shaftesbury Road, Cambridge CB2 8EA, United Kingdom

One Liberty Plaza, 20th Floor, New York, NY 10006, USA

477 Williamstown Road, Port Melbourne, VIC 3207, Australia

314–321, 3rd Floor, Plot 3, Splendor Forum, Jasola District Centre, New Delhi – 110025, India

103 Penang Road, #05–06/07, Visioncrest Commercial, Singapore 238467

Cambridge University Press is part of Cambridge University Press & Assessment, a department of the University of Cambridge.

We share the University's mission to contribute to society through the pursuit of education, learning and research at the highest international levels of excellence.

www.cambridge.org
Information on this title: www.cambridge.org/9781009650960

DOI: 10.1017/9781009650953

© Christine Grandy 2026

This publication is in copyright. Subject to statutory exception and to the provisions of relevant collective licensing agreements, no reproduction of any part may take place without the written permission of Cambridge University Press & Assessment.

When citing this work, please include a reference to the
DOI 10.1017/9781009650953

First published 2026
Cover image: A section of the audience at the opening night of the Granada Cinema, Slough, 1938. (Photo by London Express/Getty Images)

*A catalogue record for this publication is available from the British Library*

*A Cataloging-in-Publication data record for this book is available from the Library of Congress*

ISBN 978-1-009-65096-0 Hardback
ISBN 978-1-009-65093-9 Paperback

Cambridge University Press & Assessment has no responsibility for the persistence or accuracy of URLs for external or third-party internet websites referred to in this publication and does not guarantee that any content on such websites is, or will remain, accurate or appropriate.

For EU product safety concerns, contact us at Calle de José Abascal, 56, 1°, 28003 Madrid, Spain, or email eugpsr@cambridge.org

For Adam

# Contents

Acknowledgements     *page* ix

Introduction: The Historian, Critical Race Theory and
Audience Racism in Twentieth-Century Britain     1
I.1   Not Seeing Racism: Critical Race Theory and Histories of Not Knowing     8
I.2   Film, Television and the Racially Innocent Audience     17
I.3   Archives of Not Knowing     23

1   Discovering the Audience: Anxieties and Expertise     30
    1.1   The Anxieties of Screen Culture     36
    1.2   The Rise of Audience Experts     44
    1.3   Not Knowing Black and South Asian Audiences     60

2   Audience Wants: Film and the Pleasures of Racism,
    1900–1945     63
    2.1   The Pleasures of Racism: Empire Films in the Early Twentieth Century     69
    2.2   Documentary and Amateur Film: The Imagined 'Curiosity' of
          White Audiences     78
    2.3   Counter Story-telling: Audiences of Colour and Empire Films     84
    2.4   Wartime Understandings     88

3   'Expressing Their Own Point of View': Television Audience
    Research on 'Race' at the BBC, 1950–1968     95
    3.1   *Race Relations in Africa* (1952)     101
    3.2   Audience Responses to *Rainbow City* and *Till Death Us Do Part*     114

4   'A Traditional Form of Entertainment': Colour-blind
    Audiences and Blacking Up on Post-war Screens     128
    4.1   Family Viewing on the Big and Small Screens     136
    4.2   The Campaign Against Racial Discrimination (CARD) and *The Black
          and White Minstrel Show*     142
    4.3   Rangi Ram and 'The Black and White Minstrels from Jockey Mead'     154
    4.4   The End of *The Black and White Minstrel Show*     157

5   'Too Touchy': Black Audiences and the Racialised
    Everyday in the Post-war Black 'Glossies'     164
    5.1   Voices of Colour and Black Agency     167
    5.2   A 'Short-lived Fate': Black Glossies and Post-war Publishing     171

|     |     |                                                                                 |     |
| --- | --- | ------------------------------------------------------------------------------- | --- |
|     | 5.3 | 'Anti-White': Navigating White Readers                                          | 176 |
|     | 5.4 | Racialised Emotions                                                             | 184 |
|     | 5.5 | Knowing Black Success                                                           | 188 |
| 6   | \multicolumn{2}{l}{'A Sneaking Feeling': Institutional Silences, Racism and Audience Research at the BBC and ITV in the 1970s} | 194 |
|     | 6.1 | Growing Evidence: Audience Research on Racial Prejudice 1970–1978               | 199 |
|     | 6.2 | Audiences of Colour in the BBC's and IBA's Audience Research                    | 211 |
| 7   | \multicolumn{2}{l}{'Black Magic': Racially Comfortable Viewing on British Television in the 1980s and 1990s} | 229 |
|     | 7.1 | Viewing in Comfort: *The Cosby Show* and Colour-blindness in 1980s Britain       | 237 |
|     | 7.2 | *Desmond's*                                                                     | 248 |
|     | 7.3 | *The Fresh Prince of Bel-Air*                                                   | 254 |

Conclusion: 'Of the Time' — 261

*Bibliography* — 274
*Index* — 287

# Acknowledgements

This book is marked by much living and caring, and as a result my list of debts and acknowledgments is long. My thanks first to the British Academy, which supported this project twice; first through a British Academy/Leverhulme Small Research Grant that allowed me to visit the archives drawn upon for this book, and second through the considerable gift of time that is a British Academy Mid-Career Fellowship. Both grants were foundational. Time is such a valuable thing in research and almost endlessly eroded in the current landscape of higher education, and I am grateful to have received it. My thanks also to the unfailingly helpful staff at the various archives I've drawn on.

My former colleagues at Nipissing University and particularly the late Anne Clendinning, as well as Erin Dokis, made vital contributions to my early thinking. At the University of Lincoln, colleagues in the School of Humanities & Heritage have heard rather too much about this project. I want to thank Ian Packer, Chris O'Rourke, Helen Smith, James Greenhalgh, Sarah Longair, Adam Page, Jon Coburn, Ed Owens, Kristy Warren, Tom Bishop, Kate Hill, Amy Culley, Antonella Luizzo Scorpo and Krista Cowman, among others. My thanks to Kristine Alexander, Catherine Ellis and Jessica Clark for ongoing transatlantic camaraderie and intellectual engagement.

This work has been trotted out in various forms over the years as conference papers, drafts, conversations and musings with numerous historians and media scholars, and I am at pains to acknowledge them all. Thanks to Mark Abraham, Gavin Schaffer, Darrell Newton, Peter Mandler, Lucy Delap, Jodi Burkett, James Vernon, Kennetta Hammond Perry, Kieran Connell, Rob Waters, Chris Jeppesen, Marcus Collins and Karen Lury, as well as Matt Houlbrook, Elizabeth Darling and Richard Hornsey. Participants in the Cambridge Cultural History Seminar, the Utrecht Cultural History Series, the York University History Seminar, the 20s/30s network and the Citizen, Race, and Belonging network at the University of Portsmouth all offered kind feedback on different chapters. Stephen Brooke continues to provide both the gift of his own work and his unflagging support of my own, and I'm very happy to continue to acknowledge this. Peter Mandler in particular offered excellent support in the publication of this work, and Liz Friend-Smith and Sari Wastell have been lovely to work with at Cambridge University Press. My thanks to the anonymous reviewers who gave such supportive, constructive and generous feedback.

To friends in Nova Scotia, Ontario and Lincoln, my love and thanks, particularly to Miche and Beth. The support of my family in England, Mal and Joyce Houlbrook as well as Matt, Sarah, Frankie and Kitt, and their willingness to share some of their experiences of British television have been grounding and welcome. Madge was with me for almost all of this. My dad, Ron Grandy, shared this work with me in more ways than we anticipated when he was diagnosed with bone cancer in 2018 during my BA Mid-Career Fellowship. I was able to spend time in Nova Scotia with him while writing and I'm immensely grateful to have had that intense time together. We came out of that with the Grandy humour intact and for some wonderful years, including the birth of an adored grandkid, before my dad's cancer returned in summer 2024. I miss him more than I can say, and he would be so damn proud to see this book out.

To my amazing and rather miraculous daughter Zoe, thank you for continuing to be such a light and wonder. Finally, to my husband Adam Houlbrook, you are the anchor in all I do and a very patient and adept copyeditor. I have very likely not stripped out all 'the unnecessary detail' I should have but your love, support and engagement have improved this in so many ways, large and small. Thank you.

# Introduction
## The Historian, Critical Race Theory and Audience Racism in Twentieth-Century Britain

Stuart Hall, one of Britain's great thinkers in cultural studies, addressed the responses of white people in Britain to discussions of racism and empire through a series of talks he gave in 1978 and within his developing written work. In his 1979 essay on 'Race and "Moral Panics" in Post-war Britain', Hall contemplated 'the tendency to abstract race from the internal dynamic of the society' in Britain among both the 'Liberal left' and the 'Right'.[1] He captured the view common among white people on both sides of the political spectrum, which argued: 'Racism is not endemic to the structures of British social life, it has nothing intrinsically to do with the dynamic of British politics, or with the economic crisis: it is not part of English culture – it does not belong to the English ideology. It is an external virus injected into the body politic.'[2]

Through this lens, racism was something that could be solved through addressing the size or shape of the population of Black people in Britain, by applying policy measures such as controls on immigration. Hall's response to this conceptualisation of racism as external to British life was a long-form essay on Britain's imperial past and a present shaped by concerns about race, in which he ultimately argued of this conceit, 'I hope to persuade you this cannot be true.' For Hall, racism was foundational to British culture, society and state. It was part of the fabric of modern Britain and not easily separated, or faced, as a result.

As a Black viewer of television in Britain, Hall would have been familiar with the BBC's long-standing television hit, *The Black and White Minstrel Show*, which had only ceased to be broadcast in 1978. For 20 years between 1958 to 1978, the tremendously popular song and dance variety show had appeared on the BBC, the nation's central television broadcaster. Every prime-time Saturday evening, viewers

---

[1] Stuart Hall, 'Race and "Moral Panics" in Post-war Britain', in Paul Gilroy and Ruth Wilson Gilmore, eds., *Stuart Hall: Selected Writings on Race and Difference* (Durham, NC: Duke University Press, 2021), 57.
[2] Ibid.

watched the 'Mitchell Minstrels', white men who performed in blackface makeup with white circles painted round their mouths and eyes. They wore matching outfits usually consisting of white trousers, waistcoats, colourful ties and white top hats pulled over woolly black wigs and performed alongside a white female dance troupe, 'The Television Toppers'. The prodigious run of *The Black and White Minstrel Show* throughout these decades made for a remarkable hit for the BBC but it also exists like a steady and unacknowledged tick of a metronome accompanying every major race relations event that occurred from 1958 to 1978. *The Black and White Minstrel Show* came to the screen two weeks before the Notting Hill and Nottingham race riots in the summer of 1958 and had been broadcasting for not quite a year when a young Black man from Antigua, Kelso Cochrane, was stabbed to death by white youths in the same neighbourhood.[3] The show continued every week while the first Commonwealth Immigrants Act was enacted in 1962; the first Race Relations Acts were passed in 1965 and 1968; and when the 1976 Act was also passed. It was on television while the Race Relations Board struggled to appoint members to an organisation that was meant to enforce the first Race Relations Act in 1965.[4] *The Black and White Minstrel Show* was on screen when the 1968 Olympics were broadcast in October, showing Tommie Smith and John Carlos raising their fists in the Black power salute; when Black leaders in Britain were beginning to 'think Black' as Rob Waters has documented; and as Martin Luther King Jr, Malcolm X and Stokely Carmichael visited the country.[5] The show was also on – by then in glaring colour – in British homes when Enoch Powell made his 'Rivers of Blood' speech in April 1968; when the National Front made its first minor gains in politics and throughout the 1970s; and as race relations seemingly worsened in the face of rising white nationalism in the country. As Stuart Hall cemented his own critical work on class, race, politics and media at the University of Birmingham, *The Black and White Minstrel Show* went on and on.

*The Black and White Minstrel Show* was remarkable at the time for its success and longevity; to the historian, it is remarkable because it was so deeply enmeshed in racist imagery and yet was tremendously popular.

---

[3] Kennetta Hammond Perry, *London Is the Place for Me: Black Britons, Citizenship, and the Politics of Race* (Oxford: Oxford University Press, 2015), 126–152.
[4] Simon Peplow, 'The "Linchpin for Success"? The Problematic Establishment of the 1965 Race Relations Act and Its Conciliation Board', *Contemporary British History* 31, no. 3 (2017): 430–451.
[5] Rob Waters, *Thinking Black: Britain, 1964–1985* (Oakland, CA: University of California Press, 2018). King visited the country in 1961, 1964 and 1967. Malcolm X visited in 1964 and 1965, and Carmichael in 1967.

Introduction 3

1.1 Performers from *The Black and White Minstrel Show* in 1969. The programme ran on the BBC from 1958 to 1978.
Source: Fox Photos/Stringer, Hulton Archive. https://www.gettyimages.co.uk/detail/news-photo/dancers-from-the-black-and-white-minstrel-show-news-photo/2660199

Very few people in the third decade of the twenty-first century can see glimpses of the programme and deny that its premise was disturbing. It remains a rather shocking example of what was acceptable when it came to everyday attitudes towards racial imagery on screen. However, protests against the show did occur at the time, and in 1961 the show was criticised by *Flamingo*, a small magazine written by Black authors for predominantly Black readers, who recounted the offence that the show caused to these viewers. Black audiences described their experiences as viewers who chose to turn the telly off while having physical reactions of shame and disgust at the programme's overt racism.[6] However it was not until 1967, when a petition to remove the programme was presented to the BBC, that a discussion would occur in the national press about the

---
[6] 'Bad taste B.B.C.', *Flamingo*, September 1961, 22.

show's practice of blacking up. The petition, put forth by Trinidadian Clive West and supported by the Campaign Against Racial Discrimination (CARD), identified the show as a 'hideous impersonation' that was 'quite offensive and causes much distress to most coloured people'.[7] The white executives behind the show's success, the white performers starring in it, and the white audiences enthusiastically consuming the show, did not share this reaction and instead viewed it as a pleasurable, inoffensive programme featuring cheerful singers and dancers. *The Black and White Minstrel Show* was repeatedly labelled by BBC representatives, the show's stage-producer himself and audiences as a harmless 'tradition' that could not, and certainly should not, be interpreted as offensive. Black viewers, according to white viewers and supporters, were viewing this show incorrectly and seeing racism where it did not exist. Television and theatre critics such as Milton Shulman writing for the *Evening Standard* in 1967 argued that the show was actually doing a service to Black people:

In addition to the undemanding pleasure it gives me, I have always thought *The Black and White Minstrel Show* was one of the few programmes on the air that effectively preached and practised racial tolerance. It is the only programme that regularly shows coloured men – even if only in black make-up – cuddling, cooing, loving, and courting white girls.[8]

By Shulman's estimate, the programme's use of minstrelsy offered a type of vehicle for racial integration while also providing an 'undemanding pleasure' for the white television viewer.

Stuart Hall was already living in the country when the minstrels made their debut. Hall is seldom claimed as a Black audience member: his interest in the cultural formation of the imaginary vaulted academics such as Hall out of the realm of the audience and into an emerging field of 'mass communication', or in Hall's case 'cultural studies'. Yet it was his role as a Black man in the audience watching film and television in both Jamaica where he grew up and in Britain where he moved as a young man that likely prompted his close, consistent examination of what a white media taught British people about Blackness on screen and his eventual supervision of a doctoral student with the British Film Institute on the very subject.[9]

---

[7] Paula James, 'Race Rumpus Over the Black and White Minstrels', *Daily Mirror*, 19 May 1967, 3.

[8] Milton Shulman, 'Inside TV', *Evening Standard*, 24 May 1967, 5.

[9] This student was the now-Professor Sarita Malik, author of *Representing Black Britain: Black and Asian Images on Television* (London: Sage Publications, 2002); see Malik's reflections on her supervisions with Hall for further sense of him as a consumer of television: Sarita Malik, 'Reflections on Representing Black Britain', *Journal of Cultural Economy* (October 2022 online). www.tandfonline.com/doi/full/10.1080/17530350.2022.2138502.

As Hall recounted of his youth, he 'went to cinema religiously on Saturdays' with a group of friends or his Aunt Mavis on Saturday afternoons.[10] Hall's astute sense as a viewer and imbiber of popular culture contributed to his sharp arguments about race and representation in both his written work and then on screen in 1979, in a 25-minute television episode put together by the Campaign Against Racism in Media (CARM) of which Hall was a member.[11] The programme, 'It Ain't Half Racist Mum', a play on the title of the popular BBC series, *It Ain't Half Hot Mum*, then being broadcast on BBC, was broadcast on the BBC's *Open Door* series, which was ostensibly open to public broadcasting but which also saw CARM argue that organisations such as the BBC persistently equated immigrants and Black people with 'problems' in the British news cycle.[12] The master-class of media analysis that Hall and his co-presenter took the audience through showed how the language and presentation of a 'neutral' broadcaster became a powerful means of upholding Black inferiority.

A few years later, in a defence of CARM's approach and the programme, Hall wrote about the audience the organisation and the programme was attempting to reach. He discussed the decision to avoid speaking to the political left and to instead concentrate on those viewers 'struggling over the muddy and confused middle ground: the ground where Powellism, Thatcherism and the National Front have, in recent years, made such remarkable headway'.[13] For Hall, trying to change the minds of this audience was the primary purpose of the programme, even if he seemed ambivalent about the end result, noting that 'CARM's intervention could not be anything but a tiny movement in a long war of position, on the stony ground which television, regularly, delivers to the wrong side'.[14] That stony ground remained so, and the British population's deep amnesia about and avoidance of race remained a central component of the audience. Hall wrote of the act of forgetting of imperial conquest and imperial ties that were central to modern attitudes towards race and immigration in post-war Britain. He argued that the 'racism of the post-war period begins with this profound forgetfulness – the loss of historical memory, the collective

---

[10] Stuart Hall, with Bill Schwarz, *Familiar Stranger: A Life Between Two Islands* (Durham, NC: Duke University Press, 2017), 32, 36.
[11] Gavin Schaffer, *The Vision of a Nation: Making Multiculturalism on British Television, 1960–80* (London: Palgrave Macmillan, 2014): 143–177.
[12] Transcript of 'It Ain't Half Racist Mum', *Representology Journal* 1, Birmingham City Institute of Media and English: www.bcu.ac.uk/media/research/sir-lenny-henry-centre-for-media-diversity/representology-journal/articles/it-aint-half-racist-mum-transcript.
[13] Stuart Hall, 'The Whites of Their Eyes', in *Stuart Hall: Selected Writings on Race and Difference*, 116.
[14] Ibid., 117.

amnesia, the ideological repression – which has overtaken the British people since the "end of Empire" in the 1950s'.[15] This ideological repression, and that collective amnesia, is something that this book will extend to the end of the twentieth century, to investigate just how stony that ground was, and just how tiny but important a moment CARM's intervention was in 1979, the year after *The Black and White Minstrel Show* went off the air.

This is a book that is about a history of not knowing racism in twentieth-century Britain and the relationship of this not knowing to film and television content, their audiences, and how audience wants were envisioned in the period. It is about a concerted effort in the twentieth century by the vast majority of white Britons, both ordinary and extraordinary, to turn away from knowledge about racism's existence in the country and its impact upon racialised people, in an effort to maintain a racial comfort for white viewers that, in turn, allowed everyday racist imagery to flourish within television and film. This research centres on the ordinary, everyday racism that was denied by the white British public and the British media and yet was evident in both as 'what the audience wanted' was considered and provided by television and film producers, script-writers, and the nascent field of audience research. It examines racial formation in twentieth-century Britain, not through attention to the political and social spheres that have preoccupied Marc Matera and others, but through the often-overlooked constitution of British screen culture for white British audiences.[16] It posits that a look at the central television and film organs of the nation can tell us something vital about what ordinary people knew, and also wanted to know, about 'race' in the period. The remarkable 20-year run of *The Black and White Minstrel Show* on British screens, an enduring example of giving the audience what it wanted, offers an entrance to examine this overlooked story of twentieth-century British history and the considerable effort to not see racism in the country. The defences of *The Black and White Minstrel Show* by BBC and ITV executives, white British audiences, the press and television critics, censors and screen regulators, as 'not about race' but also obviously all about race marked both a consensus of effort and a pattern of evading knowledge of racism that became an enduring feature of British national identity in this period. This selective and sought ignorance about racism was sheltered in the spheres of pleasure offered to audiences by the big and small screen and informed the content and production of both in profound ways.

---

[15] Hall, 'Race and "Moral Panics" in Post-war Britain', 58–59.
[16] Marc Matera, Radkhika Natarajan, Kennetta Hammond Perry et al., 'Introduction: Marking Race in Twentieth Century British History', *Twentieth Century British History* 34, no. 3 (2023): 407–414.

To not know racism's broad contours and impact in the great age of immigration and at the end of the British empire did in fact take some work by white audiences and producers of screen culture. While historians such as Michel-Rolph Trouillot and Ibram X. Kendi have convincingly shown the inability of white enlightenment thinkers to conceive of or see Black achievement or Black emancipation in the eighteenth century, twentieth-century Britain was not such a place.[17] Knowledge about a broader spectrum of racism that went beyond the racial violence in the US was increasingly available in a century that was ever mediatising, even if that knowledge was highly contested. Erik Linstrum's work on colonial violence at the end of empire has argued effectively that that knowledge in Britain of this violence was 'never altogether absent' and existed in diverse sources such as newspaper reporting, radio broadcasts and regimental magazines.[18] Racist ideologies and actions were broadcast on the news as existing in the establishment of apartheid in South Africa; it was spoken of by Black American leaders quoted in the press and on television; it was dramatised in televised BBC plays and American films starring Sidney Poitier and a handful of other Black actors; and it was evident in the discussions of Black and Asian leaders with other white thinkers, as Priyamvada Gopal has shown.[19] Racialised immigrants themselves, as they arrived and settled across the UK, repeatedly prompted a discussion of racism's range – its contours, its sharp edges, its mild faces and blunt words, its hardening eyes through the passage of three race relations acts from 1965 to 1976. Whether it was a thing to be acknowledged, denied or rationalised, the information was uneasily out there in the world that Black men and women experienced different treatment than white people. To maintain racial ignorance in the twentieth century took some effort.

This book grapples with firstly, the imagining of audience preferences by producers and regulators of screen culture when it came to presentations of 'race' on the big and small screens and secondly, the work that film, television and the developing field of 'audience research' did in sheltering, nurturing, measuring and even creating that inability to see or know racism. The contours of that consensus around racial ignorance would significantly structure British media's inability to acknowledge and address racism and in turn deeply inform the

---

[17] Michel-Rolph Trouillot, *Silencing the Past: Power and the Production of History* (Boston, MA: Beacon Press, 1995); Ibram X. Kendi, *Stamped from the Beginning: The Definitive History of Racist Ideas in America* (New York: Random House, 2017).
[18] Erik Linstrum, *Age of Emergency: Living with Violence at the End of the British Empire* (Oxford: Oxford University Press, 2023): 2, 147–174.
[19] Priyamvada Gopal, *Insurgent Empire: Anticolonial Resistance and British Dissent* (London: Verso, 2019).

experiences of Black and south Asian women, men and children in the country. This book positions British media and its screen culture as a vital site of racial formation and a producer of a wilful racial ignorance in the twentieth century.

## I.1 Not Seeing Racism: Critical Race Theory and Histories of Not Knowing

A historical examination of 'not knowing' is not an ideal subject for historians. The topic resists methodologies in the discipline that remain wedded to the empirical and to archival spaces that are presented as sites of provision rather than obfuscation. As Trouillot wrote, the edges of not knowing are so slippery that it is almost impossible to know where the beginning and endings of this chasm of the unthinkable lie. There are also, as Trouillot has charted, myriad ways of not knowing in the past—there is that which cannot be conceived of, things to innocently ignore and realities to avoid. Trouillot's work is probably one of the best examples of a concerted history of not knowing or seeing, tracing that which was 'unthinkable' to European elites when it came to the abilities of Black men and women in the empire.[20] The history of empire remains the most notable field where some form of 'not knowing' lurks at the edges and margins of most works, occasionally coming to the centre. It is in the classic debates between Bernard Porter and John MacKenzie about Porter's 'absent-minded imperialists' who, according to him, hardly seemed to know what they were doing or reflect upon this in the massive project that was empire. MacKenzie's responses across multiple books and taken up by others point to the sheer presence of empire in the everyday as a means of questioning how much ordinary Britons did not know about empire.[21] These works argue that ordinary Britons were surrounded by an everydayness of empire and imperial products. Yet few of these works touch on what ordinary Britons could afford to ignore when it came to empire's presence in the everyday. Linstrum, on the other hand, does just that when he takes us into the post-war period and

---

[20] Trouillot, *Silencing the Past*, 70–108.
[21] Bernard Porter, 'Further Thoughts on Imperial Absent-Mindedness', *Journal of Imperial and Commonwealth History* 31, no. 1 (2008): 101–117; John M. MacKenzie (2008) 'Comfort' and Conviction: A Response to Bernard Porter', *The Journal of Imperial and Commonwealth History* 36, no. 4 (2008): 659–668. See this debate taken up in Antoinette Burton, *At the Heart of the Empire: Indians and the Colonial Encounter in Late-Victorian Britain* (Oakland, CA: University of California Press, 1998); Richard Price, 'One Big Thing: Britain, Its Empire, and Their Imperial Culture', *Journal of British Studies* 45, no. 3 (July 2006): 602–627.

argues that ordinary Britons were also surrounded by stories of the violent end of empire and the colonial conflicts that accompanied this. By his account numerous bodies including the press, the BBC and even ex-soldiers made this evidence visible and ordinary to the public if not appetising. Together this work paints a picture of ordinary Britons steeped in the material goods and evidence of empire in advertising, medicine, museums, gardening, steam travel and the bloody images of atrocities in the colonies, but still maintaining only a vague knowledge of the specific workings of empire.[22]

Priya Satia's work on 'agnatology', the study of wilful ignorance, preceded by her history of 'a state that could not see' in interwar Britain and Arabia takes the debate about how much people saw and knew of empire in different directions, uncovering what political structures embrace in the absence of knowledge about racialized people.[23] Her earliest work looked at what state actors turn to when official knowledge or intelligence of a place or people is absent, arguing that concepts of the mysterious and secretive Arab rooted in popular culture filled this space in the minds of intelligence officers. Satia's later work examines the turning away from empire among ordinary Britons that was apparent between the wars and which was, she argues, further developed by the newly democratic liberal state in order to conduct foreign policy away from the prying eyes of the masses.[24] Bill Schwarz, Wendy Webster and Jordanna Bailkin have taken this wilful absence of knowledge into the post-war period as a means of discussing popular responses to immigration rooted in the collective amnesia that Hall, as well as Paul Gilroy, had previously raised.[25] Webster starts her classic *Englishness and Empire* with

---

[22] This series is immense, but see for example, Liora Bigon and Yossi Katz, eds. *Garden Cities and Colonial Planning: Transnationality and Urban Ideas in Africa and Palestine* (Manchester: Manchester University Press, 2017); Markku Hokkanen, *Medicine, Mobility and the Empire: Nyasaland Networks, 1859–1960* (Manchester: Manchester University Press, 2017); Jonathan Stafford, *Imperial Steam: Modernity on the Sea Route to India, 1837–74* (Manchester: Manchester University Press, 2023).

[23] Priya Satia, *Spies in Arabia: The Great War and the Cultural Foundations of Britain's Covert Empire in the Middle East* (Oxford: Oxford University Press, 2008), 4.

[24] Priya Satia, 'Inter-war Agnotology: Empire, Democracy and the Production of Ignorance', in Laura Beers and Geraint Thomas, eds., *Brave New World: Imperial and Democratic Nation-Building in Britain between the Wars* (London: Institute of Historical Research, 2012), 210. See also Nicholas Owen, '"Facts are Sacred": The Manchester Guardian and Colonial Violence, 1930–1932', *The Journal of Modern History* 84, no. 3 (2012): 643–678.

[25] Paul Gilroy, *Post-Colonial Melancholia* (New York: Columbia University Press, 2005); Wendy Webster, *Englishness and Empire, 1939–1965* (Oxford: Oxford University Press, 2007); Bill Schwarz, *Memories of Empire, Volume I: The White Man's World* (Oxford: Oxford University Press, 2011); Jordanna Bailkin, *The Afterlife of Empire* (Oakland, CA: University of California Press, 2012).

a discussion of the public's widespread ignorance about empire's practicalities, and particularly the 1948 'Social Survey of Public Opinion in Britain on Colonial Affairs', to establish the lack of basic knowledge that ordinary Britons had of Britain's colonial territories and peoples in the immediate aftermath of the war.[26] Confusion reigned about which countries were colonies and more than half of the respondents did not name India or Pakistan as 'colonies, which in the past year, have been given more responsibility for governing themselves'.[27] Ordinary Britons showed a stunning lack of education about both the empire and people from the colonies, even as subsequent historians have demonstrated that elements of the colonial and commonwealth governance structured a variety of postwar public initiatives, including controls around advertising, early forms of the NHS, social care and the formation of the charity sector.[28]

However, not knowing about the specifics of empire and its workings should not be confused with not caring about empire. Ordinary Britons and even some politicians might have been confused about the differences between dominion, protectorate and colony but that did not mean that they did not care deeply and passionately about empire and attach considerable emotion to it. Book knowledge of the empire was and still is not the best way to measure whether the public cared and were invested in the British empire. Film and television producers, directors and regulators in Britain understood this when it came to imperial and racialised imagery on the screen. The empire sells. It was what film-producers and film-makers such as Stephen Tallents and John Grierson believed when they spearheaded the Empire Film Unit; it was what the film-director Korda brothers understood when they set numerous fantastical stories in the empire; and it was what advertisers imagined when they drew on often misleading and factually incorrect imagery of empire to sell their wares.[29] The details mattered little in the face of audience want when it came to empire. In particular, the triumphant story of white supremacy within empire is what brought audiences to the screen. One of the contentions of this book is that the specific elements of this emotional attachment to the empire by white Britons in the twentieth century

---

[26] Webster, *Englishness and Empire*, 4.   [27] Ibid., 4
[28] Bailkin, *The Afterlife of Empire*; Roberta Bivins, 'Picturing Race in the British National Health Service, 1948–1988', *Twentieth Century British History* 28, no. 1 (2017): 83–109, Radkhika Natarajan's forthcoming monograph *Empire and the Origins of Multiculturalism: Migrants, Citizenship, and Community in Britain, 1948–1982*; Emily Baughan, *Saving the Children: Humanitarianism, Internationalism, and Empire* (Oakland, CA: University of California Press, 2021); Rob Waters, *Colonized by Humanity: Caribbean London and the Politics of Integration at the End of Empire* (Oxford: Oxford University Press, 2023).
[29] See Anne McClintock's classic, *Imperial Leather: Race, Gender, and Sexuality in the Colonial Contest* (London: Routledge, 1995).

requires new attention by historians as part of the emotional framework of racism, including scrutiny of the pleasures associated with white superiority and racial inferiority.

The history of emotions, as it currently stands, is not particularly well equipped to address the historic intersection of emotions with racism and racialised thinking, with that field's overwhelming attention to the feelings and thoughts of white communities.[30] The ways in which select emotions, such as fear or anger, have been racialised as dominant within one minoritised group or how several emotions have been prized as particularly absent from the dominant white group have been left unexplored in the history of emotions but are touched upon in this book. Media history has also been curiously divorced from the history of emotions, perhaps an implicit acknowledgment that media as it functioned in the twentieth century traded primarily in its enormous ability to emotionally connect with or steer audiences. It was why governments invested so heavily in 'media relations', however poorly conceived, in the interwar period and during World War II, only to cede the ground to the field of advertising and audience experts in the post-war period. It is ultimately at the intersection of the history of emotions and the history of media that we encounter just how much white audiences cared about empire, all while knowing, often willingly, little of its workings.

My attention here to the history of white audiences who evaded, avoided, and actively worked to not know race and racism contributes to an existing field of scholars in critical race theory studying claims and practices of colour blindness or racial 'ignorance' and 'innocence' among predominantly white populations in a range of settings; colonial, settler, and post-colonial.[31] Most often associated with the field of legal studies in the United States, critical race theory emerged in the 1970s and 1980s to examine the seemingly 'colour-blind' systems of law in the country, an

---

[30] Katie Barclay, 'State of the Field: The History of Emotions', *History* 106, no. 371 (2021): 353–513; Rob Boddice and Mark Smith, *Emotion, Sense, Experience* (Cambridge: Cambridge University Press, 2020); Nicole Eustace, Eugenia Lean, Julie Livingston et al., 'AHR Conversation: The Historical Study of Emotions', *American Historical Review* 117, no. 5 (2012): 1487–1531. That said, it is worth noting Thomas Dixon's excellent *Weeping Britannia: Portrait of a Nation in Tears* (Oxford: Oxford University Press, 2015) and Deborah Cohen's somewhat related *Family Secrets: Shame and Privacy in Modern Britain* (Oxford: Oxford University Press, 2013), and that new directions are being addressed in the fields of global history; see Margrit Pernau, *Emotions and Modernity in Colonial India: From Balance to Fervor* (Oxford: Oxford University Press, 2019).

[31] There has been little overt engagement with CRT in the discipline of history, although see Ryan A. Archibald, 'The Rise of the Airport Metal Detector: Colour-blind Racism, Police Discretion, and Surveillance Across Borders', *Journal of Social History* 56, no. 3 (2023): 637–671.

approach which was then quickly taken up by scholars of pedagogy to grapple with university environments which also claimed colour-blind meritocracy.[32] Both strands involve a careful and meticulous unpicking of systemic racism in the courts and in educational settings through a concerted examination of not just text but repetitive meaning, implications and behaviour which highlight how deeply racialised these supposedly colour-blind sites really are. Such deep unpicking of the myriad structures of seemingly invisible race-making was not limited to the United States. In the same period, Stuart Hall, Dick Hebdige, Paul Gilroy and others working within and adjacent to Birmingham's Centre for Contemporary Cultural Studies were engaged in an similar excavation of British culture's meaning, practices and associated repetitive behaviour when it came to racialisation and empire's legacy.[33] This deep archival investigation of the manifestations and ripples of racial formation in Britain echoed what was happening in the United States.[34] Collectively this scholarship, which has since extended into philosophy and other fields, represented a burgeoning trans-Atlantic understanding of

---

[32] In legal history, see Derrick A. Bell, *Race, Racism, and American Law* (Cambridge, Mass.: Harvard Law School: 1970); Kimberlé Crenshaw, 'Race, Reform and Retrenchment: Transformation and Legitimation in Anti-Discrimination Law', *Harvard Law Review* 101 no. 7 (1988): 1331–1387; Richard Delgado and Jean Stefancic, 'Critical Race Theory: Past, Present, and Future', *Current Legal Problems* 51, no. 1 (1998): 467–491. In Education and Pedagogy Studies, see Gloria Ladson-Billings, 'Just What Is Critical Race Theory and What's It Doing in a Nice Field Like Education?', *International Journal of Qualitative Studies in Education* 11, no. 1 (1998): 7–24; A.D. Dixson et al., eds. *Critical Race Theory in Education* (London: Routledge, 2018); Nicola Rollock et al., *The Colour of Class: The Educational Strategies of the Black Middle Classes* (London: Routledge, 2015); Robin DiAngelo, 'White Fragility', *International Journal of Critical Pedagogy* 3, no. 3 (2011): 54–70. See also Reni Eddo-Lodge, *Why I'm No Longer Talking to White People about Race* (London: Bloomsbury, 2017); Eduardo Bonilla-Silva, *Racism Without Racists: Color-Blind Racism and the Persistence of Racial Inequality in the United States*, 3rd ed. (Lanham, MD: Rowman & Littlefield, 2010); Alana Lentin, *Why Race Still Matters* (London: Polity Press, 2020); Charles W. Mills, 'White Ignorance', in Shannon Sullivan and Nancy Tuana, eds., *Race and Epistemologies of Ignorance* (Albany, NY: SUNY Press 2007); Gloria Wekker, *White Innocence: Paradoxes of Colonialism and Race* (Durham, NC: Duke University Press, 2016).

[33] Stuart Hall and Tony Jefferson, eds, *Resistance Through Rituals: Youth Subcultures in Post-War Britain* (Birmingham, Centre for Contemporary Cultural Studies, 1976; Stuart Hall et al., eds, *Policing the Crisis: Mugging, the State and Law and Order* (Birmingham, Centre for Contemporary Cultural Studies, 1978; Dick Hebdige, *Subculture: The Meaning of Style* (London: Methuen & Co ltd, 1979); Paul Gilroy, *There Ain't No Black in the Union Jack* (Chicago: University of Chicago Press, 1991 [1987]).

[34] There is much mapping to be done on the intersection of Black British thought at the CCCS with the work of contemporaries in America who are more commonly associated with critical race theory, including Bell, Crenshaw and others. See one legal scholar reflecting on her training in cultural studies at Birmingham before entering the legal profession in the United States; Imani Perry, 'Cultural Studies, Critical Race Theory and Some Reflections on Methods', *Villanova Law Review* 50, no. 4 (2005): 915–924.

racialisation's operations in the 1970s and 1980s and goes beyond the common argument at the time that racist behaviour and ideology stems from a lack of understanding, or knowledge, among white people of Black, south Asian or minority ethnic experiences. Taken together as a body of work on, and adjacent to, critical race theory, this trans-Atlantic research examines strategic ignorance or lack of knowledge as central to a range of practices, concepts and beliefs that underpin the very function of law, education, culture and media in majority white societies.

Within the framework of critical race theory that this book turns to repeatedly, racial ignorance and innocence is not just 'a lack of' knowledge about race to be corrected but instead can be viewed as an active, invested and strategic means of relating to and maintaining subordinated populations. What can seem to be inadvertent oversights or lack of education are instead linked to a deliberate, albeit often unacknowledged, avoidance of new information that would unsettle or disturb. As the philosopher Charles W. Mills argues, the end result is an: '[i]nverted epistemology, an epistemology of ignorance, a particular pattern of localised and global cognitive dysfunctions (which are psychologically and socially functional), producing the ironic outcome that whites will in general be unable to understand the world they themselves have made'.[35] Shannon Sullivan and Nancy Tuana further sum up this irony: 'Even though – or more accurately, precisely because – they tend not to understand the racist world in which they live, white people are able to fully benefit from its racial hierarchies, ontologies, and economies.'[36] This lack of racial perception or knowledge of racism experienced by Black people becomes a means of preserving the social, economic and political privileges derived from it. The act of not knowing is thus wilful and ultimately serves that person who has that luxury of an absence of knowledge. Together these works formed a subset of 'whiteness studies' that can be dated back to the works of Frederick Douglas but also include David Roediger and Richard Dyer.[37] Research in anti-racism education, a field with its own blind spots, has also worked to identify what Robin DiAngelo refers to as a type of shared script among

---

[35] Charles W. Mills, *The Racial Contract* (Ithaca, NY: Cornell University Press, 1997), 18.
[36] Shannon Sullivan and Nancy Tuana, *Race and Epistemologies of Ignorance*, 2.
[37] The early development of this field can be traced to W.E.B. DuBois's *Black Reconstruction in America 1860–1880* (London: Free Press, 1998) and taken up in David Roediger's *The Wages of Whiteness: Race and the Making of the American Working Class* (New York: Verso, 2007) and Richard Dyer's *White: Essays on Race and Culture* (London: Routledge, 1997). See also Hazel V. Carby 'White Women Listen! Black Feminism and the Boundaries of Sisterhood', in Heidi Safia Mirza, eds. *Black British Feminism: A Reader* (London: Routledge, 1997) and Vron Ware, *Beyond the Pale: White Women, Racism, and History* (London: Verso, 2015).

white people; the repetitive expressions of white people's discomfort when presented with evidence, or claims, of experienced racism.[38] The field of anti-racist education and training has done much to draw attention to what white people in a supposedly post-racial world do when faced with evidence of their own participation in upholding racist systems of thought, behaviour and institution-making.

What has stood out to me as a historian, as I considered the shared scripts of whiteness identified by people such as Bonilla-Silva and Reni Eddo-Lodge were the patterns of behaviour I also saw within archival sources on twentieth-century Britain.[39] The defensiveness, the tone-policing, and the convoluted rationales or false equivalencies offered by white people in areas of law and education in late twentieth- and early twenty-first-century America when asked to consider racism and their role within it are evident in archives of history that are wide-ranging in terms of time frames and geographic coverage. In the case of Britain we have a country that has never claimed, such as the US briefly did in the twenty-first century, to be 'post-racial' but rather has asserted it was, and is, racially tolerant or racially blind instead. This claim has functioned, however, in much the same way. As Kennetta Hammond Perry has noted, these were 'the imagined antiracist ideals tethered to notions of what it meant to be British' in the post-war period and as the riots in Notting Hill broke out.[40] The resonance of these arguments in post-war Britain, which demonstrably had a 'race problem' of a dominant white population that was both hostile to visible minorities and yet claimed on public stages and at various legislative moments that it was not racist, offers a vital framework for examining this interplay of deniability and racialising practices. Indeed, some historians of post-war immigration and Black history have engaged with critical race theory's more trenchant observations. Hammond Perry, in particular, discusses the 'mystique of British anti-racism' which she sees as being in dialogue with Eduardo Bonilla-Silva's work on colour-blind racism.[41] Rob Waters' *Thinking Black*, and his talk at the Institute of Historical Research, also hints at the alternative epistemological frameworks discussed in this book and which are vital to the 'counter-storytelling' that critical race theory identifies as a key element in working against colour-blind racism (discussed

---

[38] Robin DiAngelo, *White Fragility: Why It's So Hard for White People to Talk About Racism* (London: Allen Lane, 2018), 9.
[39] Eddo-Lodge, *Why I'm No Longer Talking to White People About Race*.
[40] Kennetta Hammond Perry, '"Little Rock" in Britain: Jim Crow's Transatlantic Topographies', *Journal of British Studies* 51 (2012): 158.
[41] In conversation with Kennetta Hammond Perry, Lincoln, UK, 2017.

in Chapters 2 and 5).[42] The flexibility that historic Black communities exhibited in collapsing the distinctions between the past and present is a vital attempt to bring past and present trauma into the same framework in order to convey the emotional weight of not only thinking Black, but also feeling Black in environments claimed as racially tolerant.

If historians are already engaging with elements of critical race theory, is it particularly important to label this as such? I began drawing on critical race theory in earnest in 2016, a tremendous year in retrospect but one that did not include much, if any, public discussion of critical race theory outside of academia. Nowadays, one could be easily excused for running the other way at the very mention of it with all the negative attention it has garnered first in the US and then in the UK.[43] In part that attention indicates just how salient and sensible the work of critical race theory is to most who encounter it, and it is one of those theories of knowledge and behaviour that quickly transcends the academic in many ways.[44] My hope is that the current furore and misunderstandings of critical race theory will ultimately not turn academics away from what is a fruitful and useful field of academic study. Historians have, after all, worked across disciplinary boundaries before and have increasingly engaged with the so-called post-colonial turn ushered in by the work of Edward Said. Critical race theory offers the field something unique particularly due to the origins of its framework, where picking through the 'colour-blind' spheres of the courtroom, legal records and cultural texts invokes the historian's methodologies, scouring the archive for the spoken, the inferred, the webs of presence and absence in the historical record.

Perhaps the most practical contribution of critical race theory is firstly, its ability to identify and parse out the behaviours and patterns of white superiority and imagined racial inferiority across a range of geographical and temporal settings and secondly, to show the durability and fluidity of racist thinking in multiple settings. Critical race theory manages to cut across and work within both the post-colonial turn and the relatively new attention to settler colonialism in the field, while also accounting for the

---

[42] Rob Waters, '"Time Come": Britain's Black Futures Past', *Historical Research* 92, no. 258 (2019): 838–850; Kennetta Hammond Perry, 'The Temporal Dimensions of *Thinking Black*: A Comment', *Historical Research* 92, no. 258 (2019): 851–853; Richard Delgado, 'Storytelling for Oppositionists and Others: A Plea for Narrative', *Michigan Law Review*, 87 (1989): 2411–2441.

[43] LaToya Baldwin Clark, 'The Critical Racialization of Parents' Rights', *Yale Law Journal* 113 (8 May 2023): https://ssrn.com/abstract=4441698; H. Huw Davies and Sheena MacRae, 'An Anatomy of the British War on Woke', *Race & Class* (2023) online first: https://doi.org/10.1177/03063968231164905.

[44] Indeed, critical race theory is perhaps finding a more comfortable home in 'Black Studies' in several US universities.

persistent patterns of behaviour among white people when faced with the presence of Black people and other people of colour. It offers a map of behaviour rooted in racial superiority that can be tested in all the settings that historians explore and within the frameworks of knowledge that govern these. Marc Matera, Radhika Natarajan, Kennetta Hammond Perry, Camilla Schofield and Rob Waters have called for historians of twentieth-century Britain to place racial formation at the centre of their work as a category of analysis itself, and although they largely turn to works from sociology for frameworks to do so, critical race theory does a similar, and I would say an even more convincing, job of noting the work of whiteness across time, space, place and peoples.[45] It is less bound by national frameworks and instead oriented towards the frameworks of whiteness that sit within people, regardless of place or space. Waters' recent effort to uncover the racial framework underpinning 'racial liberalism' in post-war Britain is one such example that draws upon, perhaps unwittingly, the approach of critical race theory.[46] A direct engagement with the field and its builders could make similar explorations an accessible and vital new direction within our discipline. This focus upon how whiteness works in various settings allows us to see moments when it works against or around empire and decolonisation in the cultural imaginary, which itself is an overlooked site of political persuasion in the period I examine.

Historians have been willing to examine shifting epistemological frameworks since the so-called discursive turn, yet historical accounts that intersect with epistemologies of racial perception and its absence, in other words how social actors 'know' or 'see' codes and experiences of Blackness, are in short supply compared with works on historic epistemologies of gender and sexuality.[47] Both the relative scarcity of works doing this, and the usefulness of explicitly incorporating critical race theory into our work as historians is, I think, due in part to the whiteness of the field and university environments more broadly, as Nicola Rollock has shown.[48] In the UK, the Royal Historical Society's *Race, Ethnicity & Equality in UK History: A Report and*

---

[45] See Matera et al., 'Introduction' and 'Marking Race: Empire, Social Democracy, Deindustrialization', *Twentieth Century British History* 34, no. 3 (2023).

[46] Waters, *Colonized by Humanity*.

[47] The history of sexuality has excelled at rethinking epistemological frameworks while drawing on queer theory. See Jonathan Katz, *The Invention of Heterosexuality* (Chicago: University of Chicago Press, 1995); Mary Louise Adams, *The Trouble with Normal: Postwar Youth and the Making of Heterosexuality* (Toronto: University of Toronto Press, 1997); Judith Butler, *Gender Trouble* (New York: Routledge, 1999, 2nd ed.); Eve Kosofsky Sedgwick, *Epistemology of the Closet* (Oakland, CA: University of California Press, 1990; Laura Doan, *Disturbing Practices: History, Sexuality, and Women's Experience of Modern War* (Chicago: University of Chicago Press, 2013).

[48] Nicola Rollock (2019) *Staying Power: The Career Experiences and Strategies of UK Black Female Professors*, London: UCU. www.ucu.org.uk/media/10075/Staying-Power/pdf/UCU_Rollock_February_2019.pdf

*Resource for Change* published in October 2018 highlighted the discipline of history as an overlooked site of whiteness studies, with a disproportionate number of white academics teaching a disproportionate number of white students, in a curriculum that has been disproportionally preoccupied with the histories and experiences of white groups.[49] The report resonated throughout the profession as History departments grappled with the lack of representation of Black and minority ethnic staff and content in the discipline.[50] If one looks to the field of twentieth-century British history in the last 20 years or so this particular problem looks even more pronounced considering the role of immigration and empire in that century. What we have then are potentially colour-blind historians in Britain writing equally colour-blind histories of the twentieth century, unable to see their topic as related to race or racialised thinking in the period or cramming the experience of multiple minorities into a few pages or a slim chapter. Alongside this is the excellent work of historians working on twentieth-century Black British history.[51] But perhaps this too reflects a certain history of the country as well. Regardless, critical race theory would seem to offer historians a twofold benefit: a framework for examining the repetitive scripts of whiteness that mark out parts of British history as 'not about race'; and language and conceptual frameworks to interrogate the racialised practices, habits, and preoccupations of history-making as well.

## I.2  Film, Television and the Racially Innocent Audience

Critical race theory has a further vital place in a history of British screen culture where sites such as television have been historically tied to concerns about 'neutrality' that situate it, impossibly, as colour-blind. Neutrality became a powerful term in British media history early on, built on concepts of 'public service' attached to the birth of broadcasting in Britain and a commitment to offering both sides of every story. Lord Reith argued, on the eve of the BBC's shift from company to corporation

---

[49] *Race, Ethnicity & Equality in UK History: A Report and Resource for Change* (Royal Historical Society, October 2018). https://files.royalhistsoc.org/wp-content/uploads/2018/10/17205337/RHS_race_report_EMBARGO_0001_18Oct.pdf,

[50] Royal Historical Society Roadmap for Change Update, 2019. https://files.royalhistsoc.org/wp-content/uploads/2020/11/24094341/RHS-REEWG-Roadmap-Update-Dec-2019-FINAL2.pdf,

[51] Perry, *London Is the Place for Me*; Waters, *Thinking Black*; Bailkin, *The Afterlife of Empire*; Simon Peplow, *Race and Riots in Thatcher's Britain* (Manchester: Manchester University Press, 2019); Kieran Connell, *Black Handsworth: Race in 1980s Britain* (Berkeley, CA: University of California Press, 2019); Marc Matera, *Black London: The Imperial Metropolis and Decolonization in the Twentieth Century* (Berkeley: University of California Press, 2015); Camilla Schofield, *Enoch Powell and the Making of Postcolonial Britain* (Cambridge: Cambridge University Press, 2013).

in December 1926, that 'the BBC has tried to found a tradition of public service, and to dedicate broadcasting to the service of humanity in the broadest sense'.[52] Prime Minister Stanley Baldwin described the BBC in that same month as 'keeping itself, as it always had done, free from personal bias, from personal feeling, and was disseminated what it always does, the bare, uncoloured truth, and nothing else'.[53] This definition of public service was strengthened by the activities of the Ullswater Committee (1935) and others after it, including the Beveridge Committee (1949–1951) and the Television Act of 1954, even as a range of dailies continued to debate evidence of bias within the BBC. From 1968, *The Times* digital archive records 'neutrality' as a term openly used in letters to the editor regarding the BBC as members of the public argued for, or against, the integrity of the BBC's screen content and its independence from the state.[54] Official and public concerns about public service and neutrality, and a not unrelated vigilance against bias, while seeming to apply more to journalism than the production of film or television sitcoms, nevertheless still informed the institutional production and regulation of fictional storytelling on screen. Concerns about neutrality acted as a type of boundary-making around most programmes, marking the limits of acceptability even as the BBC marched into the 1960s. While the methodologies of cultural history and the post-structuralist or cultural turn in our discipline from the 1980s highlight the impossibility of neutral storytelling in media sources, this framework of knowledge was central to what audiences knew, or expected, particularly from the BBC. Consequently, this book concentrates on the highly racialised framework underpinning seemingly neutral spaces such as television production.

At the heart of this book are the audiences, both Black and white, who watched film and television in the twentieth century, and how these groups were imagined, served, shaped and measured by a relatively new field of 'audience research'. As I have written previously, the 'audience' has for far too long been only peripheral to the preoccupations of those working in the field of cultural history.[55] It is often only briefly

---

[52] 'The Old and The New B.B.C.', *The Times*, 31 December 1926, 5.
[53] 'New Broadcasting Era', *The Times*, 17 December 1926, 7.
[54] Vincent Tilsey, 'BBC Neutrality', *The Times*, 30 October 1968, 9. Earlier discussions in 1962 about what was termed 'political' broadcasting touched on components of this; 'Outworn System', *The Times*, 23 July 1962, 11.
[55] Christine Grandy, 'Cultural History's Absent Audience', *Cultural and Social History* 16, no. 5 (2019): 643–663. This article was a response to Peter Mandler, 'The Problem with Cultural History', *Cultural and Social History* 1, no. 1 (2004): 94–117. See the responses by Carol Watts, Colin Jones and Carla Hesse to Mandler in that same 2004 issue.

inferred or sketched out, partly because of the lack of primary sources produced by audiences about the culture they encounter, however widely conceived. What we have been left with instead are countless histories of the culture itself, the representations or texts that audiences or consumers purchase, with little sense of their experiences engaging with these. This book, in many ways, is a long-form effort to think through the audience and excavate it. It offers a multifaceted and wide-ranging approach to the audience by examining the ways film and television audiences were conceived of by the government, regulators, producers, directors and also the field of audience research, which was uniquely tasked with knowing and measuring the audience. This project certainly speaks to Adrian Bingham's invitation to historians of the twentieth century to recognise Britain as a 'mediated democracy' full of various forms of media consumed by ordinary people as a matter of course.[56] Trying to locate the audience has at times, I will admit, felt like nailing jelly to the wall. The answer that this book provides to the question of the 'absent audience' in cultural history is one that ultimately points to the audience as largely a construct of these people and organisations, and very seldom a reality. The audience was both a figment of imagination among various groups, imagined in certain ways as behaving rationally and consistently, but was also at times an awkward reality such as when Black and south Asian audiences responded negatively to what was on the screen, or when white audiences spoke bluntly of their beliefs in racial inferiority. This book chases both the image and the reality of the audience and in the process offers a view of media production and consumption in twentieth-century Britain as something quite rigid and slow to change and built on rather shaky foundations as white, middle-class executives and researchers imagined audiences that looked like them.

Producers and regulators of British screen culture at its inception had, I will demonstrate, a fairly narrow audience in mind. Not surprisingly, the imagining of this audience was directly related to the worldview of the predominantly white and middle and upper-class men producing and regulating screen culture in a country that choose to adhere to a firm two-channel model for the bulk of the twentieth century. This was the formation of the outlook of 'the white man's world' that Bill Schwarz has written about.[57] This media elite, from Stephen Tallents to Johnny Speight, claimed to know what British audiences wanted and needed in period when they had immense power and from within institutions that

---

[56] Erik Linstrum, Peter Clarke, Adrian Bingham et al., 'Forum: The Past, Present, and Futures of Modern British History', *Modern British History* 35, no. 1 (2024): 11.
[57] Bill Schwarz, *The White Man's World* (Oxford: Oxford University Press, 2011).

straddled a murky line between public service and free-market competition far before explicit tensions between these positions would structure what would come to be known as neoliberalism in late twentieth-century Britain. The creation of audience research departments within organisations such as the BBC and ITV would cement the expertise of men such as Tallents who knew the audience but also prove audience research's malleability. Other organisations with less raw production power outside the BBC and ITV would also put forward claims to knowing what British audiences wanted and needed with some rather more preoccupied with the latter. This book examines that imagining of the audience across a complex and tumultuous period in Britain, one which had a profound impact on notions of national identity. Above all the early envisioning of audiences of screen culture was actively tied to efforts to shield audiences who were imagined as white and vulnerable from the social, economic and political ills of the day. From its very inception as the first regulator of Britain's screen culture, the British Board of Film Censors, as Jeffrey Richards has argued, strove to break the connection between filmed reality and the social, economic and political reality of audiences, and this maxim was extended with the advent of television broadcasting.[58]

Central to this early desire to separate screen reality from the lived reality of British audiences was an important assumption about the impact of moving images on ordinary people that would go on to shape both film and post-war television content. I argue that audiences of Britain's screen culture in the twentieth century, with one important exception, were imagined early on by regulators and producers as fragile, impressionable and in constant need of protection by Britain's emerging media elite. The conception of the screen audience as a *tabula rasa* on which a range of images were thought to impress, prompting the need for protection, mimicked conceptions of the child in twentieth-century Britain and the state's responsibility to it.[59] This was the wayward but well-meaning child-like audience that the BBC, 'Dear Aunty', had to be attentive to. The official thinking was that if the audience saw something they would then imitate it. This attitude, as I will demonstrate, was slow to change throughout the century. This assumption about the fragility of

---

[58] Jeffrey Richards, 'The British Board of Film Censors and Content Control in the 1930s: Images of Britain', *Historical Journal of Film Radio, and Television* 1, no. 2 (1981): 95–116.

[59] As Laura King has argued, the idealised children imagined by various groups in the post-war period as future citizens were also inevitably white and middle class, embodying specific British values in the period; Laura King, 'Future Citizens: Cultural and Political Conceptions of Children in Britain, 1930s-1950s', *Twentieth Century British History* 27, no. 3 (2016): 389–411.

ordinary audiences buttressed both the decision to avoid the comparatively laissez-faire American model for producing, regulating and broadcasting screen culture and underpins the relatively late deregulation of screen culture in the UK with the passage of the Broadcasting Act in 1990. This vision of the impressionable audience accounts for the content of early cinema and the slow shifts in representation that were seen in post-war television. It is why crime could not easily be shown on screen, lest audiences learned how to engage in crime themselves. Male and female sexual acts outside of marriage or the definitions of chaste normality were treated carefully by both producers and regulators, often only finding their way onto screens through pathways of 'high culture'. British institutions from the police to the medical profession also continued to be actively depicted in largely positive ways.[60] Politicians were not criticised on film or television until the political satire *That Was the Week That Was* made its debut on the BBC in 1962. On-screen criticisms of these figures or bodies inevitably produced a flurry of memos at the BBC, the ITA, the British Board of Film Censors (BBFC) and certainly by and within organisations such as the National Viewers' and Listeners' Association (NVLA) and London Public Morality Council (LPMC). Above all, the potential reactions of British audiences had to be carefully considered both within media institutions and without.

There was an important exception when it came to conceptualising the fragility of British audiences in this period that pointed to a vital, although often unacknowledged, aspect of the imagined British audience. British audiences were envisioned as sensitive to portrayals of crime, sexuality, class conflict and critiques of British institutions; yet producers and regulators of Britain's screen culture imagined audiences as largely unaffected by negative images of Black and minority ethnic populations or spoken and physical expressions of racism by British subjects on screen. Indeed, British audiences were imagined as uniquely *unimpressionable* on this subject and this subject almost exclusively. A relatively sophisticated audience, savvy in their understanding of messages on the screen, was invoked by producers and regulators of screen culture in defence of controversial discussions or representations of race. As O. J. Whitley, chief assistant to the BBC's Director General Hugh Greene, argued in response to criticism of *The Black and White Minstrel Show* in 1967: 'It seems to be absurd to imagine that people who are not already racially prejudiced could possibly be in some way contaminated

---

[60] Christine Grandy, *Heroes and Happy Endings: Class, Gender, and Nation in Popular Fiction in Interwar Britain* (Manchester: Manchester University Press, 2014).

by the Minstrels.'⁶¹ Images of racism on the screen, in other words, could not possibly impact British audiences. Such a rationale was in place well before 1967 and allowed empire films of the 1930s featuring devious and sometimes grotesque Black and south Asian villains, usually played by white actors in blackface, to be passed without comment by the BBFC even as other films deemed too political or controversial were censored. This rationale allowed these same empire films to be rebroadcast on the BBC and ITV in the post-war period when immigration of Black and south Asian people was at its peak. This belief also supported the production of the BBC's and ITV's 'racial sitcoms' such as *Till Death Us Do Part* (BBC, 1965–1975) and *Love Thy Neighbour* (LWT, 1972 to 1976) each featuring a bigoted main character, Alf Garnett and Eddie Booth respectively. Audiences, it was argued, understood the joke and had a shrewd comprehension of racism on screen and, more crucially, were not really racist themselves anyways.

This exceptional aspect of the British audience, tied to both its imagined 'racial innocence' and 'racial ignorance', is at the heart of this project. By exploring how audience responses to racist imagery were persistently disregarded, denied, undermeasured or simply not seen as important by regulators and producers of Britain's screen culture, we further see how central the audience's presumed 'whiteness' was in this period. The blind spot of audiences, or their imagined innocent *lack* of racial perception when it came to race on screen, points to the epistemological flexibility inherent in the practice of imagining a British audience in the age of democracy and at the end of empire and during a period of growth in the immigration of racialised peoples. The white audience in this framework was painted as both innocent and knowing, but above all it was not an object of concern as potentially racist in this regard and *only* in this regard. The term 'racial innocence' is useful when discussing the way in which British audiences were imagined by producers and regulators of screen culture in Britain in the twentieth century as largely devoid of serious racism, which they defined as the type of violence-based racism that was shown in the press and on television in the US.⁶² Yet, innocence cannot be the only term in play. While Gloria Wekker makes a compelling case for the centrality of racial innocence to Dutch national identity, British national identity, bound up in the world's largest empire, has a

---

⁶¹ Memo to D. A. from O. J. Whitley, *The Black and White Minstrel Show*, 26 May 1967, R78/1, 921/1, 'Black and White Minstrel Show', BBC Written Archives Centre, hereafter WAC.
⁶² Here, I must acknowledge the work of Robin Bernstein, *Racial Innocence: Performing American Childhood from Slavery to Civil Rights* (New York: New York University Press, 2011).

more difficult claim to this term. Indeed, among the political and economic elite of Britain, there have historically been claims to a different type of understanding of Blackness based on first-hand experience of empire and tied up in the capable privileges of middle and upper-class 'absent-mindedness'.[63] Mills' foundational conceptualisation of 'white ignorance' allows for the deliberate obfuscation that white people make in order to appear innocent, while benefitting from the privileges accorded to those working to 'not know'.[64] I use, racial innocence, racial ignorance, or the less elegant 'wilful not knowing', alongside others, depending on what is at work, be it liberal wide-eyed shock at racism's existence, or a more grim irritated turning away from its reality, or something else altogether that this language can hint at. I have tried to avoid repeating variations of 'epistemology' throughout the book, although it has inevitably come in at points. All these terms have a place in discussions of racism in twentieth-century Britain and in the media produced in the period.

## I.3 Archives of Not Knowing

Finally, this book grapples with the archival silences that many a historian has grappled with, yet with some distinctive twists that speak to the twentieth-century setting and the topic of not knowing racism. The archival mix that informs this book is one rooted in the peculiar placement of screen culture in the period, as something to be fretted over and concerned about, but ultimately something with relatively little official government involvement. Concerns about the screen and its impact can be traced through the usual means in government archives such as the National Archives and through government inquiries and committees, but also in the countless non-governmental organisations that mounted their own studies of the impact of film and television such as some of the film and television inquiries discussed in Chapter 1. Non-governmental bodies that functioned adjacent to the Home Office, such as the BBFC, are also present. By far the most substantial archive consulted for this work, however, is that of the BBC. Its archive, and the much more diffuse scattering of documents related to ITV and its affiliates (primarily housed at the University of Bournemouth in the Independent

---

[63] Bernard Porter, *The Absent-Minded Imperialists* (Oxford: Oxford University Press, 2006).
[64] Charles Mills, 'Liberalism and the Racial State', in Moon-Kie Jung, João Helion Costa Vargas, and Eduardo Bonilla-Silva, eds., *State of White Supremacy: Racism, Governance, and the United States* (Stanford, CA: Stanford University Press, 2011); Vincent Chabany-Douarre, '"A Sort of Public Living Room": Ignorance and the Racial Management of Disorder in Post-war Los Angeles', *Journal of American Studies* 56, no. 4 (2022): 538–564.

Television Authority and Independent Television Broadcaster collections there) represent media broadcasters that functioned at the intersection of the private and public sectors before other parts of the public sector (such as the NHS, education and universities) began that awkward straddling in the late twentieth and early twenty-first centuries. The archives of a company such as the BBC are simply that, the archives of a company with little official duty to make their material public that is largely engaged in archiving as a branding opportunity (regardless of the excellent staff who work there) to cement their legacy and contribute to their business model, which in the case of the BBC have been under constant scrutiny in the post-war period.[65] Indeed, the BBC's written archive, started in 1936, charges academics per word for quotations from archival material. The complexities of navigating business archives are not a new challenge to the historian of the twentieth century but do raise pertinent issues when it comes to investigating a topic such as racism in the company archive. How much does a company or corporation want to know about its history? And how much does it want the historian to know what it knows?

There are moments in this research where I have come up against clear censorship in the company archive at both the BBC and ITV, such as the thin 12-page folder on *The Black and White Minstrel Show* which includes a note by an archivist from 2007 that they recognise material is missing: 'These references (to Registry Classification N0387 N0441) have been followed up, and these files were found to be destroyed as part of the BBC's Records Management programme and have never been deposited into the BBC Written Archives Centre.' This early records management programme remains a rather murky thing, dateless and unexplained.[66] These types of archival absences speak to what I think historians of the twentieth century need to discuss in greater detail – how new understandings of race, gender, sexuality and class in the late twentieth or early twenty-first centuries have shaped the archival records available to us. We know of spectacular moments of archival censorship, such as what David M. Anderson and Caroline Elkins located in their work on the Mau Mau and the subsequent discovery of the 'migrated' Foreign and Commonwealth Office files, but what of the smaller moments such as these in the BBC archives or in the archives of the Girl Guides that Kristine Alexander has written of, when an organisation's understanding

---

[65] The Boots archive, the Marks and Spencer (M&S) Company Archive and the John Lewis Partnership Heritage Centre are all examples of business archives and, it hardly need be said, employ excellent people.

[66] The current records management policy, from 2014, is available online and indicates the material that should be retained for heritage/historical value. http://downloads.bbc.co.uk/foi/classes/policies_procedures/bbc_records_management_policy.pdf.

of what is questionable or problematic in the archive causes a type of records management by company employees, however formal or informal?[67] How does knowing about racism lead to further silencing of this knowledge, as organisations and even archivists themselves work to protect their brand, reputation, or jobs? In my case, I have been relatively lucky. The written material discussing racism would be sparse anyways considering the framework of racial innocence and ignorance that I have outlined. The BBC archivists, keeping the online catalogue they consult to themselves, are pleased to provide the historian working on race with the established files on the topic. Historians of 'race' and the BBC have commiserated about being put on the same path at the BBC with the well-consulted 'Programmes for Racial Minorities' files and a few choice others. Yet without an online catalogue the proportionality of that material in respect to say, how many files exist about swearing or sexual indecency is difficult to gauge.[68]

This book ultimately builds a bridge between sometimes scarce archives of written material from media producers and consumers that largely denied racialised thinking in their production of media content and the evidence of a visual screen archive of highly racist material that spoke to the proliferation of this thinking. Although the written archives of organisations such as the BBC and ITV or those of film directors such as the Korda brothers do not easily provide evidence of racist thinking in their memos and programming decisions as that thinking was so ingrained as to be literally unremarkable, the content that was ultimately put up on the screen, large or small, speaks to a series of decisions about what audiences wanted when it came to images of Black and south Asian people. The visual legacy of these films and television material is enduring and largely intact and clearly indicates why historic film and television material is not particularly popular with contemporary audiences – this content ages badly and quickly. In the aftermath of George Floyd's murder in the summer of 2022, while most of the country was stuck at home in Covid lockdowns, a debate briefly raged in the UK about the content of shows such as *Fawlty Towers* and others, with their racist and

---

[67] David M. Anderson, 'Mau Mau in the High Court and the "Lost" British Empire Archives: Colonial Conspiracy or Bureaucratic Bungle?', *Journal of Imperial and Commonwealth History* 39, no. 5 (2011): 699–716; Kristine Alexander, 'Can the Girl Guide Speak?: The Perils and Pleasures of Looking for Children's Voices in Archival Research', *Jeunesse: Young People, Texts, Cultures* 4, no. 1 (2012): 132–145.
[68] My understanding is that this catalogue will be available at some point soon, according to Marcus Collins, closing remarks, 'The BBC at 100 Symposium', National Science and Media Museum, Bradford, 13–15 September 2022.

xenophobic content being newly aired, and this issue continues to simmer.[69]

Film and television archives of twentieth-century Britain thus present a 'difficult heritage' to grapple with that speaks of the everyday racism of ordinary white Britons. This book uses critical race theory and its attention to scripts of whiteness as a way of interrogating three archival currents: the scarce moments where race is discussed in an organisation such as the BBC or ITV and the monumental silences that can follow this (such as in Chapter 6); the often shocking content on the screen itself, which says volumes about what has been unspoken but collectively endorsed behind the screen as 'what the audience wants'; and finally the pseudo social-science world of audience research as an exceptional place within the written archives of the BBC and ITV where the silent attitudes of audiences and producers were sometimes said out loud but which was as disregarded at the time as it has been more recently by historians. These three archival currents form the shape of not knowing 'race' in twentieth-century Britain and offer a fascinating insight into the complexities of racialised avoidance, ignorance and silencing through archives of the modern.

This book also makes intermittent use of another type of audience response overlooked by historians of media: the home movie. The home movie or amateur film was in evidence from the 1920s onwards and there are currently thousands in media archives across the UK. Beyond acting as an importance source for the examination of ordinary lives in Briton, the home movie also documents how ordinary Britons engaged with existing screen culture in the period. The ability of ordinary Britons to do so increased after 1965 when Kodak's relatively affordable Super 8mm camera came onto the market.[70] British audiences made home movies and, I will demonstrate, claimed a type of racial innocence while mobilising stereotypes of Black and minority ethnic populations in domestic settings. Blackface practices were evident in a range of home movies produced by Britons from the 1920s to as late as the 1980s and perhaps beyond. Often for the sake of a pageant or parade, both children and adults blacked up as minstrels, Zulu warriors after 1964, golliwogs and as Black hobos. After 1958, when *The Black and White Minstrel Show* was airing regularly on the BBC, it was not uncommon for the home

---

[69] Jim Waterson, 'Fawlty Towers "Don't Mention the War" Episode Removed from UKTV', *Guardian*, 11 June 2022. www.theguardian.com/media/2020/jun/11/fawlty-towers-dont-mention-the-war-episode-removed-from-uktv. This debate in 2022 was not, it must be noted, requested or prompted by the Black Lives Matter movement in the UK.
[70] See Heather Norris Nicholson, *Amateur Film: Meaning and Practice, 1927–1977* (Manchester: Manchester University Press, 2012).

movie to capture floats in community parades devoted to a minstrel show enacted by adults in blackface in imitation of the television show. In this regard, home movies both demonstrate the engagement of a range of Britons with existing screen culture and seemingly affirm the premise of censorship from 1913 onwards – that if it is shown on screen, the people will imitate it. Such sources raise vital questions about the audience's own role in perpetuating the limited racial perception of the screen in Britain. Was this what the audience wanted?

**Organisation**

The following chapters examine the multiple ways in which that central question 'what does the audience want?' was considered in film and television production. It moves in and out through screen content as the ultimate authored answer to this, discussions within institutions, and decisions in response to this question and finally the creation of audience research as a means of addressing it. The book begins at the start of the twentieth century with a more prolonged focus on the interwar period when anxieties about films preoccupied various organisations and people, then moves into the post-war period with the addition of television and ends in the 1990s. This chronological movement mimics how audiences, producers and regulators of British screen culture encountered each new form of screen culture as it was presented and how this new medium influenced thinking on the central question of audience preferences. Within the book, feature films are joined by documentary films which are then joined by television. Home movies, in many ways the most stable of the screen mediums examined here, are addressed intermittently in the book. I have largely concentrated on fictional film and television, or 'narrative' content, instead of news reporting. This is partly because the excellent studies on news reporting on television by Stuart Hall, Sarita Malik, Gavin Schaffer and others make such a study redundant; however, it is also a nod to the moments when film and television producers and directors were most explicitly engaged with producing the fictions they imagined audiences wanted on screen when it came to racialised people and places.[71] Early documentary films are included in this, as an acknowledgement of the considerable shaping of content that occurred at the Empire Marketing Film Board and GPO film units.

---

[71] Malik, *Representing Black Britain*; Gavin Schaffer, *The Vision of a Nation: Making Multiculturalism on British Television, 1960–80* (London: Palgrave Macmillan, 2014); Darrel M. Newton, *Paving the Empire Road: BBC Television and Black Britons* (Manchester: Manchester University Press, 2011).

Chapter 1 examines the discovery of the audience in twentieth-century Britain and sketches out both the anxieties about audience impressionability which were voiced in various government and non-governmental committees on films and television, and the solutions that came to be offered through the developing field of 'public relations' and later 'audience research'. Chapter 2 surveys what ultimately made it to the screen when presenting racialised people, places and themes to British audiences. It concentrates on the thinking behind the production of the popular empire feature films, documentaries about empire and home movies of blacked-up Britons produced in the early twentieth century and ending in 1945, while also noting the responses of audiences of colour to some of this content. Chapter 3 moves into the post-war period and into the Audience Research Department in the BBC archive for the first time, examining two special audience research reports on a 1952 documentary series about Africa and a 1968 Audience Research Report about the BBC's first fictional television series focusing on a Black man's family in Birmingham, *Rainbow City* (1967). Chapter 4 considers how race and racism were presented in post-war television. Much of this chapter focuses on blacking-up practices on television, the related success of *The Black and White Minstrel Show* with white audiences, and its defence by white producers, audiences and the press when Black audiences in Britain protested against it.

Chapter 5 delves deeper into the perspectives of Black audiences by looking at the content of Black 'glossy' magazines produced in post-war Britain. This signals the book's primary focus on representations of Blackness and Black audiences. South Asian audiences and their voices come into this account at numerous points, and the alliance between Black and south Asian groups in the 1960s and 1970s under 'political blackness' attempted to highlight how white people and institutions conflated these groups and identities, even while also often giving disproportionate attention to differences between them. By and large, I have kept the book's attention on Blackness as the primary signifier of racial difference in the book, following the preoccupations of British media with its support of practices such as blacking up and provocations centring on Black neighbours in shows such as *Love Thy Neighbour* as well as the Black sitcoms of the 1980s and 1990s.[72] Chapter 5 takes us

---

[72] I can highly recommend Gurvinder Aujla-Sidhu's work as a comprehensive discussions of contemporary and some historic practices at the BBC, if not the broader broadcasting landscape, when it came to considerations of south Asian audiences; Gurvinder Aujla-Sidhu, *The BBC Asian Network: The Cultural Production of Diversity* (London: Palgrave, 2021).

beyond representations constructed by white people to examine how the Black press 'glossies' imagined Black audiences and their preferences, even as white readers writing into the magazines attempted to shape the relationship of Black audiences to white media culture and their own racial discomfort.

Chapter 6 moves back into the audience research archives of the BBC but also brings in ITV by examining audience research reports conducted at the BBC on *Till Death Us Do Part* in 1973 and the BBC's response to this, as well as an exceptional study of West Indian audiences and their response to *Love Thy Neighbour* conducted for ITV in 1975. It further interrogates the relationship of both institutions with Black and south Asian audiences in that decade. Chapter 7 ends the book with an examination of a seemingly golden age of television in Britain for Black sitcoms looking at three shows that were popular with British audiences: *The Cosby Show* (Channel 4, 1985–1992), *Desmond's* (Channel 4, 1989–1994) and *The Fresh Prince of Bel-Air* (BBC2, 1991–2004). It examines the response of white critics and Black viewers to the programmes both who were looking for two rather different types of racially comfortable viewing at the end of the twentieth century.

Together these chapters offer only glimpses of film and television culture in twentieth-century Britain, and as we shall see the pursuit of the audience, how they were imagined, measured and contested, is sometimes quite fragmentary in the period. The audience was sought but often remained elusive, troubling or contradictory no matter how often film and television producers chased and cajoled them. Nevertheless, across these chapters a sense of this imagining and the racially circumscribed understanding of audience wants, needs and pleasures comes to the fore in twentieth-century Britain. Knowing what the audience wanted, this book argues, was the privileged knowledge of a very few and at the expense of Black and south Asian voices.

# 1 Discovering the Audience
## Anxieties and Expertise

In January 1938, Sir Stephen Tallents, the BBC's first Director of Public Relations, struck a plaintive note in his radio broadcast about the new topic and new department of 'Listener Research' in radio at the BBC. Speaking of the BBC's obligation and the audience that it was tasked with serving, Tallents reflected on the challenges of this:

> We want to give you programmes you will enjoy, and to put on those programmes at times convenient to you. And so we want to find out what programmes you like, and what are your best listening hours. That sounds a simple enough job, I know. It is really very complicated ... Then there are so many of you. That would not matter a bit if you all had the same tastes and all did the same things.[1]

Knowing what the audience 'will enjoy', he argued, was no easy task. Tallents noted that in other forms of entertainment, 'The performer can tell, from the faces of the audience in front of him, just how things are going.' With the new mass media technologies, however, 'The broadcaster in his studio never sees or hears his audience. He can never tell at the time whether you are enjoying his performance or not.' This guessing game was the challenge facing both Tallents and the BBC. Tallents went on to discuss some of the 'new experiments' at the BBC in discovering what audiences enjoyed and did not enjoy. One of these, he explained, was a survey of 'several thousand' listeners, selected at random and asked 'simple questions about their listening'. Tallents hoped that listeners would participate, saying he was sure they would 'for this last year has proved in a very striking manner how generously listeners will help the B.B.C. if they are told, clearly, and in a friendly way, what the B.B.C. wants to know'. Tallents ended by stating that, 'It takes two to make a success of it – the BBC and those who broadcast on the one hand; listeners on the other. This is why I have been talking to you tonight not simply as listeners but as partners.'[2]

---

[1] Stephen Tallents, 'What Every Listener Knows' (Broadcast 8 January), *The Listener*, 12 January 1938, 88.
[2] Ibid.

Tallents' framing of this partnership between broadcaster and the audience in 1938 was not just a clever if somewhat obvious means of enticing ordinary Britons to fill in a survey but also marked a new approach to the public at the BBC. Tallents was specifically tasked at the BBC with thinking through how to appeal to ordinary Britons through media after having a similar role at the Empire Marketing Board (EMB). In Tallents' career he would go on to spend decades examining how best to do this, becoming a highly influential figure in the early imagining of the British public for several organisations besides the BBC including the Ministry of Information during World War II and finally as founder of the Institute of Public Relations in the UK in 1948. His 1932 pamphlet, *The Projection of England*, launched his career in the previously non-existent field of 'public relations' as Scott Anthony has noted.[3] In it, he confidently put forth the case for using various forms of media, including radio and cinema, as a means of bringing English values and products to the world. The trajectory of Tallents' career, from arguing for the use of advertising posters at the EMB to being hired by the BBC as its first Director of Public Relations, signalled the meteoric rise of the fortunes of those men.[4] Those who could self-identify as experts on the masses and who could divine what the masses wanted were heavily prized in 1930s Britain and would continue to be so during the heady days of World War II and the rise of television in the 1950s.

By 1977, however, enthusiasm for what had become known by then as 'audience research' had significantly cooled. The 1977 Report of the Committee on the Future of Broadcasting (the Annan Report) was the fifth government inquiry on broadcasting in Britain since 1923. These inquiries were conducted in rapidly evolving media contexts and the evidence gathered was ever shifting. The Annan Report was released in a time when organisations such as the National Viewers' and Listeners' Association (NVLA), led by Mary Whitehouse, had been campaigning to 'Clean Up TV' for over a decade, and had begun to conduct its own amateur and piecemeal audience research.[5] Universities were investing in 'mass communications' as a field of research underpinned by peer review; the University of Leicester's Centre for Mass Communications Research had been in existence for a decade, and the Annan Committee

---

[3] Scott Anthony, *Public Relations and the Making of Modern Britain: Stephen Tallents and the Birth of a Progressive Media Profession* (Manchester: Manchester University Press, 2012).
[4] Ibid., 131–163.
[5] Viewers' and Listeners' Association (Section 3[1]a TV Act) Vol. 1, May 1965–December 1967) ITA/ITB collection, University of Bournemouth; Lawrence Black, 'There Was Something About Mary: The National Viewers' and Listeners' Association and Social Movement History', in *NGOs in Contemporary Britain: Non-State Actors in Society and Politics Since 1945* (London: Palgrave Macmillan, 2009), 182–200.

members drew heavily on its academics for their expertise in the area.[6] Buried among the Annan Report's most significant recommendation for a fourth television channel provider in the UK (what would become known as Channel 4) was a chapter towards the end of the report devoted to the deficiencies of audience research at the BBC's and ITV's broadcasters. Chapter 29 took aim at the methodologies, staffing composition and outcomes of audience research activities at both broadcasters:

> However sophisticated the methodology, an audience rating cannot be other than an approximation ... It tells nothing about how much attention paid, or whether the programme increased his understanding, awakened his interest, pleased, irritated or bored him. These questions are not at present being answered satisfactorily because both BBC and ITV are tied to the treadmill of audience measurement.[7]

The 'treadmill of audience measurement' was of increasingly limited use by 1977. The Annan Report showed a strong understanding of the workings of audience research, including the range of publications coming out of the BBC's Audience Research Department: the weekly, short standard reports produced for all staff; the longer 'special reports' commissioned by producers or executives; the occasional loose consultation with academics in associated fields (the more specific contracting out to market research firms at ITV broadcasters) and the composition of large viewing and listening panels that were consulted daily and relied on. Crucially, the report also demonstrated clear knowledge of the often slippery role of audience research in each organisation. The committee did not shy away from direct criticism:

> We judge that, given the costs of the programmes and the problems of communicating with the audience, the research efforts of the broadcasting organisations have been too piecemeal, too narrow, and too superficial. The quality of special studies varies greatly. Some have been excellent; others ask unimportant questions use highly unrepresentative samples, resembling a public relations exercise rather than a study which will give insight into the problem under examination.[8]

By 1977, the Annan Committee deemed audience research as something that should be more substantive than a 'public relations exercise', signalling a separation of the two that was certainly not evident in the late 1930s as both fields emerged in modern Britain.

Much of the criticism in the Annan Report was directed at the BBC, indicating that the report had a more tentative grasp of ITV's audience

---

[6] Command Paper 6753, *Report of the Committee on the Future of Broadcasting* (1977), 453.6.
[7] Ibid., 453.   [8] Ibid., 452.

research conducted as it was across 14 companies licensed under ITV at the time. ITV's audience research was singled out for its piecemeal nature but was also praised for showing an engagement with research findings and changing its television content as a result. The BBC's Audience Research Department, on the other hand, was portrayed as operating at a distance from television producers, unable to offer basic answers about audience wants, obsessed with mounting large surveys of the public and dismissed by most who encountered it including television producers, academics and perhaps most damningly BBC management. The report noted that 'the department often seems to have to function like an overworked market research firm, hurriedly assembling studies with no time to bring to bear a broader perspective'.[9] Market research was another field that the Annan Committee clearly thought poorly of by 1977. The committee argued that audience research was an imprecise field, but one where the BBC's Audience Research Department should play a more credible role, noting drily that the BBC 'assured us that top management regarded it as an essential tool. That surprised us, given the few studies which BBC management had requested.'[10] These comments and the subsequent creation of the Broadcasters Audience Research Board (BARB) in 1981 to measure audience viewing for all UK broadcasters, including the emerging Channel 4, marked the end of a long period of divergence between Britain's two television broadcasters where they both separately claimed to know, and to measure, Britain's television audience. The work that the BBC had done in this regard since 1936 under its first Director of Audience Research, Robert Silvey, himself recruited by Tallents, came to an unceremonious end. New approaches, including mechanical devices fitted to televisions to measure audience interest, swept away the past approaches of the department. A new reliance on technology pre-dating the digital-based solutions for measuring audience engagement in the twenty-first century pointed to the future of measuring and anticipating what the audience wanted.

This story of the phenomenal rise of audience research expertise in Britain signals much more than just the bumpy trajectory of a uniquely twentieth-century field of interest and points to an ever-present anxiety in the period about what ordinary people saw on the screen. It signals the underpinnings of what Adrian Bingham calls 'the increasingly self-aware and self-conscious democracy' of twentieth-century Britain.[11]

---

[9] Ibid., 453. [10] Ibid., 456.
[11] Erik Linstrum, Peter Clarke, Adrian Bingham, Lawrence Black et al., 'Forum: The Past, Present, and Futures of Modern British History', *Modern British History* 35, no. 1 (2024): 11.

This consistent fretting about the public's engagement with screen culture animated numerous committees of inquiry throughout the twentieth century led by both government and private organisations and charities. Further, anxieties about the ability of the screen to profoundly impress upon viewers saw the creation of a group of expert individuals and quasi-academic fields such as audience research, market research and public relations, all which promised to address this issue. These operated in a grey area between academia, public service and business, long before the rise of neoliberalism in Britain would make such areas commonplace.[12] Together, the anxieties about audiences and the experts who promised to soothe these and the multiple inquiries on broadcasting or film which showed a government at work in this regard worked to create an imaginary audience that was deeply powerful and motivating not only in British screen culture but also British society more generally. This was no longer a public to be served but an audience to be persuaded, placated, sought and bought. The imagining of audiences and their wants became a steady pastime of large and small businesses; governments and politicians seeking re-election; and screen producers, censors and exhibitors looking to support an industry built on attention.[13] This imagined audience was also crucially envisioned as consistently white by these experts, a vision which had ramifications that the remaining chapters of this book explore.

The collective imagining of British audiences of film, television and even radio as white was an assumption so ingrained and so unremarkable within media production and regulation as to leave relatively little archival evidence except if we turn to the archives of audience research at the BBC's and ITV's affiliates. In the government inquiries that make up part of this chapter's focus, very little attention was paid to audiences of colour. The BBC's interpretation in 1975 of the Annan inquiry, which was then already taking evidence, was that 'the subject of race relations is, at first sight, a minor one in the overall context of Annan', even as the corporation took the care to marshal evidence against claims by the Wandsworth Council for Community Relations that BBC programming was alienating the Black community.[14] Across the 522 pages of the final Annan Report, only two-and-a-half pages were dedicated to the subheading of 'Programmes for Ethnic Minorities' and two-thirds of a page in the section on 'Programme Standards' addressed the 'treatment of

---

[12] This was the age of the expert, as discussed by Matthew Hilton et al., *The Politics of Expertise: How NGOs Shaped Modern Britain* (Oxford: Oxford University Press, 2013).

[13] Tim Wu, *The Attention Merchants: The Epic Scramble to Get Inside Our Heads* (New York: Knopf, 2016).

[14] Memo from Michael Starks, Secretariat, to AHS, CIS, DPA, on 'Wandsworth Council for Community Relations', Evidence to the Annan Committee, 25 March 1975, WAC.

racial minorities' in broadcasting.[15] Even in 1977, relatively little was said by the government about racism on screens (See Figure 1.1). The archives do, however, evidence some limited discussions of the whiteness of this audience in the files of the Audience Research Department. This branch of the BBC was where some of the thornier questions were posed to audiences: why they liked Alf Garnett, the bigoted protagonist of the popular series *Till Death Us Do Part* and why they did not like another series, *Rainbow City*, marking the first time a Black man was featured as a protagonist on British television screens. This chapter along with Chapters 3 and 6 delve into the archives of the audience research departments of the BBC and ITV as sites where the silent part of audience racism was spoken aloud. This will necessitate the type of revisiting of historic research data that Jon Lawrence has discussed in relation to his reuse of post-war sociological studies but with the crucial difference that audience research was not an academic field subject to peer review.[16] The issues raised by Lawrence take on rather a different complexion in the highly improvised area of audience research.

This chapter begins with a focus on the Audience Research Department's formation at the BBC, the improvisations that underpinned it and its engagement with the various government committees, inquiries and other BBC departments that made up its world. It charts three key elements that shaped the imagining of the audience. First, it examines the anxieties that existed and mutated throughout the twentieth century about the impressionability of film and television audiences that underpinned a wide infrastructure of investigation into screen content and its impact. Second, it provides an overview of the answers to these anxieties that emerged through the pseudo-academic fields of public relations, market research and audience research. Finally, the chapter scrutinises the initial imagining of the British audience as white in the interwar period and the related racial exclusion of Black and south Asian audiences. Throughout this chapter, key elements and players are introduced as are the animating anxieties that were involved in first conceiving of and then attempting to answer the central question of the age – What does the audience want?

---

[15] *Report of the Committee on the Future of Broadcasting* (1977), 351–353, 259.
[16] Jon Lawrence, 'On Historians' Re-Use of Social-Science Archives', *Twentieth Century British History* 33, no. 3 (2022): 432–444; John Goldthorpe, 'Historians' Uses of Archived Material from Sociological Research: A Response to the Commentaries on My Paper', *Twentieth Century British History* 33, no. 3 (2022): 451–459.

## 1.1 The Anxieties of Screen Culture

The power of the screen to attract, influence, ad shape the life of the ordinary Briton was no ordinary concern in the early twentieth century. Film was suddenly everywhere – speaking, inspiring, awing and also educating audiences. While concerns dawned during World War I about the influence of the screen as soldiers and civilians escaped to music halls newly exhibiting moving pictures, they gathered pace throughout the 1920s and 1930s as cinema palaces cropped up throughout the country and further intensified as television arrived in earnest in the 1950s. As multiple voices noted, British men and women were regularly consuming images of other men and women moving on screen and speaking in far-away accents in the 'talkies'. Those buying televisions in post-war Britain brought these images into the heart of the home. Both the ubiquity and the appeal of the screen prompted a persistent question: just how impressionable were audiences? The press, morality groups, censors, churches, and the government all posed variations of this question. The importance placed on potential answers to it was tied to the tightly controlled experiment that was democratic Britain. The impressionability of the public carried far greater urgency in an age when these people, this audience, were shaping Britain's political landscape and when the answer to 'what do the people want?' was raising different political answers in Europe. What prevented a full-scale moral panic regarding the screen's influence over the ordinary man and woman was a combination of factors including the immediate and widespread realisation of the profound pleasures associated with watching the projection of living people on the screen and a simultaneous understanding of the economic benefits of cinema and television in periods when the British economy seemed breathtakingly fragile. Finally, the compelling template offered by the BBC as it stepped into regulating and broadcasting radio from 1922 offered an alternative and particularly British path forward for mitigating the attractions of screen culture.[17] This was a compromise between the seeming anarchy of access to media production in the US and the state-centred film production evident in Russia.

What are often overlooked in the story of twentieth-century screen culture are the numerous inquiries and committees on film and television throughout the period which collectively captured this drumming, persistent anxiety about what an impressionable audience could and should see on screen in Britain. Between 1922 and 1999, there were seven

---

[17] Lee Grieveson, *Cinema and the Wealth of Nations: Media, Capital, and the Liberal World System* (Durham, NC: University of California Press, 2017).

Discovering the Audience 37

committees formed by the government tasked with examining broadcasting or television and producing final reports:

- 1923 (Report of the Broadcasting Committee, aka the Sykes Committee, formed in 1923)
- 1925 (Report of the Broadcasting Committee, aka the Crawford Committee, formed in 1925)
- 1935 (Report of the Television Committee, aka the Selsdon Committee, formed in 1935)
- 1936 (Report of the Broadcasting Committee, aka the Ullswater Committee, formed in 1935)
- 1951 (Report of the Broadcasting Committee, aka the Beveridge Committee, formed in 1949)
- 1962 (Report of the Committee on Broadcasting, aka the Pilkington Committee, formed in 1960)
- 1977 (Report of the Committee on the Future of Broadcasting, aka the Annan Committee, formed in 1974)[18]

Most of these committees were struck under Conservative governments, with Labour forming only two of the three post-war inquiries – the Beveridge Committee in 1951 and the Annan Committee in 1974. Two committees were also formed in economic crisis under national governments (Sykes in 1923 and Ullswater in 1935).[19] Alongside this was the odd committee established to investigate a primarily technical element of broadcasting and standards for sets and frequencies. These included elements of the Selsdon Committee of 1935 and the entirety of the 1949 Hankey Report.[20] The size of these reports mushroomed as the century progressed, becoming increasing complex as they took on larger amounts of evidence from a greater number of interested parties. The Ullswater Report of 1936 examined 79 witnesses and ran to 78 pages, whereas the Annan Report of 1977 gathered material from

---

[18] Command Paper 1951, *Broadcasting Committee Report* (London, HMSO, 1923); Command Paper 2599, *Report of the Broadcasting Committee* (London, HMSO, 1925); Command Paper 4793, *Report of the Television Committee* (London, HMSO, 1935); Command Paper 5091, *Report of the Broadcasting Committee* (London, HMSO, 1936); Command Paper 8116, *Report of the Broadcasting Committee, 1949* (Vol I) (London, HMSO, 1951); Command Paper 1753, *Report of the Committee on Broadcasting, 1960* (London, HMSO, 1962); Command Paper 6753, *Report of the Committee on the Future of Broadcasting* (London, HMSO, 1977).

[19] Party in power noted here: 1923 Sykes Committee, Conservative; 1925 Crawford Committee, Conservative; 1935 Ullswater Committee, National Government; 1936 Selsdon Committee, National Government; 1951 Beveridge Committee, Labour; 1962 Pilkington Committee, Conservative; 1977 Annan Committee, Labour.

[20] Command Paper 8116, *Report of the Broadcasting Committee, 1949* (Vol. I).

750 organisations and spent 25 days hearing evidence before producing a 538-page central report (the report and appendices A-D; a separate report on appendices E-I, which were research reports commissioned by the inquiry, was another 172-page document).[21] The Annan Committee described the huge amount of information it received as a 'pleasurable deluge' saying in the report's introduction 'we bathed in memoranda'. They noted that this evidence 'ranged from a lengthy critique of the whole system of broadcasting in the United Kingdom to a single page of comment on programmes or a view of a specific problem' and that 'several thousand letters poured in from individual members of the public'.[22] Not surprisingly the Annan Committee took three years to report its findings and recommendations and marked the last such lengthy and thorough examination of the broadcasting duopoly in the UK. The introduction of Channel 4 in 1982 at the recommendation of the Annan Committee closed out this pattern of broad-ranging scrutiny.

What followed was a new cycle of committees primarily scrutinising the public financing of the BBC.[23] The 1980s and the 1990s saw a series of consultations:

- 1986 Report of the Committee on Financing the BBC (the Peacock Committee)
- 1992 The Future of the BBC: A Consultation Document
- 1994 The Future of the BBC: Serving the Nation, Competing Worldwide
- 1999 The Future Funding of the BBC: Report of the Independent Review Panel[24]

These much more concise reports centred on the BBC licence fee payments for the most part. Gone were the large-scale considerations of the broad influence of television on the public and its role in British life. As Daniel Ruff notes, the language shifted to considering the BBC's

---

[21] Command Paper 6753-1. *Report of the Committee on the Future of Broadcasting, Appendices E-I*, Research papers commissioned by the committee (London, HMSO 1977).

[22] Command Paper 6753, *Report of the Committee on the Future of Broadcasting* (1977), 3.

[23] While writing this book, the Parliamentary Communications and Digital Committee conducted an inquiry, 'The Future of Channel 4', which reported on 26 November 2021, with a government response on 28 January 2022.

[24] Command Paper 9824, *Report of the Committee on Financing the BBC* (London, HMSO, 1986); Command Paper 2098, *The Future of the BBC: A Consultation Document* (London, HMSO, 1992); Command Paper 2621, *The Future of the BBC: Serving the Nation, Competing Worldwide* (London, HMSO, 1994); Davies, Gavyn, *The Future Funding of the BBC: Report of the Independent Review Panel* (London, DCMS, 1999). See also Daniel Ruff, 'Surviving the Committee of Enquiry: A Thriving BBC (1922–1995)', *Revue Française de Civilisation Britannique* (Online) (2021): XXVI-1.

ability to secure consumers rather than extensive scrutiny of radio or television's impact on its audience or public.[25] The audience's mental landscape was no longer to be fretted over quite as much but rather its attention was to be secured for the broadcaster. This extended the continuous pressure on the BBC into the twenty-first century in terms of scrutiny of its reliance on public funding and successive governments' willingness to protect this.

Cinema, on the other hand, had endured intense inspection in its first three decades with only infrequent moral panics about its content in the post-war period as its power relative to television waned. These moral panics were largely addressed through the mechanism of ratings produced the British Board of Film Censors (BBFC) after it came into existence in 1912. In the first decades of the century, however, numerous bodies considered the power of cinema, starting in 1917 with National Council of Public Morals (NCPM) and their Cinema Commission of Inquiry followed by the Commission on Educational and Cultural Films from 1929 to 1932 and a spate of other cinema inquiries from 1930 to 1932. The NCPM was a powerful committee formed of 22 leading figures in Britain including the future president of the Cinematograph Exhibitors' Association A. E. Newbould, the new president of the BBFC, T. P. O'Connor, Marie Stopes and Robert Baden Powell among others.[26] The NCPM heard 17 days of testimony over the winter of 1919 from various largely self-appointed experts on the influence of cinema over ordinary people.[27] Dozens of witnesses were interviewed by the committee including police officers, detectives, teachers, cinema exhibitors and even an anonymous BBFC script examiner. This was one of the first and largest inquiries into cinema but would quickly be joined by a series of investigations by local government and special interest organisations throughout the 1920s and into the 1930s.

In 1932, Stephen Tallents described a media landscape of cinema inquiries run amok in *The Projection of England* while also acknowledging that 'the moral and emotional influence of the cinema is incalculable and

---

[25] Ruff, 'Surviving the Committee of Enquiry', 10.
[26] National Council of Public Morals, *The Cinema: Its Present Position and Future Possibilities. Being the Report and Chief Evidence Taken by the Cinema Commission of Inquiry Instituted by the National Council of Public Morals* (London: Williams and Norgate, 1917), xcii.
[27] The renaming of the council was noted in *The Film in National Life: Being the Report of an Enquiry Conducted by the Commission on Educational and Cultural Films into the Service which the Cinematograph May Render to Education and Social Progress* (London: George Allen & Unwin, 1932), 4; dates of committee hearings recorded in National Council of Public Morals, *The Cinema*.

requires no demonstration here'. Tallents noted that the cinema and its content had already 'been the subject of countless investigations and committees, all of which have recognized the power and most of which have deplored the present manner of its exercise'. The Commission on Educational and Cultural Films (CECF), funded by the Carnegie Trust, made similar comments about the ubiquity of cinema inquiries and committees in *The Film in National Life* (1932) a report which would lead to the creation of the National Film Institute in Britain. The report provided a summary of inquiries and investigations into cinema's influence since World War I, starting its weighty list with the aforementioned Report of the NCPM which had since changed its name to the National Council for Race Renewal.[28] The LCC in 1921 and the Imperial Education Conferences of both 1923 and 1927 were all mentioned as inquiries into cinema's influence, and an earlier reiteration of the CECF had also commissioned a 'Psychological Research Committee' of academics who in 1925 published *The Cinema in Education* which the CECF still strongly endorsed. The CECF report of 1932 recorded with some exasperation that 'in 1930, the Commission found that there were no less than 14 bodies working in its field with which it was necessary to make contact'.[29] It noted that these inquiries included 'minor effort of different kinds, some of it valuable, some of it mischievous, but all of it uncoordinated, except in so far as the Commission has provided a link'. Summarising the inchoate nature of these inquiries both in composition and aim, the CECF argued that 'the lack of guidance and order impedes progress and wastes effort: person after person finds out what is already known but is inaccessible'.[30] The CECF's review of existing inquiries inadvertently highlighted that it too was merely the latest in a long line of bodies attempting to provide the definitive answer to cinema's influence and role in the modern age.

These prolific cinema inquiries petered out in the latter half of the 1930s but not before they and the BBFC collectively imagined the British screen audience as highly impressionable and acknowledged that film's 'indirect influence is enormous' as Tallents had himself put it.[31] At the NPMC inquiry in 1917 the BBFC script examiner who gave evidence discussed his fellow examiners' task when it came to anticipating what the audience should and should not see: 'They have to consider the impression likely to be made on an average audience which includes a

---

[28] Commission on Educational and Cultural Films, *The Film in National Life*, 4, ft. 1.
[29] Ibid., 9.   [30] Ibid.
[31] Stephen Tallents, *The Projection of England* (London: Faber and Faber, 1932), 28–29.

not inconsiderable proportion of people of immature judgement.'[32] This was the paternalist position from which the examiners, all middle- and upper-class white men at the time, imagined the 'average audience'.[33] The system of censorship put forward by the trade-supported BBFC has been interrogated by Jeffrey Richards, James Robertson, James Chapman, Christine Gledhill, Sue Harper, Justin Smith, Lawrence Napper and myself among many others.[34] Richards still offers the most convincing analysis of the preoccupations of the organisation shaping film content for exhibition to British audiences: 'The moral standards to which the cinema had to conform were essentially middle class, and in effect a largely working-class audience was being programmed to accept the concepts of propriety and decorum that prevailed amid the lace curtains and porcelain tea cups of suburbia.'[35] Certainly, T. P. O'Connor's list of 43 items to be censored, produced in 1917, was a masterful document of anxieties about what the ordinary audience member could potentially learn from time in front of the silver screen. According to the list, audiences could learn all sorts of things that needed to not be shown including indecorous dancing, cruelty to animals, unnecessary exhibition of underclothing, the modus operandi of criminals and scenes bringing British prestige in the empire into disrepute.[36] This imagined audience shifted according to anxieties about class, gender and age. It was working-class people, for example, who were likely imagined as the impressionable immature audience when the BBFC chose to prohibit scenes of 'Relations between capital and labour' in its list of censorable items and in its actions throughout the economic depression of the 1920s and 1930s.

---

[32] Statement by one of the BBFC Examiners in National Council of Public Morals, *The Cinema*, 104.
[33] On the background of the script examiners, see Christine Grandy, 'Building Character: Censorship, the Home Office, and the BBFC', in *Heroes and Happy Endings: Class, Gender, and Nation in Popular Fiction in Interwar Britain* (Manchester: Manchester University Press, 2014).
[34] Jeffrey Richards, 'The British Board of Film Censors and Content Control in the 1930's'; James Robertson, *The Hidden Cinema: British Film Censorship in Action 1913–1972* (London: Routledge, 1989); James Chapman, *The British at War: Cinema, State and Propaganda, 1939–1945* (London: I.B. Tauris, 1998); Christine Gledhill, *Reframing British Cinema, 1918–1928: Between Restraint and Passion* (London: BFI, 2003); Sue Harper and Justin Smith, eds., *British Film Culture in the 1970s: The Boundaries of Pleasure* (Edinburgh: Edinburgh University Press, 2011); Grandy, *Heroes and Happy Endings*.
[35] Richards, 'The British Board of Film Censors and Content Control in the 1930s: Images of Britain', 99.
[36] Grandy, *Heroes and Happy Endings*, 224–225.

Post-war television inquiries were just as concerned about what impressionable British audiences were likely to learn from the small screen now in their home, although these inquiries were slightly more reflective and pragmatic. The Beveridge Report on Broadcasting, reporting in 1951, acknowledged the assumptions it worked from: 'Socially, broadcasting is the most pervasive, and therefore one of the most powerful means of affecting men's thoughts and actions', a comment echoed by the Pilkington Report in 1962.[37] The Pilkington Committee presented an even darker vision of screen culture, although one that involved rather more audience agency than had previously been imagined in committee inquiries. It reported that it was audiences themselves who were full of 'disquiet and dissatisfaction' with the state of television. The power of television was immense but, according to the committee, its own audiences were crying out for some regulation of its content: 'It was perhaps largely because they realised what television had done, and could do, that people and organisations that wrote to us as viewers were conscious of what it had done badly, or failed to do at all; of how it had abused its powers, and failed to realise its possibilities.'[38] The Pilkington Report marked the zenith of concern about television audiences speaking of the 'vulnerability' of audiences watching the screen close up in their own homes. Comparisons were made to the conscious decision to go to a movie or read a newspaper versus what was inferred as a passive, inevitable and dangerous consumption of television at home:

Sitting at home, people are relaxed, less consciously critical and, therefore, more exposed. Further, audiences are often family groups and include children, who are normally protected from outside influences, and therefore especially vulnerable. Many submissions emphasised the power of television was due largely to the unique way in which it brought actuality, or the appearance of actuality, into the home.[39]

The committee outlined a dire situation of vulnerable viewers and confused ideas about the reality that television offered its viewers. This was the fragile television audience preyed upon in their own home and which echoed earlier fears about cinema audiences being able to distinguish between fiction and reality in the 1920s and 1930s.

The anxieties about television that the Pilkington report expressed were reiterated by organisations such as the NVLA, which formed in

---

[37] Cmnd. 8116, *Report of the Broadcasting Committee* (1951), 4; Cmnd. 1753, *Report of the Committee on Broadcasting* (1962).
[38] Cmnd. 1753, *Report of the Committee on Broadcasting* (1962), 14.     [39] Ibid., 15.

1964 and submitted evidence to the Annan Committee.[40] Like numerous organisations concerned with screen culture before it, the NVLA painted a vision of ordinary Britons who were heavily influenced by what they saw on screen. In the amateur audience research that the Mansfield branch of the NVLA conducted between January and March 1967, the NVLA identified the primary concerns of the organisation with what British audiences were consuming: swearing, sexuality, denigration of the family and preoccupations with money.[41] The Annan Committee noted in their report that 'Mrs Mary Whitehouse [and the National Viewers' and Listeners' Association have] in recent years campaigned indefatigably on these issues' and outlined their view of the impressionable audience: 'In their view, immoral acts corrupt, bad language degrades cultural standards, and the portrayal of violence leads if not directly to violent behaviour than to a general, and dangerous, desensitivisation [sic].'[42]

Audiences *see* and then *do* was the logic outlined by the NVLA. This was certainly not new: as the report acknowledged, such thinking had also animated previous considerations of Hollywood films and Edwardian theatre in Britain.[43] In the 1970s, it was violence on screen that particularly concerned the Annan Committee and ITV and BBC broadcasters taking prominence in the chapter on 'Programme Standards' in the Annan Report.[44] Here the impressionability of the audience was again under consideration, this time to excessive violence on screen.

Throughout all the inquiries, committees and reports outlined here, Black, south Asian, and racialised audiences were the audiences that were the least considered when it came to the screen's influence. They were rarely considered by producers and regulators of British screen culture unless they were located within the empire where they were then viewed with utmost concern. When it came to cinema in the last throes of empire of the 1920s and 1930s, as we shall see in Chapter 2, much concern was articulated over the impressionable 'native' viewer who might see an English man or woman in a compromised position doing or saying something questionable. Cinema was thought by some officials to be a harbinger of a new type of knowledge of the fallibility of white Britons – something that these officials thought they were keeping a mighty secret from the people they governed. Decisions about what

---

[40] Cmnd. 6753, Appendix A, *Report of the Committee on the Future of Broadcasting* (1977), 505.
[41] Viewers and Listeners Association (Section 3[1]a TV Act, Vol. 1, May 1965–December 1967) ITA/ITB collection, University of Bournemouth.
[42] Cmnd. 6753, *Report of the Committee on the Future of Broadcasting* (1977), 247.
[43] Ibid., 248.   [44] Ibid., ix.

could be shown to local populations in the empire and later the commonwealth were very much dictated by the content and a consideration of the excitable, immature and dangerous impressionability of racialised audiences. These groups, to the frustration of colonial officials, were not thought of often by censors and producers of screen culture in Britain itself; instead it was left to these officials to navigate the complexities of what could and could not be shown to colonial audiences. Black and south Asian audiences living in Britain itself, on the other hand, were persistently ignored even as immigration from parts of the commonwealth such as the West Indies substantially increased after World War II. Black audiences were seldom considered as viewers of film or even television in Britain itself, even by the nascent experts on audience wants.

## 1.2    The Rise of Audience Experts

As the problem of the screen and its impressionable audience was laid out in the numerous film and television inquiries of the twentieth century, a select number of men stepped forward to provide some reassuring direction. New experts on the masses emerged in the 1930s in the fields of 'public opinion', 'market research', 'audience research' and what would also come to be known in the post-war period as the academic field of 'mass communication'. These fields of inquiry would eventually become distinct from each other as the Annan Report indicated in 1977 with its dismissive comments about market research, but they collectively started out in the interwar period united by their central question of 'what does the audience want?' By 1938, Stephen Tallents had been joined by the likes of John Grierson at the EMB in 1926 and then Robert Silvey who was appointed the first ever director of Listener Research at the BBC in 1936. Silvey's role would be instrumental in shaping audience research, and he weathered numerous government inquiries into radio and television broadcasting until his retirement in 1968. Silvey's work at the BBC drew on his experience with his friend, Mark Abrams, at the London Press Exchange (LPE) whose own work in market research would significantly shape that field. From Tallents, a network developed of men of a certain common middle- and upper-class, educated, slightly left-leaning background that considered what audiences wanted and more importantly provided the answers.[45] Together

---

[45] See also Megan Faragher, *Public Opinion Polling in Mid-Century British Literature: The Psychographic Turn* (Oxford: Oxford University Press, 2021). Faragher treats these fields, alongside sociology, as part of a new preoccupation with group-thinking in the mid-century.

these men would provide much of the base of expertise on how audiences were known and imagined in the twentieth century.

Tallents' own genius was to turn concerns and anxieties about the impressionability of the British audience into an opportunity. In his pamphlet *The Projection of England* (1932), he constructed for his reader idealised domestic and international audiences all united by their consumption of British stories from newly powerful mediums.[46] The central figure of the pamphlet was a modern, middle-class English woman living in an 'English provincial town' of Cranford, with a nod to the novelist Elizabeth Gaskell, who no longer had to pore over the one periodical that came to the town 'three times a week'. Tallents outlined the speed and quantity of information that reached that woman in the modern age of the 1930s:

> A single morning's paper will give her news of revolution in Madrid, of famine and battle in China, and of murder in Chicago. Tidings of her relations in Canada and Australia are dropped casually into her letter box. She can telephone to them, if she will, from her fireside. Without moving from her chair, she can listen-in during a single evening to half a dozen European capitals. At the cost of a stroll to the cinema round the corner, she can review the lives and the loves of almost every country but her own.[47]

In this modern age this woman was consuming multiple types of media, of which the screen was an easily accessible one. What Tallents did in the opening pages of *The Projection of England* was to stress the English consumer as a familiar type steeped in tradition and taste. He not only argued that ordinary people across Britain's vast empire wanted more images of Britain but also crucially defined this audience for his readers in reassuring terms that sharply diverged from the various faces of audience impressionability that had been put forth up to this point by censors and inquiries; the fragile child, the flighty woman, the working-class hothead and more rarely the 'native' in Africa. Instead Tallents put forth the calming image of a modern rural woman yearning to learn more. She, and crucially others like her, were audience members with taste and a reasonable view of the world who wanted to both enjoy and learn from the new mediums of radio and film. Anxieties were channelled productively into opportunities instead – for businesses, government, and other organisations to shape this new mass of people. The political economy of knowing the audience started to come into view. As we shall see, the impressionability of British audiences that so had concerned inquiries up to that point was not entirely refuted by Tallents but instead recast as a positive aspect of an otherwise sensible people. Tallents' careful

---

[46] Tallents, *The Projection of England*, 1. [47] Ibid.

construction of various audiences that would benefit from projections of England made him the obvious man to place within nascent media-producing organisations.

By 1938, Tallents had taken this positive vision of impressionability to the BBC where on the surface it appeared to mesh with John Reith's concept of a public service broadcaster informing, educating, and entertaining its audience. In between, Tallents had paved the way for John Grierson at the EMB who had authored a treatise on the subject in the US for a fellowship on 'The Psychology of Popular Appeal' with the Rockefeller Foundation after spending time at the University of Chicago. Grierson provided a shortened memorandum based this earlier work, at Tallents' suggestion, for circulation to the EMB ultimately leading to his employment there under Tallents.[48] Grierson's ideas about the appeal of cinema, as we shall see in Chapter 2, were deeply influential in shaping what was and was not shown on screen when it came to representations of Black and south Asian people in documentary film. Silvey was yet another of these audience experts nurtured by Tallents when he was hired based on his previous work with Mark Abrams. Abrams was able to offer a sense of scale and professionalism to this field of knowing the audience as well as a PhD from LSE and the appropriate class background to quickly make himself well-known in those circles of newspaper men and government most interested in accessing the minds of ordinary people. Abrams' meteoric ascendency within what he called 'market research' began in the 1930s and culminated in the post-war period when he famously discovered the market for teen spending in his 1959 pamphlet *The Teenage Consumer*.[49] His PhD was on the economic origins of the industrial revolution and royal monopolies under the noted economic historian R. H. Tawney. Abrams' first post was as a Lecturer in Agricultural Economics.[50] He would go on to form the company Research Services Ltd which would continue to be used by newspapers such as *The Times* in the post-war period.[51]

The first difficulty faced by the men in the development of these fields, as Tallents put it in his message to BBC listeners in 1938, was that it was 'really very complicated'. How can one tell whether you are giving the audience what they want? Early attempts by the cinema inquiries to

---

[48] John Grierson, 'Notes for English Producers: Part 1. Cinema and the Public', circulated to the EMB, 29 April 1927, TNA: PRO CO 760/37.
[49] Mark Abrams, *The Teenage Consumer* (London: London Press Exchange, 1959).
[50] Interview with Mark Abrams (age 77) by Jean Abrams (grandson, aged 26), recorded in London 19 September 1984, Churchill Archives.
[51] Burton Paulu, *British Broadcasting in Transition* (Minneapolis: University of Minnesota Press, 1961), 164.

establish the impact of cinema content on audiences did place a spotlight on the increasing uniformity of the methods used to gauge cinema's influence. By 1932, similar methodologies involving a combination of questionnaires given to audiences and reports written by designated visitors on their experiences to the theatre were being used by the larger cinema inquiries.[52] The Birmingham Cinema Enquiry Committee distributed a written survey questionnaire to 1,439 children in elementary schools and Girl Guide groups in Birmingham. The children's responses were selectively presented as the direct thoughts and words of the child questioned.[53] The Birkenhead Vigilance Committee gave out 'an almost identical questionnaire' to 1,845 local children and gathered 46 'visitor reports' by adult cinema attendees, who recorded a narrative account of the audience's response.[54] The questionnaires included both closed questions that offered a choice of film genre and open-ended questions that asked recipients to comment on what they had learned from cinema. Together, these four inquiries surveyed 29,073 respondents about their thoughts on the cinema. This approach would also underpin other efforts by organisations such as Mass Observation to survey the attitudes of Britons during the 1936 abdication crisis.[55] Indeed, throughout the interwar period a type of mania occurred for surveying ordinary Britons on a range of topics from cinema preferences to weightier topics measured by the Peace Ballot of 1935.[56] Concern among a number of industries and organisations with knowing what the people wanted fostered a growing familiarity if not embrace of a survey culture in this period.

The approaches to surveying ordinary people that Mark Abrams would perfect under the auspices of market research in the early 1930s were not that different from the approach of these cinema inquiries. As a Lecturer in Agricultural Economics, Abrams began to study how fruits and vegetables were marketed by growers to consumers and how this could improve. In his second year he did 'research on social mobility among children of agricultural labourers' marking a shift into early sociology that would come to characterise Abrams' work and cement both his legacy

---

[52] 'Moral Panic or Flapdoodle', in Sarah J. Smith, *Children, Cinema, & Censorship: From Dracula to the Dead End Kids* (London: IB Tauris, 2005).
[53] Birmingham Cinema Enquiry Committee: Reports of Visits to Cinemas Autumn 1930–Spring 1931, received at HO, 15 May 1931, HO 45/14276 File 551004/92l, TNA.
[54] Smith, 81.
[55] Nick Hubble, *Mass Observation and Everyday Life: Culture, History, Theory* (London: Palgrave Macmillan 2006); Faragher, *Public Opinion Polling*.
[56] Faragher, *Public Opinion Polling*; Helen McCarthy, 'Democratizing British Foreign Policy: Rethinking the Peace Ballot, 1934–1935', *Journal of British Studies* 49, no. 2 (2010): 358–387.

and credibility in the world of academia.[57] Shortly after his return from a fellowship in America at the Brookings Institution, Abrams was approached by a friend and economist at Oxford, Colin Clark, to take a position in 'market research'. Abrams' response to Clark's query indicates just how little was understood about it and how little training or oversight existed within it:

> Colin Clark ... a friend of mine, phoned and said, 'Mark, do you know anything about market research?' And I said 'No'. He said, 'That's alright, ignore that question. The appointments officer here has had a request from a firm in London. They want someone who is a good economist to go and be in their market research department.' And I said, 'Well, if that's what they want, I am prepared to be an expert on market research.'[58]

As a result of this exchange, in December 1933 Abrams was hired at the London Press Exchange (LPE) on a salary of £350 a year, what Abrams called 'real money at last'.[59] Abrams developed his first study on readers of the national press for the company and would quickly come to be known in media and marketing circles as the man who understood 'market research' or what the audience wanted.

LPE was in the 1930s what Abrams identified as 'probably the biggest agency in this country'.[60] It was making significant strides in softening commercial and public attitudes towards advertising in the period by promising what *The Times* called a 'scientific method' to advertising in 1932 and chairing the Advertising Exhibition in the summer of 1933.[61] The scientific method that the LPE promised in 1932 is likely what Abrams stepped in to helm in the winter of 1933. The LPE had promised 'a new intelligence service for newspaper, advertisers, and advertising agents'.[62] *The Times* reported that this service 'is to consist of a comprehensive survey and an exhaustive analysis of the country's Press advertising and will mark a considerable advance in the application of scientific method to advertising technique'.[63] This service was envisioned at the time as involving 'monthly bulletins' on some 700 publications. With Abrams' appointment, this goal had shifted to a more manageable but still large-scale examination of nine national newspapers and readers' responses to these. Abrams' survey of national press readers significantly expanded on the smaller surveys that he had previously conducted in agricultural economics in both scale and subject. This was a study of the engagement of ordinary people with newspapers – the ubiquitous form of

---

[57] Abrams, interview, 35.  [58] Ibid., 40.  [59] Ibid.  [60] Ibid., 41.
[61] 'Plan To Advertise Advertising', *The Times*, 4 February 1932, 9; 'The Advertising Exhibition', *The Times*, 21 July 1933, 18.
[62] Ibid, 9.  [63] Ibid.

media that, as Tallents had noted, allowed an ordinary woman in a small English village to read about what was happening in Shanghai. The survey was meant to provide basic information for advertisers such as 'who were they, what did they read, what did they want to read and so on'.[64] A 'Survey of Reader Interest in the National Morning and London Evening Press 1934' laid out its major points of inquiry in each of its nine volumes in an introductory note led by the key phrase, 'What does the public want?':

> What does the public want? This is the basic question which faces all who attempt, in a competitive market, to satisfy an anonymous mass demand. It is a problem of exceptional difficulty when the commodity to be sold is a modern newspaper, for when the man in the street hands over his penny, he is buying not a homogenous [sic] product, but an amalgam of many elements.[65]

This concise opening introduced the key components of market research as it developed: first, the central deceptively simple problem 'what does the public want?'; second, the assertion that this question was in reality exceptionally difficult to answer; third, the consumer and economic transaction at the heart of this conundrum; and finally, the possibilities and potentials of the penny earned by a company or individual in possession of this expert knowledge. By 1934, this problem had been already plaguing businessmen and government officials for some time but such a concise summing up of this issue was answered by Abrams in a manner that conveyed that this study and its approach was quite novel. Abrams argued that 'in the selling of many commodities, market research has helped to reveal information of this sort' and that 'the Survey was envisioned as an attempt to apply normal market research methods to the selling of newspapers'. The methodology he outlined was not unfamiliar:

> These methods broadly consist of questioning the consumers of a particular product on their reactions to it, and from their answers drawing generalisations as to the size and nature of the available market, and the best means of obtaining this market … Each day readers of nine national papers were faced with the previous day's issue of their paper and asked whether they had read certain news items, and if so, to what degree; that is, whether they had glanced at, partly read, or completely read the items.[66]

---

[64] Abrams, interview, 40.
[65] A Survey of Reader Interest in the National Morning and London Evening Press 1934, Vol. IV, 'Readers' interest in news items', 1–2, GBR/0014/ABMS 2/1/1, The Papers of Mark Abrams, Churchill Archive.
[66] Ibid.

The survey was conducted over 50 days and included 20,000 readers. The large scale of the study distinguished it from most of the cinema inquiries and indicated the seriousness of LPE's enterprise. Yet the scale was born of Abrams' own uncertainty as he forged a path in the new field of market research. At the age of 77, looking back at his lack of experience he relayed in an interview with his grandson:

> And at one point I was asked, 'Do you think that's the right figure.' And I wasn't sure whether they meant that's too small or too big. And I thought maybe they mean it's too small. So I said 'Well of course you could always expand it afterwards if you want to.' But 20,000 turned out to be adequate, and the technique was very simple.[67]

Abrams' approach of a simple methodology of asking the consumer directly, combined with a scale large enough that the study could make plausible claims to be representative of the masses, promised to offer that key insight into what the public wanted at a moment when the new political power of the masses in Britain was of utmost concern. The promise that Abrams and LPE offered was one that few in the business of appealing to the masses could overlook. Newspaper barons, as Dan LeMahieu has argued, were working hard to understand these wants resulting in a broad simplification of language across the major dailies between the wars.[68]

If the press was partnering with the field of market research to understand what audiences wanted, it was a short leap to expect that Britain's newest form of media, radio, would likewise make use of these methods. By the mid-1930s, Reith was hard-pressed to avoid market research as a pathway to serving the audience at the BBC. Both the Ullswater and Selsdon reports of 1935 and 1936 made little reference to public wants except to note a division of Public Relations existed alongside that of Programmes, Administration and Engineering.[69] This was a fledgling division at that point at the BBC, but with Tallents arriving in 1935, a unique, tricky relationship between audience wants and BBC programming began to emerge. Tallents soon introduced 'Listener Research' as a new presence underpinned by the type of audience surveys that were already in circulation. Listener Research would emerge out of and intersect with the field of market research in key ways as Tallents appointed Robert Silvey as a new Director of Listener Research. Silvey described himself as a 'middle-class socialist' in his 1974 memoir *Who's Listening?*

---

[67] Abrams, interview, 41.
[68] Dan LeMahieu, *A Culture for Democracy* (Oxford: Oxford University Press, 1988).
[69] Cmnd. 5091, *Report of the Broadcasting Committee* (1936), 9.

*The Story of BBC Audience Research* and recounted his hiring at the BBC as an entrance into a poorly defined field that emerged through happenstance.[70] Silvey had worked with Abrams at the LPE in what Silvey called a 'happy two-year working relationship' and 'a life-long friendship'.[71] He had also, crucially, conducted a survey at LPE on the numbers of British listeners tuning into continental radio stations for potential radio advertisers. Based on this and his work with Abrams on the first reader survey, Silvey was invited for lunch at the Garrick Club in London with Stephen Tallents and his right-hand man, Pat Ryan, in 1936. This was followed by a job offer as 'the BBC had decided that it must have some listener research and was looking for someone to set it up'.[72] Silvey's qualifications included an aptitude for numbers as a statistician but little else as he noted: 'This was before the days when market research had attained the status of a recognised profession. Few were practicing it and those who did had no specialized academic training for there was none to be had'.[73] Silvey's memoir repeatedly emphasises his largely unchecked and unscrutinised development of the field of Listener Research and then Audience Research at the BBC.

Silvey was left to navigate the development of audience research in the peculiar institution of the BBC which was at that point not under the same commercial pressures that the advertisers that Silvey had previously worked with at LPE were. Silvey had had an earlier encounter with R. S. Lambert, founding editor of the BBC periodical *The Listener*, who had made passing comment that the BBC would never allow anyone in the organisation to engaged in listener research.[74] This likely reflected the hostility that Reith had to the idea of being dictated to by audience wants and his ongoing prickly relationship with Tallents himself.[75] The BBC under Reith adhered strongly to a vision of itself as part of the public sector and listener research signalled a murkiness in that role and the related pressure to please the audience as a consumer. Speaking of the task ahead of him, Silvey wrote:

It was a challenge. This was not only because no public service broadcasting system had grappled with listener research before so that one would have to devise suitable methods as well as apply them, but even more because, even though Lambert's remarks could not be taken at face value, it was obvious that

---

[70] Robert Silvey, *Who's Listening: The Story of BBC Audience Research* (London: George Allen & Unwin, 1974), 16.
[71] Ibid.   [72] Ibid., 18.   [73] Ibid., 20.   [74] Ibid., 17.
[75] Anthony notes just how fractious the relationship between Tallents and Reith was, arguing that Reith managed to stymie Tallents' career through strategic encouragement of him into posts during World War II; *Public Relations*, 131–163.

the BBC's attitude to listener research would not be the same as that of a commercial enterprise.[76]

Silvey understood that the BBC would not have the same deep desire to know 'what was in most of their customers' minds, how they behaved, or why they behaved as they did'.[77] Of commercial broadcasting and the BBC, he noted that:

> Commercially financed broadcasting stations had the same kind of basically simple objective. They could only survive if they pleased their customers – the advertisers. But the position of the BBC was different: as a public service system of broadcasting it had an obligation to the whole of its public which could not be met simply by seeking to satisfy the majority.[78]

In other words, the BBC was not beholden just to audience wants but a responsibility to shape what audiences *should* want and what amounted to good taste. Silvey also suspected that he would have to win over his new colleagues who 'might even, because of my background in advertising, be suspicious of me'.[79] Tallents smoothed the way for Listener Research in the organisation by forming an initial Listener Research Committee which he chaired and which also involved the Director of Programme Planning, Director of Features and Drama, a senior engineer, and the Director of Foreign Relations.[80] The committee was short-lived but acted as a means of introducing Listener Research and Silvey to higher-ups in the BBC without yet making it a formal department. That began collecting listener data in 1939.[81] Silvey helmed the Listener Research Unit within the Public Relations Division until World War II broke out and Listener Research was promoted to a full-fledged department with Silvey as its Director. Listener Research under Silvey became Viewer and Listener Research with the advent of regular television broadcasting, and then finally Audience Research encompassing both divisions.[82]

Throughout his time there, Silvey demonstrated an almost eerie flexibility when dealing with the varied pressures of the BBC and navigating the public/private tension that the department embodied in the organisation, while also working out how best to measure audience attitudes. Silvey's approach was to, by and large, agree with any criticism directed his way. When approached in 1948 by then Director of the Spoken Word, George Barnes, with a suggestion that Audience Research was 'ripe' for scrutiny by an 'outside expert', Silvey agreed. He acknowledged

---

[76] Silvey, 19.   [77] Ibid.   [78] Ibid.   [79] Ibid.   [80] Ibid., 24.
[81] Paulu, *British Broadcasting in Transition*, 170.
[82] I refer to this department as the Audience Research Department throughout, following Silvey's own decision in his autobiography.

of the Audience Research Department that 'the form it had taken and the methods it used were pretty well entirely what I had suggested because there hadn't been anyone else in the BBC in a position to say I was wrong'. At this point, however, Silvey noted that the 'Corporation was still stuck because this wasn't a field with which they were acquainted'. Silvey was asked to suggest an external examiner for his own department and reflected 'that the obvious choice, as the outstanding figure in market research at the time, was my old friend Mark Abrams!'[83] What resulted from Abrams' investigation were the expansion of the Audience Research department and a new budget of £10,000 a year for 'ad hoc enquiries and experiments'.[84] The department took on a statistician, Brian Emmett, who would succeed Silvey as head of Audience Research on his retirement in 1968 and several psychologists. Surveys and experiments were now conducted alongside surveying about 2,000 listeners and viewers a day and the production of thousands of daily audience research reports.[85] In this case the sheer complexity of audience research left the BBC with no choice but to rely on the department it wanted to investigate to appoint its own inquisitor. Unlike academic fields, a peer-review system was never put in place for audience research and nor could one be considering both the scarcity of practitioners at the time but also the business interests in the outcomes of the research.

Under Silvey audience research at the BBC would expand considerably. An American academic who published a book on the BBC and ITV in 1961, Burton Paulu, recorded the Audience Research Department at the BBC as housing 25 full-time staff, 60 secretarial staff, 1,200 'part-time field interviewers', and drawing on 6,000 volunteers for their listening and viewing panels; ITV operated a much different approach that relied on external contractors that could change depending on the licence holder.[86] All ITV broadcasters were wedded to data produced by a company called TAM (Television Audience Measurement) hired by ITV to record its audience share after ITV moved away from using the BBC's measures of the audience in the first year of its existence. The mechanical meter that TAM used, known as the TAM-o-meter, was installed into a television of a volunteer family that would record what channel was on when and for how long. With the advent of commercial television came these types of methodologies imported from the US.

---

[83] Silvey, *Who's Listening*, 136.  [84] Ibid.
[85] Billy Smart, 'The BBC Television Audience Research Reports, 1957–1979: Recorded Opinions and Invisible Expectations', *Historical Journal of Film, Radio and Television* 34, no. 3 (2014): 452–462.
[86] Paulu, *British Broadcasting in Transition*, 170.

William Beveridge, in his committee's Television Enquiry from 1950, acknowledged begrudgingly that 'the way in which broadcasting is financed in the US makes determination of the numbers actually listening to a programme a matter of practical importance ... Listener Research has thus been carried further in the US than in Britain', and noted that the numbers of whatever system was in use were also 'published in the trade press'.[87] TAM also used audience panels called Tamlog Panels to supplement this data. TAM's approach mimicked that of the American company AC Nielsen, formed by Arthur Neilsen Sr who had created the Nielsen ratings. It was the practice in this new heady age of market research for companies to form and then brand their methodologies or technology such that the company and method were identified as one.[88] Neilsen Sr had worked for a time in Britain before ceasing expansion there in 1959, and not before publishing a book on the topic.[89] In the UK, TAM introduced new means of measuring the audience alongside the methods of the BBC's audience research department which avoided mechanical intervention on television sets until 1981. Crucially, TAM's approach measured what the audience actually did in terms of changing the channel rather than what they said they did, which is what the BBC's data relied upon.

The methodologies that Silvey used, which mimicked those of Abrams, depended upon trusting that the audience did what it said it did. A transparent audience was key to both the methodologies developed in both early market research and audience research. This approach remained largely unquestioned until the implementation of the TAM-o-meter for ITV in 1956. For the first time, the spectre of an untruthful audience emerged and would ultimately lead to the use of focus groups by market research from the mid-1960s.[90] From 1956 until 1981, two systems of audience measurement were at play in the UK capturing an ongoing struggle among broadcasters about how best to measure audience engagement with television content. The BBC under Silvey relied on phoning viewers and listeners and asking questions about the content of the programmes they had watched the previous day. The average questionnaire involved 2,000 people who would be phoned by someone identifying themselves from Audience Research at the BBC.

---

[87] Cmd. 8116, *Report of the Broadcasting Committee*, Vol. I, Appendix G (1949), 293.
[88] The Hooper rating for radio was another example.
[89] Paulu, *British Broadcasting in Transition*, 172, fn.; Silvey saw this as a meek retreat by Nielsen in his efforts to expand; Silvey, *Who's Listening*, 176; Arthur C. Nielsen, *Television Audience Research for Great Britain* (New York: A.C. Nielsen Co., 1955).
[90] D. L. Morgan, 'Robert Merton and the History of Focus Groups: Standing on the Shoulders of a Giant?', *American Sociologist* 53, no. 3 (2022): 364–373.

Discovering the Audience 55

The BBC and Silvey's main argument against TAM's form of measuring engagement was that television was used in many households as a form of background noise. Silvey argued that measuring just what channel was on formed an incomplete measure of engagement:

> There was one glaring difference between what we and TAM respectively meant by the word 'audience'. For us it meant people and for TAM it meant TV-sets ... Our method provided no information about the number of sets which had been switched on to a programme just as TAM's meters could provide no information about the number of people who viewed it.[91]

The BBC placed the emphasis on what the audience had learned from what they had heard or watched adhering to a dual logic of audience impressionability as well as transparency in their willingness to say what they had watched.

The results of the two systems varied widely and each favoured its own broadcaster. The debate about which method was superior occasionally played out in the press, who took up a somewhat pedantic topic with only feeble enthusiasm. The initial clash of figures in 1955 made for headlines in the *Daily Mail* and included numbers-heavy reporting and discussion of methodologies.[92] ITV argued early on that the interviewee talking to the BBC in an effort to please the questioner and align themselves with its more respectable, middle-class reputation would overestimate his or her own engagement. The press continued to look in on this feud only in as much as certain broadcast events highlighted the disparity such as election night coverage. The *Guardian* in 1967 noted that the BBC claimed an audience of 16 million people on election night while also pointing out that ITV had equal shares if one measured just the number of sets or 'homes' that were watching coverage.[93] Silvey himself would occasionally release evidence of Audience Research's work.[94] When the newspapers tried to make too much of the conflict between TAM and the BBC, in a letter to *The Times* Silvey refuted reporting on the conflict calling it a 'mischievous distortion' and again belaboured the distinction between measuring sets tuned in to a channel and interviewing people on engagement.[95] Even within the BBC Silvey was careful to not dismiss the TAM methods for those who thought that ITV was 'cooking the books,' writing in his memoir 'I did my utmost to counter such views – risking

---

[91] Silvey, *Who's Listening*, 180.
[92] 'ITV clash with BBC on viewing figures', *Daily Mail*, 5 December 1955, 7.
[93] 'Home News', *Guardian*, 9 April 1966, 2
[94] 'Mr Silvey Knows the Answers', *Daily Mail*, 8 December 1945, 3.
[95] R. J. Silvey, 'Audience Measurement', *The Times*, 1 March 1966, 13.

the charge that "all you research chaps stick together".[96] In 1966, two years before retiring, Silvey talked at length about the difference between the two systems in his BBC Lunchtime Lecture on 'The Measurement of Audience'. This did little to dispel the conflict and *The Times* noted that same year that 'TV Audience Conflict Sharpened' after TAM committed to publishing the most popular television shows in nine categories, something that the BBC refused to share but which was common practice in the US.[97] In 1969, however, Independent Broadcasting Authority (IBA) began using a Television Opinion Panel of some 600 people marking a move towards a combined approach of technology and surveying in a nod to the strengths of the BBC approach.[98] The Head of Research at ITA (and later Head of Research at IBA when it was renamed 1972), Ian Haldane, discussed this briefly in the press although he proved a much quieter presence than Silvey. Regardless of the debates and shifts, in 1977 the Annan Report offered its damning account of Audience Research at the BBC, perhaps not coincidentally after Silvey had retired.

In 1981, a new organisation to assemble audience ratings from all the UK's broadcasters came into existence as the Broadcasters Audience Research Board or BARB. Peter Meneer, then head of the Audience Research Department at the BBC, changed the name of the department one last time in 1980 to the Broadcasting Research Department while acknowledging that '1980 will be the final complete year of the long-established BBC responsibility for measurement of TV audiences'.[99] An era had come to an end. What BARB consisted, and still consists, of is a combination of a viewing panel still relying on questioning viewers themselves and technical means of measuring the activity of the device that is broadcasting.[100] BARB claims to function as 'the industry's standard for understanding what people watched' and works to provide data for all broadcasters independent from them. This was the ultimate compromise that emerged in 1980 as new broadcasters such as Channel 4 were about to enter the fray. Reliable data that straddled the historic approaches of the BBC and ITV became the focus even as the mechanics of audience research migrated to yet another company. Meneers, writing in the 1980s, adhered to the BBC's other key commitment as reason for allowing this change: 'There are some broadcasting research issues that

---

[96] Silvey, *Who's Listening*, 178.
[97] 'TV Audience Conflict Sharpened', *The Times*, 21 February 1966, 6.
[98] David Wilsworth, 'Viewers to Judge ITA Items', *The Times*, 1 January 1969, 3.
[99] Peter Meneers, *Annual Review of BBC Broadcasting Research Findings*, no. 7 (1980), xi.
[100] See www.barb.co.uk.

are best undertaken outside of the BBC and its services. In this way impartiality can be assured.'[101] The department itself, however, continued at the BBC, conducting special studies as usual and releasing its annual review. Elements of the department still claimed to know what the audience wanted even if the measurement occurred somewhat at a distance.

In part, the function of appearing to survey the audience could be more important than the actual survey results because of just how difficult it was to establish the relationship between media and its impact upon viewers. The results of these surveys could be and were often dismissed by those in involved in media production and even treated with disdain by some. The very first page of Silvey's book defensively stated: 'Some will think it a more serious omission that this book contains so few examples of decisions made as a direct result of audience research findings.' Silvey could point to very few successes for audience research having much impact at the BBC under his reign, and this was a man not modest in outlining what he had done at the organisation. He went on to outline the greatest criticism of the department and his rebuttal: 'This is not because the findings of audience research were consistently ignored, my department being nothing but an elaborate facade intended to foster the delusion of that the BBC took cognisance of its public. (Had this been so the Corporation, more often hard-up than flush with funds, would long since have called the whole thing off).'[102]

Silvey was very aware of how audience research could appear to be seen and was perhaps also a bit naive about its usefulness to an emerging media giant such as the BBC in the twentieth century. Investigation of its files shows a large department within the BBC that was both easily shunted to one side in terms of programming decisions but usefully pulled out for the multiple government inquiries resulting from persistent anxieties about audience impressionability such as the Beveridge, Pilkington and Annan inquiries. It was, during the crucial time of consolidating media production in radio and television, *the* mechanism by which the BBC could demonstrate its commitment to the part of the charter that demanded that it serve the public by claiming to know the public. Silvey recounted the considerable preparation put into each broadcasting inquiry starting with Beveridge who, it was rumoured, 'was determined to find *something* wrong with an organisation which he thought, as did a good many others, had been showered with a great deal more praise than was good for it'. Silvey recounted how the then

---

[101] Meneers, *Annual Review*, xii.   [102] Silvey, *Who's Listening*, 11.

Director-General William Haley had him prepare two documents for Beveridge on audience research, one quite technical 'as a contribution to softening up the old man [Beveridge] by tickling his statistical pallet'.[103] The BBC came through unscathed but it was the Pilkington committee that most worried Silvey. Silvey was concerned that the report would offer a final decision on the validity of the two research methods now in place in the UK. He reported with pleasure upon the report's release that the BBC's audience research had been praised and noting that he appeared as a witness before this inquiry as he had for the Beveridge inquiry.[104] The Pilkington Report was largely critical of the advent of ITV and the arrival of commercial advertising and overall the BBC and the quality television it produced came off comparatively quite well within it. The Annan Report, published after Silvey retired, did not offer such a rosy view of Audience Research at the BBC. Instead, it praised ITV and its affiliates as being more reactive to the audience research it often contracted out to agencies or did in-house and for being able to work with academics. It was academia and fields such as mass communications, building upon sociology's strides, that was gaining credibility in terms of peer-reviewed quantitative and qualitative studies of ordinary behaviour. The report pointed out:

> The IBA's research, while on a considerably smaller scale than that of the BBC was in some respects better focussed. The IBA were better able to stand back from day-to-day audience research work and either themselves carry out studies or commission analyses from ASKE and academics such as Goodhardt and Ehrenberg about changes in people's viewing and outlook.[105]

IBA as representative of ITV was better embedded with academic research in this area and was, it was implied, outstripping the work of audience research at the BBC and able to act on the research it conducted or commissioned more decisively. The BBC's research department's inward focus and function was hinted at, as it had only began to make some of its findings more widely available in 1974 as the Annan committee began its inquiries and in the form of its *Annual Review of BBC Audience Research Findings* (renamed *Annual Review of BBC Broadcasting Research Findings* in 1980).[106] This publication looked like an academic journal in its format but contained material that was not subject to peer review. Television and cinema inquiries throughout the post-war period became places where the works of

---

[103] Ibid., 134.  [104] Ibid., 201–202.
[105] Cmnd. 6753, *Report of the Committee on the Future of Broadcasting* (1977), 247.
[106] *Annual Review of BBC Audience Research Findings* no. 1 (1973/74).

audience research were cited but seldom shared. As the century wore on, academic research increasingly replaced much of the company research that was being relied upon by government inquiries indicating the eroding status of these departments within broadcasting organisations.[107] This highlights a particularly salient point about audience research as it developed, which was its actual usefulness to that central question plaguing producers and organisations: 'What did the audience want?' The truth be told, Audience Research did not often seem to supply this answer.

Audience Research was expensive to mount, hard to understand, and could with the right spin often be dismissed due to the minor reach of its claims. We shall see evidence of this throughout the book. As Silvey acknowledged in his memoir, 'Audience research findings were rarely, and in the nature of things could seldom be, the only considerations to be taken into account in decision-making.'[108] Some producers hated the information that audience research could produce; those voices came to the fore in the Annan Report when it reported: 'We were not surprised to learn from many producers that they did not find the work of the research departments of much help, and from some producers that the departments had no time to do the studies they needed for their programmes.'[109] After all, knowing the audience was the producer or writer's task and the more important skill was to anticipate what they wanted. Most creatives knew that the ability to offer fresh material and new approaches to audiences was not easily measured. Yet, the murkiness of the processes that both creatives and audience research possessed when it came to knowing the audience also added a degree of flexibility to both. The development of audience experts and their methodologies across the twentieth century was ultimately a complex story of who could claim the authority to know the British audience in the age of mass media and even more importantly who could be *seen* to know this audience. Appearing to measure the audience was almost as vital as actually measuring them in this period of anxiety about audience impressionability.

---

[107] The post-war relationship between private sector market research and emerging academic fields such as mass communication is a fascinating one worthy of a sustained investigation. While academic sources seemed to be valued by the government in terms of the film and television inquiries that I have laid out here, market research still dominated in the private sector even as its methods underwent significant changes. See also Sean Nixon, *Hard Sell: Advertising, Affluence and Transatlantic Relations, c. 1951–69* (Manchester: Manchester University Press, 2013).
[108] Silvey, *Who's Listening*, 11.
[109] Cmnd. 6753, *Report of the Committee on the Future of Broadcasting* (1977), 247.

## 1.3  Not Knowing Black and South Asian Audiences

The story of audience research laid out up to this point is very much that of a privileged few who because of their class background, education, connections and skin colour were allowed to experiment on the job as they defined new fields of public relations, market research and audience research in the twentieth century. These men's careers spanned the 1930s to the 1970s, before a gradual shift saw a more definitive split between academic research on mass communication and market research. In academia, scholars working in centres such as the University of Leicester's Centre for Mass Communications Research, and Edinburgh University were heavily relied upon for their expertise by the Annan Committee.[110] In market research, new technologies for surveying the audience emerged and grew in pace in the 1980s as cable television entered the sphere and the computer age dawned. This story of development, consolidation and new innovations for getting at that key question – what did the audience want? – all seemingly pointed to what one would expect as a greater knowledge of the audience, or audiences, in the twentieth century. There was significant accrual of exact, specific, although also often unintelligible, data about a range of topics such as violence on screen, children and the screen, responses to general elections, and the type of material that preoccupied the special reports by the BBC, IBA and the cinema inquiries also referenced. Yet, the glaring omission of a lack of data and more so a lack of *interest* in Black and south Asian audiences is noteworthy. Indeed, it is why this lone sub-heading exists as a tiny addendum to the story of audience research in this chapter. In many ways, the fields of public relations, market research and audience research were built on the assumption that Black and south Asian people did not constitute the audience that they or their customers imagined.

Subsequent chapters outline how Black and south Asian television and radio audiences were in rare moments consulted by the BBC, particularly in a meaningful exchange which consisted of two days of meetings on 'Programme for Immigrants' in July 1965: one day with south Asian immigrants and another with West Indian immigrants. In the case of south Asian immigrants, a resulting 'Immigrants Programme Unit' was created for radio broadcasting but this as well as the two days of meetings were conducted without any staff present from the Audience Research Department. This absence is notable and points to the racialising

---

[110] Ibid., 6.

assumptions at play at the BBC about who its primary audience was. ITV through the ITA and ITB was no more progressive as we shall see in Chapter 6. The whiteness of the audience that the BBC and ITV imagined extended not just from audience experts themselves and executives in both organisations, but to the interviewers sent out into the field. The BBC Audience Research Department's *Handbook for Interviewers* revised edition from 1968 expected interviewers to have two hours free every day to do interviews and to be able to 'approach and question strangers in an easy but tactful manner' and be 'honest and intelligent enough to work methodically on their own to our instructions'. Interviewers were expected to interview a range of 'contacts' although a section entitled 'Contacts to avoid' stated that 'foreigners with little English' were part of this small group, alongside the 'very deaf' and 'people in a hurry'.[111] Nothing else was said about West Indian, south Asian, or other audiences of colour in the guide even though surely these groups, particularly to the rather London-centric BBC, were evident by 1968.

As Rob Waters notes, concerns about the presence of Black militants or the Black Panthers on screen for consumption by white British audiences were evident in discussions of the broadcast of the 1968 Olympics in Mexico; yet television audience research seemed immune to this broader context.[112] Black and south Asian viewers were all but invisible to audience research departments even as they fretted about white viewers responding to discussions of 'race' on screen; this is a story that will be unpicked throughout the remaining chapters. This lack of attention to audiences of colour within audience research did not always extend to other more academic fields of inquiry, and the early sociological studies of immigrants of colour into Britain contain some consideration of racialised people as a media audience as well as superficial consideration of how media representations of Black and south Asian people were impacting white audiences. Kenneth Little's 1948 study, *Negroes in Britain: A Study of Racial Relations in English Society*, pointed out that with West Indian people, 'among the younger members, and the women, film-going is by far the most popular form of entertainment … The young girls are likely to attend up-town cinemas at least twice if not three times a week, and sometimes more often.'[113] The 'glossy'

---

[111] 'BBC Audience Research Survey of Listening and Viewing: Handbook for Interviewers', R9/2, 258/1, WAC.

[112] Rob Waters, 'Black Power on the Telly: America, Television, and Race in 1960s and 1970s Britain', *Journal of British Studies* 54, no. 4 (2015): 947–970.

[113] Kenneth Little, *Negroes in Britain: A Study of Racial Relations in English Society*, revised (London: Routledge and Kegan Paul, 1972), 165–166.

periodicals discussed in Chapter 5 also drew attention to Black audiences and their cinema and television viewing habits.

It was left to audience research and its development as a field to stay persistently blind to Black and south Asian audiences as it developed, expanded, and ultimately became a central part of media production in Britain. All the conditions for surprise about the racist views of its white audiences, explored in Chapter 3, were established in the very genesis and development of audience research as a field within television and cinema. The white viewpoints of white producers thinking of what white audiences wanted on screen when it came to images of Black and south Asian people created both a type of screen content that functioned as a white 'habitus' for viewers in much of the twentieth century and the conditions of exclusion for Black and Asian talents in the media workforce.[114] If audiences of colour could seldom be imagined, neither could the need for Black and south Asian voices within visual media production. The development of audience research, born of the anxieties about what an impressionable audience would see or do if they witnessed certain things on the screen, was premised in large part on not imagining people of colour as part of that impressionable audience.

---

[114] Pierre Bourdieu, *Outline of a Theory of Practice* (Cambridge: Cambridge University Press, 1977).

## 2 Audience Wants
Film and the Pleasures of Racism, 1900–1945

At the end of the 1930s, Paul Robeson, the Black American singer, actor and activist, and Bertolt Brecht, the white German playwright of *The Threepenny Opera,* both separately contemplated the empire films that were then dominating cinemas and the central question of the age: what do audiences want? Brecht watched the US-produced empire film *Gunga Din* (1939) on the big screen, likely in Sweden, and recounted his own enthusiastic and emotional response and those of fellow audience members:

> My heart was touched too: I felt like applauding and laughed in all the right places. Despite the fact that I knew all the time that there was something wrong, that the Indians are not primitive and uncultured people but have a magnificent age-old culture, and that this Gunga Din could also be seen in a very different light, e.g. as a traitor to his people ... Obviously artistic appreciation of this sort is not without effects. It weakens the good instincts and strengthens the bad, it contradicts true experience and spreads misconceptions, in short it perverts our picture of the world.[1]

Brecht admitted that in *Gunga Din* he saw a film that moved him but also acknowledged that he possessed a different perspective on this encounter rooted in his knowledge of the anti-colonialist perspective that a growing cadre of thinkers were sharing in the interwar period. Brecht bluntly described the film from that perspective: 'I saw British occupation forces fighting a native population' and admitted that even that viewpoint did not prevent him from laughing at the film 'in all the right places'.[2] He showcased this doubled understanding of the film as he contrasted his intellectual knowledge of the British empire as oppressive in India with his and the audience's emotional response to the plot and characters:

---

[1] John Willet, ed. and trans., *Brecht on Theatre: The Development of an Aesthetic* (New York: Hill and Wang, 1964), 151. Also quoted in Jeffrey Richards, 'Boys Own Empire: Feature Films and Imperialism in the 1930s', in John McKenzie, ed., *Popular Culture and Imperialism* (Manchester: Manchester University Press, 1986).

[2] Richards, 'Boys Own Empire' in McKenzie, ed., *Popular Culture,* 151.

An Indian tribe – this term itself implies something wild and uncivilised, as against the word 'people' – attacked a body of British troops stationed in India. The Indians were primitive creatures, either comic or wicked: comic when loyal to the British and wicked when hostile. The British soldiers were honest, good-humoured chaps and when they used their fists on the mob and 'knocked some sense' into them the audience laughed. One of the Indians betrayed his compatriots to the British, sacrificed his life so that his fellow-countrymen should be defeated, and earned the audience's heartfelt applause.[3]

For Brecht, the British were clearly not a benevolent force who 'knocked sense' into a 'native population' and Indians were not 'wild and uncivilised' but this was what the screen proposed and what he and his fellow audience members responded to and enjoyed. There was an almost undeniable racial pleasure in succumbing to this thrilling narrative and consuming this imagery of white men triumphing over Indian men on the big screen.

Paul Robeson also spoke of this conflict between what he knew of the world of racialised peoples and what the silver screen told audiences about it. When Robeson joined the British film *Sanders of the River* in 1934, directed by Zoltan Korda and based on the popular short stories of Edgar Wallace, he was cast as Bosambo, a Nigerian tribal chief, who helps British Commissioner Sanders in subduing Bosambo's rival in the region. The film shows Bosambo as child-like, initially attempting to deceive Commissioner Sanders or 'Lord Sandy' about his identity before Sanders quickly sees through the deception and chastises him. References to Sanders' African 'children' throughout the film frame Bosambo's intellectual and physical abilities. Bosambo, like the character of Gunga Din, supports British efforts to prevent another indigenous figure from organising against them, in this case the old King Mofolaba. Bosambo, aided by the machine guns that Sanders brings, is able to overthrow Mofolaba's people and kill the king. Peace is ultimately restored under the British-supported rule of Bosambo. With a plot not unlike what Brecht had outlined regarding *Gunga Din*, *Sanders of the River* was heralded by the *Daily Mail* as a 'masterly film' even if the *Guardian* noted that it did not delve much 'into African psychology'.[4] The film was a considerable success with British audiences.

Robeson's motivations for making *Sanders in the River* were rooted in his hopes to educate rather than just entertain white audiences about the lives of Black people as a type of counter-storytelling to what was usually

---

[3] Ibid.
[4] F. G. Prince-White, 'Thrills in a Masterly Film', *Daily Mail*, 9 March 1935, 11; 'Paul Robeson in "Sanders of the River"', *The Manchester Guardian*, 3 April 1935.

presented on screen. As he said to the film magazine *Cine-Technician* in 1938:

I thought I could do something for the Negro race on the films: show the truth about them-and about other people too. I used to do my part and go away feeling satisfied. Thought everything was O.K. Well, it wasn't. Things were twisted and changed – distorted. They didn't mean the same. That made me think things out. It made me more conscious politically.[5]

In the same interview, Robeson spoke of being intrigued by the novel documentary footage that the Korda brothers brought back from Africa that was edited into the film and which showed indigenous dances and celebrations: '*Sanders of the River*...attracted me because the material that London Films brought back from Africa seemed to me good honest pictures of African folk ways.' Documentary film was itself a relatively new genre capturing material of the everyday that was 'real' and seemingly untouched, and which conveyed something about the lives of Black people and the Black diaspora that had not been previously presented to white audiences of empire films. This footage, much like the film camera itself at the time, was fascinating to the film industry and its players. Robeson, speaking in the third person of his celebrity status, ruminated that 'Robeson dressed in a leopard skin along with half a dozen other guys from Africa, all looking more or less the same, seemed to prove something about my race that I thought was worth proving'.

The incorporation of documentary film footage of Africans into an empire feature-film would likely produce a new story worth telling in Robeson's estimation, offering what critical race theory calls 'counter-storytelling'. Counter-storytelling or 'counter-narratives' as it is sometimes called, is most often associated with work by Richard Delgado in the field of law as a compelling means of reorienting and reclaiming narratives from those that legal frameworks impose upon racialised subjects within court systems and cases.[6] In many ways, it emphasises the usefulness of the narrative elements that historians have grown so

---

[5] Sidney Cole, 'Paul Robeson Tells us Why', *The Cine-Technician*, September–October 1938, 74–75.
[6] Works on counter story-telling within critical race theory have primarily engaged with legal studies. See Richard Delgado, 'Storytelling for Oppositionists and Others: A Plea for Narrative', *Michigan Law Review* 87, no. 8 (1989): 2411–2441; Ian Haney Lopez, *Racism on Trial: The Chicano Fight for Justice* (Cambridge, MA: Harvard University Press, 2003); Anthony G. Amsterdam and Jerome S. Bruner, *Minding the Law: How Courts Rely on Storytelling* (Cambridge, MA: Harvard University Press, 2009); Dolores Bernal, 'Critical Race Theory, Latino Critical Theory, and Critical Raced-Gendered Epistemologies: Recognizing Students of Color as Holders and Creators of Knowledge', *Qualitative Inquiry* 8, no. 1 (2002): 105–126.

uncomfortable with in the discipline's move towards scientific methodologies that still characterises much of our work. Counter-storytelling works from the premise that first, there are alternative frameworks of knowledge at work in racialised environments stemming from the differing experiences of racialised and white people. Second, voices of colour, in turn, work against these different frameworks of knowledge through community story-telling that conveys the lived historic and emotional experiences of racialised communities. Counter-storytelling thus becomes a way of understanding an event, place or time period as producing profoundly disassociated realities depending on one's racialised position with it and acknowledging that white and Black people can see and experience these very differently. Both Robeson and Brecht wrestled with the type of counter-story telling that they wanted to produce in the face of a typical empire film in the 1930s based on their knowledge of Black experiences and critiques of colonialism. As a white viewer, Brecht was unable to entirely transcend the appeal of the empire film, rooted as it was in visions of white superiority, but for Robeson, a Black man, this journey was not the same.

Robeson's effort to offer a different type of knowledge of Black people's experience through *Sanders of the River* was to him a profound failure. He spoke of his disillusionment with the story and its message and crucially couched this as a distortion of the truth he was attempting to convey:

Certain elements in a story would attract me and I would agree to play in it. But by the time producers and distributors had got through with it, the story was usually very different, and so were my feelings about it ... In the completed version, 'Sanders of the River' resolved itself into a piece of flag-waving, in which I wasn't interested. As far as I was concerned it was a total loss.[7]

The 'truth' and the story-telling that Robeson was interested in, his counter-storytelling, was lost in the mix of producers and distributors involved in the creation of the final film. The film footage of Africans became brief moments of ornamentation in a story centred on white British superiority. Robeson vowed to not work with director Zoltan Korda again, abandoning even his early interest in Korda's novel use of documentary film. He continued to be educated about the film's negative messages by a 'deputation' of uncertain origins in New York where he returned after the film's release in London:

---

[7] Sidney Cole, 'Paul Robeson Tells us Why', *The Cine-Technician*, September–October 1938, 74–75.

But I didn't realize how seriously people might take the film until I went back to New York. There I met with a deputation who wanted to know how the hell I had come to play in a film which stood for everything they rightly thought I opposed. That deputation began to make me see things more clearly. I hadn't seen the film. I was that interested. After talking to them I did go and see it and I began to realize what they'd been getting at. The films I've made since then? The same story. An idea that attracted me, a result in which I wasn't interested.[8]

The film was, by the time Robeson saw the final version, deemed harmful rather than helpful, its message the opposite of the one that Robeson thought he was bringing to the screen. Robeson's role in the subsequent *King Solomon's Mines* in 1937 as Umbopa, a figure who again helps the British in central Africa against another indigenous leader, was likewise dismissed by Robeson. The year it came out, in an interview with the *Daily Worker*, Robeson again spoke of his frustration with stories whose messages he could not control for audiences: 'I shan't do any more films after the two that are being finished now [presumably *King Solomon's Mines* and *Jericho*]. Not unless I can get a cast-iron story – the kind that can't be twisted in the making' and that he feared 'One man can't face the film companies.'[9] Robeson would go on to take starring roles in only two more films in his career; *The Proud Valley* (1940), an Ealing Studios film about a working-class coal-mining community in Wales, and *Tales of Manhattan* (1942), an American film that departed from feature-film conventions through a six-part story-telling device. Robeson was truly done with empire films and conventional story-telling about people of colour.

This chapter examines film's answer in the first half of the twentieth century to the question of what audiences wanted. It uncovers the racial assumptions that underpinned the production of that answer through the content of feature-length empire films and alongside the new documentary and amateur film produced in the period. It documents the repetitive shapes that white superiority and Black and south Asian inferiority took on the screen as film producers, directors, and writers imagined what would thrill, engage and comfort their white audiences. Even British documentary film-makers, working in an ostensibly new form of film, we shall see, considered again and again the appeal of the empire feature-film to ordinary British audiences they imagined as white. The thinking of influential film producers and shapers provides valuable insight into how they attempted to woo audiences to their particular representation of

---

[8] Ibid.
[9] Philip Bolsover, 'Why I Joined Labour Theatre', interview, *Daily Worker* (London). 24 November 1937.

empire and racialised people on screen. Black and white audiences had different responses to this film material rooted in differing experiences and knowledge of empire but also in their respective relationships to what Sara Ahmed calls 'affective economies' where 'emotions *do things*' to those consuming images on screen.[10] The affective economies of early twentieth-century empire films, bound up in both the perils and pleasures of empire for Black and white audiences, are consequently unearthed in this chapter.

Central to the answers to what audiences wanted were the collective efforts of producers and film-makers to emotionally engage audiences. A film's ability to capture its audience often hinged on this assumption of emotional involvement on the part of audiences who were also consistently imagined as white. Film-makers and film-producers were consequently highly motivated by what they imagined they knew of an audiences' emotional response to Black or racialised people on screen and the related pleasures of white supremacy. A variety of figures, including film-maker John Grierson, imagined and wrote of a type of affective economy where the imagined emotional distance between white viewers and Black subjects on screen limited the engagement of the former with the latter in the new genre of documentary film.[11] White audiences liked certain stories about empire, it seemed, and did not like others. Efforts to please this imagined preference fundamentally shaped the racist depictions and racist practices of empire films in the first three decades of the twentieth century and beyond.

The response of audiences of colour to the content of film from the 1910s to the 1940s was largely of despair and frustration and occasionally powerful laughter. The responses of racialised people, both prominent and more anonymous, to films about empire and race in this period are juxtaposed in this chapter with the racist content offered by empire films as a means of pleasing white audiences. Within a largely silent, large-scale consumption of empire films by white audiences and the comparatively rare responses of audiences of colour lies the dominant frameworks for presenting racialised people on screen. As audiences of colour contemplated what films contributed to what white audiences did not know about racism or racialised experiences, we see persistent efforts by racialised people attempting to alter the course of film content in the period. White shapers and regulators of film content in the colonies consistently fretted about the excitable responses, both real and imagined, of

---

[10] Sara Ahmed, 'Affective Economies', *Social Text* 22 no. 2 (Summer 2004): 117–139.
[11] Should be John Grierson, 'Notes for English Producers: Part 1. Cinema and the Public', 29 April 1927, p. 19. TNA: PRO CO 760/37.

audiences of colour and particularly their laughter. World War II to some extent disrupted this relationship as audiences of colour were now considered a group to persuade to new ends. Yet, this shift was slight and still rooted in concepts of racial inferiority that persistently sidelined and overlooked Black and south Asian audiences. The affective economies of early twentieth-century screen content ultimately took on a form that housed both the silent, white, large-scale enjoyment of racist imagery on screen that empire feature-films represented and the overlooked responses by audiences of colour that pointed to a different lived experience rooted in racial pain and frustration.

## 2.1 The Pleasures of Racism: Empire Films in the Early Twentieth Century

The popularity of empire films with white British audiences can be gauged in both the persistent production of these films in the 1930s and beyond and the responses of audience members surveyed at the time. I have written elsewhere about the challenges of locating what I call 'cultural history's absent audience'. This chapter illuminates some of those issues, but the sheer quantity of empire films produced in the early twentieth century, and their B-quality imitators, is certainly an indicator of audience enjoyment.[12] By and large, this was a silent, large-scale enjoyment by white audiences of plots that hinged on white superiority. When white audiences did discuss empire films, it was often to comment on the central character and to connect this character with broader characteristics of a national British identity. Cinema-goers such as Arthur Jones, 30, who responded to a Mass Observation questionnaire in Bolton in 1938, discussed the betterment of mankind evident in these histories on screen:

Films founded on History or Adventure of Men and Women will live forever and stars who by playing these parts bring to the screen the people whose lives we would never have known and whose Adventures and Lives have built Empires and made the World better for mankind.[13]

Jones's subsequent list of favourite films includes *Rhodes of Africa* (1936) and *Lives of a Bengal Lancer* (1935). The pleasure these films held for Jones seemingly resided in witnessing and emotionally aligning with the success of white empire builders; nothing was said about the depiction of

---

[12] Christine Grandy, 'Cultural History's Absent Audience', *Cultural and Social History* 16, no. 5 (2019): 643–663.
[13] Arthur Jones, interviewee, in Jeffrey Richards and Dorothy Sheridan, eds., *Mass-Observation at the Movies* (London: Routledge, 1987), 94.

colonial subjects encountered and subdued in the enterprise. Indeed, the elements of white superiority and Black or south Asian inferiority that were expressed in the films were part of the common knowledge of 'race' in the period for white audiences. Film critics for papers such as the *Daily Mail* endorsed the 'honesty of sentiment' of films such as the Korda-directed *The Drum* (1938) which made for what the paper called 'universal entertainment'.[14] The concept of a universal appeal, or the 'human interest', of the empire film was itself couched in highly racialised notions that presumed a homogeneous white audience and the pleasures this audience could experience through common understandings of white superiority.[15]

The film-maker and producer, John Grierson, known as the father of documentary film, started his career in the UK by discussing the appeal of such empire feature-films to British audiences that he consistently imagined as white. The documentary film movement arose as an alternate to this popular genre as an adjacent site for conveying knowledge about the empire and its goods to white audiences. As noted in Chapter 1, Grierson's hiring at the Empire Marketing Board (EMB) in 1927 was in large part due to his claim to know what audiences wanted. Having previously written on 'The Psychology of Popular Appeal' for the American Rockefeller Foundation, his adaptation of this into 'Notes for English Producers: Part 1 Cinema and the Public' promised to offer the embryonic EMB and its film unit important insight into the minds of the ordinary viewer. Grierson wrote at length in the memo about the difference between American films, which he saw as largely successful, and British films that were less so. Much of his treatise centred on examining the components of this American success. Grierson argued that British films were in decline because of their tendency to focus on problems or what he called 'drabness': 'Their preoccupation with Limehouse and the slums, their harping on poverty, and the tendency to represent workmen and work girls in the dismal atmosphere and setting of obvious conscious and complacent inferiority do not serve them well in the cinema market.'[16]

Grierson relayed in his 'Notes for English Producers' that 'an American once remarked to me that these English pictures "don't make you feel any good"', arguing that 'this principle I believe touches the root

---

[14] Seton Margrave, 'First Film Pre-view', *Daily Mail*, 5 April 1938, 6.
[15] Christine Grandy, 'The Empire and 'Human Interest': Popular Empire Films, the Colonial Villain, and the British Documentary Movement 1926–39', *Twentieth Century British History* 25, no. 4 (2014): 509–532.
[16] John Grierson, 'Notes for English Producers: Part 1. Cinema and the Public', 29 April 1927, p. 5. TNA: PRO CO 760/37.

of cinema success and accounts for much of the failure of English cinema in the past'. For Grierson, feeling 'good' was a vital part of cinema, and London slums full of Chinese labourers and other immigrants alongside the 'complacent inferiority' of working-class men and women, had little place in the new cinema he envisioned.[17] The aspiration and verve of American cinema had British productions beat.

Grierson outlined what he thought would make audiences feel good for the EMB's film unit in 1927. The EMB was an outgrowth of the imperial spectacle meant to attract white audiences from throughout Britain, the British Empire Exhibition of 1924, otherwise known as the Wembley Exhibition. This exhibition was meant to match the popularity of the Great Exhibition of 1851 and featured, as Daniel Stephens has documented, West African and south and east Asian people living in resident 'villages' in the exhibition or occupying these during the day for the benefit of white visitors.[18] The West African exhibition and Indian pavilion had been popular with audiences even as groups in the West African and Indian delegations came up against the expectations of white British organisers and physical restrictions on the movements and activities of those involved in the villages.[19] This event was the empire brought to life for British visitors throughout 1924 to 1925 and partly laid the groundwork for a larger impetus to fund an 'Empire Marketing Board'. The EMB's aim to advertise imperial goods to ordinary people led to a series of posters as part of one of the colonial office's first efforts to sway public opinion in what would now be termed an advertising campaign. The creation of the highly novel Film Unit was a further outgrowth.

Stephen Tallents, already working at the EMB, brought in Grierson as a presumed expert on film audiences and Grierson demonstrated this in a section of his memo entitled 'An account of audience reactions and the conditions of popular appeal in cinema'.[20] Grierson imagined an audience for the film unit's outputs when he suggested the EMB pursue 'two main types' of production: 'The first, a seven, eight, or nine reel form, ought to be dramatic in the usual sense with a powerful story and clear

---

[17] On immigrant populations in Britain in this period, see David Holland, *Imperial Heartland Immigration, Working-class Culture and Everyday Tolerance, 1917–1947* (Cambridge: Cambridge University Press, 2023); Sascha Auerbach, *Race, Law, and 'The Chinese Puzzle' in Imperial Britain* (New York: Springer 2009); John Seed, 'Limehouse Blues: Looking for Chinatown in the London Docks, 1900–1940.' *History Workshop Journal* 62 (2006); Laura Tabili, *Global Migrants, Local Culture: Natives and Newcomers in Provincial England, 1841–1939* (London: Palgrave, 2011).
[18] Daniel Stephens, *The Empire of Progress: West Africans, Indians, and Britons at the British Empire Exhibition 1924–25* (London: Palgrave Macmillan, 2013), 3.
[19] Ibid., 53–80. [20] Grierson, 'Notes for English Producers', 19.

characters carried along on the tide of a great event, a stirring adventure, or a large scale enterprise.'[21] The second type of film would be shorter, and consist of two to four reels. This one 'could afford to dispense with the powerful story [of the first category] and the main appeal would be quite frankly to the spectator's curiosity rather than to his emotions'. Grierson's elaboration of the content of the first category of imperial films included the 'stories of objective authors such as Kipling and all the stories of adventure from Conan Doyle's "African Tales" down to Ballantyne's "Coral Island"'. These stories would 'illustrate some specific phase of Imperial achievement'. Grierson suggested stories based on the 'adventures of the great explorers', 'the exploits of the Hudson Bay Company', 'or the building of a canal ... in some part of the Empire'.[22] The first category, the longer film appealing to emotions with powerful and true stories and characters, spoke to the existing domain of popular empire films and seemed to anticipate the hold they would take in the 1930s. It also elaborated on the emotional appeal of witnessing on screen white 'achievement' in an imperial setting.

In some ways Grierson's anticipation and claimed expertise of what the audience wanted was merely an astute reading of what audiences were already enjoying in Britain and the US but with an eye to what could be achieved if films oriented around images of empire were taken up primarily by British film-makers. White British audiences had, after all, already been enjoying images of racialised people in theatres for quite a long time at that point. Ben Shepherd's work on 'Showbiz Imperialism' and the often inaccurate re-enactments of Boer War skirmishes in London theatres showed how popular images of imperial war and British triumph were to white audiences in Britain at the turn of the twentieth century.[23] White men in blackface as minstrels were also evident on the stage. Michael Pickering documents just how ubiquitous both blacking up and minstrelsy were in Britain, arguing that 'variant forms of blackface caricature appeared outside the minstrel show, in media as wide-ranging as advertising, postcards, puppet shows, comics, and juvenile literature'.[24] Blacked-up minstrels featured in seaside theatrical performances or on the beaches as wandering performers before blacking up became a common sight on the big screen. Home movies housed in media archives across the UK such as the North West Film

---

[21] Ibid.   [22] Ibid., 19.
[23] Ben Shepherd, 'Showbiz Imperialism', in McKenzie, *Popular Culture*. Shephard's work on the life of Peter Lobengula is still an important piece on the limits of acceptance among white audiences consuming racialising pleasures.
[24] Michael Pickering, *Blackface Minstrelsy in Britain* (London: Aldershot, 2008), xi.

Archive (NWFA), the Yorkshire Film Archive (YFA), the Screen Archive of the South East and the Media Archive for Central England (MACE) also indicate that ordinary Britons used burnt cork and other material to black up in clear imitation of African Americans, Africans, south Asian, Chinese and Japanese communities as well as North American 'Indians'.[25] Groups of blacked-up participants can be seen wearing a range of clothing that equated blackness with poverty such as tattered topcoats and black wool wigs. The existence of such practices, a type of local theatre captured by film but not for film, indicates that the often upper-class filmmakers who could afford the expensive 'cine-camera' equipment of the time were intrigued by this spectacle.[26] For example, in footage capturing Melton Mowbray's carnival in 1938 the camera zooms in on various figures in blackface and follows them for several seconds.[27] The cutaway immediately afterwards to a different set of costumed participants indicates that the local filmmaker edited the procession footage to grant these figures considerable screen time. A blacked-up person, performed by a white person, was a point of interest for even the amateur film-maker.

The medium of film took elements of existing racial pleasures for white audiences and expanded upon them to weave a story of white superiority against the backdrop of the perils and pleasure that empire represented. Silent films on empire began to arrive in the 1920s such as the 'desert romances' *The Sheik* (novel, 1919; film, 1921) and its sequel *The Son of the Sheik* (1926).[28] Further silent films followed including *Palaver: A Romance of Northern Nigeria* (1926) and *The Green Goddess* (1930), the latter based on a popular play in Britain. But it was in the 1930s as talkies dominated the screen and both UK and US film production notably improved that British audiences saw a significant influx of empire films including *Clive of India* (US 1935), *Lives of a Bengal Lancer*, *Sanders of the River*, *Rhodes of Africa* (UK 1936), *King Solomon's Mines* (UK

---

[25] This material, while evident in the archives, has not been consistently catalogued to reference blackface or blacking up. 'Minstrel' remains a useful term for accessing this practice, but viewings of pageants and parades also almost inevitably offer examples. See Miscellaneous: Morecambe, Heysham, and North Manchester, 1936–1937/North West Film Archive, and the Screen Archive South East, whose catalogue features 'blackface' in its metadata.

[26] Heather Norris Nicholson, *Amateur Film: Meaning and Practice 1927–1977* (Manchester: Manchester University Press, 2014).

[27] 'Melton Mowbray Carnival Scenes', 1938, 35mm/MACE.

[28] See Lucy Bland, 'White Women and Men of Colour: Miscegenation Fears in Britain after the Great War', *Gender and History* 17, no. 1 (2005); Karen Chow, 'Popular Sexual Knowledge and Women's Agency in 1920s England: Marie Stopes' *Married Love* and E.M. Hull's *The Sheik*', *Feminist Review* 63 (1999).

1937), as well the other two Korda films, *The Drum* (UK 1938) and *Elephant Boy* (UK 1937) to name just a few. Alongside these films were others that used the racialised imagery of empire as central backdrops for even more fantastic plots such as *Tarzan the Ape Man* (US 1932) the first of four Tarzan films released by MGM in the 1930s (and eight more before ending in 1948). Further quantitative measures of the popularity of films from the 1930s can be traced through film historians such as Sue Harper and John Sedgwick and their work on audience figures. A film ledger located by Harper ties audience numbers to film titles, showing that a city such as Portsmouth embraced *The Drum* in 1938 with 24,572 people attending it and later *Gunga Din* in 1939 with 28,165 tickets sold, while just over 8,000 people attended the critically acclaimed World War I film, *All Quiet on the Western Front* in 1931.[29] *King Solomon's Mines* was also a hit with Portsmouth audiences, with 23,980 people attending in the third week of September 1937 and *Mutiny on the Bounty* (US 1935) brought in a sizeable 26,136 people the previous year.[30] *Tarzan the Ape Man* was the second-most popular film in 1932 in Portsmouth with 24,377 people attending it.[31] The empire film genre was also established enough to support two popular satires with *The Camels Are Coming* (1935) starring comedian Jack Hulbert, the second-most popular film in the city in 1935, and *Old Bones of the River* (1939), a scene-by-scene recreation of *Sanders of the River* with the addition of a bumbling professor as the lead, the third-most popular film in Portsmouth in 1939.[32]

The 1920s and 1930s thus saw the empire film as a regular option for British audiences. Central to all these films were the stark differentiations that Bertolt Brecht noted in 1939 between good heroic Brits and evil, villainous Black and south Asian men working to overturn the British empire. These colonial villains were usually organising and arming themselves and their forces. The organising of indigenous populations against the British, attempts at sabotage, and procuring of arms, all deemed illegal in most British territories and echoing real-life activities and anxieties, were shown again and again on screen.[33] Worries about the procurement of arms, in particular, were consistently represented in

---

[29] Sue Harper, 'A Lower-Middle-Class Taste Community: Admission Figures at the Regent Cinema, Portsmouth, UK', *The Historical Journal of Film, Radio, and Television* 24, no. 4 (2004): 565–587; John Sedgwick, *Popular Filmgoing in 1930s Britain: A Choice of Pleasures* (Exeter: University of Exeter Press, 2000).
[30] Harper, 585. [31] Ibid., 580. [32] Ibid.
[33] Priya Satia, *Empire of Guns: The Violent Making of the Industrial Revolution* (London: Duckworth Books, 2018); Martin Thomas, *Violence and Colonial Order: Police, Workers, and Protest in the European Colonial Empires, 1918–1940* (Cambridge: Cambridge University Press, 2012); William Kelleher Storey, *Guns, Race, and Power in Colonial South Africa* (Cambridge University Press, 2008).

these films – a twentieth-century extension of the concerns outlined in Priya Satia's *Empire of Guns*.[34] In *Lives of a Bengal Lancer*, which arrived on British screens in 1936, the protagonist Lieutenant McGregor, played by Gary Cooper, reports that the villain, Oxford-educated Mohammed Khan played by white Canadian actor Douglass Dumbrille in blackface, was, 'trying to stir up all the border tribes and effect a coalition of all of them ... and they're listening to him because he's promised to supply them with machines guns and two million rounds of ammunition'.[35] In Korda's *Sanders of the River* (1935), a title card at the 38-minute mark increased the dramatic tension by declaring: 'Gin and rifles are the most dangerous gifts of civilization to the natives. Their traffic is forbidden in the Territory.' This set up the audience to be appropriately appalled when Commissioner Sanders learns that the Portuguese have introduced guns into the region and to the enemy Mofoloba as a means of expelling the British.[36] Much of the drama and subsequent pleasures of these films for white audiences lay in the possibility of the British empire falling to these well-armed racialised villains. The happy resolution of these films (they were always happy endings and subject to none of the hints of ambiguity in post-war films of empire) saw the white British forces and loyal Black or south Asian forces subdue this threat with their own gunfire or quick thinking. This was David Edgerton's 'warfare state' shown in glorious tones on screen.[37]

This was also the drama of empire, as imagined for anglophone audiences, buttressed by claims to authenticity rooted in domestic reporting in England about the empire and the willingness of directors such as the Korda brothers to incorporate documentary footage, what the *Daily Mail* described as 'authentic detail', into their film.[38] For English audiences, the empire films of the 1930s were thrillingly appealing as the daily press told of real struggles to maintain colonial order in India, Kenya and the West Indies and as Gandhi and the Indian National Congress's pursuit of civil resistance told a very different, less visible story. The press were frequently willing to map these thrills onto the existing terrain of colonial conflict. For three years from 1936, the dailies found a real-life villain of the Northwest Passage as they covered the activities of Mirza Ali Khan, or the Faqir of Ipi, who *The Times* eulogised upon his death in 1960 as a

---

[34] Satia, *Empire of Guns*.
[35] Sedgwick, *Popular Filmgoing in 1930s Britain*, 269; *The Lives of a Bengal Lancer*, directed by Henry Hathaway (1935: Paramount Pictures).
[36] *Sanders of the River*, directed by Zoltan Korda (1935: London Films).
[37] David Edgerton, *Warfare State: Britain, 1920–1970* (Cambridge: Cambridge University Press, 2006).
[38] 'Best British Film of the Empire', *Daily Mail*, 7 February 1935, 9.

'doughty and honorable opponent who eluded British forces for a dozen years'.[39] The Faqir engaged British troops in irregular warfare that mimicked that showcased in empire films such as *Lives of a Bengal Lancer* or *The Drum*. Indeed, his threat also lay in his acquisition of machine guns in Waziristan. The Faqir's story was featured in not uncharitable terms by dailies such as the *Daily Mail* which reported in 1936 on the 'troops and hostile tribesman led by the "Firebrand" Faqir of Ipi'. The article painted a vivid picture of 'RAF bombers repeatedly diving on the enemy, British and Indian troops determinedly forcing their way through hills infested with equally gallant tribesman and a British major losing his life while leading his men in a counter-attack' before commenting: 'These are the pictures conjured up by communiqués issued by the India Office.'[40] In other words, this was a scene straight out of an empire film used in the national press to court readers' interest. Empire films showed a British empire that was under siege, and crucially these films acknowledged the existence of anti-colonial activity among colonial subjects but with a requisite happy ending to the conflict that reasserted British dominance. Empire films assumed that this type of conflict, replayed across film after film, would be what appealed to white Western audiences.

These films also showed British audiences the practice of blacking up. All the films discussed in this chapter, except for *Sanders of the River*, featured white actors blacking up as either Black or south Asian.[41] This was a common element of feature films in the early twentieth century with white actors wearing black or brown paint over the entirety of their faces, ears, necks and hands. The first feature-film released in Britain, *The Birth of a Nation* (1915) by American director D. W. Griffith, included white actors blacked up as African Americans in its highly racist account of post–Civil War reconstruction with the Ku Klux Klan as the triumphant heroes. As both the first feature-length film and one of the first to show historical re-enactment on screen, the British press did not comment on the blacking up or racist storytelling at its centre. These elements were unremarkable and part of the everydayness of racialised

---

[39] 'Faqir of Ipi', *The Times*, 20 April 1960, 15; Allan Warren, *Waziristan, the Faqir of Ipi, and the Indian Army: the North West Frontier Revolt of 1936–37* (Oxford: Oxford University Press, 2000); Christian Tripodi, 'Negotiating with the Enemy: 'Politicals' and Tribes 1901–47', *Journal of Imperial and Commonwealth History* 39, no. 4 (2011): 598–606.

[40] 'R.A.F.'s Rain of Bombs in India Fights', *Daily Mail*, 30 November 1936, 15.

[41] I use the terms blackface and blacking up for the practice of white people donning face make-up in order to imitate Black, south Asian or east Asian people. I think the blanket term is more useful than a colour-specific term such as brown-face, as the latter approach gives the practice rather too much credit in terms of the effect that it achieves.

thinking; what *was* remarked upon was the fantastic spectacle of a moment in history acted out. Reviewing the film in 1915, the *Daily Mail* wrote of the scene when Lincoln is shot that 'it is probably the nearest approach to complete reality in the whole of this wonderful production' and noted that 'the realism of the battle at Gettysburg is not less than that of the fight in the streets of Piedmont between the negro militia and the Ku-Klux-Klan'.[42] The blacking up in the film merited no mention, thereby forming a central part of the film landscape at the very birth of feature films. In empire films, a white lead or secondary actor would commonly wear a complete coverage of make-up throughout the film in order to 'pass' as Black or south Asian. Actors of colour often surrounded this white actor as extras, but the director and studio commonly assumed that a lead role would best be played by a white actor blacked up. This approach assumed that audiences would either not notice the extensive blacking up or share similar expectations about white actors' abilities to accurately 'act' Black or south Asian. Examples of films featuring blacked-up actors are numerous and include hits such as *The Drum* featuring Canadian actor Raymond Massey in blackface as Prince Gul alongside supporting characters such as the British-born Roy Emerton as 'Wafader' and Charles Oliver as 'Rajab'. In *Lives of the Bengal Lancers* the central antagonist, Mohammed Khan, was played by Douglas Dumbrille, another white Canadian actor, while African-American actor Noble Johnson played the supporting role of 'Prince Ram Singh'. The ubiquity of blacking up in the period is such that it is easier to identify films that featured Black or south Asian actors in speaking roles than films where blacked-up white actors occupied these roles such as *Sanders of the River* starring both Robeson and the Black American actress Nina Mae McKinney.

Little evidence exists as to whether interwar British audiences explicitly recognised the blacking up of actors, but the many popular films that used passing through blacking up as a plot device would leave audiences in little doubt as to the existence of this practice. In the empire films of the 1930s, white British officers sometimes blacked up to undertake covert intelligence work. In *The Drum*, Captain Carruthers is initially seen on screen blacked up and masquerading as an Indian man complaining about the price of a rail ticket and begging for food.[43] In *Lives of a Bengal Lancer*, Lieutenant Barrett applies blackface on screen in order to fulfil his mission to infiltrate a hostile tribe, and later in the film the lead character, McGregor, and another officer also don blackface.

---

[42] 'The Birth of a Nation', *Daily Mail*, 24 March 1916, 3.
[43] *The Drum*, directed by Zoltan Korda (1938: London Films).

In both films these officers are shown removing or donning blackface makeup in front of a mirror with the aid of a south Asian servant. The very practice of blacking up was a central part of their intelligence work. This overt blacking up emphasised the physical, linguistic and cultural authority of these British officers and their ability to easily fool the locals with their masquerade. Korda's *The Four Feathers* (1939) took this a step further and placed blacking up as central to the plot as the main English character, Henry Faversham, successfully dons blackface to rescue his friends and imprisoned officers in the Sudan. The ongoing inclusion of blacked-up actors in feature films from the period was so common that censors at the BBFC did not remark on the practice itself but rather treated the characters according to their projected racial identity.[44] Such a spectacle was part and parcel of the empire films enjoyed by white audiences in Britain.

## 2.2   Documentary and Amateur Film: The Imagined 'Curiosity' of White Audiences

Looking beyond the empire feature-film and to the new forms of film-making that were occurring in the period, such as 'documentary' films and amateur films, the racialising assumptions of a wider array of white film-makers about what the white audience wanted comes even further into view. Documentary film-makers and amateur film-makers were operating with minimal budgets for the most part but shared similar backgrounds as feature-film makers. The documentary film-makers under Grierson at the EMB and then GPO were university educated, middle- or upper-class white men, including Grierson himself educated at the University of Glasgow and Basil Wright and Humphrey Jennings, both Cambridge graduates, and Paul Rotha, privately educated but not university educated. Amateur film-makers, in comparison, were men who could afford the expensive and bulky home cinema-makers of the time before Kodak's Super-8 cine camera would make home-movie making more affordable after 1965. As Heather Norris Nicholson notes, these were primarily middle-class men, and their interests can be traced through the content of periodicals that arose in the interwar period to capture this new hobby such as *Amateur Cine World*, established in 1934.[45] Both types of film-maker faced the challenge of trying to capture the attention of audiences who were already familiar with the growing behemoth of feature-films. The documentary film movement was

---

[44] Grandy, 'The Empire and "Human Interest"'.   [45] Norris Nicholson, *Amateur Film*.

particularly working against the powerful appeal of this format of film as Grierson's early career and writings indicated.

Central to Grierson's conception of what British audiences wanted when it came to seeing empire in documentary film was brevity: a short indulgence of curiosity about people of colour is what he endorsed for early documentary films on empire. Grierson assumed that white audiences were unable to connect with Black or south Asian people on screen in 1927, recommending the documentary film as a shorter 'second category of film'[46] distinct from the 7–9-reel feature-film. The shorter 2–4-reel film was ultimately what the EMB and later the GPO film units would produce. These films tended to be just under 10 minutes long with Basil Wright's award-winning documentary 'Song of Ceylon' (1934) being distinctive at 40 minutes. Grierson declared: 'Into the second [2–4 reel] category would come those subjects that do not lend themselves to major treatment. There is a place in cinema for accounts of the lives of primitive peoples and distant civilizations [and] the main appeal would be quite frankly to the spectator's curiosity rather than to his emotions.'[47] Grierson argued: 'It is doubtful if justice is to be done to the people themselves and western motivation excluded, whether these ought to be long films … This second series too would give those simpler accounts of modern activities in commerce, industry, and research and kindred fields in which the human interest of a definite plot is not attempted.'[48] He also noted: 'A great number of pictures could be made in Africa, New Zealand, Australia, Egypt, and the East which would be cinematically fascinating.'[49] Grierson thus spun an image of short, visually interesting films for white British audiences that would not attempt to engage the 'human interest' that accompanied the stirring plots of empire films and where the lives of primitive peoples could be briefly captured and presented. Underlying Grierson's discussions was what he saw as the unemotional short film full of facts but not centred on any empathetic connection with the subject. Grierson's suggestion of shorter pieces on 'the lives of primitive peoples and distant civilisations[50]' indicated that he imagined the white British audience member as able to visit these lands on screen only briefly and not in the long engagement of feature films with the emotional investment they demanded of audiences.

Grierson's suggestion to the EMB of short documentaries devoid of deep emotional connection with racialised subjects ran counter to his personal admiration of the work of Robert Flaherty and his feature-length documentary film *Nanook of the North* (1922). This semi-fictionalised film

---

[46] 'Notes for English Producers', p. 19. [47] Ibid. [48] Ibid. [49] Ibid. [50] Ibid.

followed the daily life of an Inuk man named Nanook and presented images of him and other indigenous people identified as his family and their efforts to find food in the Canadian arctic. This was a film centred on racialised people that held Grierson as an audience member in its grip, and he repeatedly stated his respect for it and Flaherty's subsequent work throughout his life.[51] At the EMB, however, he was more circumspect about both the costs of producing feature-films and the risk of audience rejection. Grierson did not extend his own ability to connect with a racialised man on screen to the common British audience. Although he was well aware of the immense latitude that the EMB film unit enjoyed, 'a unique measure of freedom' and one of 45 sub-departments for the EMB (he pointed out that 'Research and Development interests accounted for the first twenty-four' of these sub-departments), he was also aware of his role as a 'propagandist' rather than as a commercial film-maker and drew clear distinctions between the two.[52] The feature-film maker and documentary film-maker were ultimately interested in different audience responses: 'The commercials [commercial interests] are interested only in the first results of their films: that is to say, in the amount of money a film takes in a twelvemonth. The long-range propagandists are not.' The EMB film unit was after something more enduring, and in 1933 the longevity of the feature-length film as the primary form of cinema was not quite as assured as it would be in the post-war period. Grierson, in 1933 in *Cinema Quarterly*, wrote of the EMB film unit's uniqueness as the only film-unit working in a way that emulated and countered the propaganda coming out of Russia (and the influential socialist film *Turksib* of 1929).[53] It was a film unit that was concerned with building admiration for a nation among the audience. He wrote: 'To command, and cumulatively command, the mind of a generation is more important than by novelty or sensation to knock a Saturday night audience cold.'[54]

As Grierson contemplated how to change the mind of a generation, he and his colleague Walter Creighton, who had been central to elements of the Wembley Exhibition and was also a film director, weighed up the options available to them in their new department at the EMB. Creighton chose to pursue a feature-length film and directed *One Family* (1930), a film about a young boy assembling a Christmas pudding from ingredients sourced from the empire. The film was a spectacular box office

---

[51] *Grierson on Documentary*, edited and compiled by Forsyth Hardy (London: Faber and Faber, 1966): 13, 15, 139, 170, 177, 203–205.
[52] John Grierson, 'The E.M.B. Film Unit', *Cinema Quarterly*, Summer 1933, quoted in *Grierson on Documentary*, 164–165.
[53] Ibid., 164.   [54] Ibid., 165.

failure with Paul Swann noting that it only generated £334 on its release while costing the EMB £15,740 to make and eating sizeably into its budget.[55] Grierson, writing in the aftermath of this flop, noted that his path to taking a documentary approach was instead very much influenced by financial considerations and attention to the governmental role of the unit: 'A Government department cannot, like the commercial gamblers, take a rap.' Of the small-reel documentary films, he wrote 'if it fails in the theatres, it may, by manipulation, be accommodated non-theatrically in one of half a dozen ways'.[56] The output of the EMB and later the GPO film unit, showed filmed material edited into a variety of documentary films of differing lengths and titles and occasionally for commercial use in advertising films from Shell, the Ceylon Tea Board and others. A one-time failure of a film with audiences in the usual theatre venue could be offset as it was cut into shorts to be shown ahead of a feature-length film or exhibited in other places. Grierson hinted at a new audience consuming educational material and indeed educational and scientific film also began in the 1930s.[57] Documentary films ultimately settled for a much smaller audience than feature-length films. As Grierson noted, alongside the financial exigencies, 'The fact that documentary was the genre most likely to bring method and imagination into such day-to-day subjects as we dealt with was, of course, a final argument.'[58]

Method and imagination were on ample display in the short and unique films emerging from the nascent documentary movement. For the most part this group of filmmakers wanted to dispense with conventional narrative and aimed to champion a very different type of film and a different subject in its focus on the everyday. Such a focus on the 'drama of the everyday' and a deliberate departure from existing film conventions would seem to hold numerous possibilities for a compelling vision of indigenous populations in the empire within documentary film. Was it possible that documentaries presumed to improve race relations by showing an empire devoid of sinister Rajahs? Paul Rotha, the most prolific writer of all the documentary filmmakers, claimed in 1936 that

---

[55] Paul Swann, *The British Documentary Film Movement, 1926–1946* (Cambridge: Cambridge University Press, 1989). Tom Rice offers a very good summation of the flop; Tom Rice, 'One Family', *Colonial Film: Moving Images of the British Empire*, 2010, www.colonialfilm.org.uk/node/40.
[56] Grierson, 'The E.M.B. Film Unit', quoted in *Grierson on Documentary*, 167.
[57] Max Long, 'The ciné-biologists: natural history film and the co-production of knowledge in interwar Britain', *British Journal for the History of Science* 53 (2020): 527–551.
[58] Ibid.

documentary film was in a better position to truly represent both race and class on the screen. Rotha argued that one could not expect entertainment films 'to deal impartially with such vital subjects of contemporary interest as unemployment, the problem of the machine, slum clearance, the relation of the white man to the native, or the manufacture of armaments'.[59] He further claimed that when looking at modern entertainment films: 'We can experience no surprise at the treatment of all working-class figures or coloured peoples, either as creatures of fun or as dishonest rogues, in current story-films, because it is to the ultimate interest of the dominant class that the spectator regard them as such'.[60] Basil Wright, the filmmaker behind most of the EMB and GPO's documentaries on empire including *Song of Ceylon*, was similarly sceptical of entertainment film's portrayal of the real conditions of empire, good or bad. In a review of *The Drum* for the *Spectator* in 1938, Wright had only critical remarks arguing: 'With a little more forethought, [it] could have told us something of the fundamental importance of the Empire and in particular of the political and social problems which the British Raj represents, and which the soldiers and sahibs of *The Drum* are presumably protecting.' For Wright, 'Even a slightly more liberal-minded approach would have made it valuable Imperially – which it certainly is not.'[61] Presumably Wright's own documentaries offered a new perspective on empire and colonial subjects while avoiding the pitfalls of melodrama in popular empire films.

If we look at the visual content of the documentary empire films produced by Grierson, Tallents, Wright and others what was ultimately deemed worth showing on screen was the harmonious movement of goods from the colonies to the metropole by a content and passive racialised workforce. These new types of film about empire showed white British audiences peaceable rather than violent people engaged in work that brought bananas, tea and sugar to Britain. The purpose of documentary films, as laid out by Grierson and Tallents, was not to highlight tensions in the empire. This emphasis on labour and crucially happy and content labour is evident throughout many of the EMB and GPO's films, yet in a colonial context it was not treated in the same manner by the filmmakers and producers. While *Night Mail* (1936), directed by Grierson, spotlighted GPO workers moving the post in Britain, in films such as *Cargo from Jamaica* (1933), *Windmill in Barbados* (1933), *British Guiana* (1933), *God's Chillun* (1938), *The Song of Ceylon* and the short

---

[59] Paul Rotha, *Documentary Film* (London: Faber and Faber, 1936): 45.   [60] Ibid.
[61] Basil Wright, 'The Cinema. The Drum and Damsel in Distress', *The Spectator* 15 April 1938, 671.

edited versions produced from it, *Monsoon Island* (1934), *Negombo Coast* (1934), *Dance of the Harvest* (1934) and *Villages of Lanka* (1934), the labour of indigenous populations is vital but oddly peripheral to these narratives as their work moves food produce, the star of these films, to British ports.[62] Workers often appear on the edge of the screen or just as hands moving produce or not at all. These films did not show discontented indigenous labour attempting to organise against British employers, as was the case at the time. *God's Chillun* did acknowledge these workers were poorly paid, as Marc Matera notes, but showed only images of placid workers on screen.[63] By and large these films show a content work force relatively undisturbed by British overseers and notably did not show images of the educated indigenous elites who so disturbed the peace in empire feature-films. What is striking about these films is how they do not quite fit with the dominant style of the EMB and GPO film units with their valorisation of ordinary working men and women in Britain. One does not see the narrative emphasis seen in their domestic documentaries which would often follow a particular worker in some depth as his story was revealed.[64] Only occasionally were indigenous men and women granted close-ups and never in the context of a larger narrative arc. In the empire documentaries indigenous workers were presented consecutively in turn or in groups usually in relation to the machines they operated.[65]

The belief that the development of commerce and industry among indigenous peoples should be treated on screen as distinct from feature-film plots that appealed to the emotions of white audiences is evident in the EMB and GPO's body of work. The content of the empire documentaries created by the EMB and GPO film units reflected the approach that Grierson had first outlined for the EMB in 1927, centred on 'those simpler accounts of modern activities in commerce, industry, and research and kindred fields in which the human interest of a definite plot is not attempted'.[66] These were ruminative, quiet films that quenched the imagined short-lived curiosity of white audiences. The audiences of these films were not expected to emotionally engage with the racialised people on screen but rather to focus on the products

---

[62] These films are held at the British Film Institute and the Imperial War Museum and can be viewed at www.colonialfilm.org.uk.
[63] Marc Matera, 'An Empire of Development: Africa and the Caribbean in *God's Chillun*', *Twentieth Century British History* 23 (2012): 12–37.
[64] See the GPO's *The Saving of Bill Blewitt* (1936).
[65] Lee Grieveson, 'The Cinema and the (Common) Wealth of Nations', in Colin MacCabe and Lee Grieveson, eds., *Empire and Film* (London: Bloomsbury Press, 2019).
[66] Grierson, 'Notes for English Producers', p. 19.

moving on their voyage or some of the technologies on display and connect with that endeavour as a type of racial pride at instigating such industry. Early documentary film in Britain was thus steeped in an audience logic that assumed that white audiences were primarily interested in Black and south Asian people as accessories to the goods of empire and would feel a racial pride in the achievements of white Britons within that endeavour. Implicit within the films was the dominance of the other empire films of the period, empire feature-films, which repeatedly and successfully, from a box-office point of view showed audiences a spectacle of empire meant to inspire fear, anger and then relief and ultimately pride in the audience. The preoccupations of the empire feature-film with its images of white superiority and the threats of the colonial others recounted in various and exotic ways dominated early twentieth-century answers to 'what the audience wants'. Documentary films and their servicing of white curiosity supplemented but did not disturb the racial framework of pleasures offered to white audiences.

## 2.3 Counter Story-telling: Audiences of Colour and Empire Films

The reactions of audiences of colour in the early twentieth century to both the racist content of empire films and its obvious appeal to white audiences were rooted in their own double role as misrepresented subjects and overlooked audiences. Much of the scarce archival evidence of the responses of racialised audiences is of audience members pointing out both the form of racism on film and its simultaneous impact on what white audiences would come to believe about racialised people. These accounts by viewers of colour offered fragments of counter-storytelling about the fragility of the white audience and the screen's impact on them when it came to casual and common presentations of racist behaviour, language and characterisations. Robeson's aforementioned discussion with 'a deputation [from New York] who wanted to know how the hell I had come to play in a film which stood for everything they rightly thought I opposed' indicated the response of some Black Americans to *Sanders of the River* and the presumed power of its potential impact on audiences in the United States.[67] Black Americans had organised responses to the racist depictions of Black people on screen before 1935, protesting at film theatres across the United States by the

---

[67] 'Paul Robeson Tells Us Why', 74–75.

NAACP in response to screenings of *Birth of a Nation*.[68] The deputation that met Robeson existed because of the acknowledged power of the screen to shape white frameworks of knowledge about Black people. Performers of colour such as Robeson sat in an uncomfortable space between white audience expectations, available work and their own efforts to assert Black agency in public.[69] Franz Fanon wrote about American films shown in France or Martinique and the stereotypical way in which 'good' Blacks were consistently shown in positions of servitude, noting that 'Out of every Negro mouth comes the ritual "Yassuh, boss."' This persistent stereotype on film haunted the highly educated Fanon as a Black man in the audience:

I cannot go to a film without seeing myself. I wait for me. In the interval, just before the film starts, I wait for me. The people in the theatre are watching me, examining me, waiting for me. A Negro groom is going to appear. My heart makes my head swim.[70]

Fanon suffered through this depiction on screen of the servile Black man and what Fanon imagined as the white audience's willingness to extend this framework of what they knew about Blackness to himself. Fanon wrote movingly and consistently in his life about the weight of these white expectations and the related inability of the Black man to be at ease in the world. His comments and his obvious distress at such imagery on the screen stand as a counterpoint to Brecht, a white man, giving in to the enjoyment of what he knows is a distorted depiction of racialised subjects. For Fanon, the Black man had little relief even as he noted the positive emotional engagement of Black children with the white heroes of children's comics and their negative reactions to the Black evil cannibals in the same story: 'Since there is always identification with the victor, the little Negro, quite as easily as the little white boy, becomes an explorer, an adventurer, a missionary "who faces the danger of being eaten by the

---

[68] See chapter 6 in M. Stokes, *D.W. Griffith's* The Birth of a Nation: *A History of the Most Controversial Motion Picture of All Time* (Oxford: Oxford University Press, 2007). See also Stephen Weinberger, 'The Birth of a Nation and the Making of the NAACP', *Journal of American Studies* 45, no. 1 (2011): 77–93. Weinberger notes that there were no less than 120 challenges to the showing of the film by the NAACP between 1915 and 1973.

[69] Maurice Hunter, an in-demand Black man who modelled in American advertisements for whiskey, cigarettes and other goods that necessitated a Black man holding or serving them, expressed his own discomfort with this work through the scrapbook he kept. This primarily featured photos of him in respectable suits and largely ignored the dominant images of loin cloths or livery that he wore in his modelling; Clare Corbould, 'Race, Photography, Labor, and Entrepreneurship in the Life of Maurice Hunter, Harlem's "Man of 1,000 Faces", *Radical History Review*, no. 132 (2018): 144–171.

[70] Franz Fanon, *Black Skin, White Masks* (New York: Grove Press, 2007), 140.

wicked Negroes.'".⁷¹ This identification and then the realisation that these young Black readers are themselves the 'wicked' Black aggressors came in encounters with white people who brought that knowledge to bear in those moments. Fanon considered the story-telling and the imagery that accompanied it to be formative for both white and Black audiences. Trinidadian cricketer turned civil rights activist Learie Constantine echoed Fanon's frustration and directly referenced Kipling's character of Gunga Din when he wrote in 1954 on cinema in his book *Colour Bar*:

> It is hard to make it understood by white people how much we resent – and fear! – this perpetual undercurrent of jeering, this ingrained belief in the white mind that the coloured man, woman, or child is a matter for mirth – or at the very best – a kind of devoted, loyal dog to a white all-powerful master, the Kipling conception.⁷²

Constantine touched on the vast chasm in understanding between audiences consuming this imagery and the emotional pain this caused Black people, themselves also part of the audience. The lived reality of Black people did not match what was presented on the screen for white people. The screen became a powerful site for not knowing about Black experiences and Black people.

Moving beyond the responses of middle-class Black subjects such as Robeson, Fanon and Constantine to mass media and to those racialised subjects who are too often presented as voiceless in the archive, we see other examples of colonial subjects of colour responding to the empire feature films that were shown in settings of empire. Black and south Asian audiences offered alternative readings of the drama of white superiority under threat that empire films were anchored on much to the dismay of the British authorities where these films were exhibited. In a letter received by the Colonial Office in June 1932 about the banning of the film *Tell England* (1931) in Baghdad, the Inspector-General of Police recommended the film's withdrawal based on the inappropriate response of audiences to certain scenes:

> [The film] depicted scenes of fighting at Gallipoli between British and Turkish Troops and those scenes aroused considerable excitement among the Iraqi members of the audience who loudly applauded representations of British reverses and British casualties.⁷³

---

[71] Ibid., 145–148.
[72] Learie Constantine, *Colour Bar* (London: Stanley Paul and Co., 1954): 175.
[73] Letter from Acting Commissioner for Iraq to Secretary of the State for the Colonies, 23 May 1932, Colonial Office (CO) 323/1168/1, TNA.

Iraqi audiences in this case, instead of being horrified by British casualties at the hands of villainous Turks, were cheering on their moments of defeat. Mr F. Arnol, 'the Baghdad agent of British International Pictures Limited' who very much wanted his films to be distributed widely, argued to the acting High Commissioner of Iraq that the cheering was due to 'the natural excitement normally occasioned in an Iraqi audience by any rousing "action" film' and was not 'of a partisan nature'. Authorities present at the film, citing the support of English audience members that included RAF rank and file, overturned his views: 'Colonel Prescott ... decided that every ingredient of disturbance was present and that it was very undesirable on political grounds to permit the film to be shown again.'[74] The excitable audience of colour was invoked on both sides of the discussion with the argument about the impressionability of this audience winning out.

Reports in the colonies of deliberate misreading of empire films by audiences of colour continued to find their way to the Colonial Office. In September 1932, a letter to the Royal Empire Society concerning 'a matter that has been the subject of serious discussion' was forwarded to the Colonial Office. The letter, by a clerk in Mombasa, Kenya, related that:

> A friend of mine saw recently a film called *The Green Goddess*, the villain in the story of which is an Indian Rajah. My friend's car driver either went in as an Arab and was allowed in the cinema, or slipped in as a Swahili waiting for his English master. On driving my friend home, he remarked what a fine fellow the 'Rajah' was, one of the points of his 'fineness' being that a white girl has been on her knees to him.

The writer does not elaborate on the other points of the Raja's 'fineness' for what was clearly disturbing them was that the submission of a white woman to a native was noted and celebrated by an Arabic or Swahili viewer. The clerk further commented that 'apparently local film censors are not sufficiently careful of the distorted views that will be propagated among people of a different civilization'.[75] This 'distorted' reading of an empire film's villain was of deep concern in the colonies with racialised audiences in India, Iraq, Kenya and elsewhere consistently viewed as more impressionable and less sophisticated than English audiences. Subsequent recommendations to the Colonial Office from the Government House in Kenya for a new rating of 'N' to indicate suitable viewing for natives were rejected by the Colonial Office as overly

---

[74] Ibid.
[75] Letter from Government House, Nairobi, Kenya to Secretary of the State for the Colonies, 5 April 1932 and memorandum, 9 June 1932, CO 323/1168/1, TNA.

complicated and 'not practicable'.⁷⁶ Censorship in the empire continued to be enforced at an ad-hoc local level based on either appropriate or inappropriate responses by indigenous audiences to the film's content. Empire feature films would continue to trade in stereotypes that featured Black and south Asian men and women as violent or servile, cunning or infantile, and rarely to be trusted while the superiority of white characters was consistently confirmed. Black or south Asian audience members could seldom expect anything different.

### 2.4 Wartime Understandings

The outbreak of World War II saw the British state's earnest engagement in film production resulting in both ruptures and important continuities in representations of racialised people and how screen audiences were imagined. This period included a new and novel effort to consider audiences of colour in the film-making supported by the government. However, it also saw the persistence of the racialising pleasures of the screen that had been established for white audiences in the decades prior. The content of feature films that were produced in America, where film-making production remained largely untouched by the war, continued to feature imperial settings and Black and south Asian people as exotic and fantastic foils against upright English protagonists, even if the pace of production slowed somewhat. In documentary films, however, some evidence can be seen of new thinking around Black and south Asian audiences and a related consideration of what was put on the screen in terms of representation.

The mobilisation of the British empire prompted new thinking about reaching and motivating Black audiences and potential soldiers and workers in the empire through film. Tom Rice's excellent monograph documents the 'special films' that William Sellers argued were necessary for engaging Black audiences in the colonies and Africa in particular.⁷⁷ While previously a colonial official working in sanitation and health in Lagos, Sellers had experimented with educational films as a means of conveying information to Black audiences. As the first director of the newly formed Colonial Film Unit in 1939, he was the logical person to consider what Black audiences both needed and wanted to see on screen.⁷⁸ Sellers wrote explicitly in both the *Documentary News Letter*,

---

[76] Ibid.
[77] Tom Rice, *Films for the Colonies: Cinema and the Preservation of the British Empire* (Berkeley: University of California Press, 2019).
[78] Ibid.

published by the Film Centre, and later the Colonial Film Unit's own newspaper *Colonial Cinema* about an 'illiterate, semi-literate, or otherwise backwards population' that would not understand existing documentaries circulating in the English educational system. He argued that 'existing English educational films are of little use except for more advanced natives, who usually represent a very small proportion of the population. For the great majority, special films must be made'.[79] Sellers outlined five principles for creating films for colonial audiences, all steeped in highly racialised thinking about this audience's intellectual inferiority. These films had to be 'slow, and the length of individual scenes must be twice or three times as long as is usually considered for English school audiences'.[80] Content and composition of the shot must be simple, without too many objects in the frame; accuracy was needed regarding customs as 'mistakes at once turn serious film into comedy'; no camera tricks must be used; there was to be a clear continuity of events; and films must be silent. Such a framework assumed an African audience that was childish in their viewpoint, understanding, and ability to learn. As Rice notes, ten years after the creation of mobile film units in the country Sellers finally admitted that African audiences were ready for more sophisticated material. Initial responses of African audiences to films such as the 'Life History of the Mosquito', which had audiences reportedly worried after seeing a giant mosquito in close-up on screen, became not just an initial audience response to a new medium but rather orthodoxy as to how African audiences would *always* respond to extant cinema techniques.[81] The highly racialised thinking about what Africans could learn from the screen entirely formed the output of the Colonial Film Unit which Rice has amply and richly covered and which I will not repeat here except to note several continuities in how audiences of colour were imagined.

Within the framework of knowledge that Sellers spun around African audiences encountering film were hints of oppositional readings of screen content by racialised audiences. Sellers shared his ongoing thinking about film and colonial audiences in the *Colonial Cinema* periodical produced from 1942 to 1954 and circulated throughout the colonies.[82] Sellers' concern with avoiding the laughter of Black audiences warranted an entire article 'On Laughter' in the November 1943 issue, and it was

---

[79] William Sellers, 'Film for Primitive Peoples: A New Technique', *Documentary News Letter*, no. 3 (March 1940), 10.
[80] Ibid.   [81] Rice, *Films for the Colonies*, 53.
[82] The entire run of *Colonial Cinema* has been digitised and is available at http://cinemastandrews.org.uk/archive/colonial-cinema.

clear he found the laughter of African audiences consistently troubling.[83] Audience response and the importing of commercial films into colonial settings had to be managed carefully for reasons similar to those of local colonial officials between the wars. A long discussion of the desire for more Charlie Chaplin films from staff in the colonies was featured in the second issue of *Colonial Cinema*.[84] The article recounted the efforts of those involved to find suitable Chaplin films for both white and racialised audiences and the initial assumption by staff in the Colonial Film Unit that most Chaplin films would be appropriate: 'We retain very vivid recollections of these masterpieces and are quite certain that all or any of them are exactly what should be shown.'[85] On reviewing the films, staff instead found that 'the first few films were a shock', ultimately deciding that 'not one was suitable for the particular purpose for which the investigation was being made'. The root of this concern lay in the themes of conflict with authority that Chaplin pursued in his films. The article selected some of the tamer examples of unsuitably to discuss but it became clear that while Chaplin could test the limits of local authority on film for white audiences, this could not be shown to Black audiences: 'We had to decide to rule out certain things; for instance Chaplin or some other character dressing ... up as a woman; scenes which showed the police in a bad light; scenes in which a priest or a clergyman was a figure of fun ...'[86] The Colonial Film Unit settled on one Chaplin film that was found suitable (*Charlie the Rascal*) and indicated this would be circulated to colonial audiences. The laughter of colonial audiences at this film was deemed appropriate.

While the Colonial Film Unit made the response of Black and racialised audiences its primary object of concern in its post-war life and its educational films, in domestic Britain wartime attempts to speak to Black audiences living in the country can be measured within a small collection of documentary films. Indeed the scarcity of positive representations of people of colour on screen and the marginalisation of audiences of colour can be read through the very form of the medium; short documentary films rather than costlier feature films. The 14-minute documentary *Africa's Fighting Men* (1943) was meant primarily for Black and white audiences in Britain. It highlighted Black soldiers in war service in a variety of settings culminating with an image of Pilot Officer Peter Thomas boarding his plane.[87] Rank and respectability were on display

---

[83] 'On Laughter', *Colonial Cinema*, November 1943, 4.
[84] 'Charlie Chaplin Films', *Colonial Cinema*, December 1942, 3.   [85] Ibid.   [86] Ibid.
[87] Martin Francis, *The Flyer: British Culture and the Royal Air Force, 1939–1945* (Oxford: Oxford University Press, 2011).

in what Wendy Webster has noted was a concerted effort to portray a unified notion of Empire during the war that incorporated, however uneasily, racialised members of the empire as active, if not yet equal, contributors.[88] White audiences of the film could feel assured about Black soldiers in settings curtailed by white structures of colonial or military power.

At the very outset of the war on 18 September 1939, documentary filmmaker Basil Wright, already working under the auspices of wartime footing for the Ministry of Information, conceived of a documentary called, at the time, 'Men of Africa' as filling three needs.[89] The first was 'films for propaganda in neutral countries' which would use film to illuminate what the records referred to as the 'trusteeship' relationship Britain had with its colonies. A confidential memorandum from Sir William McLean confirmed this: he complained that during a trip to the US in the summer of 1939 on 'a mission of thanks to America for co-operation in the social development of our colonies' and even in university circles in the US there was a belief that 'the United Kingdom gets taxes from the Dominions and raw materials for next to nothing from the Colonies'.[90] McLean was at pains to outline 'the silken threads of the Crown holding the British Empire together' and the '"trusteeship" for the colonies, the people of which are being trained to govern themselves eventually', as a counter to these conceptions in America. The second need that Wright identified was 'films for native populations, dealing with the simpler aspects of Great Britain and other part of the Colonial Empire'. This was how the Colonial Film Unit was formed, centring on how Sellers imagined Black audiences responded to films in Africa as part of the war effort.

The third reason outlined for a film such as 'Men of Africa' stepped lightly and carefully towards what would be a topic of great discussion and angst for post-war television. Wright outlined a novel type of wartime film that would increase a white audience's understanding of Black people in Britain: 'Films for showing in this country, both theatrically and non-theatrically stressing economic aspects and also the importance of closer sympathies and understanding between the citizens of Great Britain and the citizens of the various colonies'.[91] This seemingly benign

---

[88] Wendy Webster, *Englishness and Empire 1939–1965* (Oxford: Oxford University Press, 2008).
[89] Basil Wright, 'Memorandum on the use of colonial films under war conditions', 18 September 1939, CO 852/228/1, TNA.
[90] 'Memorandum on the need in the US for propaganda explaining the nature of the British Empire and the position of the Colonies', 21 September 1939, CO 852/228/1, TNA.
[91] Wright, 'Memorandum on the Use of Colonial Films Under War Conditions', 18 September 1939, 4.

outline of the need for 'closer sympathies and understanding' between white citizens of Great Britain and the racialised citizens of 'various colonies' articulated the great task of not only wartime but also postwar film and television. How could the screen work to foster understanding and sympathies among white audiences for Black people and bridge divides that could not yet be named as racism in the UK? 'Men of Africa', which would become *Africa's Fighting Men*, spoke to white audiences through the language of class to stress the existence of middle-class Black respectability but also carried through the film the soothing presence of white supervision articulated through a middle-class Englishman's voiceover. A rather different film, *West Indies Calling* (1943), would also draw on middle-class Black men and women in Britain to populate the screen. Una Marson, Learie Constantine and a range of prominent Black artists and talent in Britain were shown as travelling, living and working in Britain all while speaking in posh accents.[92] Yet the film stressed again and again to the white British audience that these men and women were merely 'visitors' and that their stay was a temporary one to help and fortify Britain. The presumed whiteness of Britain, and indeed the maintenance of this, was never questioned in the film. This stress on the visiting nature of these West Indians was much more persistent than it was in the longer film from which much of the footage was taken, *Hello! West Indies*, which was aimed primarily at a West Indian audience instead. In *Hello! West Indies*, the national and imperial belonging that Kennetta Hammond Perry has written of was not presented as inconceivable on screen.[93]

Film in the period, as Webster and others have discussed, offered a coming together under wartime conditions that saw racial divisions subsumed to some extent in the wartime project. This mimicked efforts in the US as directors, such as Frank Capra, of popular interwar feature films also tried to incorporate Black Americans into images of the war effort and into the film audience. Capra's 43-minute film *The Negro Soldier* was released in 1944 and opened with images of well-dressed Black teachers, doctors, lawyers and soldiers attending church. This was the effort, albeit late in the war, of film-makers to consider new audiences and to bridge what could not yet be acknowledged as racism among white audiences but could be recognised ever so carefully as the need to build 'sympathy and understanding' as Wright put it in 1939. Wartime

---

[92] Webster, *Englishness and Empire*, 41–43. See also the entry on the film authored by Tom Rice at www.colonialfilm.org.uk/node/5733.
[93] Kennetta Hammond Perry, *London Is the Place for Me: Black Britons, Citizenship, and the Politics of Race* (Oxford: Oxford University Press, 2015).

conditions created these bridges but we also have evidence from Black soldiers during the war of the persistent racism they encountered in their interactions with white Britons. Webster's most recent work and that of Lucy Bland point to a population that was 'mixing it' but sometimes with vast gulfs of experiences stemming in part from the misunderstandings sown by empire films about Black and south Asian men and women.[94] The post-war period would see what was only cautiously approached during wartime – the everyday racism of white Britons – examined rather more directly within film and television, if not successfully, as the following chapters will show.

## Conclusion

Producers and directors of film content in the early twentieth century, such as Grierson, Sellers and the Korda brothers, offered their answer to what they thought white audiences wanted by producing images of Black and south Asian people rooted in stereotypes and empire thrillers that imperilled and then affirmed white superiority. These stereotypes and narrative arcs would offer a template for empire films that endured long after the period in which they were largely formed. This chapter has investigated the content of that material and the thinking behind it as well as the responses of racialised audiences as they increasingly contemplated what white people seemed to enjoy watching. The events of World War II introduced new complexities through the highly circumscribed possibilities of white producers and directors speaking to audiences of colour and their tentative use of film as a means of creating sympathy among white audiences for Black and south Asian visitors and immigrants where little seemed to exist. The story of post-war screen content, as we shall see, is very much one that was informed by these structures of presentation and the affective economies of race on screen that were laid out in the early twentieth century.

For a Black actor such as Paul Robeson, the legacy of the empire films of the early twentieth century would be manifold. His work in them quickly stopped, but films such as *Sanders of the River* would have a second life in the post-war world of television, repeated as a 'classic' of the time, as discussed in Chapter 4. Audiences of colour who despaired in the interwar period over such material on screen would see these films

---

[94] Wendy Webster, *Mixing It: Diversity in World War Two Britain* (Oxford: Oxford University Press, 2018); Lucy Bland, *Britain's Brown Babies: The Stories of Children Born to Black GIs and White Women in the Second World War* (Manchester: Manchester University Press, 2019).

continue to shape what white audiences knew and did not know about empire and racialised people and what they thought was harmless entertainment. The counter-storytelling that Robeson attempted through his art continued, however, even as Black and south Asian audiences found themselves more formally marginalised in the new scientific push to measure what audiences wanted when it came to television content. The legacy of the early twentieth-century empire films and their answer to what audiences wanted was a sticky one – difficult to dislodge from the minds of white audiences who would come to see empire films as innocent, harmless pleasures of the past; unable and unwilling to acknowledge the pleasures of white superiority they were rooted in.

## 3 'Expressing Their Own Point of View'
Television Audience Research on 'Race' at the BBC, 1950–1968

In March 1968, the BBC's Audience Research Department circulated to other departments a confidential 'Special Audience Research Report' on the television series *Rainbow City* broadcast the previous year in July and August 1967. Darrell M. Newton, Gavin Schaffer and Stephen Bourne have all noted *Rainbow City* was the first television series broadcast in Britain that featured a Black man as its protagonist.[1] The Trinidadian actor Errol John played John Steele, an upright barrister from Jamaica, living in Birmingham and married to a white woman, Mary, played by Gemma Jones. As Steele grappled with an interracial marriage, his legal practice and the numerous challenges facing West Indians living in post-war Britain, the series failed to extend into a second season and ending as Schaffer writes, 'in discord and uncertainty'.[2] In the aftermath of the programme's broadcast, an extended six-page special audience research report was released that was not the usual standard audience research report of one or two pages in length, the latter which were produced at a rate of 700 a year between the 1950s and 1980.[3] The introduction to the special audience research report on *Rainbow City* indicated the high stakes involved for the BBC when it came to the production of the series and the role of audience research in establishing its impact on viewers: 'Since [*Rainbow City's*] avowed purpose was to contribute to the reduction of inter-racial tensions and to promote a sympathetic understanding of coloured immigrants, plans were made for an elaborate study of its impact and effects.'[4]

---

[1] Gavin Schaffer, *The Vision of a Nation: Making Multiculturalism on British Television, 1960–80* (London: Palgrave Macmillan, 2014); Darrel M. Newton, *Paving the Empire Road: BBC Television and Black Britons* (Manchester: Manchester University Press, 2011); Stephen Bourne, *Black in the British Frame: The Black Experience in British Film and Television* (London: Bloomsbury, 2005).
[2] Newton, *Paving the Empire Road*, 148–151; Schaffer, *The Vision of a Nation*, 245–247.
[3] Billy Smart, 'The BBC Television Audience Research Reports, 1957–1979: Recorded Opinions and Invisible Expectations', *Historical Journal of Film, Radio and Television* 34, no. 3 (2014): 452–462.
[4] 'Race Relations and *Rainbow City*', An Audience Research Report, 4 March 1968, BBC Audience Research Special Reports Television, R9/10/15, p. 1, WAC.

A twofold endeavour at the BBC was revealed in this statement: firstly, the monumental and explicit effort to change audience attitudes when it came to attitudes towards immigrants and secondly, the ability of audience research to measure this change. *Rainbow City* was thus revealed as a self-conscious attempt by its producers to use the screen to shape an impressionable audience. David Porter, Head of Programmes for the BBC's Midlands Region, relayed in an interview with *Radio Times* that the purpose of the show was to demonstrate that 'immigrants have the same recognisable egos and psyches, hopes, fears, and difficulties as the rest of us, plus a few problems of their own'.[5] Porter, alongside the two writers for the show – John Elliott, who was white, and Horace James, a Black Trinidadian writer and actor – imagined television as something that could change the minds and outlooks of impressionable audiences. This was an opportunity to bring new stories about immigrants to white audiences. The Audience Research Department on the other hand had to prove that it could measure such a shift and quantify something like the changing racial viewpoints of British audiences. It was the job of Audience Research at the BBC to know what audiences preferred on the television screen in 1960s Britain.

As was often the case, scheduling decisions made outside of the Audience Research Department shaped its ability to mount the proposed study and further emphasised the somewhat marginal place of audience research within the BBC. The report's authors noted with some degree of frustration that 'unfortunately a sudden decision to bring [the programme's] transmission forward by several weeks torpedoed this plan' and 'from the wreckage a more modest one was hastily put together'. This new modest plan was again 'pursued by bad luck' as the study depended upon a large number of group sessions and 'only 164' people showed up for these which limited the ability of the Audience Research Department to directly compare the effects of the programme on viewers and non-viewers. At the time the department was accustomed to conducting surveys with almost a thousand respondents. Even more pressing than the small numbers was the fact that most of the participants surveyed had not even watched *Rainbow City*. Only 58 of the 164 people interviewed, or 35.4 per cent, of the respondents had actually seen the show, providing an early indication of just how unsuccessful the series was with British audiences. Nevertheless the study was undertaken, and in a passing comment at the end of the introduction the report noted the racial composition of those surveyed: 'The 164 people who took part

---

[5] Quoted in Newton, *Paving the Empire Road*, 148; Original quote, 'Rainbow City', *Radio Times*, 29 June 1967, 35.

were all Londoners and all white, but in terms of age, sex, and social status, they constituted a broadly representative group.'[6] The survey went ahead as it was 'felt worth while to subject the data collected to a thorough analysis, not least because they would have a value in throwing light on the problem or race relations'.

What resulted from this survey of 'a broadly representative group' made for sobering reading for the Audience Research Department. When faced with 23 statements regarding race relations in Britain produced by staff in the department, the 164 white Londoners indicated whether they agreed or disagreed with each one. The statements chosen by the Audience Research Department 'about coloured people/immigrants' were selected in part for their extreme views: 'Some of the statements represented attitudes which were, in varying degrees, hostile and others represented favourable attitudes.' This approach uncovered a strong endorsement of some of the more excessive statements put to those interviewed. So striking were the outcomes that the Audience Research Department led in the report with the data on 'Anti-colour/immigrant statements and the proportion *agreeing* with them' (emphasis in original).[7]

> 84% If an immigrant is offered a good job in the country he came from, he should take it and go home
> 79% One of the troubles with this country is that there are too many foreigners living there
> 78% It was a mistake to allow so many coloured people to settle here
> 66% The type of person who immigrates to this country is only interested in money
> 56% If jobs are scarce it's only fair that immigrants be the first to be laid off work
> 53% The standards of behaviour of coloured people are lower than those of white people
> 50% Most immigrants just do not fit into the British way of life[8]

In the spring of 1968, 138 of the 164 white Londoners surveyed thought that immigrants should go home if they had a good job offer; 130 saw 'too many foreigners' as constituting a problem for the country; and 128 indicated that allowing the settlement of people of colour in Britain had been a mistake. When presented with statements explicitly discussing the abilities of people of colour rather than settlement, the responses

---

[6] 'Race Relations and *Rainbow City*', 1.   [7] Ibid., 2.   [8] Ibid.

were no less troubling. The Audience Research Department professed itself shocked by the outcomes of the survey in its analysis of the data: 'The startling, but inescapable, impression left by these results is that *most* of these people showed anti-colour/immigrant attitudes in at least some degree and that what can only be described as racial prejudice proved to be alarmingly common.'[9]

The report's findings circulated through the BBC on 4 March 1968, six weeks before Enoch Powell's 'Rivers of Blood' speech on 20 April, as a second Race Relations Act was making its way through parliament and exactly one month before the assassination of Martin Luther King Jr. in the US. The data captured within the special report echoed viewpoints that had driven the passage of the two exclusionary Commonwealth Immigrants Acts of 1962 and 1968 and which had been evident in towns such as Smethwick during the 1964 general election and further indicated that London's urban cosmopolitanism was no buffer against anti-immigrant and anti-Black sentiment.[10] This group of all white Londoners endorsed much of the thinking laid out in the survey's extreme statements as the majority view while the Audience Research Department's own seemingly tolerant attitudes were hinted at in their expression of shock and surprise.

The Audience Research Department's alarm at the outcomes of the report sat alongside another claim by the department that the racial prejudice they had measured and quantified in the study was new. The attitudes of white British audiences towards race on screen had changed since the department's last study of these in 1952 according to staff writing the report: 'This picture is depressingly different from that presented in a not dissimilar Audience Research inquiry made before Christopher Mayhew's TV series on *Race Relations in Africa* in 1952. At that time, which was before the influx of coloured immigrants into Britain, the sentiments expressed by the public were predominantly liberal.'[11]

Between 1952 and 1968, according to the Audience Research Department, something had happened to shift audience attitudes towards Black people on screen, and the authors speculated that this was due to increased immigration. The report used the language of 'influx' to characterise this growth as sudden and complete even as the

---

[9] Ibid.
[10] Nadine El-Enany, *(B)ordering Britain: Law, Race and Empire* (Manchester: Manchester University Press, 2020); Rachel Yemm, 'Immigration, Race and Local Media: Smethwick and the 1964 General Election', *Contemporary British History* 33, no. 1 (2019): 98–122.
[11] 'Race Relations and *Rainbow City*', 1.

authors expressed discomfort with the report's findings of racial prejudice among most viewers. No other editorialising was evident in the report and nor was there any consideration, methodological or otherwise, of the incongruous comparison between the pre-broadcast responses of British audiences to a documentary series on *Race Relations in Africa* and the response to a fictionalised dramatic series centring on a Jamaican barrister living in Birmingham. An equivalency between the two was established that drew attitudes towards empire and immigration into the same frame; this was simply 'race' on television. Nor was a discussion or justification offered for the large gap of 16 years between these two studies which encompassed the formal end of empire and increased immigration from current and former colonial territories. A discussion was also absent of the BBC's other successful 'racial sitcom', *Till Death Us Do Part*, on television in the same year as *Rainbow City* and which constituted the BBC's other primary means of discussion race relations on screen in a fictionalised setting. A number of the extreme views offered to those in the *Rainbow City* survey directly mimicked statements made by the protagonist of the *Till Death Us Do Part*, Alf Garnett. Instead, shock and dismay were professed by the BBC's Audience Research Department in the face of a white British viewership that had somehow become 'depressingly different' from those 'predominantly liberal' audiences of 1952.

As we shall see in this chapter's examination of audience research on 'race' at the BBC from 1952 to 1968, audience racism had in fact been a factor in the field of audience research from the very advent of small-screen broadcasting in Britain. The prospect of audience racism, or what would most likely have been termed 'racialism' among white British viewers at the time, had informed the creation of the 1952 special audience research report on 'Race Relations in Africa' at the BBC. In 1952, both a BBC producer and the Audience Research Department closely considered the potential responses of white audiences to a programme series that would consistently feature Black people on screen. This chapter examines the assumptions that underpinned the production and comparison of the two special audience research Reports of 1952 and 1968 and related standard audience research reports to reveal a moment when the assumed colour-blindness of white British audiences slipped to reveal something more troubling. Audience racism came to the fore in 1968 in the findings of the Audience Research Department in a 'depressing' manner that indicated the following: firstly, how limited the BBC's notion of race on screen was; secondly, how little audience research was prepared to encounter the variety of responses of white viewers towards Black people on the screen; and thirdly, how the mechanisms of audience research began to silence and evade evidence of racism among ordinary Britons in the post-war period. As this chapter demonstrates, varied audience responses to racialised people on screen were rooted in notions of white superiority that encompassed paternalist attitudes, vigorous anti-immigrant sentiments, or silent disengagement. Audience research witnessed this mind-frame through its clunky examination of racial attitudes and recoiled from it in 1968 even though elements of it can be seen in the earlier study of 'race' in 1952 and in the related enthusiasm for the racial sitcom *Till Death Us Do Part*.

The two special studies at the heart of this chapter, alongside the standard audience research reports of *Till Death Us Do Part*, made use of approaches and methodologies that would likely not see the light of day in current sociological or even market-research approaches. As I indicated in Chapter 1, the field of audience research worked in the grey margins of adjacent areas including market-research, sociology and an emergent academic knowledge of mass communications. Given the latitude and lack of oversight over audience research at both the BBC and ITV, this material was unlikely to stand up to close scrutiny even then and accounts for much of the closed discussions in the Audience Research Department at the BBC. As a result, my revisiting of this material is not quite part of the 'social scientific turn in modern British history' that Lise Butler discusses.[12] This is moving through much murkier territory due to the questionable, unscrutinised, non–peer reviewed methods of audience research in comparison to sociology. As discussed in Chapter 1, audience research's decision to ask answers and expect honest questions from its interviewees was its driving methodology during its life. I am primarily interested in what audiences choose to reveal in light of such a blunt methodology. However, I am also interested in the racialised assumptions at work which have received rather less scrutiny in this turn.[13] Certainly the types of questions that the Audience Research Department asked audiences about 'race' were themselves highly racialised and racist. When the Audience Research Department put statements to its respondents such as 'It was a mistake to allow so many coloured people to settle here' or 'It's a mistake to try to

---

[12] Jon Lawrence, 'On Historians' Re-Use of Social-Science Archives', *Twentieth Century British History* 33, no. 3 (2022): 432–444; Lise Butler, 'The Social Scientific Turn in Modern British History', *Twentieth Century British History* 33, no. 3 (2022): 445–450.

[13] See Gurminder K. Bhambra, *Rethinking Modernity: Postcolonialism and the Sociological Imagination* (London: Palgrave, 2007); Gurminder K. Bhambra and John Holmwood, *Colonialism and Modern Social Theory* (London: Polity, 2021), and George Steinmetz, *The Colonial Origins of Modern Social Thought: French Sociology and the Overseas Empire* (Princeton, NJ: Princeton University Press, 2023).

educate the black people' (from the 1968 and 1952 reports respectively) and asked them to agree or disagree we see the racialised infrastructure of the very field. This chapter, then, is about that developing infrastructure, yet is also explicitly about a moment when the Audience Research Department faced the racism of white audiences that it had assumed were racially tolerant.

## 3.1  Race Relations in Africa (1952)

Presenting Black people on the small screen to predominantly white British audiences is an overlooked experiment in the history of early television broadcasting in Britain and one that signals just how racialised thinking was at the time when it came to imagining Britain's screen audiences. Historians of television have demonstrated that audiences were imagined as monarchists, sports-lovers and also increasingly as housewives when television returned in the UK after World War II, from 1946.[14] Much attention was paid to the class composition of viewers, evidenced by a paper presented by Brian Emmett to the Royal Statistical Society in 1956 who was then working in the Audience Research Department under Robert Silvey.[15] Yet even in this study, coming as it did after eight years of substantive immigration from the West Indies, the unspoken assumption was that British audiences were entirely white. Although Black and south Asian voices had been heard on BBC radio throughout the 1930s and into the early 1950s as musical guests or in programmes such as 'West Indies Calling', the prospect of actors and entertainers of colour on the television screen was treated as a different challenge within the BBC.[16] The broad and baggy definition of 'race' used by both BBC and ITV broadcasters in the 1950s and 1960s worked to house a huge diversity of topics on screen. The term 'race' encompassed Black men and women occupying different social, economic,

---

[14] Tim O'Sullivan, 'Researching the Viewing Culture: Television and the Home, 1946–1960,' in Helen Wheatley, ed., *Reviewing Television History: Critical Issues in Television Historiography* (London: IB Tauris, 2007): 159–170; Tim O'Sullivan, 'Television and the Austerity Games: London 1948', in J. Hill, K. Moore and J. Wood, eds., *Sport, History and Heritage: Studies in Public Representation* (London: Boydell and Brewer, 2012); Helen Wood, 'Television – the Housewife's Choice? The 1949 Mass Observation Television Directive, Reluctance and Revision', *Media History* 21 no. 3 (2015): 342–359.

[15] B. P. Emmett, 'The Television Audience in the United Kingdom', *Journal of the Royal Statistical Society* Series A (General) 119, no. 3 (1956): 284–311.

[16] Michael Pickering, 'The BBC's Kentucky Minstrels, 1933–1950: Blackface Entertainment on British Radio', *Historical Journal of Film, Radio, and Television* 16, no. 2 (1996): 161–195; Amanda Bidnall, *The West Indian Generation: Remaking British Culture in London, 1945–1965* (Liverpool: University of Liverpool Press, 2018).

geographic and political contexts, but 'race' on screen also signalled subjects that were thought of as only impacting Black and south Asian communities including racism or 'racial prejudice' and 'racialism'. The imagined whiteness of the audience, as this chapter demonstrates, informed a cautious approach within Audience Research at the BBC to presenting both Black people and racism on the small screen. In examining this caution through the lens of critical race theory and its attention to what white people tend to do when faced with discomfiting evidence of racism, what becomes evident is television's and audience research's early role in sustaining the segregated and privileged world of the white everyday.

The BBC was, from its early broadcasts, cautiously alert to moments when white audiences encountered 'race' on screen and consistently imagined these moments as ones that could lead to audiences changing channels. This caution had been instilled early on in broadcasting history at the BBC by Norman Collins as the first Television Controller through what he viewed as an initial misstep in the production of a variety programme, now lost, called *Black Magic*. In 1950, four years into the BBC's broadcasting of television and two years prior to the push to mount the series *Race Relations in Africa*, Collins issued a stern memo to the Heads of Television Production and Television Light Entertainment after *Black Magic's* broadcast, stating 'We must be extremely careful in the matter of employment of white and coloured artists in the same show. In particular, love songs between white and coloured artists must be scrupulously considered, and the settings, ages, gestures, and costumes *all* taken into consideration' (emphasis in original).[17] Collins himself found watching the programme, which featured what he called 'a coloured man's songs to a white girl', a negative experience citing his viewpoint as an audience member: 'I watched the whole of this production and I thought it was quite deplorable.' He found the production itself 'chaotic' but couched the Black singer's song to the white woman as a 'question of good taste' and invoked the responses of other audience members to support his view: 'There have been a number of letters complaining about this point, even though some of the correspondents are badly confused by the lightness of some of the coloured artists.' The skin colour of Black entertainers was questionable to some white audiences but Collins himself bore no such confusion and

---

[17] 'Use of Coloured and White Artists on Any Future Occasions', memo from Norman Collins, Controller, Television to Head of Television Light Entertainment and Head of Television Production, 2 February 1950, TV Policy: Race Relations, File 1/1950–54), T16/175/1, WAC.

recommended the termination of not only the programme itself but also of the variety entertainment producer Walton Anderson's employment. Collins further demanded a meeting with the Head of Television Programming on the subject of the programme. Collins sharp criticism of the content, his simultaneous invocation of his own strong response, and the discomfited response of other audience members to interracial screen content was likely felt throughout the corporation.

Two years after Collins memo had been issued regarding *Black Magic*, the BBC revisited the issue of audience response to representations of Black people on screen in light of the prospect of a production of a five-part documentary series on race relations in Africa. The proposed series was one that was quite different from the musical programme that had offended Norman Collins but it was another moment when white British audiences would be seeing Black people on television. The programme would involve a presentation and discussion of race relations and anti-Black racism in a number of commonwealth countries in Africa. *Race Relations in Africa* was the brainchild of Christopher Mayhew, the then-Labour MP, who proposed to host the series spotlighting racial segregation in the Union of South Africa while also visiting Kenya, the Gold Coast and the Sudan. The series was to be prefaced by a stand-alone programme entitled *Race and Colour: A Scientific Introduction to the Problem of Race Relations* featuring the perspectives of a number of white scientists in Britain on contemporary racial categorisations.[18] The structure of the weekly series drew heavily on the documentary film tradition developed by Basil Wright and others such as Paul Rotha at the Empire Marketing Board and GPO film units throughout the interwar period.[19] The presence of a white British narrator, in this case Mayhew, also provided continuity for British audiences familiar with the public information films and educational documentaries produced during World War II. Mayhew's narration offered white British audiences a trusted, familiar figure – upper-class, male and white – who would visually and aurally guide the audience through these diverse African countries and tricky discussions of race relations and racism.

The question for the BBC, however, as they considered the programme was: is this what audiences wanted and would they be offended by the topic? Just as John Grierson considered this in 1927 as he

---

[18] See Darrell Newton's excellent discussion of the stand-alone programme, *Paving the Empire Road*, 57–61.
[19] See Marc Matera, 'An Empire of Development: Africa and the Caribbean in *God's Chillun*', *Twentieth Century British History* 23 (2012): 12–37, and Colin MacCabe and Lee Grieveson, eds., *Empire and Film* (London: Bloomsbury Press, 2019).

contemplated white audiences of documentary films, so did the BBC wonder about the appetites of white television viewers for watching Black people on screen. This was a particularly pressing question at the BBC because of the relative fragility of television's role in the organisation in comparison to radio. Television producers such as Grace Wydnham Goldie needed to demonstrate the worth of the medium itself by either pointing to the prospect of significant audience numbers or by demonstrating a programme's moral and educational impact upon an audience.[20] Television producers vacillated between these two arguments as they attempted to get programmes made and to find their feet in a volatile landscape for television within the corporation. Goldie had been appointed to the BBC's Television Talks Department in 1947 as a rare female voice in the field, and in 1952 she was involved in bringing Mayhew's vision of the documentary series to life.[21] By then Goldie's efforts to bring politics into television broadcasts was making inroads with higher ups at the BBC who were reluctantly considering television's reach with audiences.[22] Yet when it came to Mayhew's proposed series Goldie expressed reservations about the willingness of white British audiences to embrace such a programme. Even accounting for the television monopoly the BBC was then enjoying, the risk posed by the presentation of 'race' on screen was enough to prompt Goldie to involve the Audience Research Department, renamed from the Listener Research Department in 1950, in an effort to establish what audience response was likely to be. In a memo directed to the Audience Research Department Goldie laid out her concerns about the potentially negative attitudes of white audiences: 'Is there such a hostility, and what is its cause and should we expect it any particular groups or areas? Is there alternatively any sort of predilection towards hearing about Race Relations? Is there a prejudice for or against seeing coloured people in television expressing their own point of view?'[23]

Goldie's concerns did not just centre on the presumed fragility of white audiences when it came to race relations and racialised bodies on screen but instead on something stronger – what she anticipated as

---

[20] James Curran and Jean Seaton, *Power Without Responsibility: Press, Broadcasting, and the Internet in Britain*, 8th ed. (London: Routledge, 2018).

[21] Mary Irwin, 'Grace Wyndham Goldie at the BBC: Reappraising the "First Lady of Television"', *Critical Studies in Television* 17 no. 3 (2022): 284–296; John Grist, *Grace Wyndham Goldie: First Lady of Television*. (London: New Generation Publishing, 2006).

[22] Goldie recounts the early marginal place of television in her autobiography; Grace Wyndham Goldie, *Facing the Nation: Television and Politics, 1936–76* (London: The Bodley Head, 1977).

[23] Grace Wyndham Goldie to Audience Research Department, 15 September 1952, T/32/209, WAC.

audience 'hostility' towards both and a hostility that she did not think the fledgling television wing could easily weather. The study that the Audience Research Department mounted in response to Goldie's concerns incorporated one of these questions when it laid out its central research questions:

a) To what extent is this 'audience' aware of the problems of race relations?
b) To what extent is the audience hostile towards the subject as such?
c) Is there a prejudice for or against 'seeing coloured people in television expressing their own point of view'?
d) What are this audience's attitudes on:
   (i) alleged innate differences between black people and white people?
   (ii) existing black/white issues in British Africa?
e) What is the state of the audience's general knowledge of Africa and of the factors around which African race-relations issues revolve?[24]

These questions taken together also pointed to a readiness by the BBC and Goldie to identify a white British audience that knew next to nothing of Black experiences and world views.

The broad final research question posed by the Audience Research Department about the audience's 'general knowledge of Africa and of the factors around which African race-relations issues revolve' and the potential of a reaction that might include hostility or prejudice against 'coloured people in television expressing their own point of view' left room for the BBC to be directed by the discomfort of white people confronted with evidence of the larger structures of racism and their own white privilege. Although the proposed programme conformed to the existing patterns of empire documentaries the programme would, as Goldie and Mayhew well knew, still feature Black people expressing themselves and speaking on screen instead of silently being filmed as had been the case in 1930s and 1950s empire documentaries. Television had the capacity to allow multiple voices to speak within an extended programme and it was the combined televisual and aural presence of Black people on screen that forged a new component of the series and which prompted the Audience Research Department's first foray into examining white audience responses to 'race' on screen. When Goldie put forth the idea of the documentary to the BBC's Audience Research

---

[24] 'A pre-broadcast study of the opinions and the knowledge of the "target audience" for the projected television series *Race Relations in Africa*', Part I, p. 1, 24 October 1952, Audience Research Department, Audience Research Special Reports Television/December 1949–1954, R9/10/1,WAC.

department and asked it to measure potential responses to it she raised basic but important questions about what the impact of this desegregated hour on television would mean to the existing white comfort and white spaces of television audiences.

The pre-broadcast study of *Race Relations in Africa* conducted in 1952 as a result of Goldie's concerns was representative of the occasional special report that the Audience Research Department would pursue at various points in its history when producers requested this. It was not until the release of the 1977 Annan Report, that the quality of these reports for the BBC would be seriously questioned as either 'excellent' or 'unimportant' and dependent on 'highly unrepresentative samples'.[25] In 1952, the production of special reports was still in its infancy under Robert Silvey, and for this particular study 230 viewers were interviewed at Broadcasting House individually through a paper questionnaire.[26] The sample was described as a 'cross-section' of the 'general adult television population' although the Audience Research Department in October 1952 noted that this group was 'biased slightly upwards in respect of both intelligence and occupational levels'. The department nevertheless concluded, perhaps based on the costs and rarity of television-set ownership at the time and the demographic of those interested in empire, that 'the audience which is likely to view the series when it is broadcast will in all probability be a similarly based group'.[27] Part II of the report circulated at the BBC a month later and indicated that participants were interviewed in groups of 15–20 people.[28] Part I offered a summative discussion of the report's findings alongside the most relevant statistical data while Part II included all of the statistical data in graph form and a fuller discussion of the methods used. For the purposes of programming decisions by BBC executives, the first report seemed to be key. The initial report noted that 'Adorno's adaptation of the Likert method'[29] was used when putting together the written questionnaire which was defined as 'the method of so padding a relatively nasty statement as to

---

[25] *Report of the Committee on the Future of Broadcasting*, Cmnd. 6753 (London, HMSO, 1977), p. 452.
[26] As opposed to 218 viewers surveyed about the first stand-alone programme, *Race and Colour*.
[27] Chris Jeppesen, '"Sanders of the River, Still the Best Job for a British Boy". Colonial Administrative Service Recruitment at the End of Empire', *The Historical Journal* 59, no. 2 (2016): 469–508.
[28] 'A pre-broadcast study of the opinions and the knowledge of the "target audience" for the projected television series *Race Relations in Africa*, Part II', p. 2–3, 28 November 1952, Audience Research Department, Audience Research Special Reports Television/December 1949–1954, R9/10/1, WAC.
[29] Ibid., 3.

allow the ordinarily defensive respondent to admit it as his own ... e.g. I'm afraid we have to admit that the "black man is born less intelligent than the white man"'.[30] This type of softer language around the production of racist sentiments was meant to put respondents at ease so that their true opinions could be freely aired. The Audience Research Department assumed, even in 1952, that racist beliefs would need to be coaxed out of white Britons and confessed to rather than confidently claimed indicating the power the labels of 'racialist' or 'racial prejudice' was already wielding within the largely middle-class London BBC staff if not the country more broadly.

The statements that white audiences were asked to respond to in the survey gives us considerable insight into race relations at the time in Britain as well as the crude methods that audience research possessed for unearthing racial attitudes among viewers. The *Rainbow City* survey would make use of very similar phrases in 1968 and likely account for some of the direct comparisons that the Audience Research Department was so willing to make between the two special reports. The 1952 study separated respondents' answers along four lines of agreement or disagreement and included the chatty or 'padded' voice of a friendly questioner alongside the more extreme statements:

> Given a fair chance, the black man can become equal to the white man in all things. The only real difference is the colour of his skin.
> *Very strong agreement*
>
> We have to admit that the black man is born less intelligent than the white man.
> *Fairly strong disagreement*
>
> Black men and whites have a different kind of blood.
> *Fairly strong disagreement*
>
> In some important ways, the black man is born better than the white man.
> *Fairly strong disagreement*
>
> The black man is born more savage than the white man and no matter what we do for him he will always be savage under the skin.
> *Strong disagreement*

---

[30] Ibid., 3.

It may seem an awful thing to say, but the black man has not advanced very far from the animal stage.
*Very strong disagreement*

I dislike the idea of marriage between blacks and whites.
*Strong agreement*

Personally, I dislike black men.
*Strong disagreement*

I must admit I dislike the idea of mixing with black people.
*Fairly strong disagreement*

I wouldn't like to have black people living in my street.
*Strong disagreement*

It's a mistake to try to educate the black people.
*Very strong disagreement*

Even if there *are* real differences between black and whites we should overlook them because black men are just as human as we are.
*Very strong agreement*

Somehow, I just can't help disliking black people.
*Strong disagreement*

I would be quite willing to have a black man visit me in my home if he was educated or civilised.
*Very strong agreement*[31]

Many of the questions that were posed were rooted in what was assumed knowledge among those surveyed of pseudo-scientific conceptions of racial difference as linked to intellectual capacity, originating in blood and kinship. The belief in intellectual inequality as a valid scientific justification for racial prejudice and difference was largely rejected by those providing responses with questions concerning the education of Black people eliciting strong responses in favour of it from potential white audiences of *Race Relations in Africa*. A British audience of 1952 seemingly favoured concepts of educational, intellectual and social capacity, if not equality, among Black people and the willingness to embrace a universalist colour-blind sentiment. Statements related to the potential of white people mixing with Black people such as those about an 'educated or civilised' Black man visiting one's home or living on one's street were largely validated in favour of such interactions.

---

[31] 'A Pre-broadcast Study', Part II, 7.

The results of the pre-broadcasting report by the Audience Research Department offered a strong endorsement by audiences for the future documentary series and according to its unnamed authors the survey's outcome offered a hopeful vision of the future of race on screen at the BBC. Ninety per cent of those surveyed had an interest 'in the general subject of the relation of black and white people in Africa' and 60 per cent were 'strongly interested'. In a seemingly direct refutation of Goldie's initial concerns about the programme the report relayed that 'about three-quarters of the viewers said they didn't mind seeing coloured people in television giving their own point of view and about a third strongly denied any antagonism towards the idea'. Some of the respondents were indeed offended at the very notion that they should object to seeing and hearing Black people expressing their 'own point of view' on screen. Alongside this there was also enthusiasm among those surveyed for 'seeing coloured people as entertainers on television', affirming the tradition of Black singers on BBC radio and offering a possible pathway for future versions of the *Black Magic* variety programme. The potential outcome of the broadcast seemed clear; *Race Relations in Africa* was likely to be a success with an interested audience. The report went one step further in tentatively noting that the responses of those surveyed may well capture the attitudes of ordinary Britons towards race relations more widely: 'This evidence does seem to point to a certain overt liberalism about black/white relations.'[32] Television content could, it seemed, become rather more racially integrated than it was without alienating white audiences. The vast majority of respondents reacted strongly to the most extreme statements put before them and the Audience Research Department pointed out that 'there was a general rejection of the idea that black people are innately inferior to whites'.

The survey also, however, indicated the limits of white British audiences when it came to Black people on screen. It showed a strong rejection of the prospect of interracial marriage on screen with 'strong agreement' among respondents to the statement: 'I dislike the idea of marriage between blacks and whites.' This was in keeping with the attitudes that Bland has uncovered in her work on World War II and even as Black and white men and women continued to, as Webster has argued, 'mix it' during the period.[33] In 1952, the Audience Research

---

[32] Ibid., 3.
[33] Lucy Bland, *Britain's Brown Babies: The Stories of Children Born to Black GIs and White Women in the Second World War* (Manchester: Manchester University Press, 2019); Wendy Webster, *Mixing It: Diversity in World War Two Britain* (Oxford: Oxford University Press, 2018).

Department noted that this robust negative response to the idea of interracial relationships stood out among the racial tolerance of those surveyed: 'What is more, this opposition came in the midst of a considerable liberalism about blacks mixing with white people in public places and entering one's own home. This could be an expression of a deep-rooted belief in the superiority of a white skin.'[34]

The report further noted that 'racism is not, of course, the only explanation of opposition to inter-marriage', opening the possibility for the softer and apparently benign concern among the respondents about the racism of others. The considerable antipathy demonstrated by survey respondents to mixed relationships were addressed directly, although awkwardly, through the 'social problem' feature-films on interracial romances of the late 1950s and early 1960s such as *Sapphire* (1958) and *Flame in the Streets* (1961).[35]

A further examination of the survey's findings indicates that respondents housed anti-immigrant attitudes distinct from pro-empire ones and which anticipated the results of the 1968 report. Race relations in Africa were, after all, not race relations in England. The 1952 survey pointed to audiences who were thinking of race in highly circumscribed ways that equated Blackness solely with the British empire and further identified race relations and racism as a potentially uncomfortable topic for the white British viewer. After noting the 90 per cent of the audience in favour of 'the general subject of the relation of the black and white people in Africa' the report commented: 'At the same time, there was evidence that this attitude springs partly out of a certain sense of duty towards Africa and coloured people and that it is tinged in a large number of cases with an undercurrent of feeling that to examine the subject would be somewhat unpleasant.'[36]

The survey's explicit questions about Britain's historic and contemporary role in Africa were listed towards the report's end:

> In the British colonies in Africa, the treatment of the black people is generally good.
> *Fairly strong agreement*
>
> The British are only in Africa for the good of the black people.
> *Fairly strong disagreement*

---

[34] 'A Pre-broadcast Study', Part I, 3.
[35] Clive James Nwonka, 'Love Knows No Colour Bar: Windrush, Racism and *Flame in the Streets*', *Ethnic and Racial Studies* 43, no. 12 (2020): 2199–2216; Amanda Bidnall, *The West Indian Generation: Remaking British Culture in London, 1945–1965* (Liverpool: Liverpool University Press, 2017).
[36] 'A Pre-broadcast Study', Part I, 2.

> The British should give the black people of their African colonies self government as soon as they are ready for it.
> *Very strong agreement*
>
> Britain has done a lot for Africa so she is entitled to get all she can out of it.
> *Fairly strong agreement*
>
> The black people in Africa are like children and it's the whites who have to tell them what's good for them.
> *Some measure of disagreement*
>
> Black people in Africa are better off now than they were before the whites came.
> *Some measure of agreement*

This was the confused legacy of empire for ordinary, albeit London-based, Britons. Black Africans were imagined as better off than they had been before colonisation by Britain, and the infantilising narratives of progress that accompanied decolonisation still had some purchase with those surveyed, while the audience also registered some awareness of the negative effect of empire on African territories and the exploitation that accompanied this with their moderated responses to what the impact of empire actually was. Yet questions on further exploitation within the empire were then rejected in favour of answers that prioritised progress, education and welfare.

The anonymous authors of the 1952 Audience Research department survey were also careful to highlight the hypothetical nature of the survey even with its initial 'liberal' results and to point out that the reality of Black people appearing on screen could prompt a different outcome with audiences: 'It is important to point out, however, that any question dealing with 'feelings about seeing coloured people' is inevitably hypothetical and is not be taken as a prediction of what will in fact happen.'[37] The report also noted in a prominent position on page two that audience discomfort at the topic of race relations was clearly signalled in the data through the large amount of 'no opinions' expressed. When faced with the statement 'Somehow I feel that this subject would be a little unpleasant', only 7 per cent agreed strongly and 15 per cent agreed, but a relatively large proportion in comparison to the rest of the report – 25 per cent – chose 'no opinion'. Two further statements related to this bore similarly large 'no opinion' responses: 31 per cent chose 'no

---

[37] 'A Pre-broadcast Study', Part I, 2.

opinion' in response to the statement 'To tell the truth, I simply don't know how I'd feel about it' and 25 per cent chose 'no opinion' to the sentence 'It's probably a good thing to know about race relations in Arica, but I just don't happen to be interested' and 48 per cent disagreed with the statement.[38] The large 'no opinion' percentages for these statements stood out as significant to the Audience Research Department and among a survey where audiences had been largely happy to profess opinions one way or the other. This was a shrug of unease among viewers that could point to something of significance. It is impossible to ascertain in the results whether this shrug sheltered a broader antipathy among white British audiences to Black people appearing and speaking on screen or to stirrings of white fragility as audiences were faced with the prospect of a sustained examination on screen of structural racism that might not favour the paternalist workings of colonial development or colour-blind racism. Discussions with white viewers of the possibility of Black people expressing themselves on screen and related discussions of racism were merely hypothetical at this point but carefully considered by the Audience Research Department.

The general enthusiasm for the documentary series by potential viewers resulted in its production under Goldie in the *International Commentary* umbrella at the BBC. The Audience Research Department traced a healthy audience endorsement of the five episodes hosted by Mayhew in their standard Audience Research Reports after overcoming a fairly negative initial response by audiences to the *Race and Colour* programme helmed by the scientists. This programme gave a 'disappointing reaction index of 54' when a numeric value in the high 60s was rated as ideal and a Reaction Index in the 70s indicated a 'hit'.[39] The dry content and jargon of the scientific experts was described by one viewer as 'like listening to a lot of doctors at a medical confab'.[40] The standard report was quick to note at the outset of their summation that 'The widespread feeling of dissatisfaction with the programme had little to do with the subject itself,' yet they also noted an audience response that hinted at the findings of the pre-broadcast study: 'Admittedly, some viewers were inclined to regard the theme – race and colour – as tedious, or unpleasant, and therefore unsuited to television …' Yet the audience research report may have stretched beyond the evidence itself when the

---

[38] Ibid., 2–3.
[39] It is worth noting that the ongoing calculations and permutations of the Reaction Index and how it was calculated and read could be a study unto itself. By the 1960s, a score in the sixties was considered a success.
[40] A Viewer Research Report: 'Race and Colour', p. 1, 26 November 1952. VR 52/513, R9/10/1, WAC.

authors noted that most of the viewers were 'clearly not averse to a programme that promised to enlighten them on a subject which struck many as being of paramount importance'.[41] Future episodes set in Africa and hosted by Mayhew garnered a much more positive Reaction Index of 75 (Union of South Africa), 73 (Kenya), 72 (The Gold Coast), 73 (The Sudan), and 73 (Summing Up). The series was a hit with white British viewers and affirmed both the initial findings of the Audience Research Department and Goldie's approach.

Within the series itself Mayhew's performance and 'neutrality' were consistently praised particularly in light of what Goldie, the Audience Research department, and audiences themselves saw as controversial subjects. A 'Company Secretary' was quoted in the report as saying 'both sides of a highly controversial matter appear to have been fairly presented', while 'A Student' praised Mayhew's 'complete impartiality' and noted that it was 'a difficult task extraordinarily well carried out'. This fair presentation and impartiality were emphasised repeatedly in the weekly standard Audience Research Reports. The first episode on South Africa noted a debate between an anti-apartheid Miss Jabavu and a pro-apartheid Mr Biermann. The Audience Research department noted some criticisms from British audiences: 'Viewers were, however, rather surprised that the speakers chosen to represent "two diametrically opposed points of view" were not more evenly matched, for it seems that Mis Jabavu put her case for racial equality much more lucidly and persuasively than Mr Biermann, who spoke for the principle of apartheid.'[42]

Gavin Schaffer's description of the BBC's willingness to position extreme racial views against reasonable ones for the purpose of balance and impartiality was evidently already in play in 1952.[43] This programming commitment was underpinned by what the BBC's Audience Research department identified as an audience preference for such counterbalance. A lucid and persuasive argument in favour of racial equality was seemingly expected to exist alongside an equally lucid and persuasive argument for apartheid. This expectation by white British audiences is noteworthy but not unique in the period. White audiences in 1952 preferred to see discussions of racial equality and apartheid represented as a debate where arguments put forth by white proponents of apartheid would be considered seriously and presumably calmly. Such an exchange would ideally not arouse an emotional response among the viewer but

---

[41] Ibid.
[42] A Viewer Research Report: 'International Commentary, 1 Union of South Africa', p.1, 24 November 1952. VR 52/538, R9/10/1, WAC.
[43] Schaffer, 96–102.

rather would be logically presented as something that needed addressing or debating. This too built upon a long tradition in British media that carefully positioned the subject of racial injustice as devoid of the type of emotional framing that could naturally accompany accounts of racism's and apartheid's impact. Black people, in other words, were inferred in the responses of these audience members as more likely to be emotional or unbalanced about racism and its impact while white people and white narrators such as Mayhew were seen as devoid of such emotional baggage and consequently able to present bare facts to white audiences.[44] Audiences imagined white narrators such as Mayhew as another member of this (un)emotional white community, to borrow Barbara Rosenwein's phrase, and noted it when other members of this white community failed to adhere to this particular presentation of racial conflict.[45] Television's segregation of white and Black spaces maintained the viewer's emotional space as well, where Black people were accepted only if adhering to the emotional norms of that community. Overall, the programme was a considerable success working against the fears of Goldie and offering the corporation a sense of a British audience with liberal sentiments able to accommodate the BBC's particular definition of 'race' on screen.

## 3.2  Audience Responses to *Rainbow City* and *Till Death Us Do Part*

In the aftermath of the broadcast of Mayhew's series in the winter of 1953, the BBC did not wholeheartedly embrace representations of race on screen, but British television audiences did have other, albeit scarce, opportunities to see Black people on television. Sarita Malik and Gavin Schaffer have pointed out repetitive news coverage that equated immigrants with crime and other social problems and further marginalised the speaking presence of racialised immigrants in favour of stories of white British anxieties about imagined threats.[46] News reporting from both the BBC's and ITV's franchise holders after 1955 regularly featured images of immigrants that emphasised their problematic presence in Britain, and as 'dark strangers' arriving into a local area.[47] Kennetta Hammond Perry

---

[44] Eduardo Bonilla-Silva, 'Feeling Race: Theorizing the Racial Economy of Emotions', *American Sociological Review* 84, no. 1 (2019): 1–25.
[45] Barbara H. Rosenwein, *Emotional Communities in the Early Middle Ages* (Ithica: Cornell University Press, 2006).
[46] Sarita Malik, *Representing Black Britain: Black and Asian Images on Television* (London: Sage, 2002); Gavin Schaffer, *The Vision of a Nation*.
[47] Chris Waters, '"Dark Strangers" in Our Midst: Discourses of Race and Nation in Britain, 1947–1963', *Journal of British Studies* 36, no. 2 (1997): 207–238.

and Kathleen Paul have also outlined the racist discourses that underpinned government efforts throughout the 1950s and early 1960s to limit immigration from Afro-Caribbean members of the commonwealth in what would become the Commonwealth Immigrants Act in 1962.[48] This act and its subsequent amendment as the 1968 Commonwealth Immigrants Act newly excluded those who had previously been positioned as members of Britain's colonial 'family' through the imposition of a three-pronged voucher scheme tied to one's newly classified and recognised skills as a worker. The aim and outcome of this legislation was a severe reduction in the immigration of Black men, women and families into Britain as workers and settlers and the ongoing allowance of largely white immigration.

Alongside media coverage of the movement of these bills through parliament and perceptions of a growing crisis around immigration by people of colour in the period, was a very small number of programmes about race featuring racialised people that were broadcast on British screens in this period. Media historians have already done excellent work in itemising and examining these limited offerings and it not my intention to repeat that work here.[49] By and large what this works demonstrates is that television continued to primarily be a space for white audiences to encounter other white people but with some scarce chances for audiences to engage with visualisations of Black experiences in post-war Britain. Televised theatre that would inform the 'social issue' films of the late 1950s and 1960s developed in this period, alongside some stand-alone episodes of existing programmes such as *Z-Cars* 'Place of Safety' episode in 1964, featuring the experiences of immigrants in Britain. Earl Cameron would star in the first BBC television film to portray immigrants from the West Indies adjusting to life in Britain in *A Man From the Sun* (1956). Cameron, born in Bermuda, would become the most high-profile Black British actor in the period and was joined by Johnny Sekka from Senegal, Errol John, and Harry Baird from Guyana who himself largely occupied minor speaking roles. These four Black actors would dominate the small amount of roles on offer in the 1950s and 1960s, later joined by actors such as Norman Beaton and Carmen Munroe in the 1970s.

---

[48] Kennetta Hammond Perry, *London Is the Place for Me: Black Britons, Citizenship, and the Politics of Race* (Oxford: Oxford University Press, 2015), 153–186; Kathleen Paul, *Whitewashing Britain: Race and Citizenship in the Postwar Era* (Ithica: Cornell University Press, 1997), 143–189.

[49] Malik, *Representing Black Britain*; Stephen Bourne, *Black in the British Frame: The Black Experience in British Film and Television*, 2nd ed. (London: Bloomsbury, 2001); Jim Pines, *Black and White in Colour: Black People in British Television Since 1936* (London: BFI, 1992); Newton, *Paving the Empire Road*; Schaffer, *The Vision of a Nation*.

From the Audience Research Department's perspective, however, the transmission of *Rainbow City* would be only the second time majority-white British audiences had encountered immigrants of colour on screen within the structure of a television series which favoured and indeed required weekly audience investment in the programme's protagonist. The format of a television series rather than a television play or film again raised the risks that Goldie had broached in 1952 of the prospect of audiences switching the channel over multiple weeks rather than just avoiding one or two hours during a televised play. This particular risk, taken as it was almost twenty years after Windrush's arrival and fourteen years after the *Race Relations in Africa* series was broadcast but also in a period when restrictions to immigration were front and centre in the political sphere, did not prompt the production of a pre-broadcasting study. Yet the production of the series, as the introduction to the special audience research report on *Rainbow City* indicated, bore the pressure of being an experiment in presenting racialised communities and experiences on screen for British viewers.

Before turning to *Rainbow City*, it is crucial to highlight that this second experiment with 'race' on screen was also broadcast in 1967 alongside a highly compelling treatment of immigration that was available for audiences at the time, *Till Death Us Do Part* (1965–68, 1972–1975). Julian Critchley, writing for *The Times* in July 1967 while *Rainbow City* was airing, offered his own views of both programmes. He noted with enthusiasm 'the return of popular villain' Alf Garnett while observing in the same column that *Rainbow City* was marching towards its conclusion and 'means well', but was 'dull'.[50] Critchley enthused instead about Alf Garnett:

It is ironic that Alf Garnett, who is supposed to be the villain of the piece, should be so popular. Johnny Speight has given him all the unfashionable prejudices. He is a caricature of a Tory working man. He is anti-Semitic, anti-black, and contemptuous of foreigners. He is also a blusterer and a bully. Yet even so he is strangely endearing ... Alf Garnett is one of the great comic characters of television, although not perhaps in the way that Mr Speight may have originally intended.[51]

Critchley's enthusiasm for Garnett reflected the interests of audiences of the programme, the latter which was measured by the same Audience Research Department tasked with evaluating *Rainbow City*'s success. The shock of staff in the Audience Research Department at the responses of white British audiences to *Rainbow City* was, no doubt, authentically felt,

---

[50] Julian Critchley, 'Return of Popular Villain', *The Times*, 15 July 1967, 7.  [51] Ibid.

yet evidence of audience racism was apparent in other research conducted by the department on *Till Death Us Do Part* in its standard weekly reports. If we take a closer look at standard audience research reports on *Till Death Us Do Part* conducted in 1968, we start to see the persistent presence of post-war audience racism. This research indicates just how frequently white audiences rejected the intended message of scriptwriters and producers of these programmes and instead offered their own alternative and sometimes highly prejudiced take on the presence of Black and south Asian subjects and racism on screen.

*Till Death Us Do Part* commenced broadcasting on the BBC in July 1965, predating *Rainbow City* by over two years and in the same month that the papers were documenting reactions to proposals by John Selwyn-Lloyd, as chair of the Conservative Policy Group and Conservative MP, for a one-out and one-in scheme for immigration, health tests for immigrants and the possibility of repatriation 'of those who obviously do not fit into our community here'.[52] The popularity of *Till Death Us Do Part* (hereafter *TDUDP*) was largely anchored in the series' protagonist, the bigoted and reactionary Alf Garnett played by Warren Mitchell, and Garnett's interactions with his wife, daughter and son-in-law. The programme has been examined by numerous academics including Brett Bebber and Schaffer for its use of comedy to frame anti-immigrant anxieties and sentiments in the 1960s and 1970s.[53] The complexities of a comedic framework, Speight argued, allowed the programme to satirise existing racist attitudes and subsequently improve race relations as a result of this treatment. Schaffer's study of *TDUDP*'s script-writer Johnny Speight's intentions seemingly affirm that these were largely altruistic. Yet Speight's missteps with programmes such as the notorious *Curry and Chips* and his own biography indicate that Speight himself and those higher-ups who promoted him often mistook Speight's own confidence and comfort in speaking about race as his greatest strength. Speight's experiences as a young writer and musician in London had afforded him a much more desegregated life than most BBC executives but also produced a common occurrence among whites in Black spaces in the 1960s of appropriating the language and expressions of racialised communities in order to speak authoritatively about them to other white people. Regardless, *Till Death Us Do Part's* messages

---

[52] From Our Political Correspondent, 'Cabinet Reaction to Selwyn Lloyd Plan", *The Times*, 5 July 1965, 10.
[53] Schaffer, *The Vision of a Nation*; Brett Bebber, "*Till Death Us Do Part*: Political Satire and Social Realism in the 1960s and 1970s." *Historical Journal of Film, Radio and Television* 34, no. 2 (2014): 253–274.

on racial relations were not interpreted as Speight seemingly intended by most of its white British audience. Bebber has pointed to the special audience research report that would finally be conducted on the programme in 1973 (further discussed in Chapter 6) as proof of this but earlier standard audience research reports also offered signs that audiences overlooked the programme's satirical intent to instead strongly identify with a main character whose beliefs about immigrants and racial difference were familiar. In the winter of 1968, while the Audience Research Department was conducting its research on responses to *Rainbow City*, a standard report on *TDUDP*'s return to the BBC emphasised that much of the affection of audiences for the series was rooted in common audience experiences and attitudes:

Several went on to remark, there were people around just like the Garnetts and much of the programme's attraction lay in the fact that reflected so accurately how they might think and react in certain circumstances, even down to the swearing, etc, which may not have been pleasant to the ear but was nonetheless true to life as here presented.[54]

This point regarding the programmes ability to be 'true to life' was stressed again and again in the weekly audience research reports produced on the programme's final series. It was commented upon so much that one suspects this pointed to the BBC's ongoing difficulty in producing programming that registered life as most Britons knew it. The report for the final episode of the 1968 series again stressed this relatability even as it noted that the toilet humour of the episode, revolving around a bug caught by Alf that caused him to need constant access to the neighbour's toilet, raised eyebrows among viewers. While acknowledging that 'a number of those reporting evidently felt that the subject of tonight's episode … was hardly in the best taste', the report ended on a familiar note: 'Vulgar as it undoubtedly was, at times, it was said, but the episode reflected life as it really was and, as such, had a strong appeal.'[55]

*Till Death Us Do Part*'s visual manifestation of racial prejudice and racist behaviour on screen was, from the evidence of these standard reports, not a strong concern for producers, audiences, or the Audience Research Department. Passing mention was made of the programme's 'racial element' but this aspect and any impact on audiences was minimised in favour of concerns about the implications of the character's strong language instead. The final episode of 1968, 'Alf's

---

[54] '*Till Death Us Do Part*' Week 1, An Audience Research Report, 11 February 1968, VR/68/12, Till Death Us Do Part, Part I, R78/2.811/1, WAC.
[55] '*Till Death Us Do Part*' Final Episode, An Audience Research Report, 23 March 1968, VR/67/136, Till Death Us Do Part, Part I, R78/2.811/1, WAC.

Dilemma, or Cleaning Up TV' which so vexed some viewers with its toilet humour also contained a sub-plot that had Alf repeatedly ascribing disease and infections to immigrants who he characterised as natural 'carriers' of viruses. Agreeing with Mary Whitehouse and the National Viewers' and Listeners' Association's campaign to 'Clean Up TV', Garnett argued she needed to prevent diseases coming from abroad, 'They ain't English bugs' and that she should go further in 'getting rid of all these dirty foreigners and all their bloody diseases'.[56] This followed on from the airing of such sentiments by local broadcasters such as ATV Midlands who gave ample screen time to people living in Smethwick airing their stubborn insistence that homes occupied by West Indian immigrants in the Birmingham area were rife with tuberculosis.[57] The mobilisation of this narrative in the season finale was countered by the discovery at the end of the episode that Alf was himself a 'carrier' of a bug and the subsequent need to destroy the paper material he had touched in the household. This outcome, from the perspective of the writers and the producers, cast Alf's previously expressed racist views of immigrants as carriers of disease as deeply ironic. How audiences responded to this irony is difficult to ascertain in the standard audience research report as the racial element of the programme raised little response: 'Indeed, a few dismissed it as a new 'low' in entertainment – lavatory humour at its worst – and found the whole episode thoroughly distasteful, one, for instance declaring: "Subject in the past have been acceptable but reference to the function of the human bowels, when treated in[58] this fashion, is totally unnecessary."'

Such a 'new low' had no place in front of the average Briton this respondent indicated. Alf's articulation of his racist theory of contamination and infection, however, gained less of an outcry according to the report merged as it was with seemingly more frequent concerns about cursing: 'There were objections, too, to the racial element and the inevitable bad language which, it was often held, spoiled what would otherwise have been an amusing programme.'[59] It was the bad language that tended to show up repeatedly in the standard audience research reports, averaging three to four mentions per report, as opposed to the racist language which merited one mention on average in an episode where it featured. This supports David Hendy's argument that the BBC was

---

[56] 'Alf's Dilemma' *Till Death Us Do Part*, Season 2, Episode 10, March 1968, Disc 2 DVD, BBC Worldwide Ltd, 2016.
[57] Yemm, 'Immigration, Race and Local Media: Smethwick and the 1964 General Election'.
[58] '*Till Death Us Do Part*' Final Episode, An Audience Research Report, 1.   [59] Ibid.

overwhelmingly preoccupied with whether 'bad language' could be aired or not in the 1960s and 1970s.[60] The audience research report on *TDUDP*'s finale saw a reaction index of 70, above the series' average of 67. An extensive examination of the impact of Alf Garnett's racism on British audiences was not undertaken by the Audience Research Department in the first stretch of the series' broadcast ending in 1968 but only later in 1973, two years before the show ended, as will be discussed in Chapter 6.

It was in this climate of race on screen that *Rainbow City* was broadcast in 1967. The arrival of *Rainbow City* on British television screens, while *TDUDP* was exciting critics and audiences alike, was immediately accompanied by press coverage pointing to the novel and potentially controversial elements of the programme. Brian Dean from the *Daily Mail* introduced the prospect of the series to the paper's readers in February 1967 as word emerged of the programme's scheduling at the BBC. Writing in an article entitled 'BBC clash over mixed marriage', Dean immediately framed the show with controversy and wrote that the first three episodes of a programme were provoking a conflict between BBC's Midland Region and BBC chiefs in London over 'a new television serial about a mixed marriage' and whether it should be showed outside of the Midlands.[61] There was no evidence cited in the article that the controversy over which arm of BBC television should show it stemmed from the programme's content, regardless of the inference by Dean. Dean highlighted, without actually seeing the programme, what he thought would be noteworthy for his reading audience: 'In one episode, Mr John and Miss Jones are seen in bed, discussing the problems of mixed marriages.'[62] Dean also included a quote by John Elliott, the lead writer of the show, who was recorded as denying the possibilities of the programme to discomfort audiences: 'It is not sensational and not about racialism.' No further mention was made of the programme or Elliott's co-writer James in either the *Daily Mail* or *The Times* at that point but this conflict between executives, minor as it was, warranted a further headline in April that signalled 'Go-ahead for TV mixed marriage' in the *Daily Mail*. This article claimed that 'Six trial episodes will be shown to test audience reaction before a decision is taken on whether to continue the serial *Rainbow City*.'[63] No such pre-broadcasting report exists at the BBC, and it was presumably replaced by the post-broadcasting special

---

[60] David Hendy, 'Bad Language and BBC Radio Four in the 1960s and 1970s', *Twentieth Century British History* 17, no. 1 (2006): 74–102.
[61] Brian Dean, 'BBC Clash Over Mixed Marriage', *Daily Mail* 21 February 1967, 7.
[62] Ibid.    [63] 'Go-ahead for TV Mixed Marriage', *Daily Mail*, 4 April 1967, 7.

report instead, but the eagerness of the *Daily Mail* to point to the importance of white audience reactions to the content of the series signalled both the potential for audience discomfort with the subject of interracial romance and what the *Daily Mail* promoted as their key role in judging this content. Crucially, this also pointed to the press's understanding of the risks that the programme posed for the primarily white viewing space of British television.

The programme itself garnered mixed responses from critics that pointed to the difficulties that the BBC had in presenting instances of racism on screen and representations of immigrant life that rang true to white viewers. Peter Black, another of the *Daily Mail's* television critics, was initially one of the more positive endorsers of the programme but with some qualification. Calling it a programme 'concerned with how the pink bumpy-faced race is getting on with the smooth brown one', Black noted that 'the production carried instant conviction as to settings and dialogue' and singled out the script-writers: 'I look forward to watching where John Elliott producer, director and script-writer with Horace James, will take it next.'[64] Black continued his support of the programme into the second episode saying this one, 'set mainly among the local culture in Jamaica, raised still higher my expectations of the serial'. Focusing primarily on Elliott's contribution again, he wrote 'from the size of John Elliott's canvas and the quality of his writing it is evident that this is to be a major survey of the brown and pink dilemma'.[65] Yet by episode three, Black began to present a range of complex reactions to the programme's content. On the one hand, he found the pace too slow and the programme's reluctance to show racism on screen frustrating: 'The actual physical difficulties of living among a community basically hostile are presented in a low key.'[66] Black noted that one of the characters who experienced discrimination in his appeal for promotion at work was 'off to Canada' and that 'the hostility was reported, not shown, and the thought that it will be as bad in Canada was not spoken'. Black speculated on the authenticity of this representation in his column, ruminating on what the racialised every day would include for West Indian immigrants: 'This is right in one sense. Probably they don't talk about a difficulty they meet every day. And to present the white society around them so anonymously, as a

---

[64] Peter Black, 'Real Trouble Hits an Illusion Called *Rainbow City*', *Daily Mail*, 6 July 1967, 3.
[65] Peter Black, 'Rediffusion's Half-Hour Story Is Doing Distinguished Work in Finding Writers Who Do Not Want Merely to Fill a Half Hour', *Daily Mail*, 13 July 1967, 3.
[66] Peter Black. 'TV', *Daily Mail*, 21 July 1967, 3.

kind of enveloping presence that develops sharp edges only when they put pressure on it, offers the same kind of truth.'[67]

Yet the mundane elements of everyday racism offered little narrative arc nor dialogue according to Black and was not even actually recognised by him as racism itself. What Black wanted was some visualisation of racism which he defined solely as violence-based and which the BBC as a whole shied away from at this point. Black conceded that 'despite the absence of punch-ups, I want to know what happens' but then went on to state that 'on the whole it has deepened my conviction that it's a damned shame they have to come here, to queue up for the jobs that the whites don't want to do'.[68] This then was an audience member, a critic, who both wanted to see violent racist interactions on the screen but also felt a deepening sense of sadness while watching the programme, which only affirmed his commitment to a primarily white British society. Black concluded this column on *Rainbow City*, which was the last he would write on it, with a dual reference to the debts of empire and the impossibility of imperial belonging that Hammond Perry has so deftly shown animated the immigration of many men and women from the West Indies: 'Nothing is truer than that Britain owes them a debt. But the place to repay it was in their own country, not in Birmingham.'[69] For Black the programme had only cemented an idea that this was a community emerging from poverty which was rooted in the legacies of colonialism but poverty that should not be alleviated through immigration and instead through the policies of commonwealth development that had been pursued through the interwar period and after World War II.

For Peter Black, racism was envisioned as a dramatic event, a punch-up, with a narrative arc rather than the 'enveloping presence' with its sharp edges evident only every now and then to those experiencing it. The latter vision of everyday racism was dull and encompassing on television. Other critics went further in noting the lack of appeal of racism's representation on screen. Critchley for *The Times* labelled the show the 'Boredom of Good Intentions', writing that 'Its attitudes are commendably liberal, its purpose is plainly to influence those who watch it in the direction of racial tolerance, its effect, unfortunately is one of boredom.'[70] Critchley criticised the programme's earnestness saying 'it was in all probability conceived by a committee at Lime Grove' but mildly condemned the project's aims and executions by declaring, 'if

---

[67] Ibid.  [68] Ibid.
[69] Ibid; Kennetta Hammond Perry, *London Is the Place for Me: Black Britons, Citizenship, and the Politics of Race* (Oxford: Oxford University Press, 2015), 126–152.
[70] Julian Critchley, 'Boredom of Good Intentions', *The Times*, 6 July 1967, 8.

we must do good in this way, it should at least be better done', arguing that 'the plot was predictable, action enervating, the characters made of cardboard'.[71] The good intentions of the programme, it was inferred, ultimately made the content dry and dull. Ultimately, the *Daily Mail's* other television critic, Barry Norman, wrote that the end of 'the BBC's experiment in multi-racial soap opera' was 'regrettable' particularly due to its even-handed discussion of the 'upbringing of a half-caste child'[72] in the programme's final episode. Noting that 'quite rightly, it took no sides. The English father-in-law, trying hard but not always successfully to be "liberal", was no less sympathetic than the educated but still prickly West Indian son-in-law.'[73] The programme had dramatised the discussion of racial prejudice in a way that played to the idealised unemotional framework for discussing racism that white audiences and the BBC favoured but ultimately without raising the sustained interest or sympathies of white viewers in Black Britons.

The short standard audience research reports on *Rainbow City* in 1967 also foreshadowed the negative response of the 1968 special report. The failure of the *Rainbow City* experiment was evident early on through the small viewer numbers for the programme and a relatively minor 'Reaction Index'. Staff in the Audience Research Department commented on the small audience in light of a fairly favourable viewing time: 'The first episode of *Rainbow City* (Wednesday 7.30pm) had a disappointingly small audience, 4.5%.' Staff summarised the response of audiences that did watch the first episode noting that it was too violent, too negative, and too slow:

While there was sympathy with this 'courageous attempt' to bring the subject of racial integration out into the open, there were doubts about whether this was an effective way to do it. Was it wise to begin with an incident that showed all the violence and bad feeling simmering beneath the surface? Was the story strong enough? (Some thought it slow moving with too much talk and a very self conscious cast.) The Reaction Index was a not very impressive.[74]

The broad range of reactions outlined here, and the responses of television critics – that it was too violent, too unpleasant, not unpleasant enough, too slow, and just too racist and everyday – signalled the uneasy unwillingness of white audiences to engage with such a show, particularly when there was a wide range of racialising pleasures on screen as the next chapter demonstrates. Barry Norman, writing in the *Daily Mail* upon *Rainbow City's* end, ruminated:

---

[71] Ibid.  [72] Barry Norman, 'TV', *Daily Mail*, 10 August 1967, 3.  [73] Ibid.
[74] Audience Research Report, 58, VR/67/433, WAC.

As a series it was hardly flawless but it was always intelligent and at least had the virtue of breaking new ground. Possibly that's why it didn't last very long. Not cosy enough, I suppose. At 7:30 on a summer's evening and full of tea and chips or whatever, who wants to grapple with the real problems in our midst? Much nicer to be soothed by the real unrealities of *Coronation Street*.[75]

Racism on screen, perpetrated by white Britons who were not the outrageous but true-to-life Alf Garnett, was a hard sell for British audiences in other words. The show was not gripping, it was predictable, and it made white audiences turn away. The BBC after it mounted the special audience research report almost seven months after the programme aired had further confirmation that the experiment of *Rainbow City* had failed.

The resulting data from the 1968 special report was damning. While a majority agreed with statements such as 'One of the troubles with this country is that there are too many foreigners living there' and 'The standards of behaviour of coloured people are lower than those of white people', the tally of statements that respondents did not agree with were steeped in explicit concepts of racial inferiority. The report's authors wrote in their summation that 'as many as one in five did *not* [emphasis in original] agree with the statement that "coloured people are the equals of whites and must be given equal opportunities in all ways – political, economic, and social"'. One in five respondents also did not agree with further statements documented in the report which included: 'For the most part, coloured people are good workers', and 'A coloured man is just as likely to make a good foreman or an inspector as a white man'. This was a refutation of racial equality and the underpinning aims of the 1965 Race Relations Act but certainly an expression of the hostility towards immigrants that animated the passage of both Commonwealth Immigrants Acts in 1962 and 1968.[76] Older, white women in the lower half of the occupational scale and those with a 'pessimistic' outlook on life were more prone to be prejudiced but the differences were, the report stressed, small and subsumed within evidence of widespread racism among audiences. As the report relayed, 'These results ... were more impressive in suggesting that hostility existed with depressing frequency even among those groups who were least pre-disposed to share it.'[77] Perhaps even more worrying was that the survey found that of those viewers who had seen the programme were 'if anything, *more* hostile to

---

[75] Norman, 'TV'.
[76] Simon Peplow, 'The "Linchpin for Success"? The Problematic Establishment of the 1965 Race Relations Act and Its Conciliation Board', *Contemporary British History* 31, no. 3 (2017): 430–451.
[77] 'Race Relations and *Rainbow City*', 4.

coloured people/immigrants than were the non-viewers and it is unlikely this was due to mere chance'.[78] The programme had raised the possibility of audience prejudice actually increasing due to its broadcast. This element was not further explored in the BBC's rush to abandon its approach but one viewer, who identified as an Italian Vice consul, wrote a letter to *The Times* in the programme's aftermath that argued: 'It is evidently more convenient to satirise Italians (albeit gangsters) rather than coloured people, who instead need to be glorified in propaganda programmes (I am thinking of *Rainbow City*).'[79] The programme pointed to audience racism that was provoked by this favourable presentation of the 'good immigrant' on screen.[80] The very presence of Black immigrants expressing themselves on screen was enough to raise the anger of viewers who saw this 'propaganda'.

## Conclusion

The comparisons between *Race Relations in Africa* broadcast in 1953 and *Rainbow City* in 1967 came to an uncomfortable end with the publication of the special audience research report on the latter in March 1968. As Enoch Powell crystallised the thinking of anti-immigrant sentiment throughout Britain that same spring to the professed horror of Britain's political class, the country's own media professionals faced an awkward junction. The BBC's own experiment in producing and promoting positive representations of immigrants for white viewers in the sustained and established form of the programme series on television had backfired. This apparent failure illustrated a number of flaws in the BBC's approach, including its broad definition of race for audiences, its avoidance of the racial prejudice of many ordinary Britons, and its clunky presentation of both immigrant life and racism on the small screen. The approach of both BBC executives and its Audience Research Department to *Rainbow City* had equated audience affection for empire in the 1950s with a broad and enduring support by white audiences for seeing people of colour on screen. Both drew false equivalencies between enthusiasm and duty to the empire among white Britons with tolerance of West Indian men and women from that same empire living in Britain itself. What the *Rainbow City* 1968 report revealed was evidence of racial prejudice deeply rooted in concepts of white racial superiority that were

---

[78] Ibid.
[79] Carlo Ungaro, Vice Consul for Italy, 'Italian as She is Shown', *The Times*, 4 August 1967, 9.
[80] Nikesh Shukla, ed., *The Good Immigrant* (London: Unbound, 2016).

held by casual viewers in Britain and which situated settled, racialised immigrants as outside of this empire-adjacent realm of duty, tolerance, and crucially 'Englishness'. These results seemingly affirmed the earlier concerns of white producers of screen culture such as John Grierson articulated initially in 1927 and Grace Wyndham Goldie in 1952 that British audiences were unlikely to connect with representations of people of colour on screen. While Grierson and Goldie conceived of this uninterest in ways that benignly naturalised it, the data of the BBC's Audience Research Department pointed to something much more definitive than uninterest in favour of blunt anti-Black racism rooted in concepts of social, political, intellectual and economic inferiority. The Race Relations Act of 1965 which had supposedly affirmed a tolerant Britain very different from the US could just as easily been seen as an act meant to address what was already present in Britain. The Audience Research Department, by doing what it was meant to do, pulled back the curtain on this secret. British racism sat awkwardly present and quantified in the report.

How the report on *Rainbow City* and its evidence of widespread racism among British audiences was received is harder to track within the opaque archive of the BBC. As Sara Ahmed has noted, the discomfort of white people when faced with evidence of racism and related discussions of structural change often results in institutional silences.[81] What is clear is that the BBC retreated from trying to direct the sympathies of white audiences towards immigrants through the medium of a programme series, although the BBC would go on to reference the existence of the series as proof of its liberal attitudes towards race. In March 1975, eight years after *Rainbow City* had been televised, the BBC was still pointing to the programme as the broadcaster's noble and mighty effort to 'contribute to the reduction of racial tension' as it faced criticism from the Wandsworth Council for Community Relations in the midst of reporting to the Annan Committee about the state of British broadcasting.[82] This one experiment would be all that the BBC would pursue outside of the work of news reporting until the broadcasting of the series *Empire Road*

---

[81] Sara Ahmed, *On Being Included: Racism and Diversity in Institutional Life* (Durham, NC: Duke University Press, 2012). There is some evidence that points to the BBC deciding to cover 'race' primarily in the Current Affairs Group programming, which included shows like *Panorama* and other investigative reporting, but this is not definitive. The Audience Research Department did work for this group in March 1968 and Darrell Newton's work indicates that audience racism may have been evident in that work as well; see Newton, *Paving the Empire Road*, 151.

[82] Response of Michael Starks on the '*Report of The Wandsworth Council for Community Relations to the Annan Committee*', March 1975. File R782 538/1 WAC.

featuring a primarily Black cast in October and November 1978. This was eleven years after *Rainbow City* aired and two years after *The Fosters*, a sitcom featuring a West Indian cast and modelled on an American counterpart, began broadcasting on ITV's London Weekend Television.[83] This programming silence spoke volumes of the organisation's discomfort with what the Audience Research Department had uncovered. The racially tolerant audience that the corporation and Audience Research had previously imagined showed itself to be a fiction rather than a reality.

---

[83] Gavin Schaffer, 'Framing *The Fosters*: Jokes, Racism and Black and Asian voices in British Comedy Television', in Sarita Malik and Darrel M. Newton, eds., *Adjusting the Contrast: British Television and constructs of race* (Manchester: Manchester University Press, 2017); Newton, *Paving the Empire Road*.

# 4 'A Traditional Form of Entertainment'
Colour-blind Audiences and Blacking Up on Post-war Screens

On 19 May 1967, a concerted response to a petition by the Campaign Against Racial Discrimination (CARD) calling for *The Black and White Minstrel Show* to be removed from television screens occurred in both the halls of the BBC and in the British press. In the press, newspapers as diverse as *The Times*, the *Daily Mirror* and the *Daily Mail* released similar stories about the petition putting a strong defence of the programme by the BBC as 'a traditional show enjoyed by millions for what it offers in good-hearted, family entertainment' front and centre in their coverage.[1] George Inns, the producer and writer for the show, was featured by *The Times* declaring himself 'astonished at the protest' and stating: "How anyone can read racialism into this show is beyond me."[2] Kenneth Lamb, director of Public Affairs at the BBC, wrote to David Pitt, the chairman of CARD, in response to the petition on the same day as the press reporting emerged and in line with the BBC's ongoing practice of responding to the complaints of individual viewers and various groups.[3] By 1967, *The Black and White Minstrel Show* had already been broadcast for nine years on the BBC, and its popularity with television viewers was well established. As the introduction of this book noted, *The Black and White Minstrel Show* would continue to be broadcast by the BBC into British homes until 1978 over an astonishing twenty-year span. The petition by CARD, signed by 200 people, provoked an immediate response from Lamb who was now occupying the role first held by Stephen Tallents in 1935. Lamb was both enjoying a hit programme and functioning within a large organisation accustomed to ongoing scrutiny by government, the press and the public. Lamb replied in a manner that situated Pitt as 'new to this country', writing: 'As many of the signatories are no doubt new to this country they will perhaps not be aware that black-faced minstrels performing a song and dance act have

---

[1] Ibid.  [2] 'BBC Asked to Ban the TV Minstrels', *The Times*, 19 May 1967, 3.
[3] Kenneth Lamb, BBC to David Pitt, CARD, 19 May 1967, File 3995803, ITA/IBA Archive, University of Bournemouth.

been a traditional form of entertainment in the British Isles for a great many years.'⁴ Lamb lectured Pitt and CARD members on the appropriate perspective one should bring to viewing *The Black and White Minstrel Show*, emphasising that minstrelsy had a long history, steeped in tradition, that immigrants would likely 'not be aware' of. While arguing that the practice of minstrelsy was both historic and not inherently racist, Lamb implied that this was something native, white British audiences already understood. Inns took a stronger line when talking to the press and invoked his own inability to see 'racialism' or racism within the programme itself.

Lamb was confident that both his response and that of Inns reflected broader attitudes towards the programme among British audiences. In the thin twelve-page file on *The Black and White Minstrel Show* available at the BBC Written Archive Centre, a consensus in defence of the show is also evident across both the BBC and its competitor the Independent Television Authority (ITA) overseeing ITV and its affiliates. On the same day that Lamb wrote to Pitt at CARD, Stephen Murphy, Senior Programme Officer at the ITA, privately wrote in support of the BBC's rebuff of CARD's complaints to someone he thought could influence the situation further, E. J. B. Rose as Director of the Survey of Race Relations, an organisation affiliated with the National Committee for Commonwealth Immigrants (NCCI). To Rose, Murphy jokingly acknowledged 'I should make it clear that I have no personal interest in this: *The Black & White Minstrel Show* is a BBC programme, and an unhealthily successful one at that!'⁵ Still, Murphy argued 'I doubt if anyone takes stereotypes seriously anyways, but if they do, then the Black and White Minstrel stereotype is rather a helpful one – warm, friendly, affectionate and gay.' He went on to state, 'Blacking up is a theatrical convention so old that is has lost any derogatory meaning. All that this group of CARD members is doing – though I understand the petition has the official backing of CARD – is to create a racial issue where none exists.' Murphy ended with a nod to Rose's influence with the NCCI: 'I doubt if this campaign will ever get off the ground: but if it does, then I hope that the NCCI will dissociate itself from it.' This letter to the NCCI acted as another attempt to educate immigrants through organisations that represented them on the appropriate response to *The Black and White Minstrel Show*.

---

⁴ Ibid.
⁵ Stephen Murphy (Senior Programme Officer, ITA) to E.J.B. Esq. (Director, Survey of National Committee for Commonwealth Immigrants), 19 May 1967, 'Black & White Minstrel Show', R78/1, 921/1, WAC.

Murphy and Lamb's invocation of minstrelsy as simultaneously historic and not a 'racial issue' for audiences put forth a powerful post-war conception of a colour-blind white audience in Britain, one that both justified the ongoing presence of blackface on popular film and television and left the racial sitcoms of *Till Death Us Do Part* and ITV's *Love Thy Neighbour* firmly in place. In 1962, five years prior to the controversy of spring 1967, Kenneth Adam, then Director of Television at the BBC, described minstrelsy as 'a perfectly honourable and uncondescending convention' in a published booklet about *The Black and White Minstrel Show* for the programme's fans.[6] When *Flamingo*, a monthly magazine aimed at West Indians and Africans living in Britain (and discussed in detail in the next chapter), ran a piece criticising *The Black and White Minstrel Show* in September 1961, the next two issues featured some of the letters that, according to its editors Edward Scobie and Ellis Komey, 'came pouring in' to *Flamingo*'s offices.[7] One Black reader, P. Okuri from Birmingham, recounted the reaction of white people in his office when he showed them *Flamingo*'s story: 'They could not understand why we should feel so badly about the programme. They kept telling me it was good fun and full of entertainment.'[8] Okuri's office-mates, such as George Inns, did not see racism in the programme, and Okuri's invocation of the collective negative response of Black viewers was ignored in their repeated presentation of it as 'good fun'.

From the perspective of Kenneth Lamb, the white acquaintances of readers of *Flamingo*, and those defending *The Black and White Minstrel Show* in the press, minstrelsy and blacking up was an established custom within British entertainment that was not, and indeed could not, be seen as racist by its white British producers or its majority white audience. Yet the intervention of CARD and the petition against the programme raised troubling questions about British audiences in the post-war period who could not 'see race' in a programme whose platform hinged on the practice of white men imitating Black men as 'warm', 'affectionate' and 'gay'. The presence of the petition opened up the possibility of other frameworks of seeing and knowing race and racism on television in post-war Britain and also pointed to the existence of racialised audiences that were being alienated by the BBC. These troubling questions and this

---

[6] Kenneth Adam, 'Foreword', *The Black and White Minstrels* (London: BBC, 1962), quoted in Gavin Schaffer, *The Vision of a Nation: The Making of Multiculturalism on British Television, 1960–1980* (London: Palgrave Macmillan, 2014), 206.

[7] 'Bad taste B.B.C.', *Flamingo*, September 1961, 22–24; Dear Flamingo, 'Those Minstrels', *Flamingo*, October 1961, 2.

[8] Dear Flamingo, 'Those Minstrels', 2.

audience of 200 petitioners were ultimately as we shall see dismissed through a collective response to the campaign by white BBC executives, white reporters in the press and white audiences writing to the press about the petition. This was an impressive consensus of effort rooted in the outlook and experiences of white viewers to not see or acknowledge the racialised practice of blacking up on screen as just that. Thus this chapter uses *The Black and White Minstrel Show* and the controversy of 1967 in particular as an entrance into both a survey of a highly racialised practice on screens in post-war Britain which formed part of the answer to the question of what audiences wanted and the efforts of British consumers and producers of screen culture to position British audiences as colour-blind and racially innocent.

It has been an unfortunate result of this project that once I started looking for evidence of blacking up on screen in British film and television as an overlooked component in the answer to the book's central question of 'what the audience wanted', more examples came my way than I can possibly acknowledge here. Michael Pickering likewise talks about the abundance of minstrelsy in late nineteenth- and early twentieth-century press culture.[9] The practice of white actors and singers donning blackface and performing 'blackness' is thought to be an import from the US and a form of entertainment with a history rooted in the practices of slavery and post-abolition anxieties about reconstruction. Scholars such as Eric Lott, Stephen Johnson and Aryana Thompson, working in diverse fields, have charted the multiple meanings that white audiences and performers ascribed to blacking up in the nineteenth and early twentieth centuries while noting the stereotypes that these performances consistently relayed.[10] The transatlantic transference of this practice into a British context demands attention to what blackface and minstrelsy offered to majority white audiences consuming these within a framework that also included the pleasures and performances of empire. In the British context Tom Scriven notes minstrelsy's formation in the nineteenth century of 'the archetype of black people as dim-witted, oddly framed and fundamentally comical' as white actors in blackface articulated British anxieties about Black men in urban settings and the

---

[9] Michael Pickering, *Blackface Minstrelsy in Britain* (London: Aldershot, 2008).
[10] Stephen Johnson, ed., *Burnt Cork: Traditions and Legacies of Blackface Minstrelsy* (Amherst: University of Massachusetts Press, 2012); Eric Lott, *Love and Theft: Blackface Minstrelsy and the American Working Class* (Oxford: Oxford University Press, 1993); William J. Mahar, *Behind the Burnt Cork Mask: Early Blackface Minstrelsy and Antebellum American Popular Culture* (Urbana: University of Illinois Press, 1998); Aryanna Thompson, *Blackface* (London: Bloomsbury Academic, 2021).

slippages of class and racial formation that accompanied this.[11] Pickering documents just how ubiquitous both blacking up and minstrelsy were, arguing that 'variant forms of blackface caricature appeared outside the minstrel show in media as wide-ranging as advertising, postcards, puppet shows, comics and juvenile literature'.[12] The sheer wealth of material documenting the existence of minstrelsy he concludes provides 'abundant evidence not only of its apparent constancy but also of its cultural acceptability'.[13] Blackface was widely enjoyed by British audiences through a variety of mediums even before the age of the big and small screen.

In post-war Britain blacking up on screen did, as Lamb claimed, continue an existing tradition in British entertainment even as the practice was doing a different kind of labour in film and television. In practical terms the practice meant the ongoing marginalisation or absence of Black or south Asian actors on screen. In epistemological terms it indicated a tangled commitment to 'traditional' ways of entertainment built on a commitment to avoiding alternative frameworks of knowledge about Black experiences that were increasingly circulating in the post-war period. Race, even broadly defined to include any discussions of Black and south Asian people, was more obvious in the post-war period. The impact of immigration by people of colour and a related rise in racial prejudice was certainly harder to ignore for the average viewer of television or reader of the local or national news.[14] As Kennetta Hammond Perry has shown, politicians from both Labour and the Conservatives debated how to curb the arrival of visibly racialised groups through the Commonwealth Immigrants Act of 1962 and further amendments to it in 1968.[15] Both newspapers and televised news highlighted the presence of immigrant children in schools, immigrant homeowners and renters in neighbourhoods and workers in the public sector and across the country. Roberta Bivens has noted national institutions

---

[11] Hazel Waters, *Racism on the Victorian Stage: Representation of Slavery and the Black Character* (Cambridge: Cambridge University Press, 2007); Tom Scriven, 'The Jim Crow Craze in London's Press and Streets, 1836–39', *Journal of Victorian Culture* 19, no. 1 (2014): 94; Anne McClintock, *Imperial Leather: Race, Gender, and Sexuality in the Colonial Conquest* (London: Routledge, 1995).

[12] Pickering, *Blackface Minstrelsy in Britain*, xi. [13] Ibid.

[14] On local news depictions of the 'race problem' see Rachel Yemm, 'Immigration, Race and Local Media in the Midlands, 1960–1985' (PhD diss., University of Lincoln, 2018); Shirin Hirsch, *In the Shadow of Enoch Powell: Race, Locality, and Resistance* (Manchester: Manchester University Press, 2018); Benjamin Bland, '"Publish and Be Damned?" Race, Crisis, and the Press in England during the Long, Hot Summer of 1976', *Immigrants & Minorities* 37, no. 3 (2019): 163–183.

[15] Kennetta Hammond Perry, *London Is the Place for Me: Black Britons, Citizenship and the Politics of Race* (Oxford: Oxford University Press, 2016),187–243.

such as the NHS grappled with how best to introduce white patients in Britain to the fact of Black and south Asian workers in hospitals as nurses.[16] One could not easily ignore immigration into London or other areas around the country including Birmingham, its neighbouring villages or places such as Liverpool and elsewhere even if one chose to ignore the multiple ways in which Britain's colonial wars abroad were discussed within Britain itself as Erik Linstrum has demonstrated.[17] International Black experiences were making it onto screens in the 1960s through the Hollywood films of the Black actor Sidney Poitier, televised news coverage of the civil rights movement in the US or the push for independence in British colonial territories. The collective effort of white British television and filmmakers, regulators and audiences of screen content to avoid grappling with 'race' or racism started to fray ever so slightly in the face of greater discussions of both. Yet the racial innocence and colour-blindness of the white British audience was articulated forcefully during the controversy about the petition against *The Black and White Minstrel Show* in 1967, capturing a moment when the sheer effort of claiming to not know or see racism was laid bare in the British press, in broadcasting institutions and for Black audiences who were marginalised in the process. A post-war adherence to 'tradition' by audiences and television-makers in Britain began to look more like a deliberate strategy of avoidance in order to protect and sustain racialising pleasures for white audiences.

This refusal to see race and racism among executives and shapers of British screen culture is evident in both the written and visual archives of *The Black and White Minstrel Show*. Episodes of *The Black and White Minstrel Show* are not deployed on nostalgia-based television programming these days in the UK and scarce clips on YouTube are the primary visual evidence of the show. *The Black and White Minstrel Show* file at the BBC Written Archive Centre contains just twelve pages in contrast to the relatively thick files on other broadcasted programmes, which house multiple exchanges of memos. A note from an archivist at the BBC, deposited in 2007, confirms that material relating to the programme was removed at some unknown point:

In the exchange of memos between Barrie Thorne (Chief Accountant) and Oliver Whitley (Chief Assistant to DG) on 19th May 1967 and 26th May 1967, there are handwritten notes (made by Registry staff) referring to where other related

---

[16] Roberta Bivins, 'Picturing Race in the British National Health Service, 1948–1988', *Twentieth Century British History* 28, no. 1 (2017): 83–109.
[17] Erik Linstrum, *Age of Emergency: Living with Violence at the End of the Empire* (Oxford: Oxford University Press, 2023).

papers are filed within Management Registry. These references (to Registry Classification N0387 N0441) have been followed up, and these files were found to be destroyed as part of the BBC's Records Management programme and have never been deposited into the BBC Written Archives Centre.[18]

In this case it is unclear what the priorities of 'records management' were but what has been left behind offers a taxonomy of the various responses of white people to discomforting discussions or accusations of racism. Lamb's indignant response to the show being considered racist is included as well as three pages detailing the relaying on a one-page letter written on stationary from a Hilton hotel in Ocho Rios, Jamaica from an Elizabeth Duben, a singer from Surrey who was touring the Caribbean.[19] Her note said 'I thought (in view of recent controversy) you'd be interested to know that one which is watched with absorbed attention and great enjoyment by the local people – is the Black + White Minstrels!' The letter was received with gratitude by Tom Sloane, who it was addressed to as Head of Light Entertainment, and then passed on to Lamb who responded 'Thank you for a most useful addition to the file!'[20] The one-page letter seemingly proved that Black audiences approved and appreciated the show. One further letter of the twelve pages left in the file is from Barrie Thorne, accountant at the BBC, registering his protests against the programme and his plea that US viewers get involved in evaluating it, which I will examine later in the chapter.

Contemporary discussions of *The Black and White Minstrel Show* are willing to largely abandon it as an odd moment of poor taste. A *Radio Times* interview in 2011 with Ronnie Corbett, comedian and star of the popular show *The Two Ronnies* (BBC, 1971–1987), which produced a satirical sketch 'The Short & Fat Minstrel Show' in 1976, featured his ruminations on *The Black and White Minstrel Show*: 'How outdated that seems.'[21] A *Guardian* review in 2015 of a television show based on the Black actor and comedian Lenny Henry's life noted that scenes depicting his performance as a member of the touring theatrical version of *The Black and White Minstrel Show* in the 1970s 'make difficult viewing' in the

---

[18] James Codd, Dep Written Archivist, 27 June 2007, 'Black & White Minstrel Show', R78/1, 921/1, WAC.
[19] Letter from Elizabeth Duben to Tom Sloane, 14 July 1967; Ibid.
[20] Tom Sloane to Kenneth Lamb, 25 July 1967 and response by Kenneth Lamb, 26 July 1967; Ibid.
[21] 'Ronnie Corbett in His Own Words', *Radio Times*, 31 May 2016, Original interview 2011, www.radiotimes.com/news/2016-03-31/ronnie-corbett-in-his-own-words; *The Two Ronnies*, BBC, Series 1, Episode 7, 22 May 1971.

contemporary period.²² Lenny Henry himself is asked regularly about the programme and has indicated that performing on it as a young man impacted his mental health.²³ Yet the show was immensely popular in the period, representing more than a brief hiccup in programming and giving the audience what it wanted for twenty years on the BBC. It was, as we shall see, one part of a broader landscape of blacking up by white actors in post-war British screen culture.

It should be noted that the term 'screen culture' is doing more work here than in previous chapters as we survey the screen culture of the period in this chapter and blacking up as an important overlooked component of this. It has been expanded to include the numerous types of moving-image media produced and exhibited in post-war Britain including feature-films, the arrival of television and the 'home movies' that were increasingly accessible to a range of domestic consumers. Such a broad focus on what ordinary Britons were likely to see in their everyday lives highlights popular customs such as minstrelsy and blacking up as an important on-screen practice that originated in the early twentieth century but persisted well into the post-war period. What is clear if we take this wide-ranging approach to screen culture is that 'blackness' was presented and imagined on screen multiple times in post-war television without Black people necessarily being present. This wide attention to both race through blacking up and a broad screen culture moves us beyond both what has been a traditional approach of historians and media scholars of looking at what could be termed the 'social-issue' programmes that the BBC and ITV produced about racialised immigrants in the period and the archives that have informed these.²⁴ The focus on a narrow range of activities, programmes and archival material during the 1960s and 1970s or what occupies the files of 'Programmes for Racial Minorities' and similar at the BBC Written Archive Centre or the ITA collections has caused us to overlook the historic existence of blackface as a type of racialised custom in British entertainment over a much longer period from the 1920s through to the late 1970s. Blacking up for entertainment was indeed as Kenneth Lamb stated, 'a traditional

---

²² Stuart Jeffries, 'Last Night's TV, *Danny and the Human Zoo*', *Guardian*, 1 September 2015, www.theguardian.com/tv-and-radio/2015/sep/01/danny-human-zoo-lenny-henry-enfield-whitehouse.
²³ 'Episode 4: Lenny Henry', *Grounded with Louis Theroux*, BBC Radio 4, Broadcast 18 May 2020.
²⁴ Sarita Malik, *Representing Black Britain: Black and Asian Images on Television* (London: Sage, 2002); Stephen Bourne, *Black in the British Frame: The Black Experience in British Film and Television*, 2nd ed. (London: Bloomsbury, 2001); Darrell M. Newton, *Paving the Empire Road: BBC Television and Black Britons* (Manchester: University of Manchester Press, 2011); Schaffer, *The Vision of a Nation*.

form of entertainment in the British Isles for a great many years' among professional actors and ordinary Britons and one that was newly affirmed, defended and amplified in the post-war period when this practice was routinely featured on British television and films. Audiences wanted this particular racial pleasure on screen. Makers of film and television delivered and defended it.

## 4.1   Family Viewing on the Big and Small Screens

In post-war British television and film, the Minstrels made up just one part – albeit deeply popular – of a wider habit of blacking up on screen for audiences. Chapter 2 argued that British audiences regularly encountered blacked-up actors in the 1920s and 1930s through popular 'empire films'. When we look forward to the post-war period we see that the advent of television broadcasting gave these empire feature films a new lease on life as wholesome family viewing. While some feature films produced in the 1950s and 1960s made use of Black West Indian actors living in Britain such as Earl Cameron, Carmen Munroe and Errol John among others, the interwar empire films were rebroadcast on both the BBC and ITV. The two broadcasters brought historic blackface practices to new generations of television viewers, including examples of both minstrelsy with the customary white rings around the eyes and mouth of the person donning it and blacking up to pass as a Black or south Asian person, which involved a more thorough application of black or brown make-up. Popular minstrel singers such as Al Jolson could be seen in blackface on screen in American feature films such as 1927's *Jazz Singer* and 1939's *Rose of Washington Square*, in both of which Jolson sang 'My Mammy', as well as in the post-war biographical film *The Jolson Story* (1946), all broadcast anew on television.[25] This screen culture went largely unremarked upon except by a few voices of colour taking up the burden of declaring this material's broadcasting as problematic. The BBC and ITV both continually scheduled programme content that featured blackface and asserted that this content was harmless and wholesome, offering an important counterpoint to Rob Waters' spotlight on the British Black and south Asian audiences eagerly consuming images of the Black Power

---

[25] *The Jazz Singer*, directed by Alan Crosland, Warner Brothers (US, 1927; United Kingdom release, 1928). *Rose of Washington Square*, directed by Gregory Ratoff, Twentieth Century-Fox (1939). *The Jolson Story* (1947) had a respectable 15,118 filmgoers for its first showing in February 1947 at the Regent Cinema in Portsmouth and increased this total to 18,413 in July 1948; Sue Harper, 'Fragmentation and Crisis: 1940s Admissions Figures at the Regent Cinema, Portsmouth, UK', *Historical Journal of Film, Radio and Television* 26, no. 3 (2006): 361–394, 92–94.

movement in the US or within events such as the 1968 Olympics in Mexico.[26] This ongoing presentation of blacking up on screen to audiences through the 'classic' film is an important and overlooked aspect of the wider custom of highly racialised practices on screen that informed later defences of *The Black and White Minstrel Show.*

Broadcast listings indicate just how frequently films featuring white actors in both obvious minstrel makeup and in blackface in order to pass as Black or south Asian people could be seen on British televisions. The central place of empire films in television broadcasting was signalled early on when the BBC televised an adapted theatrical performance of W. P. Lipscombe and R. J. Millney's 'Clive of India' for viewers on New Year's Eve 1956.[27] It was ITV, however, that broadcast the bulk of empire films from 1957 and throughout the 1960s through its wide array of regional broadcasters.[28] In autumn 1957, ITV began a Saturday programme, *The Great Pictures of Alexander Korda*',[29] on ABC, its Midlands weekend broadcaster. The draw of Korda's films had been stressed by ABC in a feature in *The Times* aimed at potential advertisers on television that highlighted ABC programming decisions 'carefully measured by audience research' that translated into 'more viewers' and included 'live plays, outside broadcasts, sport, serials, the great Korda film classics, and variety'.[30] In 1958, the same films were again broadcast as a Saturday programme and called *Great Movies of Our Time.* Evidence indicates that the timing of such films fell within the 'watershed' period of family viewing. In 1961, ITV regional broadcasters Tyne Tees, South

[26] Rob Waters, 'Black Power on the Telly: America, Television, and Race in 1960s and 1970s Britain', *Journal of British Studies* 54, no. 4 (2015): 947–970.
[27] 'Clive of India' was adapted for performance on BBC Television, 'B.B.C. Television', *The Times*, 31 December 1956, 3.
[28] On the numerous broadcasters holding regional licences, some with weekday but not weekend privileges, see Catherine Johnson and Rob Turnock, *ITV Cultures: Independent Television Over Fifty Years* (London, Open University Press, 2005). From the audience perspective and more, see Joe Moran, *Armchair Nation: An Intimate History of Britain in Front of the TV* (London: Profile Books, 2013) and Helen Wheatley, ed., *Re-Viewing Television History: Critical Issues in Television Historiography* (London: IB Tauris, 2007).
[29] I.T.A. Associated Television 10.5: The Great Pictures of Alexander Korda – 'The Drum', 'B.B.C. Programmes for The Weekend To-Day', *The Times*, 28 September 1957, 4; I.T.A. Associated Television 10.5, 'The Great Pictures of Alexander Korda presents Sabu in "Jungle Book"', 'B.B.C. Programmes for The Weekend', *The Times* 2 November 1957, 4; ITA, Associated Television, 10.5, 'The Great Pictures of Alexander Korda Presents "Sanders of the River"', 'B.B.C. Programmes for The Weekend', *The Times*, 16 November 1957, 4; ITA, ABC Midland, To-Day. 'The Great Pictures of Alexander Korda Presents "Sanders of the River"', *The Times*, 7 December 1957: 3; I.T.A. A.B.C. Midland, 10.05pm 'The Great Pictures of Alexander Korda presents Sabu – "The Elephant Boy"'. B.B.C. Programmes for The Weekend. *The Times*, 28 December 1957, 4.
[30] ABC Television Network, *The Times*, 21 June 1957, 13.

Wales and West of England all featured *Sanders of the River* as 'Sunday Television' at 3pm and 4pm while a perennial favourite with broadcasters, *The Thief of Baghdad* (1940) with Indian child-actor Sabu and a blacked-up John Justin as the Sultan of Baghdad, was shown in July, September and December of that year.[31] The BBC began to include both interwar and post-war empire films in its programme listings in 1966 with Richard Burton in blackface as Dr Rama Safti in *The Rains of Ranchipur* (1955) and the Russian actress Eugenie Leontovich as the Maharani, broadcast in the prime slot of 7.25pm on a Sunday.[32] *Clive of India* (1935), featuring the American actor of Spanish descent, Cesar Romero, blacked up as the Indian Nawab Mir Jaffar, was broadcast on BBC1 in 1970 at 3pm on a Saturday and described in *The Times* regular television programme listings as 'a film for the family'.[33] The American film *Swanee River* (1940), featuring Al Jolson's minstrel show, was also broadcast on BBC2 in 1973 at the family viewing time of Saturday afternoon from 3pm to 4.20pm.[34] These are just some examples of the presence of blackface on television framed by scheduling that positioned this content as classic and wholesome entertainment and suitable for audiences of all ages.

When broadcasting hours for the BBC and ITV were extended after 1972, the pressure to provide programming resulted in a marked increase of films featuring blackface on television. In 1975 alone the following films were featured on ITV's various regional broadcasters (of which some audiences, particularly in the south and the Midlands, could access more than one) and on the BBC: *The Four Feathers* (1939) featuring blackface as a central plot point with a British officer masquerading as Black, deaf and dumb was shown twice in the year on Anglia on 22 March, at the outset of Easter vacation, and on London Weekend on 28 June; *The Thief of Baghdad* (1940) three times, on 29 March on Easter weekend in the Midlands, on 26 May on Thames broadcaster and on 25 August again on Thames; *Khartoum* (1966) twice in the year, on Grampian on 29 March and Southern on 12 April; *Sanders of the River* (1935) on Westward on 31 May; *Go Into your Dance* (1935) (with

---

[31] Tyne Tees, 3pm Film Festival, *Sanders of the River*, Sunday Television. *The Times*, 22 July 1961, 5; South Wales and West of England, 4pm Sunday Matinee, *Sanders of the River*, Sunday Television. *The Times*, 9 September 1961, 5: ITV, South Wales and West of England, 2.45pm *Thief of Baghdad*, Sunday Television. *The Times*, 16 December 1961, 5.

[32] 'Weekend Television and Radio', *The Times*, 24 September 1966, 3.

[33] 'Saturday Broadcasting', *The Times* 25 April 1970: II. Indeed, *Gunga Din* (1939) was broadcast on BBC iPlayer, BBC Two in March 2018, after two broadcasts in 2015, one in 2012, and one in 2011.

[34] 'Broadcasting' *The Times*, 14 July 1973, 8.

Al Jolson blacked up as a minstrel) on BBC2 on 29 July; *Elephant Boy* (1937) on Tyne Tees on 9 August; *Lives of a Bengal Lancer* (1935) also featuring British officers donning blackface in order to fool the locals and gain intelligence was shown on BBC1 on 11 October; and *Arabian Nights* (1942) on BBC2 on 20 December.[35] All of these broadcasting times except two were Saturday or Sunday viewings and all but two also fell within the watershed. Crucially the Easter holiday of 1975 was awash in these films as part of family viewing programming.

The timing of these broadcasts is itself a key indicator of how producers and programmers imagined the responses of British audiences to such films. Anamik Saha has noted the consistent marginalisation of minority programming in the schedules of British broadcasters in the twenty-first century, yet programming from 1955 to 1978 indicates that both empire films and films featuring overt blackface on television continued to be imagined as a site of audience consensus.[36] This is what a range of audiences could agree to watch according to programmers. British audiences in BBC and ITA files and press coverage seldom protested the prime viewing slots granted to such films by producers. It was a lone voice in 1957 that spoke out when *The Times* quoted a letter by Matthew T. Mbu, the first High Commissioner for Nigeria in the United Kingdom, to Associated Television of the Midlands, arguing that 'The film *Sanders of the River*, which was shown in the organization's programme "The Great Pictures of Korda" last Saturday night is "most damaging" to Nigeria.'[37] *The Times* reported on the complaint in small

---

[35] The most reliable programme listings for both ITV and BBC are featured in *The Times*, although the *Daily Mail* also includes programme listings. Anglia, 7.55pm, *The Four Feathers*, Sunday. *The Times*, 22 March 1975, 10; Granada, Border, Midlands, *Thief of Baghdad*, Grampian, *Khartoum*, Pick of the weekend TV films *Daily Mail*, 29 March 1975, 16; Southern, 6.45pm Film: *Khartoum*, *Daily Mail*, 12 April 1975: 16; Thames, 4.35pm *Thief of Baghdad*, Broadcasting. *The Times*, 26 May 1975, 8; Westward, 10.55pm *Sanders of the River*, Broadcasting Saturday. *The Times*, 31 May 1975, 8; London Weekend, 3.05pm Film: *The Four Feathers* Broadcasting Sunday. *The Times*, 28 June 1975, 8; BBC2, 9.00pm *Go Into Your Dance* (1935) with Al Jolson, Ruby Keeler, Glenda Farrell, Helen Morgan. Broadcasting. *The Times*, 29 July 1975, 23; Tyne Tees, 10.30am, *Elephant Boy* with Sabu, Broadcasting Saturday. *The Times*, 9 August 1975, 6; Thames, 4pm, *Thief of Baghdad*, Holiday sport, of course, predominates (BBC1 10.55am, ITV 1.5. *The Times*, Monday, August 25, 1975, 8; 1.55pm. *Lives of a Bengal Lancer* (1935), BBC1 Sunday. *The Times*, 11 October 1975, 8; BBC2, 2.45pm, *Arabian Nights*, with Sabu. Broadcasting Saturday. *The Times*, 20 December 1975, 8.
[36] Anamik Saha, 'Scheduling Race', in Sarita Malik and Darrell M. Newton, eds., *Adjusting the Contrast: British Television and Constructs of Race* (Manchester: Manchester University Press, 2017): 50–70; John Ellis, 'Scheduling: The Last Creative Act in Television?' *Media, Culture, and Society* 22, no. 1 (2000): 25–38.
[37] 'Film "Damaging To Nigeria"', *The Times*, 22 November 1957, 6.

notice: 'The letter asks of what use this film, "allegedly shot in 1935 or thereabout" could be to anybody in 1957 "when all efforts are being directed to better understanding among nations of the world, particularly the British Commonwealth of Nations."' Mbu saw the rebroadcasting of such a film as working against 'better understandings' of other nations and pointing out that this is what the Commonwealth was ostensibly pursuing in the period. That 'better understanding' pointed directly to the racial framework of knowledge outlined in *Sanders of the River* where white people ruled inferior, childish Black people. In a denial of Mbu's effort to name the film and its broadcasting as racist, *The Times* pointed out that Mr Mbu's response was not the majority response, arguing that 'Many British viewers who saw the film would describe it as thrilling.' Mbu's unsuccessful argument for the complete 'withdrawal of this obsolete film' was firmly aligned only with a minority of viewers who would not see the film as 'thrilling' first and foremost.[38] Even Mbu's considerable standing as Nigeria's first high commissioner did not protect him from being offered a lesson by *The Times* in how to properly view and respond to the film, and deny his own expressed view of it as ignorant and lacking an understanding or race or racialised people.

New empire films were also produced in the period and overshadowed the production of the social-problem films created by Basil Dearden and Michael Relph and Roy Ward Baker. As Wendy Webster has documented, new types of empire films such as *Guns at Batasi* (1964), *Bridge on the River Kwai* (1957) (Christmas viewing in 1974) and *Lawrence of Arabia* (1962) found receptive British audiences in both cinemas and on television.[39] Although the director Basil Dearden had made efforts to examine anti-immigrant prejudice in *Pool of London* (1951) and *Sapphire* (1958) and had cast Earl Cameron in both, Dearden's creation of *Khartoum* (1966) featured the white English actor Laurence Olivier in blackface playing the Mahdi. Dearden's willingness to hire a white actor to don blackface indicates that this custom was well entrenched among directors of a variety of political persuasions. The British Board of Film Censors also did not note Olivier's blacking up in June 1964 when they considered the film but were instead preoccupied with 'some of the belly-dancing' and 'shots and sounds of panic, carnage and corpses' in the film.[40] Yet Olivier's performance and the practice of

---

[38] Ibid.
[39] BBC1, 8.45pm, 25 December broadcast, *Bridge on the River Kwai*, *Daily Mail*, 24 December 1974, 16–17; Wendy Webster, *Englishness and Empire: 1939–1965* (Oxford: Oxford University Press, 2007).
[40] Letter to Harold Buck, Production supervisor, Julian Blaustein Productions, 4 June 1964, 'Khartoum' BBFC/Soho Square.

blacking up were not without comment on its release in 1966. *The Times'* film critic referenced British comedian Peter Sellers who had, along with the comedian Spike Milligan, impersonated Indian accents as Mr Lalkala and Mr Banerjee respectively on the popular BBC radio show *The Goon Show* (1951–1960) and had blacked up on screen as Dr Ahmed el Kabir in the 1960 British film *The Millionnairess*: 'We are given a formidable display of eye-rolling and lip-licking, a weird Peter Sellers-oriental accent and a valiant but unsuccessful attempt to disguise Sir Laurence's all too English features with false hair and green lipstick.'[41] This did not prevent *The Times* from concluding that this was an 'intelligent film', and *Khartoum* found a steady success with audiences in both cinemas and on television.[42]

In comparison a social-problem film such as Roy Ward Baker's *Flame in the Streets*, an adaption of a play, *Hot Summer Night*, featured on ITV's *Armchair Theatre* and showcasing a number of Black actors in the UK, had a relatively modest life on television regardless of the amount of attention it has received from historians.[43] The film tackled an interracial romance between a Black teacher, Peter, played by Johnny Sekka, and Sylvia Sims as his white girlfriend, Kathie, and the disapproval of Kathie's family. It offered a visualisation of the ordinary racism experienced by West Indians in Britain through a range of characters including Sekka as the teacher and Gabriel, a foreman at a local factory where Kathie's father worked, again played by Earl Cameron.[44] After three broadcasts in 1968 (on Southern, Rediffusion and Grampian) it was shown only three times in the entire 1970s: on Sunday 8 April in 1972 at 7.55pm on the Midlands Westward broadcaster, then for the first time in Yorkshire in 1973 at the dubious time of 11pm on a Friday, and on Westward in 1973, again in a late-night slot of 10.35pm on a

---

[41] 'An Intelligent Film about Gordon of Khartoum. From Our Film Critic', *The Times*, 9 June 1966, 8.

[42] The film was shown in the prime slot of Christmas Eve in 1972 on multiple broadcasters (ITV London, Anglia, Southern, Westward, and Yorkshire, all at 7.25pm) and on New Year's Day in 1976; Christmas Eve. *Daily Mail*, 23 December 1972, 16–17; Television: Two Page Guide. *Daily Mail*, 29 December 1976, 16–17; New Year's Day TV. *Daily Mail*, 31 December 1976, 18–27. See also Max Jones, '"National Hero and Very Queer Fish": Empire, Sexuality and the British Remembrance of General Gordon, 1918–72', *Twentieth Century British History* 26, no. 2 (2015): 175–202.

[43] Raymond Durgnat, 'Two 'Social Problem' Films: *Sapphire* and *Victim*', in Alan Burton, Tim O'Sullivan and Paul Wells, eds., *Liberal Directions: Basil Dearden and Postwar British Film Culture* (Wiltshire: Flicks Books 1997); Amanda Bidnall, 'The Race Relations Narrative in British Film', In *The West Indian Generation*, 162–203; Clive James Nwonka, 'Love Knows No Colour Bar: Windrush, Racism and *Flame in the Streets*', *Ethnic and Racial Studies* 43, no. 12 (2020): 2199–2216.

[44] Webster, *Englishness and Empire*, 164–171.

Friday.⁴⁵ In this regard, the social-problem films of the 1960s should be firmly placed within a broader context that indicates the frequency and regional broadcasting of these films. Sympathetic depictions of immigrants through fictionalised feature-films were simply not presented to audiences as often as the empire films of the past or present were and which were finding audiences in the consensus-driven timeslot awarded to 'family viewing'.

## 4.2 The Campaign Against Racial Discrimination (CARD) and *The Black and White Minstrel Show*

The broadcasting of both historic and contemporary films featuring actors in blackface had been established as a racialised custom in British television from 1957 onwards; nevertheless, this custom took on a more virulent life within original made-for-television programming in Britain. The previous popularity of Al Jolson films and radio acts such as the Kentucky Minstrels with British audiences led to the BBC's trialling of a discrete one-hour programme in 1957 entitled *The 1957 Television Minstrels* that featured the Mitchell Minstrels helmed by the popular musical director George Mitchell.⁴⁶ Reaction to the programme was positive with Ronald Camp, television reviewer for the *Daily Mail*, referencing his own experience of blacking up: 'Tradition dies hard – and it is a long time since I blacked my face and sang *Swanee* …' *The Black and White Minstrel Show* began broadcasting on 14 June 1958 with an initial 8pm Saturday evening slot before moving to 7.30pm in 1959. It was a prime-time showcase for its mix of highly choreographed dance pieces; regular solo performances by blacked-up minstrels Leslie Crowther and George Chisholm; and guest appearances by comedians, actors and singers who did not don blackface. By 1963, the BBC's Corporation Handbook reported that 16.5 million viewers were watching the show on Saturday evenings, making it the broadcaster's top programme and easily dwarfing the 5 to 7 million viewers of *Till Death Us Do Part*.⁴⁷ The

---

⁴⁵ Grampian 7.25pm. Weekend Broadcasting Programmes. *The Times*, 9 March 1968, 14; Rediffusion 10.30pm Television and radio. *The Times*, 21 June 1968, 18; Southern Television, 8.10pm. Weekend Broadcasting. *Times* 26 October 1968, 19; 7.55pm Westward. Sunday. *Daily Mail*, 8 April 1972, 21; 11pm. Yorkshire. Entertainment/1 TV in Detail *Daily Mail*, 25 May 1973, 22; 10.35pm Westward Entertainment/1 TV. *Daily Mail*, 3 August 1973, 18.

⁴⁶ Michael Pickering, 'The BBC's Kentucky Minstrels, 1933–1950: Blackface Entertainment on British Radio', *Historical Journal of Film, Radio, and Television* 16, no. 2 (1996): 161–195.

⁴⁷ 'To-Day. BBC Programmes for the Weekend', *The Times*, 16 August 1958, 3; Gander, L. Marsland, Daily Telegraph Television and Radio Correspondent. '16 1/2m Saw

television show spawned a series of successful records featuring music from the minstrels and the travelling theatrical show playing in community halls and theatres across the UK that Lenny Henry had briefly been a part of after the show had already featured in the West End of London, 'breaking every box-office record'.[48] Regular stories in the press about the minstrels, such as the *Daily Telegraph*'s 'Minstrels Run Out of Make-Up', headline in 1962 were featured as light human-interest stories.[49]

The popularity of *The Black and White Minstrel Show* did not, however, extend to Black audiences. The petition to ban the show was put to the BBC in May 1967 by CARD and 32-year-old Clive West, who was identified as Trinidadian by *The Times* and as 'an unemployed stoker' by the *Daily Mirror*.[50] West's original petition is not in evidence and can only be reconstructed through the reporting of the press at the time.[51] The petition's content was selectively quoted throughout the dailies with two lines from it repeatedly presented in the press coverage: 'This hideous impersonation is quite offensive and causes much distress to most coloured people [and] moreover it creates serious misunderstanding between the races.'[52] West pointed out the profound impact of the show upon racialised viewers using the strong terminology of 'distress' to do so. West further noted, as Matthew Mbu had also done so in his protest about *Sanders of the River* from 1957, that this was a false representation of Black people on screen that could only lead to white audiences misunderstanding the reality of Black people. Reporting on West's role in bringing the petition to CARD vacillated between identifying the petition as purely a CARD initiative and hinting that West was a rogue affiliate.[53] CARD as an organisation was two years old at the time but encompassed a group of Black and south Asian men and women who had been highly active in campaigns and organisations supporting immigrants of colour in Britain throughout the 1950s and into the 1960s.[54]

---

BBC "Black and White Minstrels"', *Daily Telegraph*, 25 January 1963, 13. JICTAR rankings for *Till Death Us Do Part* from 1965 to 1968, ITA/IBA collection, cited in Brett Bebber, '*Till Death Us Do Part*'.

[48] 'The Magic of The Minstrels', *The Times*, 8 November 1969, 3.
[49] Daily Telegraph Reporter. 'Minstrels Run Out of Make-Up', *Daily Telegraph*, 12 January 1962, 13.
[50] 'BBC Asked to Ban the TV Minstrels', *The Times*, 19 May 1967, 3; Paula James, 'Race Rumpus Over the Black and White Minstrels', *Daily Mirror* 19 May 1967, 3.
[51] I have been unable to locate this petition in the Institute of Race Relations, the George Padmore Institute, the National Archives, or the BBC Written Archive Centre.
[52] James, Ibid.
[53] 'BBC Asked to Stop "Offensive" Minstrel Show', *Birmingham Post*, 19 May 1967, 9.
[54] See Hammond Perry's excellent history of CARD in *London Is the Place for Me*, 203–229.

David Pitt, CARD's chairman and a physician and originally from Grenada, was also a London County Councillor for Hackney and had been primarily preoccupied with campaigning for a Race Relations Act that would offer genuine protection and recourse for racialized people facing discrimination in house, employment and public spaces. Pitt clarified in a letter to the editor of *The Times* that the petition 'was drafted and circulated without our prompting' by one of the 200 signatories but that it nevertheless had CARD's support.[55] West himself explained to *The Times*, 'I requested to C.A.R.D that the show should be taken off as it depicts my race as a singing, dancing, laughing, idiotic people.' He went on to elaborate both the reasoning and process behind the petition: '[*The Black and White Minstrel Show*] is a laugh at the expense of a minority and it causes distress to coloured people by showing them as a race that cannot be taken as serious-minded citizens. The petition was a spontaneous effort and both white and coloured people have signed it.'[56] Contacted for comment by the *Daily Mirror*, West was further quoted as saying that the show 'makes a monkey out of us'.[57] For West, the racism within the show and its portrayal of Black people ran counter to efforts by CARD and other organisations to have West Indians treated as intelligent citizens of Britain and as viewers who could only be negatively impacted by the laughing, dancing portrayal of the minstrels. Although CARD had not occupied itself with media representation at this point, as one of the most visible organisations campaigning against racism in the country the petition found its way to an association with them.

West's comments built upon views of the programme within the West Indian community that had previously been voiced in the Black press. The Dominican-born journalist, historian and publisher, Edward Scobie, was instrumental in the creation of magazines that catered to what Scobie termed 'a Negro voice' that united 'West Indians, British Guianese, Americans or Africans' while also aiming to attract white readers.[58] Scobie's fourth and most successful magazine publication, *Flamingo* (which followed 1948's *Checkers*, *Bronze* (1954–1955), and *Tropic* (1960) which are examined in the next chapter) ran from 1961 to 1963 and circulated throughout the UK from its base in London. *Flamingo* featured an article on the Black and White Minstrels in its very first issue of 1961 entitled, 'Bad Taste B.B.C.!'[59] The piece opened with interviews with a number of West Indians of various

---

[55] David Pitt, Chairman, '"The Wrong Target", Campaign Against Racial Discrimination', *The Times*, 23 May 1967, 9.
[56] 'BBC Asked to Ban the TV Minstrels', 3; 'Race Rumpus', 3.   [57] 'Race Rumpus', 3.
[58] *Flamingo*, September 1961, 1.   [59] Ibid., 22–25.

professions, including a writer, theatrical agent and actress, and businessman discussing their reactions to the show:

> Lloyd Squires, a young West Indian businessman in Brixton has this to say of *The Black and White Minstrel Show*: 'I feel ashamed and disgusted when I see the antics of these coons on the programme. No one whom I know likes it. Some have told me that they switch off the moment the show starts and then feel uncomfortable and miserable for the next 30 minutes when they know that "the fastest show in black and white" as the producers call it, is on the air.'[60]

Squires' reaction and his shame and disgust with the show anticipated similar expressions by West in 1967. This was not harmless media representation but a programme that elicited strong emotional and physical responses from Black audiences experiencing the opposite of white audiences who viewed the programme as pleasurable and enjoyable. *Flamingo* also quoted 'a young Englishman, Bob Dawbarn', presumably white, who noted 'I just do not understand how Auntie B.B.C. which seems only too willing to ban folk songs or stop comedians from imitating politicians, can continue to put out this insulting show which is offensive to many people.'[61] In the pages of *Flamingo*, the consensus of those interviewed in the article was that this was not a show that should be on the air in post-war Britain.

Responses to *Flamingo*'s piece, however, raised a familiar refrain from *Flamingo*'s white readers. One reader, James Graham from Glasgow, wrote in response to the article, 'If we are to achieve better racial understanding in this country, it will be despite the complex-ridden "Bad Taste B.B.C.!" of your September issue ... The "attack" on Negroes in the "Black and White Minstrel Show" is manifestly no more degrading to Negroes than are the other countless show-business parodies degrading to us Scots ... Bad taste Flamingo!'[62] November's issue featured a comment by the editors noting that 'the following letter sums up the position of a substantial number of readers'. The letter stated:

> Most of my friends and I think that the 'Black and White Minstrel Show' is first-rate entertainment. I strongly disagree with your criticism and I am sure that it displays over-sensitiveness ... In any case, 'Black and White Minstrel Show' surely should be regarded as a compliment by your West Indian and African readers. It shows how dominant people of Negro descent are in the entertainment world for the B.B.C. to emulate.[63]

The argument that the stereotypes deployed on the show benefitted Black immigrants preceded similar sentiments put forth by Stephen

---

[60] Ibid., 22.  [61] Ibid.  [62] *Flamingo*, October 1961, 2.
[63] 'Minstrels: A Defence. K.S.T', *Flamingo*, November 1961, 3.

Murphy at the ITA. Both statements argued that this particular form of representation on British screens, which ran counter to negative news coverage of immigrants documented by Schaffer, was a beneficial one.[64] This show did not feature 'black' people as a problem, but rather as a source of entertainment and skilled performance. White people were thus also positioned as offering a better, more positive, performance of Blackness than Black people themselves. In both arguments, the blacking up of white bodies as black bodies in order to achieve these distorted emotions of warm cheerfulness was not addressed; rather the minstrelsy was treated as a form of accurate imitation or passing.

*Flamingo*'s article did not reach the BBC, according to existing records; however protests against the programme also became evident within the BBC itself. The BBC's own satirical programme *That Was the Week That Was* (1962–1963) made a point in 1963 about violent anti-Black racism in the US and the broadcast of *The Black and White Minstrel Show* when actors impersonating the minstrels sang a morbid song about lynching. Prior to this in 1962, Barrie Thorne, who would be Chief Accountant by 1967, complained to Kenneth Adam, then Director of Television, about the show. Although the original complaint is not in *The Black and White Minstrel Show* file at the BBC Written Archive Centre, Adam's indignant response is: 'I yield to no one in my detestation of apartheid and the Little Rock philosophy. But to suggest that to continue a perfectly honourable theatrical tradition of the British music hall is a "disgrace and an insult to coloured people everywhere" is, I submit, arrant nonsense.'[65] When CARD submitted its petition in May 1967, such arguments in defence of the programme were again mobilised. The BBC kept an eye on the press as a site of public feeling over two days on 18 and 19 May.[66] It is unclear whether CARD or the BBC itself raised the story to reporters but the papers unanimously endorsed the BBC's position that *The Black and White Minstrel Show* was a harmless 'traditional' programme devoid of racist implications. The *Daily Mail*'s coverage made a headline of the petition's argument, 'This hideous impersonation distresses coloured people', before featuring a further sub-heading 'Tradition' above the BBC's rationale for the blacking up within the show.[67] An unnamed 'BBC official' stated 'The Corporation

---

[64] Schaffer, *Vision of a Nation*.
[65] Kenneth Adam to Barrie Thorne, 11 September 1962, T16/175/2 TV Policy-Race Relations, File 2 (1955–1968) WAC. Adam's response is housed in the file, as is Thorne's rejoinder.
[66] Extract from Minutes, Board of Management, 21 August 1967, R78/1,921/1 'Black and White Minstrel Show' WAC.
[67] Brian Dean, 'Ban Them!' *Daily Mail*, 19 May 1967, 6.

has a strict attitude about the presentation of racialism in its programmes and we do not think the Black and White Minstrels offend in any way.' The official continued, 'The show is not about race. It is traditional, enjoyed by millions for what it offers in good-hearted family entertainment. The series is one of the few BBC shows that holds a regular place in the Top Twenty.' The *Daily Mirror* followed with 'Traditional' again forming the subheading and a rather more incendiary headline, 'Race Rumpus Over the Black and White Minstrels'.[68] The content of the *Mirror*'s reporting mimicked that of the *Daily Mail*, quoting the official at the BBC regarding 'good-hearted family entertainment' and that the show was 'not about race'.

The *Daily Mirror* took its reporting a step further when it described the signatories as 'immigrants' and added further evidence that the show was beloved by what it identified as 14.5 million viewers by citing approval of the programme by a prominent Black woman, 'Lady Constantine, wife of Sir Learie Constantine, the West Indies cricketer and diplomat', who had been contacted regarding the story. Lady Constantine is quoted as saying, 'My husband and I take it as a show and have no objection to it at all. You might say we were fans.' Lady Constantine's endorsement of the show, while Sir Learie was a member of the BBC's General Advisory Committee, offered what the *Mirror* positioned as definitive proof of the BBC's own argument that the show was not about race. The show was, by the *Mirror*'s estimation, approved by Black people and something that the singer from Surrey, Elizabeth Duben, also conveyed when she dashed off her note to Tom Sloane from a Hilton in Jamaica in the same time period. Yet Sir Learie, for his part, had also expressed concern two years prior over blacking up in the film industry at the BBC's 'Second Conference on Immigrants (West Indies)' held in July 1965. Constantine stated to the Chairman of the BBC and participants that 'in films, I have always objected to white people blacking their faces to present certain pictures when we can get naturally coloured faces to do the job. There is something obnoxious about it to me' before going on to endorse the BBC's efforts at 'looking in on coloured people'.[69] Echoing *Flamingo*, it was the overlooking of Black actors in favour of blacked-up white actors and the subsequent lack of employment that was the more immediate and offensive issue for Sir Learie.

---

[68] 'Race Rumpus', 3.
[69] The British Broadcasting Corporation: Second Conference on Immigrants (West Indies) held at Broadcasting House, London, W1, Tuesday 13 July 1965, *Report of Proceedings*, p. 25, WAC.

The refrain that *The Black and White Minstrel* show was 'not about race' was persistent among producers and audiences of the programme, overriding the efforts of Black viewers to put forth their own points of view. *The Times* quoted George Inns as 'astonished by the protest', saying, 'How anyone can read racialism into this show is beyond me.'[70] Letters to the *Daily Mail* collectively grouped in a feature, 'The Red Pink and Blue Minstrel Show!' overwhelmingly favoured this argument as well.[71] Of the five responses printed (one by three signatories), only one endorsed CARD's assessment of the programme. A letter writer, named as 'Patience Jeeves' wrote, 'I was not surprised to read that coloured people have protested. Surely it is time that the "chocolate covered coon" image was finally ended?' The remaining letters, however, drew on familiar strategies meant to maintain the colour-blind racial innocence of the programme and those viewers watching it. D. A. Lockhart from Surrey attacked an emergent political correctness proposing that the show be renamed the Red and Blue Minstrel Show before declaring, 'Wait a minute though! Red and blue are political so we can't risk that. Pink and green would be out for similar reasons.' E. Allison-Webb, in an approach similar to Lamb's, suggested that members of CARD were not properly viewing the programme and as such were not seeing the fun in the show: 'Have the campaigners against Racial Discrimination [sic] have no sense of humour? Or do we have to change our every way of life?' This last element, that this misreading of the programme and the broader accommodation of immigrants into Britain negatively impacted the lives of white Britons, was also implied in the other letters. T. Oxlade from Islington wrote, 'If these people wish to be absorbed into the community, they should take the chip off their shoulders and join in the fun.' The three signatories of the last letter, K. M. Ross, M. Grant and R. M. York were rather more threatening regarding the consequences of reading racism into the programme's innocent fun: 'Has it occurred to the campaigners themselves that they themselves induce far more resentment by continually provoking the people of this country to anti-racial feelings?' On 22 May, the Head of Programming at the BBC had noted in a confidential meeting of the Management Board that 'the Press had been severely critical of the basis of the petition and letters printed in the *Daily Mail* [that] reflected the general view that the programme was not racially offensive.'[72] When the

---

[70] 'BBC Asked to Ban the TV Minstrels', 3.
[71] D. A. Lockhart et al., 'The Red Pink and Blue Minstrel Show!' *Daily Mail*, 22 May 1967, 6.
[72] Board of Management, Minutes of 22 May 1967, R78/1,921/1 'Black and White Minstrel Show', WAC.

controversy was revived on 11 August by an article critical of the programme by Elizabeth Thomas in the *Tribune*, the Assistant Head of Programming had noted in another meeting of the Management Board that letters to the editors in the article's aftermath had 'all been strongly critical of the view expressed by Elizabeth Thomas'.[73] The press and the majority public sentiment that it seemingly represented was still with the BBC and its defence of the programme as not about race.

What these discussions ultimately centred on was a struggle over who could legitimately identify and name racism in post-war Britain. West and CARD's campaign highlighted how contentious this struggle was and how little power Black and south Asian people in Britain had to author definitions of racism. The controversy pointed to the emergence of what was coming to be known as 'political correctness' as white viewers and producers voiced frustrations with the naming of racist practices by Black audiences and their own thoughts and feelings about these representations. Further arguments outlined *The Black and White Minstrel Show* and popular culture more widely as an arena that should be overlooked in favour of areas that obviously impacted the quality of life of immigrants in Britain, such as employment and housing. The oft-quoted memo from Oliver Whitley, chief assistant to the Director General, fell into the latter camp: 'The best advice that could be given to coloured people by their friends would be: "On *this* issue, we can see your point, but in your own best interests, for Heaven's sake shut up. You are wasting valuable ammunition on a comparatively insignificant target."'[74] Even for CARD, this issue was not at the forefront in its battle for non-segregated spaces in Britain and equal opportunity in housing, employment and public services. The scale of issues facing organisations such as CARD were referenced by Pitt in a letter to *The Times* about its editorial of 19 May, titled 'The Wrong Target':

For over two years, we have documented the extent of racial discrimination in employment, housing, and services and have pressed the case for effective legislation to cover these fields. CARD published a detailed report last month on 43 of our cases, but the only part of it that received publicity in the press were 5 cases of complaints about police conduct. In contrast, the present petition is given widespread newspaper coverage and is then criticized for attacking the wrong target.[75]

---

[73] Board of Management, minutes of 21 August 1967, Ibid.
[74] Memo to D. A. from O. J. Whitley, *The Black and White Minstrel Show*, 26 May 1967, R78/1, 921/1, 'Black and White Minstrel Show', BBC Written Archives Centre, hereafter WAC.O. J.
[75] Pitt, 'The Wrong Target'.

Pitt was referring to the report that it had submitted to the Race Relations Board noting ongoing discrimination in the wake of the Race Relations Act. Further, Pitt noted that CARD's 'main target is racial discrimination', and his acknowledgement in the same letter that *The Black and White Minstrel Show* was nevertheless an important 'side issue' points to the difficulties in identifying the impact of popular culture on audiences' construction of race in the period and also the need and expectations of Black people living in Britain. For Pitt, the battle was in the living conditions of Black people in Britain and not on the screens that white people watched. Dominant television programmes were shunted to the side in such a context. That Clive West turned to CARD as a natural home for this protest against the BBC programme indicated just how much work CARD had on its plate. CARD would be effectively dissolved come December of that same year as Black Power contested and shaped agendas for campaigning and education on racial discrimination in Britain.[76]

While Pitt saw the goings-on of the screen as a side issue for CARD in the busy spring of 1967, producers and regulators of screen culture in Britain, as I have shown in Chapter 1, had spent years and in some cases decades imagining the screen's impact on audiences. The BBFC, the BBC and ITA were very well attuned to audience responses and a raft of non-governmental organisations such as The London Public Morality Council, The National Viewers' and Listeners' Association and formal government inquiries such as the Pilkington Committee reminded these organisations of the fragile impressionability of British viewers.[77] The advertising industry also depended on this very element.[78] Yet, when it came to a defence of *The Black and White Minstrel Show* and the blacking up at the centre of it, the audience logic articulated within these organisations was inverted to present audiences as deeply unimpressionable. O. J. Whitley's memo on *The Black and White Minstrel Show* also included his

---

[76] Hammond Perry, *London Is the Place for Me*, 233–243.
[77] Jeffrey Richards, *The Age of the Dream Palace: Cinema and Society in 1930s Britain* (London: IB Tauris, 2009); James C. Roberston, *The Hidden Cinema: British Film Censorship in Action 1913–1972* (London: Routledge, 1993); Sian Barber, *Censoring the 1970s: The BBFC and the Decade That Taste Forgot* (Newcastle: Cambridge Scholars Press, 2011); David Hendy, 'Bad Language and BBC Radio Four in the 1960s and 1970s', *Twentieth Century British History* 17, no. 1 (2006): 74–102; James Curran and Jean Seaton, *Power Without Responsibility: Press, Broadcasting, and the Internet in Britain*, 8th ed. (London: Routledge, 2018); Lawrence Black, 'Whose Finger on the Button? British Television and the Politics of Cultural Control', *Historical Journal of Film, Radio and Television* 25, no. 4 (2006): 547–575.
[78] Sean Nixon, *Hard Sell: Advertising, Affluence and Transatlantic Relations, c. 1951–69* (Manchester: Manchester University Press, 2013).

estimation of the British audience: 'It seems to be absurd to imagine that people who are not already racially prejudiced could possibly be in some way contaminated by the Minstrels. People who are already racially prejudiced are more likely to be exacerbated by the protest itself than the object of the protest.'[79] In Whitley's account, the longevity of this practice in British entertainment resulted in audience immunity to the racist elements of the practices and little chance of audiences absorbing these attitudes; all of which was in stark contrast to the careful treatment that the BBC gave to images of politics, class conflict, sexuality or bad language on screen and on air and which were consistently viewed as potentially shaping audience behaviour. The young Englishman Bob Dawbarn noted this race-based exception in his aforementioned comment in *Flamingo*: 'I just do not understand how Auntie B.B.C. which seems only too willing to ban folk songs or stop comedians from imitating politicians, can continue to put out this insulting show which is offensive to many people.'[80]

The audience of *The Black and White Minstrel Show* referenced by the press and the BBC was articulated as white, British and devoid of the racial lens that American audiences were presumed to possess based on the historic presence of African Americans in that country and a perceived absence of Black people in historic England. *The Times* editorial 'The Wrong Target' argued against CARD's characterisation of the show: 'These are certainly not criticisms that come readily to the minds of most viewers of the show. The B.B.C. regards it as a wholesome family entertainment, and it is doubtful whether any but a handful of the 14,500,000 viewers who regularly switch on had previously considered that it had racial undertones.'[81] This 'handful of viewers' was thus the aberration and not the norm. *The Times* acknowledged: 'It is true, for example, that a show of this kind would not be shown on American television but this is for obvious historical reasons. The "nigger minstrel" show springs from the old South and Uncle-Tom-like acceptance of the divisions between white and black.'[82] In this argument, 'historic reasons' act as a euphemism for the acknowledged presence of Black audiences in the US and the presumed related racial sensitivity of American audiences. *The Times* went on to argue, 'Again, it is doubtful whether this strikes the average viewer in Britain.' Yet as Waters demonstrates, the BBC and ITV both carefully considered the impact on white television audiences in Britain of images of the Black Power movement in the US.[83] White British audiences were imagined as fragile and impressionable

---

[79] Whitley, *The Black and White Minstrel Show*.   [80] *Flamingo*, September 1961, 22.
[81] Pitt, 'The Wrong Target'.   [82] Ibid.   [83] Waters, 'Black Power on the Telly'.

when consuming this particular representation of Blackness on screen as one that highlighted systemic anti-Black racism and organised, as well as militant, responses to it. America's race problem and its presentation to white viewers in Britain had to be handled sensitively according to the BBC but blacking up did not.

The spectre of America, however, served other functions in the debate over *The Black and White Minstrel Show* when a BBC staff member attempted to highlight diverging treatments of blackface on screen in post-war America and Britain. Barrie Thorne at the BBC used the controversy raised by CARD and the BBC's own argument about the racial innocence of the programme to request that an American and specifically Black audience have the final say on whether the show was racist or not:

> One way of testing responsible opinion would be for the BBC to send the Black and White Minstrels book and the coloured *Radio Times* front cover of them to the National Association for the Advancement of Coloured People and the Urban League and ask for their opinion. The BBC might also ask the three American networks, since it is only a theatrical show, what reaction they think the series would have on responsible coloured opinion in the United States if it was put coast to coast.[84]

Thorne ended by arguing that 'the theatrical tradition of the show could then be measured against the historical background and the continued fight against segregation going on in the US, here, and elsewhere in the world'. This is a fascinating moment in the scant records on *The Black and White Minstrel Show* in the BBC archive. Thorne posited African-American audiences and organisations representing them such as the NAACP as likely able to 'see' racism in ways that white British audiences and British producers were unable to do so. Thorne's reasoning on this likely lay in two areas: firstly, that it was Black Americans who could educate the BBC on why blacking up was unacceptable and secondly, that blacking up was becoming less common on screen in the US context. An increase in Black actors on screen in the US in both film and television was indeed edging out the practice of blacking up on screen as was the work of the NAACP and various organisations and individuals lobbying against film and television studios for better representation. The American press offered a cool response to British films such as Zoltan Korda's remake of the *Four Feathers* in 1955 as *Storm over the Nile* with the newspaper *Variety* stating: 'Battle sequences filmed in the Sudan have

---

[84] Barrie Thorne to C.A. to Director General, 19 May 1967, 'Black and White Minstrel Show' WAC.

a convincing look. The same can hardly be said of the disguise effected by Anthony Steel in posing as a native to purge his cowardice and return the four feathers he received on his resignation from brother officers and fiancée.'[85] Thorne was relying on this national shift in attitudes towards blacking up as well as the presence of a Black organisation to help the BBC see blacking up as racist when he suggested sending material on *The Black and White Minstrel Show* to the NAACP. This, he thought, would be a more effective means of educating BBC executives than anything else – the growing presence of immigrants of colour in Britain was clearly not enough to help BBC executives see anti-Black racism while Americans with their imagined expertise on the subject could. America could function, in Thorne's reasoning, as both solution and spectre.

The BBC did unsuccessfully attempt to address some elements of the controversy in the two years following CARD's petition. *The Black and White Minstrel Show* incorporated two Black performers into the minstrels on 5 August 1967, drawing a swift internal rebuke from the Board of Management indicating that the inclusion 'of two real negroes had broken the well-established convention of the coloured coon' and as Mr Whitley noted, 'This might seem to run counter to the grounds on which the BBC had rebutted the recent petition by CARD.'[86] A show that was 'not about race' threatened to acknowledge the opposite as it suddenly included two Black entertainers. Two subsequent efforts to mount programmes that featured the Mitchell Minstrels without their blackface make-up were also short-lived. In September 1968, Brian Dean, television writer for the *Daily Mail*, made reference to the past controversy with CARD when he reported on the production of a new programme, *Masquerade*, in an article entitled 'The White-and-White Minstrel Show'. Even then, the BBC was reported as saying of *The Black and White Minstrel Show*, 'It is not about race. It is traditional and enjoyed by millions for what it offers.'[87] In 1970, it was again Dean who reported on the BBC's failed efforts to avoid blackface on screen:

Two years ago, the BBC tried out a new Minstrel show *Masquerade* in which the men left off the dark-brown stage make-up and appeared, as it were, in the raw. They did it again in *Music, Music, Music*. But although it probably pleased the show's critics, it didn't please the viewers. The fact is that the traditional blacking-up *is* the Minstrel show.[88]

---

[85] From *Variety*, 28 November 1955 clipping in 'Storm over the Nile, Columbia 1956', Margaret Herrick Library, US.
[86] Extract from minutes of meeting held on 14 August 1967, Board of Management, Confidential, 'Black and White Minstrel Show' WAC.
[87] Brian Dean, 'The White-and-White Minstrel Show', *Daily Mail*, 19 September 1968, 3.
[88] Brian Dean, 'A New Funny Man for the Minstrels', *Daily Mail*, 14 March 1970, 4.

The Minstrels returned to their Saturday night slot on BBC1, while *Music, Music, Music* which had been broadcast on Sundays on BBC2 at 7.25pm disappeared. The minstrels blacking up was what the audience wanted.

### 4.3 Rangi Ram and 'The Black and White Minstrels from Jockey Mead'

The publicly acknowledged 'tradition' of blacking up, however, continued in both film and television in the late 1960s and throughout the 1970s. As well-known white comedians fully blacked up their faces, necks and hands on screen the celebrity of these actors in Britain tipped passing into a form of modern minstrelsy. Peter Sellers was a particular fan of the practice in comedy. In Seller's film *The Party* (1968) the *Daily Mail* reported that Sellers 'darkens his face, puts on his favourite funny accent, and plays a ham-fisted Indian actor at large in Hollywood' and starred as an extra in an old-fashioned empire film remarkably similar in its opening scene to the interwar empire film *The Lives of a Bengal Lancer* (1935).[89] *The Party* was released in 1969 in Britain to tepid reviews yet none, barring the *Daily Mail*'s brief reference, made any comment on Sellers blacking up.[90] The comedian Spike Milligan who had worked opposite Sellers on *The Goon Show* blacked up as an Irish-Asian immigrant, Kevin O'Grady, in ITV's short-lived series, *Curry and Chips*, developed by Johnny Speight in 1969 (Figure 4.1). Central to the show's comedy was O'Grady's inability to fit in to the various quintessentially British scenes of a factory floor, boarding house, pubs and other settings. O'Grady was a truly outlandish and ridiculous character with a mangled sense of British life and customs or no knowledge at all. This was the licence Milligan had as a white man acting south Asian. Building on the success of *Till Death Us Do Part*, the new series still quickly ran afoul of the Independent Television Authority as Brian Dean reported that viewers protested 'at the use of words like "wog," "Sambo" and "coon" in the 30 minute comedy'. Jagmohan Joshi, secretary of the Indian Workers' Association, was quoted in Dean's report as saying 'My association will do everything in its power to get the show stopped.'[91] As Brett Bebber has documented, internal audience surveys at the ITA demonstrated that the show was widely viewed but audiences refused to

---

[89] Cecil Wilson, 'Film', *Daily Mail*, 6 March 1969, 14.
[90] Ibid.; John Russell Taylor, 'A Director's Reputation and Achievement', *The Times*, 6 March 1969, 13.
[91] Brian Dean, 'Curry and Chips Starts TV Colour Row', *Daily Mail*, 22 November 1969, 1.

4.1 Kenny Lynch, Spike Milligan and Eric Sykes in 1969 in a scene set in the novelty factory that all three characters were employed at in *Curry and Chips*. Source: Mirrorpix, www.gettyimages.co.uk/detail/news-photo/television-programme-curry-and-chips-with-spike-milligan-news-photo/1450839834.

acknowledge that the show's racial attitudes could influence their own.[92] Milligan's Kevin O'Grady showed up again in blackface in an episode of *Till Death Us Do Part* in 1974 entitled 'Paki-Paddy'. The BBC would not shy away from blackface on television as new sitcoms featuring blacked-up actors such as *It Ain't Half Hot Mum*, set in colonial India during World War II, debuted in 1974 and ran until 1981. The white British actor Michael Bates played a leading role in that series as 'Bearer Rangi Ram' alongside two south Asian actors, Dino Shafeek and Babar Bhatti, as a trio of Indian servants. Often shown slyly subverting the wishes of the British officers, the characters were deeply rooted in stereotypes familiar to British audiences. Again, however, the blacking up that was central within the series merited little comment by commentators either within the BBC or the press.

It is when we turn to home movies from the period that we see how impressionable viewers actually were when it came to seeing the practice

---

[92] Brett Bebber, 'The Short Life of *Curry and Chips:* Racial Comedy on British Television in the 1960s', *Journal of British Cinema and Television* 11, no. 2–3 (2014): 213–235.

of blacking up on screen. In the post-war period, local residents blacked up in explicit imitations of British screen culture as entire floats in parades and carnivals featured men and women performing songs as black and white minstrels. In 1961 in the North West of England, Dr Derek Nuttall a local filmmaker, captured the Bacup carnival procession that included children dressed as *The Black and White Minstrels* among numerous other costumes.[93] In 1963 near Brighton, amateur filmmaker Cecil Cramp filmed the Horsham carnival procession that featured 'The Black and White Minstrels from Jockey Mead' on a float dancing and wearing boater hats and blackface.[94] On 25 August 1979, a local film-maker in Rocester, Staffordshire, known as Humphries, took footage of the village festival and another float featuring adults blacked up in what appears as a hybrid of both the black and white minstrels and the golliwog that featured in advertisements and labelling for Robertson's Golden Shred marmalade. The parade also featured two men blacked up with one wearing a feminine dress and carrying a large handwritten sign saying 'Wogs of Rocester' while the other was dressed as a baby and being pushed in a pram.[95] A film-maker in Kegworth who shot films of local carnivals over a number of years from the late 1970s into the early 1980s captured a marching band blacked up and costumed such as the black and white minstrels in one year and a different float in a subsequent year titled 'Mississippi' that featured adults blacked up and engaged in song and dance in imitations of *The Black and White Minstrels Show*.[96]

Further films showing adults dressed as minstrels are also evident in collections in the Yorkshire Film Archive.[97] The Moving Image Archive of the National Library of Scotland also holds remarkable footage of 200 primary school pupils performing in woolly wigs and garish costumes as the Black and White Minstrels for an audience at the Bo'Ness Fair in 1974.[98] I suspect that much more exists in media archives as practices of blacking up as either minstrels or other figures are not always identified in current cataloguing practices in a uniform manner, or at all. The existence of such footage indicates evidence of the very impressionability that normally preoccupied producers and regulators of screen

---

[93] Dr Derek Nuttall, 'Bacup Carnival 1961'/North West Film Archive (NWFA).
[94] Cecil Cramp collection, 'Carnival; Last Train to Brighton; West Street' 1963; October 1964; February 1965/Screen Archive South East.
[95] 'Humphries: Rocester Festival 1979'/Media Archive for Central England (MACE).
[96] 'Sharpe: Kegworth Easter Market and Carnival Parades 1977–1980s'/MACE.
[97] 'Carleton Gala', 1972 DB 319/Yorkshire Film Archive (YFA) is one such example.
[98] Bo'Ness fair, Reference #7793, 1974, Director: Michael Alexander, Pelicula Film, 16mm, The Moving Image Archive/The National Library of Scotland, footage commencing at 26:08.

culture in Britain but which was ultimately refuted by decisions to place the black and white minstrels and other blacked-up actors on screen. The evident fun and pleasure that local actors experienced when blacking up spoke of to all the contradictions of colour-blind racism that has been discussed by Eduardo Bonilla-Silva and others working within critical race theory and which has long been associated with family entertainment in Britain.[99] In the case of the Kegworth carnivals, which explicitly signalled a Mississippi setting, blacking up also continued to be associated with references to the American Deep South.

## 4.4 The End of *The Black and White Minstrel Show*

In July 1978, *The Black and White Minstrel Show* finally ceased broadcasting on the BBC for reasons that seemed to speak to its declining popularity with most, if not all, audiences and a growing discomfort with the show among BBC executives. In 1975, according to the entertainment trade magazine, *Stage and Television Today*, JICTAR ratings (Joint Industry Committee for Television Advertising Research) for the programme still placed it in the top three programmes of eight regional broadcasters in the UK and in the top 10 of three others.[100] However by 1978, it registered only within the top 10 in London and not at all in other regional broadcasters.[101] In July 1977, the *Daily Mail* went as far as to run an article titled 'That Old Black Magic Gone and Lost its Spell?' with a subheading that stated somewhat inaccurately 'Now in its twentieth year, *The Black and White Minstrel Show* has survived rock, the Beatles, the Race Relations Board. But how much longer can it go on?'[102] Martin Jackson, the article's author, claimed that much of the Minstrels' enduring appeal lay in the lack of change evident in the programme for viewers, even likening it to an essential part of Britishness: 'It has become like a National Institution like Big Ben or the Tower and like them, a kind of monument to British durability and a comforting reassurance that all is not yet up with the world.' The 'comforting reassurance' of this British institution offered a vision 'recalling an

---

[99] Eduardo Bonilla-Silva, *Racism without Racists: Colour-Blind Racism and the Persistence of Racial Inequality in America*, 5th ed. (London: Rowan and Littlefield, 2017).
[100] Jictar's ratings, *The Stage and Television Today* (Archive: 1959–1994); 5 June 1975; 4912.
[101] Jictar's ratings, *The Stage and Television Today* (Archive: 1959–1994); 29 June 1978; 5072.
[102] Martin Jackson, 'Has That Old Black Magic Gone and Lost its Spell?', *Daily Mail*, 16 July 1977, 13. *The Black and White Minstrel Show* was never investigated by the Race Relations Board as media fell outside of its purview.

age that never was, and a nostalgia beyond memory' and reassurance for white viewers that a show built on nostalgia for a simpler time could continue on and on undisturbed. White viewers could listen to old show standards and be entertained by a type of performance and racial pleasure that was frozen in time. The blacking up at the heart of it and the implications for modern racial representation and race relations merited barely a mention in the article beyond the one reference to the Race Relations Board in the subheading except by George Mitchell himself: 'The black make-up, which offends no one, enables you to do outrageous things with the lads that you could never get away with if you could see their faces.' While acknowledging that the minstrels could do 'outrageous things' with the make-up of blackness on Mitchell maintained that no one was offended by it. Black audiences were silenced in this statement and the article as a whole.

Mitchell did go on in the article to engage in an oblique way with some of the criticisms of the show, that it portrayed Black people as silly and infantile, by defending the manliness of his performers: 'How else could a lot of sequinned fellows prance around and still look manly ... They are also the beefiest and toughest-looking dancers on any TV show.'[103] Any inference that these were effeminate, childlike dancers was rejected by Mitchell who was happy to talk about the skill involved while still staunchly rejecting any possible offence that the blacking up could cause. Both the *Daily Mail* and Mitchell himself did not acknowledge the changes in race relations and indeed in audience understandings of racism that may have contributed to the decline of the minstrel's fortunes at the BBC. Mitchell was himself an institution by 1977, and the show's appeal with some audiences continued to persist. The *Daily Mail*, continuing its defence of the show in the age of tabloidisation went so far as to name the programme its 'pick of the day' on television on 21 July 1978 when it played at 7.45pm on BBC1. Yet this was as far as the paper went in endorsing the continuation of the programme at that point. For the most part, *The Black and White Minstrel Show* slipped off screens, and with hardly a murmur from the Audience Research Department at the BBC which tended to pay particular attention to the final broadcast of other long-standing series such as *Z-Cars* and *Dixon of Dock Green* in its weekly standard audience research reports. While the end of *Dixon of Dock Green* had prompted a reflection on current audience figures and audience responses as a last farewell, the end of *The Black and White Minstrel Show* (which outlived the other two programmes) did not merit a revisit.

[103] Ibid.

The silence around *The Black and White Minstrel Show*'s end was, no doubt, due to an increased discomfort among BBC executives and viewers that accompanied a dawning understanding within the media that anti-Black racism could be defined more broadly than it had been in Britain up to that point and that there was a new approach worth exploring on the small screen. On Good Friday, April 1977, Alex Haley's *Roots*, the popular six-part miniseries produced by the American broadcaster ABC and based on Haley's novel about multiple generations of a family grappling with enslavement and its legacy in the United States, debuted on BBC1 to enthusiasm amongst both audiences and critics. The *Daily Express*'s James Murray pointed out, 'For once, a dominantly white audience has to consider the Negro as something more than a comic appendage or a background hanger-on in TV drama,'[104] The *Times* critic Fred Emery praised *Roots*' unique presentation of Black people on screen noting 'The blacks in *Roots* are clever as well.'[105] The *Daily Express*'s Murray ultimately claimed 'The great impact of "Roots", the American saga on BBC 1 over Easter weekend is the revelation of the black man as a hero.'[106] This was a new form of 'race' on screen in Britain, with compelling acting by a Black cast and with no blacking up in sight. Such representations were building upon other successful American programmes featuring primarily Black casts, including the weekly comedy series *The Jeffersons* (CBS 1975–1985). The following year in 1978 those involved in television production and broadcasting in Britain were increasingly brought into discussion about racism; learning about it, contesting it and also often denying the role of media in contributing to racialised thinking among white British audiences.

Just weeks after *The Black and White Minstrel Show* ceased broadcasting in 1978, the annual Edinburgh International Television Festival featured panels on 'Race' and 'Stereotyping' that brought these new ways of thinking more firmly into the sphere of production and industry events. The panel on 'Stereotyping' was reported on in outlets beyond the trade magazines such as *The Times* with a headline: 'Jokes About Irishmen Not Funny to TV Writers'. The debate about whether jokes

---

[104] James Murray, 'A New Lesson: Black is Noble', *Daily Express*, 12 April 1977, 17.
[105] Fred Emery. 'TV history of slavery sets viewing records', *Times*, 17 February 1977, 6.
[106] Murray, 'A New Lesson: Black is Noble'. For more on the British response to *Roots*, see Martin Stollery, 'The Same, but a Step Removed: Aspects of the British Reception of Roots', in Erica L. Ball, Kellie Carter Jackson and Henry Louis Gates Jr., eds. *Reconsidering Roots: Race, Politics, and Memory* (Athens, GA: University of Georgia Press, 2017. The Audience Research Department also conducted a survey of British responses to the programme almost a year after it was broadcast, An Audience Research Report, 'A Study of British Viewers' Reactions to the "Roots" Series', BBC, February 1978, R9/788/1, VR/78/029.

defused anxieties about certain issues and communities, which was the well-worn argument of Johnny Speight and Vince Cable and the racial sitcoms they helmed, came up against a new critique: 'Several speakers made a distinction between jokes about oppressors and jokes about oppressed.' The newspaper coverage quoted John Bowen, writer of the television series *Rock Follies*, who argued 'Comedy that diminishes the already powerless, I find despicable and increasingly obscene.'[107] *The Black and White Minstrel Show* was also mentioned by Brian Winston, a journalist and academic in the still relatively new field of mass communications, who pointed out the shame of the show's existence in 1978:

> It was appalling, he said, to find programmes like *The Black and White Minstrel Show* or *Mind Your Language* being broadcast in a multi-racial society under strain, when what they did was reinforce stereotypes of black and brown people as being loveable but ridiculous. Producers of comedy in those sensitive areas needed to exercise a greater degree of care.[108]

For Winston these programmes were baffling, offensive and a site of embarrassment and shame; indeed this is how more and more producers and viewers such as him and Bowen were characterising the racial stereotyping on British screens. The session on 'Race' was also fraught with varied opinions including a magistrate in the crowd who felt along with his friends that there were 'far too many' Black and south Asians on the screen and the Indian-British actor Mardav Sharma who noted that his name alone had prevented him from access to roles in Britain, arguing to the producers in the room: 'What I am saying is that you are driving people like me, whom V.S. Naipaul would quite rightly describe as mimic men and who fell for the con that a middle class lad with a background of public school and university would be all right, to extremism.'[109] *The Times* noted that Sharma was told after the panel by two people 'in a position to give him work' that 'He had perhaps gone over the top and in his speech, which wouldn't do him any more favours in finding work.' The panel included critiques by Gerry Hines, head of the BBC Asian Programme Unit, of the argument that 'there is no talent' as justification for the lack of Black and south Asian staff in production positions: 'That there is no talent is too easy. After all, we've promoted enough whites who have little enough talent.'[110] Even Peter Ansorge, the

---

[107] Michael Church, 'Jokes About Irishmen Not Funny to TV Writers', *The Times*, 30 August 1978, 2.
[108] Ibid. Brian Winston was a tireless campaigner against racism in the media throughout his academic career.
[109] RACE Broadcast (Archive: 1973–2000); 11 September 1978, 979; *Entertainment Industry Magazine* Archive, 20
[110] Ibid., 21.

white producer of the television programme *Empire Road* on BBC, noted that 'it was difficult for white writers to write about West Indian domestic scenes because they have no experience of them'. He then went on to argue rather tangentially that it was also difficult to find young Asian actresses willing to kiss a man on screen.

These conversations in 1978 were contentious and fraught with little in the form of solutions offered but a certain consensus did seem to emerge that what was being broadcast on 'race' on British television was insufficient. As Gerry Hynes surmised, 'We are in charge of the most powerful, most persuasive medium in history and what are we doing? We're doing *Curry and Chips* and *Love Thy Neighbour*.'[111] This frustration and increasingly evident discomfort were part and parcel of the media industry beginning to shift its understanding ever so slightly of how stereotypes functioned. Tim Cotton, the Controller of the BBC, also pointed to the most vital issue that had been overlooked by the BBC for decades as he maintained the decision that *The Black and White Minstrel Show* be taken off the air and in the face of fans protesting its departure: 'It's all very well people who are not black saying "I didn't think about it that way", but that by then, the perspectives of "the people who are black" also mattered.'[112] Black audiences and their protests and disgust with the long-running programme were in the last moments of the show acknowledged and cited as a reason for its departure even if this audience, as we shall see in Chapter 6, was consistently ignored by audience research in the corporation. In 1979, a year after *The Black and White Minstrel Show* disappeared from British screens, Stuart Hall and the Campaign Against Racism in Media (CARM) would bring their arguments to the viewing public on BBC's 'Open Door' through the documentary 'It Ain't Half Racist Mum' as they tried to help the ordinary British viewer see racism in the current broadcast offerings.[113] The programme seemed to have little immediate impact and the minstrel's departure was rather offset by the touring version's ongoing and deep popularity into the 1980s in seaside towns and music halls across the UK. If television was increasingly willing to entertain Black audiences and the changing racial attitudes of white audiences as a driving force, pantomime theatre and its audiences seemed to reject such shifts in thinking.

---

[111] Ibid., 20.
[112] www.bbc.com/historyofthebbc/100-voices/people-nation-empire/make-yourself-at-home/the-black-and-white-minstrel-show.
[113] Gavin Schaffer, 'What's Behind the Open Door? Talking Back on Race in Public Access Broadcasting', in *The Vision of a Nation*.

## Conclusion

The ongoing presence of blackface and minstrelsy on both British film and television in the twentieth century indicates the role that film producers and organisations such as the BBFC, BBC and ITV played in shaping the inability of ordinary white Britons to acknowledge racism. The broadcasting of 'traditional' wholesome pleasures of blacking up televised on a weekly basis for 20 years until 1978, when *The Black and White Minstrel Show* went off the air, and buttressed by other material discussed here that pre-dated the existence of *The Black and White Minstrel Show* ultimately silenced discussions of racism in screen culture and society more widely under the guise of colour-blindness. Black and south Asian people who were asked to deny or more rarely affirm minstrelsy and blacking up as racist were thus burdened with the task of naming racism to organisations and audiences who clearly did not want to name it as such and were highly defensive of this custom. Identifying blackface as racist prompted the cries of white audiences and producers who denied or resented both the authority of immigrants of colour to name British customs as problematic and who denied their own central roles as a majority white audience catered to by a media which was itself highly dependent on the appeal of racialised screen content to audiences. Efforts by *Flamingo*, CARD and others to acknowledge anti-Black racism in screen culture were accompanied from the late 1960s onwards by complaints within media organisations and the press about an emergent language of political correctness which further characterised Britain's own audiences of colour as a highly sensitive minority that suffered from seeing race everywhere. The next chapter discusses this accusation in greater detail.

This popular custom of blacking up on British screens was largely untouched by discussions in the 1970s about the responsibility of television to the shaping of audience prejudices, something which will be discussed in Chapter 6. Further entreaties from the 1960s by Sir Learie Constantine and others to increase the presence of racial minorities on screen as actors seemed to have little effect. By 1972 a confidential report produced for the BBC's Audience Research Department by an American academic, Professor Bradley S. Greenberg of Michigan State University, entitled 'Non-Whites in British Television' showed a woeful lack of racial diversity on British television as measured over a week's viewing in 1971. The report's aim was to gather data because it admitted that 'both the BBC and the ITV have been approached by groups advocating greater presentation of non-whites on television [and] no meaningful data exist as to the current practice'. Just 0.04 per cent of the actors in drama, variety and feature film programming were identified as 'non-white' in comparison to a Black and minority ethnic population at the time that was stated in the report as 2.5 per cent.[114] Of this 0.04 per cent representation, the majority were actors in American shows which included Hawaiians featured in *Hawaii Five-0*, broadcast on ITV at the time, and the overwhelming majority of these existing roles were identified as non-speaking. The minstrels were not included, nor was the blacking up evident among other programmes at the time. White British people in blackface may have felt they were embodying blackness but the visiting American academic in 1971 did not feel compelled to measure this as such. Blacking up allowed a largely white screen culture to remain as such throughout the 1950s to the 1980s and allowed audiences that could not and would not see racism to continue to consume on-screen pleasures that were in fact highly racist.

---

[114] R78/2,538/1 'Programmes for Racial Minority: General' An Audience Research Report (Confidential) VR/72/56, 16.02.72 'Non-Whites in British Television', WAC.

# 5 'Too Touchy'
Black Audiences and the Racialised Everyday in the Post-war Black 'Glossies'

In October 1961, the team at the recently launched glossy magazine *Flamingo* used their second editorial to argue that the magazine represented the overlooked 'Coloured Voice' in Britain:

> The white papers of Fleet Street and the rest of Britain do not cater for the Black man – for all aspects of his life. They splash him on their pages only when he is a problem; only when he is 'popped' with drugs; or running a noisy backstreet club; or when he has run foul of the law. In other words, the picture of the coloured man is it appears in the white Press is not one that will cause his white neighbours to love him. He will be looked upon as a nuisance; as someone who is not wanted and sometimes, which can be worse, someone to laugh at.[1]

This built on the approach outlined in the inaugural September issue which introduced *Flamingo* as 'A Negro Voice' within a sea of white voices in post-war Britain. *Flamingo* claimed that 'up until now these Negro citizens of Britain have been denied a Voice' and arguing that 'most newspapers and periodicals in this country present a prejudiced and harmful view of them'.[2] By the October issue, *Flamingo's* editor, Dominica-born Edward Scobie, was able to celebrate *Flamingo's* early success noting that the 20,000 copies printed for the first issue had sold out in the UK, and a further 15,000 had been sold abroad. For Scobie this vindicated not only the success of the magazine and its voice but also his involvement in similar ventures in England since 1948. As a doctoral student in history Scobie had contributed to or edited many publications for Black readers that this chapter examines, including *Checkers* (1948–1949), *Bronze* (1954–1955), *Tropic* (1960) and *Flamingo* (1961–1965), all of which ran alongside better-known ventures such as the *West Indian Gazette* (1958–1965) edited by Claudia Jones. *Bronze* had taken a similar approach to *Flamingo* in identifying the desire for Black readers to engage with a space for their voice with one of its more well

---

[1] 'Coloured Voice', *Flamingo* (October 1961), 1.
[2] 'Editorial', *Flamingo* (September 1961), 1.

known contributors, the African-American choreographer Buddy Bradley, outlining both their imagined audience of the magazine and what the editorial team thought that audience most wanted to read about: 'We are going to keep you posted on the activities of all the coloured people associated with the show business in general'.[3] This was a magazine for Black readers wanting to know about Black talent in Britain and how and where to support them.

Yet as the *Flamingo* editorial from October 1961 indicated, producing a magazine in post-war Britain that spoke for and to audiences of colour was no easy task. These magazines were produced specifically for Black West Indian and African audiences in a publishing climate that 'did not cater for the Black man' and largely ignored Black audiences as Buddy Bradley had pointed out in the pages of *Bronze* in 1954. The perspectives and wants of Black audiences were largely invisible to the dominant white press, making the production of magazines such as *Flamingo* welcome within Black British communities but also fraught with heavy expectations and the burdens of speech within this context. The exact reach and impact of these magazines remains difficult to gauge. While their letters pages and editors' introductions spoke of success and a reach within and without England, the short publishing lives of each of these magazines, barring *Flamingo*, indicate the difficulties of speaking to and for audiences of colour in the post-war period. Yet it is in these magazines which share similar publishing styles and preoccupations that we see audiences of colour spoken to and engaged with by Black authors and editors. Black audiences were imagined and acknowledged in these pages as interested in film, television, theatre, history, music, politics, fashion and the local spaces of London where these magazines were published.

These magazines presented a Black perspective and a Black understanding of racism in relation to film and television and popular culture more broadly and were adjacent but never entirely divorced from discussions of politics. The perspectives of the glossies offered both Black and white readers an alternative framework of knowledge of post-war race relations and British media, one where Britain too had a 'race problem' and where racism was experienced and acknowledged by Black people. The content of these periodicals also elevated Black audiences as avid consumers of media in all its forms. The pages offered readers a rereading of the dominant narratives in white media and screen culture and identified the racist tropes and stereotypes at work in these – that Black figure, as *Flamingo* noted on Fleet Street coverage, 'as a problem',

---

[3] Buddy Bradley, 'Entertainment', *Bronze* 1, no. 1 (June 1954), 20.

'popped with drugs' or 'foul of the law'. While the scarce social-problem films and television of the late 1950s and 1960s were busy constructing the figure of the racist on screen as embodying only extreme, physical acts of racist violence most often associated with the US, the glossies relayed a racialisation of Britain's Black community as an everyday occurrence blindly and unthinkingly pursued by ordinary white Britons. These magazines present a different narrative, or story, about the experiences of Black Britons in Britain and their knowledge of daily racism at work in the country. Even though this story ran counter to what many white Britons were willing to acknowledge as a reality for Black people in the country, these magazines offered a powerful space where that account came to the forefront. The features in the glossies merged an analysis of anti-Black racism within white media and the everyday and attention to Black success as a counterpoint to these. These magazines identified Black success in broad ways that included Black men and women working across the entertainment world, but also as both ordinary and extraordinary Black Britons working and getting by in contemporary Britain.

The editorials, features and letters to the editors in these magazines also spoke of the emotional impact of racism within the media on Black audiences. As noted above, *Flamingo's* second editorial stated frankly that the image of the Black man in the white press was 'not one that will cause his white neighbours to love him'. This was a particular, local environment of emotional meaning for the Black immigrant in Britain where the Black man or woman was not 'wanted' by white neighbours and would sometimes be laughed at, 'which can be worse', because of popular representations in the white media. While the BBC and ITV hesitated to argue that images on the screen directly influenced audience behaviour, contributors to the Black 'glossies' discussed here were less reluctant to make these connections. The impact of racist imagery on Black Britons was clearly articulated again and again in publications surveyed in this chapter as part of the daily life of the immigrant of colour. Strain, stress, frustration, exhaustion, anger and what has been called 'racial battle fatigue' by William Smith were articulated repeatedly throughout the pages of the magazines that I examine here.[4] The

---

[4] The psychologist William Smith has discussed racial battle fatigue as a feature of Black people living in historically white spaces, a perspective that has been taken up in critical race theory. William A. Smith, et al., '"You Make Me Wanna Holler and Throw Up Both My Hands!" Campus Culture, Black Misandric Microaggressions, and Racial Battle Fatigue', *International Journal of Qualitative Studies in Education* 29, no. 9 (2016) 1189–1209. See Nicola Rollock's excellent work on this in the UK context; Nicola Rollock, '"I Would Have Become Wallpaper Had Racism Had Its Way": Black Female

emotional turmoil of relating to and resisting racist ideology is something that has gained attention as a contemporary phenomenon yet is seldom investigated as a historic experience. In these magazines post-war racism in Britain, and screen culture in particular, was openly spoken of, navigated, rejected and bargained with as the writers of these periodicals and the readers who wrote into them traversed an environment that saw openly racist attitudes towards immigrants coincide with an emergent discourse of liberal colour-blindness that brought its own emotional burdens. The persistent intrusion of white voices into these magazines in the form of letters to the editors or the invited contributions of white authors likewise highlights the privileges and freedoms that white Britons claimed when commenting on Black emotional expression in post-war Britain. This freedom by white people to examine Black emotional expression, in fact, formed a vital plank of the colour-blind racism of post-war Britain.

## 5.1  Voices of Colour and Black Agency

Before proceeding further it is worth reflecting on the role of this chapter in the book and its larger story. While Black and racialised audiences have been discussed in the previous chapters, this is the sole chapter that examines media authored by Black people and which spoke explicitly to Black audiences. It is tempting when examining the magazines at the centre of this chapter to situate these Black voices as pushing against or resisting the predominantly white media landscape that I have so far outlined and which privileged the racialised perspectives of white British audiences. I initially approached this chapter through a traditional social history framework that situated Black and south Asian audiences and voices as exercising a type of agency within twentieth-century media environments. Yet as I grappled with this material and the broader contours of this racialised screen culture I reconsidered the position of these voices and the very concept of Black agency. The pervasive expressions of casual racism on screen outlined in the previous chapters, alongside the wilful racial ignorance that underpinned decisions by producers and regulators to cater to both imagined and demonstrated audience racism, caused me to re-evaluate the usefulness of the term 'agency'. The identification of agency within such a deeply racialised environment of screen culture seems inadequate in the face of both the daily lived experience of Black subjects as a demographic minority in

Professors, Racial Battle Fatigue, and Strategies for Surviving Higher Education', *Peabody Journal of Education* 96, no. 2 (2021): 206–217.

post-war Britain and the position of a powerful and predominantly white British media within this.

Here I revisit Walter Johnson's essay on agency.[5] Working in the field of slavery studies, Johnson points out that historians have been too eager to equate and align Black agency primarily with resistance. This equation Johnson cautions invokes a particular liberal subject or community in the past that strove against all odds finding various moments and strategies to push back in the way that historians tend to *want* their subjects to push back. Johnson notes that this particular type of liberal subject defined by their pursuit of humanity and their striving are ones that are also most easily imagined and sought out by white historians such as myself, working in a field dominated by white academics. Saidiya Hartman and Marisa Fuentes have also both noted this impulse as a central component of the historiography of enslavement.[6] Displacing class as the primary lens through which agency was first imagined, Johnson argues that the particular constraints of societies that social history has imagined since the 1960s has not always sufficiently acknowledged the daily conditions of Blackness informed by racialising structures at work.[7] Elevating stories of subjects that pushed back social history thus threatens to overlook the dense web at work in daily life that circumscribes agency for Black and ethnic minority actors and communities in the past. Johnson's critique offers us a valuable means of moving beyond what I see as insufficient frameworks within social history for discussing the lives of Black audiences and the Black everyday that were outlined in these magazines. These frameworks of 'resistance' threaten to diminish the very experience of the everyday as a form of success unto itself for racialised people.

The stories that were highlighted in the Black press that is at the centre of this chapter are stories of a Black every day that is often overlooked in favour of examinations of political movements or moments of conflict. In light of this emphasis, it is worth revisiting the concept of 'counter-storytelling' within critical race theory that I discussed in Chapter 2. That chapter concentrated on individual

---

[5] Walter Johnson, 'On Agency', *Journal of Social History* (Fall 2003): 113–124.
[6] Marisa J. Fuentes, *Dispossessed Lives: Enslaved Women, Violence, and the Archive* (Philadelphia: University of Pennsylvania Press, 2016); Saidiya V. Hartman, *Scenes of Subjection: Terror, Slavery, and Self-making in Nineteenth-Century America* (Oxford: Oxford University Press, 1997).
[7] Lucy Delap considers related points, and Johnson's essay, when discussing working-class women; see Lucy Delap, 'Agency and Domestic Workers', in Nitin Sinha and Nitin Varma, eds., *Servants' Pasts: Late Eighteenth to Twentieth-Century South Asia*, Vol. 2 (Hyderabad: Orient BlackSwan, 2019), 265–278.

protests by audiences of colour against racist film content that was scattered across the press, only occasionally encompassing powerful story-tellers in their own right such as Paul Robeson or the collective responses of audience who laughed at this content. These efforts attempted to rewrite what was seen as not racist to white audiences as eminently racist to audiences of colour viewing them. In the current chapter I examine the sustained efforts of Black people living in Britain to author and present their own stories of their experience of the everyday within the Black press as a response to what critical race theory calls 'majoritarian' story-telling.[8] Counter-storytelling points to the invisible assumptions that inform and uphold the majoritarian storytelling and allows the overlooked experiences of racialised people to come to the fore. In this case, the counter-storytelling in the glossies provided an alternative narrative of Britain tied to different experiences of a time and place by racialised people. In the historians' toolkit, counter-storytelling asks us not to only consider new actors within an existing story but rather to consider the very foundations of that story in favour of a new one altogether. In this chapter, Black-authored publications present an alternative story, and crucially an alternative framework of knowledge, about British media, society and empire. This alternative framework of knowledge was deeply rooted in the repetitive experiences of racism in the post-war period documented in these magazines but also in demonstrated understandings by Black authors and letter writers of the longer histories of white media representation of Blackness. The Black readers and writers of these magazines were drawing on and developing their own study or taxonomy of white people and their pleasures and prejudices. Counter-storytelling in the magazines was also attentive to the emotional labour involved in experiencing an alternative understanding of media and society. Working from this perspective I am struck by a description of the Black everyday that the psychiatrist Chester M. Pierce coined in 1974 to capture the daily experience of racism among African Americans in the US.[9] Pierce referred to the experience of Black Americans living with everyday racism, small and large, as living within a 'mundane extreme environment'. Historic film and television in Britain with its repetitive and casual racism also strikes me as embodying a type of 'mundane extreme

---

[8] Danile Solórzano and Tara Yosso, 'Critical Race Methodology: Counter-storytelling as an Analytical Framework for Research', *Qualitative Inquiry* 8, no. 1 (2002): 23–44; Richard Delgado and Jean Stefancic, *Critical Race Theory: An Introduction* (United Kingdom: New York University Press, 2012).

[9] Chester M. Pierce, 'Psychiatric Problems of the Black Minority', in S. Arieti, ed., *American Handbook of Psychiatry* (New York: Basic Books, 1974): 512–523.

environment' that was part of the twentieth-century Black everyday that historians such as Kennetta Hammond Perry, Radhika Natarajan, Kieran Connell and Stephen Brooke have also explored.[10]

This chapter examines the alternative world of British screen culture that was presented in the pages of the Black press and the expressed emotions that accompanied this unveiling for Black audiences. The chapter's explicit focus on Black audiences builds upon Rob Waters' account of the impact of televised images of the Black Power movement on both Black and white audiences in Britain in 1968 and engages with scholarship on Black television viewers in the US.[11] It must be stressed, however, that there is no need to perform a Thompsonian 'rescue' of Black television audiences in post-war Britain as an absent audience within the archive as Black audiences attempted to make themselves visible over and over again to producers and regulators of screen culture. This chapter further concentrates on the emotional work done by Black audiences and writers in the pages of *Checkers*, *Bronze*, *Flamingo* and *Tropic* as they steered through the everyday of a highly racialised post-war British media from the 1940s into the 1960s. This focus contributes to the developing field of the history of emotions which, as I have noted, currently offers rather unsatisfying and even problematic engagements with racialised communities. I am deeply reluctant to apply existing terminology in that field which includes language of 'emotional practices', 'emotional cultures' and 'emotional communities' to Black and minority ethnic communities whose experience of racial discrimination, we shall see, was bound up in pseudo-scientific concepts of Black people as 'naturally' emotional. Thus my discussions in this chapter largely rely upon the methodologies of critical race theory instead to examine the type of boundary-work that white readers imposed on Black feelings and the related efforts of Black readers and writers to navigate this.

---

[10] See chapter 4, 'Leisure and Sociability: The Black Everyday', in Kieran Connell, ed., *Black Handsworth: Race in 1980s Britain* (Berkeley: University of California Press, 2019); Stephen Brooke, 'Space, Emotions and the Everyday: The Affective Ecology of 1980s London', *Twentieth Century British History* 28, no 1 (2017): 110–142; Kennetta Hammond Perry, *London is the Place for Me: Black Britons, Citizenship and the Politics of Race* (Oxford: Oxford University Press, 2016), Radhika Natarajan, forthcoming monograph. I am also indebted to Adele Perry and Mary Jane Local McCallum's discussion of the indigenous everyday in *Structures of Indifference: An Indigenous Life and Death in a Canadian City* (Winnipeg: University of Manitoba Press, 2018).

[11] Rob Waters, 'Black Power on the Telly: America, Television, and Race in 1960s and 1970s Britain'. *Journal of British Studies* 54, no. 4 (2015): 947–970; Beretta E. Smith-Shomade, ed., *Watching While Black: Centring the Television of Black Audiences* (New Brunswick: Rutgers University Press, 2012).

## 5.2 A 'Short-lived Fate': Black Glossies and Post-war Publishing

The Black magazines that this chapter examines span a seventeen-year period, from 1948 after the arrival of the *Windrush* to 1965 when both *Flamingo* and Claudia Jones's *West Indian Gazette* ceased publication. Multiple publications emerged within this period. Donald Hinds, former staff-writer at the *West Indian Gazette*, described post-war Black publishing as consisting of a mix of newsletters for various civil rights organisations such as *Keys* (the newsletter for Harold Moody's League for Coloured People), the *West Indian Gazette* following on from other smaller ventures such as *Magnet*, and finally, the 'glossies' which were often in colour and featured photography. Hinds noted that the latter 'made their appearance simultaneously' with the more overtly political Black publications.[12] The work of Claudia Jones at the *West Indian Gazette* has been well documented by Marika Sherwood, Hammond Perry and Bill Schwarz among others with relatively little attention paid to the glossies barring some excellent work by Naomi Oppenheim.[13] Alongside these magazines and newspapers were other ventures by Black publishers including New Beacon Books, formed in 1966, and Bogle L'Ouverture formed in 1968.[14] This chapter primarily focuses on four post-war glossies that Hinds characterised as not 'overtly political' but which nevertheless featured a mixed focus on politics and the entertainment world. Historians have by and large approached what Waters calls the 'Black political press' in the spirit of Hinds' assessment, as a marginal expression of that which emerged in the 1960s.[15] Publications such as *Black Voice*, the *West Indies Observer*, *Link*, and *Magnet* mapped out a political network at work through the movement of various writers

---

[12] Donald Hinds, 'The West Indian Gazette: Claudia Jones and the Black Press in Britain', *Race & Class: A Journal on Racism, Empire and Globalisation* 50, no. 1 (2008): 88–97.
[13] Marika Sherwood, *Claudia Jones: A Life in Exile* (London: Lawrence and Wishart, 2000); Bill Schwarz, 'Claudia Jones and the West Indian Gazette: Reflections on the Emergence of Post-colonial Britain', *Twentieth Century British History* 14, no. 3 (2003): 264–285; Perry, *London is the Place for Me*. On the glossies, see Naomi Oppenheim, 'Popular History in the Black British Press: Edward Scobie's *Tropic* and *Flamingo*, 1960–64', *Immigrants & Minorities* 37, no. 3 (2019): 136–162. Oppenheim's AHRC PhD project also supported the digitisation of part of the first issue of *Flamingo* for the British Library.
[14] Colin A. Beckles, '"We Shall Not Be Terrorized Out of Existence": The Political Legacy of England's Black Bookshops', *Journal of Black Studies* 29, no. 1 (1998): 51–72; Natalie Thomlinson, '"Second-Wave" Black Feminist Periodicals in Britain.' *Women: A Cultural Review* 27, no. 4 (2016): 432–445; Karen Sands-O'Connor, *Children's Publishing and Black Britain, 1965–2015* (London: Palgrave, 2017).
[15] Rob Waters, *Thinking Black: Britain, 1964–1985* (Berkeley: University of California Press, 2018), 61.

and activists in meetings and campaigns and in their editorials. The glossies, on the other hand, have consistently been overlooked in this mapping even as they participated in this and shared a mutual interest in identifying and speaking to Black audiences that saw culture as deeply political. Historians working on Jones's *West Indian Gazette*, for example, rarely acknowledge that the paper regularly featured coverage of the Black entertainment world. Although this coverage could be dismissed as lighthearted distraction within the *West Indian Gazette*, these magazines' focus on the entertainment world engaged with and developed the persistent argument among Black Britons that representation mattered.

What connects this range of publications was not only their audience and the time period in which they emerged but also the very real difficulties they faced in making it into their readers' hands. These magazines were published in London and sometimes only lasted for a half dozen, usually monthly, issues before folding. They were available at booksellers and magazine sellers willing to carry them at a range of prices, from 1s6d for both *Checkers* (released in 1948) and *Flamingo* (released in 1961); 1s for *Bronze*'s debut in 1954; and the short-lived *Tropic* cost 2s6d per monthly issue in 1960. Many, however, featured letters to the editor that stressed the international reach of subscribers in the Caribbean and elsewhere. Most of the opening editorials also maintained a patter of success for their readers that only occasionally acknowledged the difficulties facing these editors. Yet they all faced challenges in terms of production, circulation and durability. Hinds noted that even the *West Indian Gazette*, the most successful and long-running of these publications, often could not cobble together the £100 it needed to pay the printer.[16] The second issue of *Checkers*, self-identified in 1948 by editor J. Y. Lovegreen as 'the first Magazine of its kind to our knowledge to be published in this country', was frank about the publication challenges it faced and its hopes for a smoother production in the future:[17]

The first copy of this journal was printed under great difficulties, inadequate premises, obsolete machinery, lack of staff and many other essentials which are necessary for launching such an organ. Gradually, however, we will be able to equip ourselves with better machinery, and with the thought always with us that we are really doing something worthwhile, each month will bring new improvements.[18]

*Checkers* was printed in black and white throughout its five issues dating from July 1948 to December of the same year, but its mix of news from

---

[16] Hinds, 'The West Indian Gazette', 95.
[17] 'Editorial', *Checkers* 1, no. 1 (July 1948), 5.
[18] 'Editorial', *Checkers* 1, no. 2 (October 1948), 2.

the Black community in Britain and abroad, its focus on entertainment and use of photography throughout, and a cover photo consistently featuring a Black actor or celebrity was a template that future magazines would follow. When *Bronze* launched in June 1954 and published six issues, ending with the April–May issue of 1955, the magazine seemed to have acquired, at least temporarily, a white editor even as its contributors were primarily Black, including Edward Scobie and Buddy Bradley, himself well-connected in Hollywood.[19] *Bronze* was also printed in black and white but relied more heavily on photographs including press images from films such as the American musical *Carmen Jones* (1954), which featured a primarily Black cast led by Dorothy Dandridge and Harry Belafonte, and British film company Rank's 'Mau Mau movie' *Simba* from 1955.[20] The story on *Simba* featured five still photos from the film; three featuring Bermudan actor Earl Cameron and the other two also featuring Black actors from the film. The publication had good connections with the Black Hollywood community and Black writers such as Scobie in London as well. *Bronze's* ties to the entertainment world were not enough, however, to combat the publication difficulties that most Black magazines faced. *Bronze's* penultimate issue countered the cynical view of some readers that it was merely out for profit with a swift rejoinder: 'If anyone would like to come to the *Bronze* office and present us with a cheque to cover the considerable financial loss on each issue, plus a reasonable profit, then they will be at liberty to say we are publishing *Bronze* to make money!'[21]

When *Bronze* was followed in March 1960 by the debut of *Tropic*, Edward Scobie was now at the helm as co-editor, alongside Patrick Williams, for the magazine's duration of eleven issues which ended in December 1960. The magazine's cover was in colour, and after that first issue regularly featured a Black 'cover girl'. *Tropic* was rather more political in its outlook than *Bronze* with stories on independence movements in several African countries and the colour-bar in Britain, alongside regular coverage of film, theatre and music; historical subjects (usually produced by Scobie); short stories by emerging Black authors such as Samuel Selvon; and occasional discussions of clothing and

---

[19] Stephen Bourne, 'Buddy Bradley and Elisabeth Welch: Harlem Comes to London', in *Black in the British Frame: The Black Experience in British Film and Television*, 2nd ed. (London: Bloomsbury Press, 2001), 47–58; Sean Mayes and Sarah K. Whitfield, 'Clarence "Buddy" Bradley and Clarence Robinson', in *An Inconvenient Black History of British Musical Theatre 1900–1950* (London: Bloomsbury, 2021).

[20] *Bronze* 1, no. 5, February–March (1955), 'Mau Mau Movie', *Bronze*, 1, no. 3 (October–November 1954).

[21] 'Editorial', *Bronze* 1, no. 5 (February–March 1955), 3.

recipes. *Tropic* also focused increasingly on television in Britain, a focus which *Flamingo* (with Scobie now as Editor in Chief alongside Ellis Komey, a Ghanaian writer, as Assistant Editor) would also take up when it was first published in September 1961. *Flamingo* proved to be the most enduring success of these magazines, publishing almost monthly for six years and even after Scobie stepped down as editor in January 1964 and took up the position of contributing author instead.[22] The second volume of *Flamingo* included a weary acknowledgement in the letter bag that this was not the first venture aimed at Black audiences with a reader stating that 'I read the first issue with much enjoyment and I hope you will keep up the good work ... I only hope your magazine does not suffer the short-lived fate of the many coloured magazines that have from time to time appeared in Britain.'[23] Magazine publication for Black audiences was not an easy venture.

As these magazines struggled to maintain a regular publishing schedule and move beyond a five- or six-month lifespan, the visibility of this Black voice in print in Britain was nevertheless bringing new and troubling challenges in the form of violent responses by organisations and individuals. The front window of the London offices of *Tropic* was pierced by what appeared to be a bullet in the summer of 1960. A description of the event and a black and white photo of the window were published in the September 1960 issue with a statement by the publishing team that explicitly tied the attack to tense race relations in Britain: 'These attacks do not only occur in places like South Africa and the American Southern States. They can happen right here in London. And they do. Just take a look at the editorial picture and you'll see for yourself.' The night's events and the police response were laid out for *Tropic's* readers:

The police were called. The Managing Director (Charles I. Ross) of *Tropic* was contacted. After taking a formal statement, the police left, saying they'd report the matter for investigation. To date nothing has happened. We, of the *Tropic* office, like the thousands of coloured people all over Britain are worried. We feel it's time the police did something so that coloured people in this country won't keep saying: 'The police are not on our side, man'.[24]

The fragility of the publication's position was emphasised in this moment as part of the wider fragility facing Britain's Black community who identified violence as racist to a police force largely unwilling to

---

[22] 'Edward Scobie', *Flamingo* 3, no. 5 (January 1964), 2.
[23] 'Letters', *Flamingo* (October 1961), 2.
[24] 'Coloured People and the Police', *Tropic* (September 1960), 3.

acknowledge it as such.²⁵ Subsequent issues did not report on any follow-up to the incident by the time the magazine ended in December of that year.

When *Flamingo* emerged not long after *Tropic* ceased publishing, the magazine's editors and publishing team were also subject to harassment which the magazine again brought to the attention of readers as a vital counter-narrative to the relative invisibility of white nationalism in the media in early 1960s Britain. After *Flamingo* ran a piece on white nationalist organisations in Britain in its very first issue of September 1961 titled 'The Lunatic Fringe', the offices received a letter in December postmarked from Waco, Texas, claiming to represent the 'Aryan Knights Ku Klux Klan of Britain' identified in the article. Directed to 'My dear Black Savage', the letter professed a growing membership and stated:

> Many groups have turned to us for help, and we are training them patience [sic] to wait for that DAY when by a combined effort, we will drive the Black brother crawlers from the shores of Britain. It is said that fire purifies and we intend to purify. Perhaps your office is high on the list. Have you heard of one Black bas […] called Kelso Cochrane?²⁶

The reference to Kelso Cochrane's death at the hands of a number of white youths in Notting Hill in 1959, an event that London police refused to label as racist, was claimed by the letter writer as the work of the Klan and in conjunction with police. The writer further invoked the recent anti-colonial struggle in Kenya: 'What did the police do? They did not help the foul-mouthed Mau Mau oath taker. They turned their head the other way. You have been warned – Black Jungle Brute. We act Fast.' The letter combined diverse occurrences such as colonial uprisings in Kenya, immigration by Black people in Britain and crucially the lack of police support in crimes against this group into a powerful cocktail of Black invasion that was wholly unacceptable to the white writer. The editors included the letter in *Flamingo's* letters page with the brief note: 'We have no comment other than to say the matter has been placed in the hands of the police.' Black readers likely would have read both the action and the police intervention in significantly different ways than white readers. Racialised harassment and violence increased for London's Black bookshops in the early 1970s as white nationalism, including organisations such as the National Front, stepped into public spaces. Black bookshops and publishers, including Unity Bookshop, Grassroots

---

²⁵ See Kennetta Hammond Perry's forthcoming work on the relationship between the postwar carceral state, the welfare state, and David Oluwale, as well as Perry, *London is the Place for Me*.
²⁶ 'Letters', *Flamingo* (December 1961), 1.

Bookshop and Bogle Books, had windows smashed and spray-painted and firebombs mailed to them throughout the 1970s according to Colin Beckles' communication with the bookstore owners, all of whom reported police and media uninterest in the events.[27]

## 5.3 'Anti-White': Navigating White Readers

The staff at these magazines voiced their experiences with racist harassment and violence as an alternative account of tolerant Britain that both openly acknowledged the racism that existed in the country and assumed that these experiences were shared by Black readers. This airing of experiences of racial harassment and violence ran counter to the dominant tropes that preoccupied screen culture in the period and which labelled Black subjects, within and without the empire, as naturally prone to violence and as troublemakers. The transparency *Flamingo* and *Tropic* displayed in relaying the hostile publishing landscape they faced opened up an alternative understanding of race relations in Britain rooted in these racialised encounters experienced by immigrants. The magazine offered spaces for the sharing of these experiences, as part of the 'mundane extreme environment' that Pierce wrote about in the 1970s, and the related frustrations, hurt and anger that emerged from this but always with an emphasis on a racially inclusive readership. Indeed, we see within these Black magazines the difficulties the editors faced in attempting to explicitly court Black audiences and also encourage white readers to consume the alternative knowledge of race relations in Britain laid out in these pages. The healthy circulation of the periodicals was at stake in such an effort. Claiming and subsisting on a Black readership alone was seemingly not imagined as feasible throughout the 1950s and early 1960s in Britain.

The delicate balancing act that the post-war Black press navigated can be seen in how these magazines initially revealed their target audience of Black readers. All the glossies signalled their intended readership through their cover photo subject which usually featured a Black woman, and very occasionally a Black man, as a form of representation that was unheard of in glossy magazines at the time. The first issue of *Checkers* featured a glamorous headshot of Hilda Simms, the African-American stage actress, while the second issue featured Harrison Dilland and Lorenzo Wright, two African-American members of the US Sprint Relay Team, and Erling Kaas, the white Norwegian pole vaulter, posing

---

[27] Beckles, 'We Shall Not Be Terrorized Out of Existence', 64.

in tracksuits for the camera with their arms around each other's shoulders. Subsequent issues only featured female cover girls, an approach that *Bronze*, *Tropic* and *Flamingo* would mimic. The first issue of *Tropic*, however, departed from this tradition and featured a Black toddler talking into a telephone and the most explicit appeal on a cover to a Black readership with its tagline next to the toddler's smiling face of 'Hello! Seen our new magazine for coloured people?' *Checkers* did not declare its readership in text until its second issue, with 'Britain's Premier Negro Magazine' as a subtitle under the magazine's name, and *Bronze* did not do so at all beyond the Black faces on its cover. *Tropic*, however, identified its readership clearly from the outset. Its first editorial placed *Tropic's* birth in the context of independence for Ghana in 1957, 10 West Indian territories becoming federated or gaining dominion status, and the upcoming independence of Nigeria in October 1960. It stated: 'TROPIC, as the voice of the 250,000 coloured people in Britain, could not have chosen a more opportune time to make its appearance. For we stand for coloured people everywhere in their struggle for Independence. In their fight to live with dignity and freedom.'[28]

*Tropic's* explicit appeal to Black readers who *Tropic* called 'coloured' was met by dismay by some readers, so much so that Tropic's staff responded to this in the next issue writing that 'West Indians especially – and we emphasise this – seem to be thoroughly ashamed of the word "coloured". They wrote in no uncertain terms that we shouldn't have used the word "coloured" because it would put off white readers.' The etymology of the term was further laid out by one writer, L. E. Williams of Hampstead, London, who noted that 'coloured' was associated by most whites with being 'sub-standard' and which threatened to impact the magazine's readership.[29] The staff at *Tropic* strongly resisted this criticism and did not engage it as a shifting usage of descriptive, race-based language and argued for self-pride among Black populations in Britain, the West Indies and Africa where they stressed that *Tropic* was being sold. They also felt compelled to point out that 'We are not – repeat NOT – anti-white. Any decent-thinking white person who believes in the freedom of human dignity is our friend and ally. We will also write about him.'[30] The need to express this, shortly after declaring in Black and white that the periodical was aimed at people of colour, indicated a potential outcry by readers about racial exclusion – a position white readers were quick to take as we shall see. *Tropic* was thus presented as an inclusive space for both Black and white readers and one where the quality of its output would not suffer due to it being aimed at audiences of colour.

[28] *Tropic*, no.1 (March 1960), 1.    [29] *Tropic* (April 1960), 38.    [30] Ibid.

Other glossy magazines echoed this inclusive sentiment in their editorials. *Checkers* stated in its first issue that 'we aim to bring people from the four corners of the world closer together through the medium of this magazine, and to give to all our readers a truer understanding of the races throughout the world'.[31] *Bronze* stated quite late in its publication life: '*Bronze*, while acting as the voice of the coloured people in Britain, hopes to further its ideal of racial friendship and equality in every way, regardless of race, colour or creed.'[32] *Flamingo* also included white readers in its remit but with a more explicit statement by Scobie about the magazine's aim to uncover Black experiences as a type of counter-storytelling:

> It is my belief that the thousands of coloured people here have a right to express their views; have a right to read the news from an unbiased viewpoint; have a right to a knowledge of the facts as they really are. In *Flamingo* we will present these facts and these views. By publishing ... this monthly magazine, we will fight prejudice and present a clear, unhysterical view of our 'problems' to white readers.[33]

While Black readers were the focus of these magazines white readers were again and again also included as readers. The pursuit of Black audiences alone did not sit comfortably with either the social landscape of post-war Britain, or a business model of a magazine aimed at a minority readership. The stated inclusivity of these magazines offered a window into an alternative understanding of racism in Britain that they wished to share with white readers. This was the Black British press explicitly willing to engage in the dialogic teaching that Priyamvada Gopal charts in nineteenth- and early twentieth-century encounters between Black and white activists examining racism and racialisation in imperial contexts.[34]

White audiences in the pages of *Tropic*, *Bronze*, *Checkers* and *Flamingo* were explicitly acknowledged as part of the readership of these magazines, and it is worth examining the terms by which white readers intruded upon and attempted to shape the counter-storytelling offered in the relatively short lives of these magazines. White readers wrote in and were featured regularly enough in the letters pages that the magazines' staff were clearly either eager to publicly demonstrate the racial inclusivity they proclaimed or felt compelled to do so in the fraught publishing environment laid out above. In other words the pressures facing Black magazines to include white voices within them as evidence of not being 'anti-white' were tied to a post-war economic, political and social environment that was highly racialised. White voices entered the magazines and offered their

---

[31] 'Editorial', *Checkers* 1, no. 1 (July 1948), 5.
[32] 'Editorial', *Bronze* 1, no. 6 (April–May 1955), 3.   [33] *Flamingo* (September 1961), 1.
[34] Priyamvada Gopal, *Insurgent Empire: Anticolonial Resistance and British Dissent* (London: Verso, 2019).

perspective on this counter-storytelling in a way that deployed a type of repetitive boundary-making that scholars of critical race studies have identified as hallmarks of white discomfort with discussions of racial bias.[35] These works recount that white people's unease with acknowledging white racial bias often leads to an evasion of the topic, the drawing of false equivalencies between racialised and non-racialised groups, emphasis on individual rather than collective experiences and a centring of white emotions about racism.[36] This shared pattern of responses among white readers, the often invisible work of collective racial ignorance and avoidance, is evident within this post-war archive of Black glossies as white readers stepped into a Black space that was unequally constituted from the beginning in terms of the readership it could claim and even the physical safety of its publishing team.

The response of white readers included discomfort with the alternative presentation of Black experiences in post-war Britain offered in the magazines which manifested in a variety of repetitive ways, including the policing of Black contributors' tones; an emphasis on racial progress upheld and delimited by white progressives; and a lack of individual responsibility among whites in a racialised society. The latter feeling of helplessness was expressed by a number of readers who viewed buying one of the magazines as a positive step towards remedying anti-immigrant sentiments in the period. Mrs Joan M. Twigg's letter was featured in the third issue of *Checkers* when she argued that a lack of 'fighting organisation' in Britain to address racism left her purchasing the magazine as a sign of support for her own racial attitudes that she had acquired during wartime exposure to Black GIs in Britain:[37]

Since the war when I met many coloured G.I.'s [sic] serving in the army, I have had a sincere liking and respect for coloured people as a whole, and I wait for the day when equality for all includes Negroes and Jews, not just self-appointed super men. Waiting is not a very lucrative way of assisting a cause, but in England there is no fighting organisation to deal with this problem. It seems a good idea to do my little best and support your magazine, an heroic project if I may say so.[38]

---

[35] Robin DiAngelo, *White Fragility: Why It's So Hard for White People to Talk about Racism* (London: Allen Lane, 2018), 9.
[36] Eduardo Bonilla-Silva, *Racism without Racists: Colour-Blind Racism and the Persistence of Racial Inequality in America*, 5th ed. (London: Rowan and Littlefield, 2017); Reni Eddo-Lodge, *Why I'm No Longer Talking to White People about Race* (London: Bloomsbury, 2017); Alana Lentin, *Why Race Still Matters* (London: Polity Press, 2020).
[37] Lucy Bland, *Britain's 'Brown Babies': The Stories of Children born to Black GIs and White Women in the Second World War* (Manchester: Manchester University Press, 2019).
[38] Letter from Mrs Joan M. Twigg, Craven Park, N.W. 10, *Checkers* 1, no. 3 (November 1948), 2.

In the absence of something like the NAACP in Britain and ahead of the formation of CARD, Mrs Twigg purchased this magazine instead. In December 1960, when *Tropic* released what would be its last issue, Miss C. R. Crossley from Walthamstow voiced a similar sentiment after reading about the attack on Tropic's office.

> It makes me ashamed to admit I am white ... it's time something was done about this Fascist organisation. I thought S.C.J.F. was doing something to help but I have heard nothing of them for some time. It's hard for individuals to improve relations between Whites and Coloured – for myself I go to parties and clubs where I am sure of meeting coloured people because I love to be among you but although I have a few West Indian women friends, for the most part any white woman going to coloured clubs is regarded as rather low.[39]

Miss Crossley spoke of her own racial discomfort and shame at the attack, but also her helplessness. For both Mrs Twigg and Miss Crossley there was a stated admiration and also perhaps a fetishisation of Black Britons and an expectation that external organisations would address racism in Britain. Both white women acknowledged the presence of racism within British society but placed their own anti-racist activities as passive and linked to buying *Checkers* or *Tropic*.

Other white women claiming rather circumscribed anti-racist positions were also highlighted in *Tropic* including a feature story, 'The Negroes in the "White" Theatre' by Joan Clarke.[40] Clarke was part of a handful of efforts by white theatre producers to foster Black voices in the national theatre scene. She was a producer for the West Indian Drama Group which mounted classic plays by white playwrights with all-Black casts. Clarke's motivations became clear in the story as she relayed her surprised discovery of the acting ability of immigrants alongside admonishments that Black actors must learn discipline: 'My experience has convinced me that in emotional range and flexibility, the Negro actor is second to none – also that if he applies himself to learn the basic training necessary to every actor, that he can acquire the discipline and consistency vital to a really great performer.'[41] Clarke advocated a key component of colour-blind racism, an abstract emphasis on racial progress that centres the activities and aid of white progressives, while overlooking evidence of the persistent lived experiences of racism by Black communities.[42] Clarke positioned Black actors as students in need of study and discipline that she and the white community could offer. Black progress would be aided by white instructors. She ended her piece by emphasising

---

[39] Letter from 'Miss C.R. Crossley at Walthamstow', *Tropic* (December 1960), 1.
[40] Joan Clarke, 'The Negros in the "White" Theatre', *Tropic* (April 1960), 6–8.
[41] Ibid., 7.   [42] Bonilla-Silva, *Racism without Racists*, 142–158.

her own place in providing the necessary training for Black actors: 'Let the coloured actor therefore take heart: the time is ripe for change in the theatre. Let him learn his craft thoroughly, as he would learn that applying to any other profession, and then campaign for his right to play parts where he can apply himself with dignity, and with artistic satisfaction to himself and his audience.'[43] This then was a future of dignity, skill and range, uniquely supported by a white theatre producer who nevertheless openly recognised the primarily white world of British theatre and claimed an anti-racist stance within this.

The other way in which white readers made their presence felt in the post-war Black glossies was in their comments on the emotional registers of the Black staff-writers and letter-writers contributing to these magazines. This tendency became more pronounced in the early 1960s in the pages of both *Tropic* and *Flamingo* as white Britons expressed a growing concern with immigrant populations. Mrs Pam Walton from London, identified by *Tropic*'s editors as 'one of the many English people who liked our first issue', praised the positive tone of the publication, while condemning the possibility of negative expressions by Black writers: 'I think you have done an excellent job, particularly in the presentation of your views without bitterness or rancour.'[44] After *Flamingo*'s article criticising *The Black and White Minstrel Show* was published in its first issue of September 1961, a more overt discussion by white readers of appropriate Black emotional responses to racism on the screen occurred in its pages. The stated discomfort of a number of Black men and women at the show's existence was aired in the pages of the magazine, allowing a Black perspective on the programme which put blacking up at its centre. Ellis Komey, the poet who is identified in the article as a 'Ghanaian writer working in London' was quoted as saying of the programme: 'It's degrading to our race ... I don't have a television set but if I did there's one programme I couldn't bear to see.' Pearl Connor, the well-known theatrical agent bemoaned the lack of Black people in the production of the show: 'As it is, white performers with black faces only look ridiculous—and make me feel ashamed.' Lloyd Squires, that young West Indian businessman in Brixton also recounted the show's impact on himself: 'I feel ashamed and disgusted when I see the antics of these coons on the programme.'[45] These were the feelings of a number of Black viewers that were aired in print and in the pages of a Black glossy. The article itself supported these comments and laid out a history of

---

[43] Clarke, *Tropic* (April 1960), 7.
[44] Letter from Mrs Pam Walton, London, *Tropic* (April 1960), 1.
[45] *Flamingo*, September 1961, 22.

blackface minstrelsy in the United States as the exploitation of enslaved Black people by white entertainers for their own profit. Offering a deep archival examination of the history of minstrelsy, the writer who is likely Edward Scobie, identified the first successful minstrel performer in the United States as Thomas Dartmouth Rice, a white man who witnessed an enslaved street-cleaner engaged in a 'twist and turn dance' to keep warm while working. Rice then went on to adapt the dance to a successful show that would allow him to die a wealthy man, according to the research underpinning the article. The article's opening sentence indicated nothing but scorn for the show, 'In this Age of the African and so-called progress it seems fantastic that an organisation like the British Broadcasting Corporation can continue to run the Black and White Minstrel Show series,' and went on to label it a 'piece of outdated and degrading rubbish.'[46]

White readers of *Flamingo* had very different responses to the programme and again demonstrated their inability to see the racism that the show depended upon. In the second issue of *Flamingo*, the editors acknowledged the avalanche of comments that accompanied the article: 'Many from white readers who thought Negroes "too touchy."'[47] The subsequent issue saw another white reader characterise the emotional responses of Black audiences to *The Black and White Minstrel Show* as overly sensitive, and noted the Black audience's misunderstanding of the programme:

I strongly disagree with your criticisms and I am sure that it displays over-sensitiveness. Scotsmen, Irishmen, and mothers-in-law are always having fun pointed at them throughout the world. I notice no particular sensitivity of these people. In any case, 'Black And White Minstrel Show' surely should be regarded as a compliment by your West Indian and African readers. It shows how dominant people of Negro descent are in the entertainment world.

This white reader explicitly resisted the alternative viewpoint and experience of the show that *Flamingo* relayed in its account of Black audiences reacting negatively and viscerally to *The Black and White Minstrel Show's* broadcasting on the BBC. The pain of Black audiences was dismissed as 'over-sensitiveness'. The reader drew false equivalencies between the racism experienced by Black immigrants in Britain with the experiences of the Scottish and Irish communities, as well as mothers-in-law who endured joking at their expense on the big and small screen. Collectively these white readers argued that racism would not be experienced or seen if Black audiences could just see and experience the programme as white

---

[46] Ibid.  [47] Letters, *Flamingo* (October 1961), 2.

audiences did, without 'particular sensitivity'. White readers urged these Black viewers to not see the racism they identified, inviting them instead into the easy and more comfortable emotional work of not knowing prejudice. Steps beyond this into 'bitterness or rancour' were highly discouraged by white readers and letter-writers.

In 1964, *Flamingo* again featured a female white reader, Margaret McCarthy from London, who was responding to a critical stance towards white people within the magazine and expressing her concern about what she saw as a bitterness of tone:

> As a white person, when I read the very interesting article about Arctic explorer Matthew Henson, I was distressed by the author's reference to the white conscience as 'hypocritical and un-Christian'. Racial intolerance makes it hard to keep from bitterness; when a group of people are oppressed and treated unjustly, it is easy for them to hate not only the oppressor but all those who are in any way associated with him, however remotely. Black people must remember that it is only a certain proportion of white people who are against them. Others reject this attitude with scorn – this was demonstrated at the anti-apartheid meeting in Trafalgar square, London, at which a large proportion of those present were white. I entreat all black men and women to be generous. Let us remember that before we belong to the black or white race, we belong first of all to Mankind.[48]

McCarthy's urging of a 'generous' approach to white Britons subscribed to a colour-blindness that rejected the existence of systemic racism and racialisation in the country and instead identified racial bias as the work of a small minority. McCarthy spoke of the visible anti-racist demonstrations by white people that she knew of but ultimately emphasised the responsibilities of Black communities to not express bitterness within the counter-storytelling that they were offering in *Flamingo's* pages. This policing of tone, itself a historic preoccupation of white communities hearing the frustrations of Black communities, was something that white readers of the Black press expressed again and again. Racism should be discussed in particular ways, it was inferred, and certainly without emotion. Black contributors also inevitably spoke to issues of tone among Black people in their efforts to be heard by white people. In other words, we see in these pages the development of and encouragement towards unemotional responses to racism as a vital part of the code-switching that Black immigrants took on when discussing racism in Britain. By the release of the third issue of *Checkers* in 1948, the lengthy editorial stated firmly: 'We are a friendly magazine. We bear no malice, hold no grudges. Our aim at all times is to present a true picture of the dark man's

---

[48] Letter, 'Belonging to Mankind', *Flamingo* (January 1964), 2.

problems. We take no sides but merely state the facts as they are.'[49] Facts rather than emotions would speak. *Flamingo's* opening editorial message in 1961, previously mentioned in this chapter, also acknowledged the tone that Black counter-storytelling had to abide by in order to discuss racism: 'By publishing ... this monthly magazine, we will fight prejudice and present a clear, unhysterical view of our "problems" to white readers.'[50] White audiences demanded unemotional responses and an unemotional tone that was constructed as neutral in order for racism to be discussed and for their own discomfort to be alleviated.

### 5.4 Racialised Emotions

*Flamingo's* aim to present a 'clear, unhysterical view of our "problems"' to both its white and Black readers in 1961 signalled the pressure that the Black press, and immigrants more widely, carried when they experienced racial prejudice and attempted to discuss these experiences and related emotions with white Britons. The simultaneous experiencing of racism by Black Britons and the inability to share these experiences at pain of silence and indifference was and still is common to majority white societies, as Eduardo Bonilla-Silva has written.[51] In a televised roundtable on an American radio station in 1961, James Baldwin memorably outlined the interior emotions of a Black man in America:

> To be a Negro in this country, and to be relatively conscious, is to be in a rage almost all the time. So that the first problem is how to control that rage so it won't destroy you. Part of the rage is this: It isn't only what is happening to you, but it's what's happening all around you all of the time, in the face of the most extraordinary and criminal indifference, the indifference and ignorance of most white people in this country.[52]

Baldwin's excavation of the Black everyday was one acknowledging the emotional responses of Black Americans to common experiences of racism alongside the 'extraordinary ... indifference' of white people. He sketched out a situation of almost constant stress as Black communities operated within an experiential and epistemological framework separate to that of whites. Bonilla-Silva outlines the work of various critical race theorists who have examined 'the dynamic through which

---

[49] 'Editorial', *Checkers* 1, no. 3 (November 1948), 3.
[50] 'Negro Voice', *Flamingo* (September 1961), 1.
[51] Eduardo Bonilla-Silva, 'Feeling Race: Theorizing the Racial Economy of Emotions', *American Sociological Review* 84, no. 1 (2019): 1–25.
[52] James Baldwin et al., 'The Negro in American Culture', *CrossCurrents* 11, no. 3 (Summer 1961), 205.

the emotions of the dominant race become authoritative', and by which the emotions of the subordinate are 'deemed dubious'.[53] This dynamic has, predictably enough, archival echoes. The glossies that aimed to offer a space for Black readers to be at ease in were still rife with the contradictions that accompanied the daily production of just such a racialised hierarchy in post-war Britain. Woven throughout the stories in these magazines that outlined strategies for navigating British life, including the search for accommodation that was Black-friendly with appropriate manners of speech and ways of dressing, was an intense anxiety about entry into that life. 'Bitterness and rancour' were indeed expressed and shared in these pages regardless of the emotional surveillance that white readers introduced into the publications and alongside efforts by the magazines to emphasise stories of Black success in daily life.

Racist incidents, racist language and racist representations were recounted by contributors in each of these magazines from *Checkers* onwards and accompanying these stories was a recounting of the emotions of Black subjects involved, both in the moment and afterwards. *Checkers'* third lengthy editorial noted that 'people here in England know next to nothing of the lives of the dark loyal races', referencing the recent involvement of Black and south Asian Britons in the war effort. The editorial, written by either J. Y. Lovegreen or Edward Scobie, recounted incidents of racism and racial ignorance from white Britons: 'It can be particularly distressing to be asked by an English R.A.F. Officer whether the black man has a tail coiled beneath his trousers. You feel perplexed when a passport official says, "Oh, yes, Trinidad. That is a town in Jamaica isn't it?"' Encounters with curious children on the street in 1948 were relayed as fraught, in an echo of Fanon's description in *Black Skin, White Masks*:

> Child education in these matters should not be left to a chance remark in the street by some half-drunken illiterate. When a kid wants to know why the black man's skin is black tell him TRUTHFULLY. Do not offer the black man as an object of ridicule. He cannot help the colour of his skin in the same way that the English child has no control over his colour.[54]

The various explanations that had been provided to children regarding the colour of a Black man's skin was provoking enough in this exchange to cause *Checkers* to break into capitals. The hurt and dismay of such encounters caused the writers to repeatedly theorise the reasons for such statements. White ignorance rather than racism was initially proposed by

---

[53] Bonilla-Silva, 'Feeling Race', 6.
[54] 'Editorial', *Checkers* 1, no. 3 (November 1948), 3.

the magazine and also initially treated as separate: 'It occurs to you that there is not so much intolerance as a lack of awareness and certain wrong teachings in the schools and press.' The broader institutional implications of such incorrect teachings were addressed by the alternative knowledge of race relations that *Checkers* itself hoped to offer in 1948 and 1949.

*Bronze*, with its mix of a white editorial voice for the first four issues of 1954 and Black contributors from the world of entertainment, also relayed incidents of everyday racism. The self-described 'white European' editor ran a feature called 'Mr Bronze' which relayed his astonishment with the racism he encountered when he was accompanied by his Black friends, who he himself tended to fetishise. The first issue featured a story called 'Mr Bronze in Search of a Room' that relayed the shifting attitudes of white British landladies when they rented to a white man who later brought home friends of colour. His mixing with West Indian men and women caused multiple landladies to ask him to leave which Mr Bronze relayed in detail: 'I told [the landlady] in no uncertain terms that if I rented that flat I must be allowed to entertain all my friends, regardless of their colour. Her answer to this was short and to the point, "I don't want Blacks in my house ... I have to think of the neighbours."'[55] Mr Bronze was consistently appalled by the racist landladies he encountered but did not advocate legislation against discrimination but rather the promotion of a universal colour-blindness that largely sidestepped the discrimination he himself had witnessed. Other Black contributors, however, felt free to discuss their disappointment and exhaustion with the racist experiences and racist tropes they witnessed. Scobie, writing in 1954 about the televised BBC play 'Halcyon Days' written by James Dyrenforth, 'a white American born in Chicago', laid out what he called 'the usual stock characters, both coloured and white' in the play:

The loyal ageing coloured retainer and his simple wife who have been keeping house for the sympathetic white judges; the Negro minister; the northern-trained coloured doctor; the city-slicker all sweet-talk, fancy clothes, and marijuana; the white Negro-hatin' miser and his sick wife; the Colonel whose contempt of the North is not lessened when he finds out that Northerners do not shave the ice when fixing mint juleps; his pretty daughter in love with a good-looking Philadelphian, and a retinue of 'good neggras' (to use a pet Southern phrase) who sing about their old Kentucky home, go to church, eat fried chicken and drink gin at the annual picnic, and generally earn a meagre livelihood by 'growing tobacco for industry' without 'too much industry'.[56]

---

[55] 'Mr Bronze Goes in Search of a Room', *Bronze* 1, no. 1 (June 1954), 6–7.
[56] Edward Scobie, 'TV's Vintage Play', *Bronze* 1, no. 2 (August–September 1954), 23.

Scobie's account of the dominant stereotypes within theatre, film, and now television indicated a weary repetitive knowledge of these. He wrote: 'It seems sad that a play written in 1954 for television audiences should have followed the old pattern with the usual cliches about "good neggras" and "bad neggras" "de Lawd," "Massa", and the scores of other relics of an unhappy past which the Negro race would rather not dig up and expose even in the guise of entertainment.'[57] This was exhaustion, a mournful note that such imagery was now to be repeated on the modern platform of television, and also shame at such cliches being newly exposed to British audiences. Buddy Bradley, the entertainment writer for the magazine and choreographer, also noted this is in his coverage of Hollywood film and theatre, remarking in 1954: 'Maybe one day the world will realise that all coloured people are not servants and minstrels.'[58] Bradley imagined a different type of material for both Black and white audiences.

Weariness with racialised tropes on screen and on the page were also laid out in *Tropic* and *Flamingo* alongside increasingly hard-hitting reporting on racism experienced by Black men and women in Britain. Articles in *Tropic* that investigated 'Who Killed Kelso' and 'Landlords' Terror Tactics' ran alongside articles about the Caribbean 'rock singer Ricky Wayne'.[59] In June 1960, *Tropic* ran an article entitled 'Negroes Say Cut Uncle Tom Films' which featured an image of the Black scheming but dim-witted bar-tender in the social-problem film *Sapphire* (1958) as its cover and the label 'The stereotype Negro of films ... ever smiling. Not thinking too much for himself, as long as he's on the right side of the boss'.[60] As mentioned previously, *Flamingo*'s article on *The Black and White Minstrel Show* also laid out in detail a history of minstrelsy in the US and the racist context and meaning of the practice while explicitly highlighting the emotions the variety show prompted in audiences of colour including feelings of shame, degradation and disgust.[61] In the detailed history of minstrelsy that *Flamingo* provided, it also relayed the response of the British novelist William Thackeray in 1865 to a minstrel show that he confessed 'moistened my spectacles' and set his heart 'thrilling with happy pity'. Thackeray mused on the appeal of blacking up to such a white audience member: '"Happy pity" – an apt and telling phrase. Perhaps it is this emotion that has made "black-face" so

---

[57] Ibid.
[58] 'Buddy Bradley's Show Talk', *Bronze*, 1, no. 2 (August–September 1954), 26.
[59] *Tropic* (June 1960); *Tropic* (July 1960).
[60] 'Negroes Say Cut Uncle Tom Films', *Tropic* (June 1960), 14–16.
[61] 'Bad Taste BBC', *Flamingo* (September 1961), 22.

popular.'[62] Within the pages of the magazine, the pleasures of racism for white audiences were thus investigated in great detail, alongside the more violent expressions of prejudice in post-war Britain. Two visions of minstrelsy were laid out – efforts by Black audiences to understand the racialised emotions of white audiences enjoying minstrelsy, and then the shame and disgust felt by Black audiences themselves. The space that these magazines offered for the articulation of the negative emotions accompanying persistent racialisation, regardless of the policing of tone by white readers searching for evidence that these magazines were 'anti-white', was a vital, yet intermittent and fragile one, for audiences of colour in post-war Britain.

## 5.5    Knowing Black Success

It was not only the emotions that accompanied the Black everyday experience of racial bias that was featured in the post-war Black glossies; the magazines also offered a path for readers to celebrate the success of both ordinary and exceptional Black men and women who were making their way in Britain and the US. These magazines aimed to capture a sense of pride and celebration for their Black readers but within the existing framework that acknowledged that such success could often take the form of merely existing and being at ease in predominantly white spaces. Success in the Black everyday was often, but not always, related to the work that was featured in the magazines. What all four magazines pursued as a strategy for noting and defining Black success for their readers was the production of a veritable rollcall of men and women working in the entertainment world and who were otherwise invisible in the white press coverage of entertainment. They made a point of 'seeing' Black people in the everyday and recognising their existence even as the magazines simultaneously excavated the structures at work which often prevented this entrance into the everyday except as racialised workers engaged in menial tasks.

The primary way in which the magazines invited their readers to see Black success was through its visual production on their covers and in photospreads that were regularly featured in the glossies. Black actresses, many of whom had brief careers or small parts on screen or on the stage, were featured on the front covers. Carmen Manley, who played a character titled 'Samoan' in the BBC's *Sunday-Night Theatre* televised play 'Tusitala' from 1950, may have had a minor role in the production but

[62] Ibid., 24.

occupied the cover of the first issue of *Flamingo* in 1961. The African-American singer Muriel Smith was on the cover the first issue of *Bronze* in June 1954 while other more well-known actresses were also featured, such as Lena Horne on the cover of the fifth issue of *Checkers* in January 1949. Aspiring actresses and singers were also featured in some of the glossies with *Bronze* being very willing to publish photos of 'Bronze Beauties' such as 'Vivacious Louise Carty, formerly of St. Andrew, Jamaica' in 1954 who 'brings a happy personality to the serious vocation of nursing' and 'is at present a student at Archway Hospital'.[63] These images, such as the techniques that the press had been using since the interwar period, were meant to boost readership by inviting readers to imagine themselves as starlets in their own right.[64] While never pursuing the possibility of recruiting starlets all four magazines featured both female and male actors occupying roles, no matter how small, in the entertainment world.

The actors Earl Cameron, Errol John and Johnny Sekka were featured in all four magazines, with Cameron's 'Mau Mau Movie' garnering multi-issue and multi-image coverage in 1955.[65] Errol John had both his acting and playwriting career supported by *Tropic* when his play *Moon on a Rainbow Shawl* was televised on ITV's broadcaster in the Midlands, ATV, in 1960. The broadcast had been criticised by a fellow West Indian, a doctor, which caused *Tropic* to speculate that 'perhaps all these years away from home … have dulled his sensibilities as well as his sense of balance'. *Tropic* went on to vigorously defend the televised version and argue that it was superior to the 'fairly innocuous' *A Hot Summer Night* which had received rave reviews by British audiences.[66] The magazine professed enthusiasm for the complexities captured in the play which presented its all-Black cast as 'very real people'.[67] Similar celebrations of well-rounded Black characters that moved beyond the thin stereotypes on screen were echoed by Buddy Bradley in his immense enthusiasm for *Carmen Jones's* release and what he saw as a complex multi-faceted presentation of Black lives by an all-Black cast. The film was covered extensively by Bradley who hoped that 'if it is a resounding box office success we might expected a spate of all-coloured films for it is an old Hollywood trick to follow one box office success with another film of the same type'. Bradley's attention to Italian cinema, which he positioned as

---

[63] 'Bronze Beauties', *Bronze* 1, no. 1 (June 1954), 17.
[64] Chris O'Rourke, *Acting for the Silent Screen: Film Actors and Aspiration between the Wars* (London: I.B. Tauris, 2017).
[65] Mau Mau Movie', *Bronze* 1, no. 3 (October–November 1954), 22.
[66] *Tropic*, no. 1 (March 1960), 6–7.   [67] Ibid, 7.

much more equitable in its use of Black actors, became a backdrop for this hope that the West Indies would have their moment on screen: 'Once the ball starts rolling I can see them making pictures in the beautiful and natural surroundings of Jamaica and Trinidad. The West Indies would seem to be a paradise for film producers and I can't think why they have not made more use of them.' These dreams were ultimately not realised in Britain or the US despite the success of the film.

Cinema and television stars were not the only Black people who were trumpeted within the Black glossies: ordinary Black Britons making their way and at ease in London and elsewhere were featured in their pages. *Checkers* featured aspiring sculptors and painters in 1948 such as Benedict C. Enwonwu, a Nigerian living in Britain.[68] Edna Barnes, a Black Canadian training as a nurse in London, was presented in *Checkers*' 'Meet the People' section as was Maurice the hairdresser in a subsequent issue.[69] *Bronze* ran stories on local events and Black presence at them such as a story on London's Portobello Market and Peddie's Barber Shop, identified as 'the only coloured barber around these parts who can cut a coloured man's hair with artistry and skill'. Alongside Peddie, the story featured photographs of Black Britons shopping, including '28-year-old Miss Stillie Betty who has come to London to study dress designing' and Staff Sergeant Price 'who has been with the U.S.A.A.F. at East Kirkby for three years' who posed smiling, respectively buying weekend supplies and King Cole's latest record at the market.[70]

While *Bronze* kept its focus and its photographs in the 1950s on the entertainment world that it so thoroughly documented, *Tropic* and *Flamingo* took up this practice of featuring ordinary Black Britons at work or on the streets. In its first issue of 1960, a middle-aged Black woman identified as 'Gloria' was 'whipped off smartly to Winifred Atwell's new hair-dressing salon in Berners Street' and the makeover documented in a photospread.[71] Subsequent issues featured photographs of 'Ghana's Air Girls', stewardesses training to work for Ghana Airways; the textile designer Althea McNish from Trinidad; and of a prone and hospital-bed bound 22-year-old Felix Alphonso Samuels, an immigrant from Jamaica working for the London Underground who had been 'publicly

---

[68] 'Dark Man with a Bright Future', *Checkers* 1, no. 1 (July 1948), 14.
[69] 'Meet the People', *Checkers* 1, no. 2 (October 1948), 11; 'Meet the People', *Checkers* 1, no. 4 (December 1948), 10.
[70] 'Portobello Market', *Bronze* 1, no. 3 (October–November 1954), 6–7.
[71] 'Steps to Beauty', *Tropic* (March 1960), 22–23. Winifred Atwell, the Trinidadian pianist, had opened the salon in 1956. Atwell was also featured in other *Tropic* issues offering recipe and beauty tips.

thanked on television' after he guided passengers off a train that filled with smoke after a malfunction.[72] In keeping with *Flamingo*'s increased attention on television broadcasting, its May 1962 issue featured a four-page spread on Winnie Cameron who they labelled 'TV Girl' and 'the only girl from the Caribbean who is employed in this type of work'. Cameron, originally from Guiana, was a production assistant for Associated Rediffusion, one of ITV's London broadcasters. Cameron relayed her working day in the Features department for the film and television director Rollo Gamble, emphasising the rather unglamorous side of the job. The story nevertheless recounted the multiple places she had travelled to, including Vietnam, Norway and America, while regularly living at a hostel in South Kensington. It featured her in photos with Gamble and crew members at Associated Rediffusion and in a fur coat fixing her hair, all of which emphasised her relative success, ultimately concluding that 'she was trying to enter a field completely untried by any West Indian girl … and she succeeded'.[73] Although Cameron declined to acknowledge the existence of a colour-bar when interviewed, the story's dual positioning of her success and rare place in the field of broadcasting told a slightly different one of success against great odds.

The emphasis in these magazines on ordinary and extraordinary Black Britons told a story of Black visibility and ease when both were sorely lacking in the British press.[74] Black people in post-war Briton were rarely acknowledged as viewers or consumers to engage with by either the BBC's Audience Research Department or even Mark Abram's market research. As the Black glossies repeatedly noted the representations on screen or in the press were largely negative and stereotypical, hinging on a one-dimensional and incomplete understanding of most Black experiences and cultures. These magazines overtly worked to rectify this for Black audiences through positive representations of the everyday for Black people in Britain and through a press space that also emphasised that a glossy magazine could 'see' and know its readers and gauge their desire and need for positive representation and related feelings of aspiration and celebration. Bradley's first column at *Bronze* in 1954 invoked a chatty style that invoked and acknowledged Black audiences who were as

---

[72] Anne Townsend, 'Ghana's Air Girls', *Tropic* (April 1960), 14; Pat Blair, 'Althea McNish-Fabric Designer', *Tropic* (April 1960), 32; 'Jamaica Hero', *Tropic* (September 1960), 8.
[73] 'TV Girl', *Flamingo* (May 1962), 23–26.
[74] Smith-Shomade notes that one of the early successful advertising campaigns in the early twenty-first century for the Black-owned American television network TV ONE stated simply 'I See Black People.' Smith-Shomade, 'I See Black People', in *Watching While Black*, 1–18.

interested in entertainment as he was while noting the precise cataloguing and Black visibility that the column would offer:

> Hello, hello, hello to all our friends who are interested in the show business, who are in the show business, or would like to be in the show business. We are going to keep you posted on the activities of all the coloured people associated with the show business in general. That is to say – if we learn that Mattiwilda Dobbs is doing a concert, Pearl Primus giving a dance recital or Mary Lou Williams a jazz concert, we will let you know about it and hope you find time to attend. We wonder how many of you saw Miss Dobbs on T.V. a few weeks ago, or Claude Marchant's Company at the Embassy, Swiss Cottage ... Quite often, those things of interest to coloured people in general, do not receive sufficient publicity.[75]

Bradley spoke to a Black audience, 'all our friends,' who were imagined as particularly interested in other Black people in the entertainment world. Working from this assumption, Bradley's championing of singers, dance troupes, theatre, and film stars and even Black bullfighters in Spain was repeatedly featured in *Bronze*. Under Edward Scobie's direction at *Tropic* and *Flamingo*, Black history would also be illuminated for readers as Black intellectuals, artists, and writers were photographed alongside those working in the entertainment world. The first issue of *Flamingo* put a spotlight on Errol Edwards who the magazine called 'the only Negro taxi driver in Britain who has his own fleet of cabs', a seven-car business.[76] Black men and women working in Britain were presented as part of the positive visual everyday constructed for Black readers by *Flamingo*. *Flamingo* highlighted the well-rounded, multi-faceted, and working Black community alongside tales of white discrimination towards the Black community and the occasional awkward interjection of white readers. Black agency within these pages was thus the construction of the Black everyday which itself was cause for witnessing and celebrating in magazines that could nevertheless only speak intermittently to Black audiences due to the precarious place of the Black press.

## Conclusion

A survey of the Black glossies that emerged in post-war Britain and continued sporadically within a difficult publishing climate illuminates a Black audience in Britain that was largely ignored by producers and regulators of film and television and by audience research as well. The invisibility of Black audiences to these shapers of screen culture and the

---

[75] Buddy Bradley, 'Entertainment', *Bronze* 1 (June 1954), 20.
[76] 'Coloured Cabby', *Flamingo* 1, no. 1 (September 1961), 32.

British media left Black glossies with a particular path of connection to their readers. They simultaneously acknowledged, traced, and historicised the patterns through which white people shaped this invisibility and this otherness as part of a counter-narrative pursued by all four magazines. Even as white readers and contributors placed themselves among Black audiences of these magazines and affirmed patterns of colour-blind racism at work in post-war Britain, these publications maintained a persistent format that witnessed and knew Black people on multiple levels: as navigators of profound and mundane racism in Britain, as immigrants in a new environment, and as cinema and television watchers. Together these magazines affirmed the politics of representation as vital to Black people in Britain and presented their own images of the ordinary and extraordinary Blackness and the wider entertainment world. This was a political and epistemological undertaking that exposed the alternative viewpoints and experiences of Briton's Black community and which was nevertheless open to white readers willing to engage with it.

These Black glossies also, crucially, opened spaces for the articulation of the emotions that accompanied experiences of the extreme mundane every day for immigrants in post-war Britain. Frustration, incredulity, and anger at white ignorance and white racism was aired in these pages. Theories of whiteness were articulated in the letter bag and in columns by contributors. As white contributors and readers attempted to police the tone of Black writers and audiences and as white violence attempted to forcibly silence these publications altogether, we see a new emphasis on a contained type of composure for speaking of racism. A need for a neutral presentation of the facts of racism was articulated by Black writers and readers themselves. White Britons had little tolerance for Black people who spoke of white racism angrily or with frustration. These glossies highlighted the colour-blind practice and language of whiteness in the 1950s and early 1960s, long before the visibility of the Black Power movement would re-animate white fears of Black anger and action through a new medium of television. It was in this context that both the BBC and ITV and other shapers of British screen culture began to engage with audiences of colour in order to occasionally acknowledge and also circumvent accusations of media and audience racism as discussed in the next chapter.

## 6 'A Sneaking Feeling'
Institutional Silences, Racism and Audience Research at the BBC and ITV in the 1970s

In 1976, David Glencross, Head of Programmes at the Independent Broadcasting Authority (IBA) and responsible for much of ITV's output across its various regional franchises, circulated to IBA staff a memorandum that argued that 'the events of 1976 have added a new sharpness to the question of race relations in the UK'.[1] Glencross listed in the memo the 'widely publicised activities of [white nationalist] Robert Reilf'and 'the growth in support for the National Front and the National Party in by-elections and local elections', alongside disturbances at the Notting Hill carnival and Enoch Powell's ongoing activities which collectively 'contributed to unease, uncertainty, and an atmosphere in which prejudice is easily stimulated and mutual racial suspicions increased'.[2] The tumultuous atmosphere of the 1970s, as numerous historians have noted, did indeed lend itself to a feeling of crisis among institutions and individuals in power.[3] Characterised by Thatcher herself as a decade of decline with the government barely in control of powerful unions that indulged the British worker, the work of historians has done much to uncover the move towards deindustrialisation, neoliberalism, and

---

[1] 'Memorandum by Mr Glencross', 10 November 1976, p. 1, Race Relations in Independent Television, ITA/ITB Collection, University of Bournemouth.
[2] Ibid.
[3] Lawrence Black, Hugh Pemberton and Pat Thane, eds. *Reassessing the 1970s Britain* (Manchester: Manchester University Press, 2013); Aled Davies, Ben Jackson and Florence Sutcliffe-Braithwaite, eds. *The Neoliberal Age: Britain since the 1970s* (London: UCL Press, 2021); Matthew Worley, *No Future: Punk, Politics and British Youth Culture, 1976–1984* (Cambridge: Cambridge University Press, 2017); Callum Brown, *The Battle for Christian Britain: Sex, Humanists and Secularisation, 1945–1980* (Cambridge: Cambridge University Press, 2019); Robert Saunders, *Yes to Europe! The 1975 Referendum and Seventies Britain* (Cambridge: Cambridge University Press, 2018); Jim Tomlinson, 'De-industrialization Not Decline: A New Meta-narrative for Post-war British History', *Twentieth-Century British History* 27, no. 1 (2016): 76–99; James Vernon, 'Heathrow and the Making of Neoliberal Britain', *Past & Present* 252, no. 1 (2021): 213–247; Stephen Brooke, *Sexual Politics: Sexuality, Family Planning, and the British Left from the 1880s to the Present Day* (Oxford: Oxford University Press, 2011); Peter Mandler, *The Crisis of the Meritocracy: Britain's Transition to Mass Education Since the Second World War* (Oxford: Oxford University Press, 2020).

individualism that were already at work in the period.[4] Race relations in the 1970s has had somewhat less attention than these issues although recent work by Benjamin Bland and James West points to the growing role of the tabloid press in fostering negative representations of racialised people in the decade.[5] Glencross's memo took a longer view and considered the particular role of independent British television in fostering a rise of anti-immigrant feeling: 'With the admittedly faded wisdom of hindsight, therefore, it now becomes appropriate to ask whether some of Independent Television's approaches to racial matters in the recent past has been as well-judged as we would wish.'[6]

Glencross described broadcasters' treatment of 'coloured immigration into Britain' as steeped in what he called the 'benign neglect' of the postwar period. This reflection came in 1976, a year after Britain reaffirmed its commitment to the European Economic Community, five months ahead of the release of the findings of the Committee on the Future of Broadcasting (the Annan Committee) and two years after the committee began hearing evidence from bodies such as the Race Relations Board about the state of British television and the audience research that sat within it. It came as various working men's clubs were articulating their own relationship to race, locality and white working-class sociability in the 1970s as Camila Schofield has noted.[7] A growing unease within organisations such as ITV and the BBC prepared the ground for Glencross's memo and his reconsideration of racism's role in British society and television audiences. As Glencross hinted, the National Front's voting gains in 1973 and 1974 were shocking for many executives and staff within the primarily white, middle- and upper-class London-based media elite that had emerged in the twentieth century, many of whom considered themselves aligned with anti-racist viewpoints.[8]

---

[4] See above as well as Lawrence Black, 'An Enlightening Decade? New Histories of 1970s' Britain', *International Labor and Working-Class History* 82 (2012): 174–186; Jim Tomlinson, 'Deindustrialisation and "Thatcherism": Moral Economy and Unintended Consequences', *Contemporary British History* 35, no. 4 (2021): 620–640.

[5] Benjamin Bland, '"Publish and Be Damned?" Race, Crisis, and the Press in England during the Long, Hot Summer of 1976', *Immigrants & Minorities* 37, no. 3 (2019): 163–183; E. James West, 'Hunt the Wizard! Race, Immigration, and British Tabloid Coverage of David Duke's 1978 Tour', *Contemporary British History* 35, no. 1 (2021): 100–124.

[6] 'Memorandum by Mr Glencross', 2.

[7] Camilla Schofield, 'In Defence of White Freedom: Working Men's Clubs and the Politics of Sociability in Late Industrial England', *Twentieth Century British History*, 34, no. 3 (2023): 515–551.

[8] Gavin Schaffer, *The Vision of a Nation: Making Multiculturalism on British Television, 1960–80* (London: Palgrave Macmillan, 2014).

The series of events that Glencross outlined in 1976 raised a thorny dilemma for screen production in Britain and the relationship of television broadcasters to British audiences. Firstly, it presented a compelling indictment of the media's existing treatment of racial prejudice on screen as ineffective and secondly, the groundswell of political support for the anti-immigrant platform of the National Front and related anti-immigrant sentiments voiced by Enoch Powell indicated the possibility of an audience with specific, anti-immigrant concerns that had not sufficiently been accounted for by broadcasters. Powell's 'Rivers of Blood' speech from March 1968 increasingly looked less like the ravings of a man who would go on to be isolated by the national, if not local, media for his racist views and instead looked representative of a large audience of men and women in Britain who were possibly racially prejudiced.[9] As Anna Marie Smith has noted, widespread support for Powell among disparate groups in the country actually proved a help to the Conservatives and not a hindrance.[10] Glencross, ruminating on this situation, laid out a tale of two audiences, one white and one of colour, in his memo to IBA staff:

It is likely that, whatever view is taken of the virtues and faults of Independent Television in handling racial matters, the Authority and the programme companies are going to come under further pressure from two opposing sources. The first is those who say that Independent Television has, along with the BBC and most of the Press, concealed the truth about the impact of coloured communities in those areas where they have grown up in considerable numbers. The second is the coloured communities themselves and their sympathizers who will argue that such efforts as have been made by the broadcasters to assimilate the coloured communities into the fabric of the television output are no more than tokenism.[11]

Glencross did what broadcasters had hitherto been reluctant to do and acknowledged television as an influential tool able to conceal, tell the truth or pursue tokenistic representation when it came to race. Glencross

---

[9] For local treatments of Powell's speech, see Rachel Yemm, 'Immigration, Race and Local Media in the Midlands, 1960–1985', (PhD diss., University of Lincoln, 2018); Amy Whipple, 'Revisiting the "Rivers of Blood" Controversy: Letters to Enoch Powell', *Journal of British Studies* 48, no. 3 (2009): 717–735; George Kassimeris and Leonie Jackson, 'Negotiating Race and Religion in the West Midlands: Narratives of Inclusion and Exclusion during the 1967–69 Wolverhampton Bus Workers' Turban Dispute', *Contemporary British History* 31, no. 3 (2017): 343–365; as well as Camilla Schofield, *Enoch Powell and the Making of Postcolonial Britain* (Cambridge: Cambridge University Press, 2013).

[10] Anna Marie Smith, *New Right Discourse: Britain 1968–1990* (Cambridge: Cambridge University Press, 1994), 129–182.

[11] 'Memorandum by Mr Glencross', 3.

also outlined firstly and sympathetically a white audience experiencing the 'truth about the impact of coloured communities' in Britain. This audience's 'opposing source' of 'the coloured communities themselves and their sympathizers' would have a very different view of ITV's contributions. This account of two audiences and two perspectives, as well as two points of pressure upon the broadcasters, pointed to what would be a main point of tension for British television broadcasters from 1973 onwards. The racism of white British audiences began to be acknowledged and discussed in institutions of television broadcasting in the 1970s simultaneous to conversations about serving the concerns of this audience. Glencross was already doing institutional work within the IBA to understand a perspective that was imagined as largely silent, and instead re-interpret it as something rooted in a rational defence of whiteness. This audience was imagined not as racist but rather as concerned about the true impact of immigrations.

The awkward role and the awkward findings of audience research in maintaining the racialising output on ITV and the BBC during the 1970s and the ongoing presence of programmes such as *Till Death Us Do Part*, *Love Thy Neighbour* (ITV Thames Television, 1972–1976), *Mind Your Language* (ITV LWT, 1977–1979) and *It Ain't Half Hot Mum* BBC, 1974–1981) has been largely overlooked by historians working on the period.[12] As this chapter argues, the audience research that occurred at both the BBC and ITV continued to discover and then evade evidence of anti-Black and south-Asian audience racism in Britain, a story that had begun with the 1968 Special Audience Research Report on *Rainbow City*. Audience research departments, those central if flawed branches of television and radio broadcasting in twentieth-century Britain, were increasingly collecting evidence throughout the decade of racial prejudice among white audiences against people of colour. This emerging story in audience research also dovetailed with the unwillingness of these institutions to engage with racialised groups who could offer their own account of the impact of BBC's and ITV's television content on people of colour. Such a reluctance was increasingly commented on through the mechanisms available to organisations such as the Race Relations Board

---

[12] Catherine Johnson and Rob Turnock, *ITV Cultures: Independent Television Over Fifty Years* (London: Open University Press, 2005); Sarita Malik, *Representing Black Britain: Black and Asian Images on Television* (London: Sage Publishing, 2002); Stephen Bourne, *Black in the British Frame: The Black Experience in British Film and Television*, 2nd ed. (London: Bloomsbury, 2001); Darrell M. Newton, *Paving the Empire Road: BBC Television and Black Britons* (Manchester: University of Manchester Press, 2011); Schaffer, *The Vision of a Nation*.

when its evidence was summarised for the Committee on the Future of Broadcasting, the Annan Report, in 1975:

> The Board conclude that 'there is no indication that an adequate policy, let alone provision exists to cater for the needs, of the disparate and scattered ethnic minorities of Britain'. Among other things, they propose formal liaison meetings between broadcasters and the Board and that more races should be represented in viewing and listening panels.[13]

The Race Relations Board recognised that the viewing and listening panels that underpinned the broadcasters' understanding of the audience was not racially diverse. The two belated and brief attempts that did exist in audience research to engage Black or south Asian audiences in the latter half of the 1970s give us sharp insight into how racial diversity was discussed or avoided within both organisations. It points to institutions that were in Sara Ahmed's words 'stuck' and how areas such as audience research operated as both a site of knowledge about race and a place where the racial innocence of audiences and institutions were maintained.[14]

This chapter continues the close examination of the Audience Research Department at the BBC laid out in Chapter 3 but with the addition of the IBA's work in audience research to give us a clearer picture of just how ill-equipped both broadcasters were to face growing evidence of racism among their highly scrutinised white audience. Drawing on critical race theory, related and relatively recent work on 'decolonising' institutions and Ahmed's work on racism and institutional life in particular, this chapter examines what occurred in the 1970s when institutions as large and public-facing as the BBC and ITV were at the time starting to grapple with a growing awareness of racism as something beyond racial violence and as something that touched them directly.[15] I highlight a simultaneous process of uncovering the racism of white audiences within Britain's two television broadcasters, the cosy 'duopoly' of the 1970s and the institutional silences that followed this. Six special

---

[13] J. M. Goose's cover letter for the Race Relations Board's evidence and summary to the committee, 26 November 1975, Race Relations Board's Evidence to the Committee on the Future of Broadcasting/HO 245/1568, TNA.

[14] Sara Ahmed, *Being Included: Racism and Diversity in Institutional Life* (Durham, NC: Duke University Press, 2012), 84–85.

[15] Ahmed, *Being Included*; Priyamvada Gopal, 'On Decolonisation and the University', *Textual Practice* 35, no. 6 (2021): 873–899; Eve Tuck and K. Wayne Yang. 'Decolonization Is Not a Metaphor', *Decolonization: Indigeneity, Education, & Society* 1, no. 1 (2012): 1–40; Leslie M. Harris, James T. Campbell and Alfred L. Brophy. *Slavery and the University: Histories and Legacies* (Athens, GA: University of Georgia Press, 2019).

audience research studies were mounted on the racial prejudice of white audiences at both the BBC and ITV throughout the 1970s indicating that racism among white viewers was measured according to audience research's practices and interpretation of data and was quantifiable by their means. That initial discovery in 1968 of widespread racial prejudice among British audiences of *Rainbow City* by a startled BBC Audience Research Department would prove to be just the first report that captured problematic, highly racialised and racialising views of British audiences towards 'race' on screen. In subsequent acts of under-researching and 'not knowing' related to this emerging pattern, Black and south Asian audiences were consistently represented by audience research within their respective institutions as too difficult to access for audience research. This occurred first at the BBC where audiences of colour were largely invisible in the audience information that informed programming decisions there and secondly at ITV where Black and south Asian audiences were marginalised within ITV's own versions of audience research. As the chapter demonstrates, when Black and south Asian audiences were finally invited into audience research in the latter half of the 1970s the terms by which this invitation was extended indicated just how wedded both broadcasters were to maintaining a dominant image of television audiences as white. The whiteness of audience research in terms of staffing, methodology and institutional sheltering in both organisations led to an interpretation of data that upheld notions of a racially innocent white British audience while racialised voices with potential understandings of racism that threatened to puncture this colour-blindness were sidelined. In 1975 at ITV and 1979 at the BBC, Black and south Asian audiences were finally brought into the methodologies of audience research but in exceptional and questionable ways that confirmed these audiences as ever outside the audience that both television producers still imagined.

## 6.1   Growing Evidence: Audience Research on Racial Prejudice 1970–1978

The 1968 Special Audience Research Report *Rainbow City*, that first television series of a primarily Black cast on a topic of immigrant life, had by their own admission left the Audience Research Department at the BBC startled and depressed with what they had uncovered about the attitudes of white viewers towards immigrants. The series was followed by a long programming silence at the BBC when it came to presenting another series that would feature a primarily Black cast. The Audience Research Department, however, continued much as it had done, weathering the retirement of its founder and head, Robert Silvey, and the appointment of Brian Emmett in his stead in 1968. Meanwhile audience research progressed rapidly in the 1970s at the BBC's competitor, the Independent Television Authority (ITA) which oversaw ITV and its affiliates until it was superseded by the new organisation of the IBA in 1972. ITV's reliance on the Tam-O-Meter device as the primary means of measuring audience behaviour continued but merged with new audience survey methods that were not unlike what was pursued at the BBC. At the ITA, these initial audience studies emerged as the Television Opinion Panel (TOP) and then as the Audience Reaction Assessment (AURA), the in-house research team at IBA beginning in 1974. AURA would go on to develop two sub-panels called the Children's AURA and Teenager AURA.[16] Under the auspices of AURA a London-based audience panel of 1000, picked to be representative of ITV viewers, was regularly used for studies with the occasional incorporation of regional panels as well. Just as the programming offerings of the two broadcasters quickly began to look alike during the period of the duopoly, so too did audience research.

From 1970 these two audience research branches made some effort to examine links between depictions of people of colour on television and racism among white viewers, primarily at the behest of producers responding to external pressure to defend their television content and its approach to race on screen. The racial sitcoms broadcast in the decade saw particular scrutiny by both branches. Of the six Special Audience Research Reports conducted on race between 1970 and 1979 across both institutions, two were conducted for ITV franchises and four for the BBC. At ITV a study was conducted on the cancelled and disastrous Johnny Speight racial sitcom *Curry and Chips* for ITV-London Weekend Television in 1970; the second in 1975 by AURA on ITV's popular Thames Television production of the hit racial sitcom *Love Thy Neighbour*. The latter also captured a new and novel methodological approach stated in the title of the report: 'Love Thy Neighbour: What Coloured Immigrant Viewers Think'. Four other Special Audience Research Reports were conducted by the BBC's Audience Research department: one in 1973 on the BBC's hit racial sitcom *Till Death Us Do Part* during the second stretch of the show from 1972 to 1975; another in 1972 conducted by an outside research team from the

---

[16] AURA evolved out of what was initially called the Television Opinion Panel or TOP which was run by external contractors and awarded in 1969; Jeremy Potter, *Independent Television in Britain, Volume 3: Politics and Control 1968–80* (London: Macmillan Press, 1989), 212–215.

University of Michigan on the broader topic of 'Non-Whites on British Television'; a further Special Audience Research Report in 1978 on white audience reactions to the BBC's broadcast of the American television series *Roots*; and finally in 1979, another pre-broadcast report on potential responses to a BBC programme in development referred to as 'Multi-Racial Britain'. The latter study, such as the 1975 study at IBA of *Love Thy Neighbour*, included audiences of colour as invited participants for the first time in the history of BBC's Audience Research Department. Both are discussed in detail here. Together this range of Special Audience Research Reports points to new thinking, if not action, about the screen's role and responsibility in shaping audience attitudes and the frailty of 'racial innocence' as an animating logic for British broadcast programming. This chapter will pay particular attention to the special reports addressing the popular racial sitcoms penned in Britain and the two reports that incorporated audiences of colour for the first time.

It was two short years after *Rainbow City* met a negative response among British viewers on the BBC that ITV saw a brief and seemingly disastrous run in 1969 of a new racial sitcom called *Curry and Chips*. This was ITV's attempt to imitate the success of the BBC's *Till Death Us Do Part* while capitalising on its show-writer Johnny Speight's mounting frustration with restrictions at the BBC and his willingness to work elsewhere. *Curry and Chips* premiered on 21 November 1969 on LWT but was also broadcast on other franchises including Westward, Harlech Television, Border Television and Channel Television.[17] It was initially broadcast at 8.30pm and then pushed back to 9.30pm as complaints against the programme were immediately registered as historian Brett Bebber has noted.[18] The cast included the Black British actor and musician Kenny Lynch playing Kenny, whose own claims to Englishness was a subject of comedy throughout the series, but the star of the show was the blacked-up actor and comedian Spike Milligan as a Pakistani man named Kevin O'Grady. O'Grady's lack of belonging and his obliviousness to this fuelled the series' comedy, all punctuated by profane language directed towards O'Grady by other factory workers, including the free use of racial slurs such as 'sambo' and 'coon'. Across the six episodes various controversial topics were explored, including an emphasis on the indolence of British factory workers and the propensity for striking by

---

[17] 'Television Today', *The Times*, 21 November 1969, 19; 'Television Today', *The Times*, 20 November 1969, 19; 'Television Today', *The Times*, 27 November 1969, 23; 'Television Today', *The Times*, 28 November 1969, 19.
[18] Brett Bebber, 'The Short Life of *Curry and Chips*: Racial Comedy on British Television in the 1960s', *Journal of British Cinema and Television* 11, no. 2–3 (2014): 228–230.

union members. Episode four was also set in the context of a race riot on the way to a football match which Kevin becomes accidentally entangled in.

In the new year of 1970, after the series was pulled after its six episodes, the programme was reported to the Race Relations Board by Clive Jenkins, joint general secretary of the Association of Scientific, Technical and Managerial Staffs (ASTMS), a Welsh white man and head of the powerful new union who seemingly took issue with the presentation of the shop steward in the fictional factory. Bebber has noted the sheer number of complaints from both white men and women that poured into the IBA from the very first episode with immigrants of colour also strongly objecting to the programme.[19] Speight's response was well publicised in the press, including in *The Times* where he invoked a non-racist audience understanding the show's function as satire: 'Most intelligent people had seen the point of the series, which was simply to send up a common British attitude towards immigrants.'[20] Spike Milligan's anti-racist credentials, primarily linked to his birth in India, were further cited by Speight as proof that the show was not racist: 'We did not set up the series to be offensive and Spike would never have agreed to play the part if we had.'[21] Nothing came from the complaint, and an official from the Race Relations Board was reported in the *Daily Mail* as saying that 'whatever Spike Milligan does on the show, I can't see the Board getting involved'.[22] The positioning of both the BBC and ITV and media institutions more widely as outside the remit of the Race Relations Act left the board with little to do as both broadcasters well knew. The show was, however, brought to a quick end and not renewed seemingly based on the public outcry.

Bebber has ably examined the programme in detail, but it is worth focussing further on the Special Audience Research Report on *Curry and Chips* and drawing it into the broader trajectory of audience research on race from 1968 and into dialogue its slow, intermittent unveiling of racist thinking among white viewers in this period. Remarkable similarities exist between the surveys conducted in 1968 at the BBC on *Rainbow City* and the one in 1970 on *Curry and Chips* within IBA's Television Opinion Panel.[23] After the November debut of the programme, the January 1970 study was led by Dr Ian Haldane (Head of Research at

---

[19] Ibid., 228–230.
[20] Chris Dunkley, 'Programme Reported to Race Board', *The Times*, 1 January 1970, 3.
[21] Ibid.  [22] 'No Race Probe into *Curry and Chips*', *Daily Mail*, 21 November 1969, 9.
[23] TOP Market Research Report, *Curry and Chips Questionnaire*, 15 January 1970, in IBA/409, Folder RK/3/64, ITA/IBA Collection, University of Bournemouth.

IBA) and made use of the same basic premise of the BBC's but with some key simplifications.[24] A range of men and women made up the television viewing panel, the TOP, drawn from London and Lancaster in this case, making a total of 673 respondents (55 per cent of whom had seen the show) and all who were noted as being white.[25] Viewers were asked only five broad questions about episode two of the programme instead of the multi-question approach at the BBC's Audience Research department. IBA compiled their statistics from this data. Viewers were asked to complete the statement, 'I found the way the programme showed coloured people ...' from a choice of responses such as 'very objectionable' to 'not really objectionable at all'.

What resulted was a very different picture of viewer response to *Curry and Chips* from that represented in the mailbag to ITA. In contrast to the numerous complaints received in the mailbox, the research report recorded that 88 per cent of those surveyed decreed the episode of *Curry and Chips* 'not really objectionable at all' with only 2 per cent finding it 'very objectionable' and 9 per cent 'quite objectionable'. What emerged from the 1970 study was an audience that was *not* outraged by the bad language or the racist statements made in the programme. The television panel was conducted after the negative coverage of the programme in the press, which may well have led to viewers responding to this and asserting the programme as being racially innocent in the aftermath. Much as had been the case with the *Rainbow City* report, viewers also indicated that existing attitudes towards immigrants were not likely to shift because of the programme. *Curry and Chips* did not, in other words, increase sympathy towards immigrants tolerating the racist abuse featured in the programme but simply enforced existing attitudes. Analysis of the TOP surveys showed British audiences as mostly content to endorse the programme as largely unremarkable and even ordinary in 1970. In this case and in a moment that reflected the political if not popular exile of Enoch Powell, the mailbag and the loud complaints as the programme aired spoke more loudly than the TOP results communicated to ITA after its broadcast, causing the show to not be renewed at ITV and for LWT to distance itself from it. At ITV, this particular racial comedy came to an end, but ITV would revisit the racial sitcom in another less crude format in the new comedy series *Love Thy Neighbour* three years later in April 1972 for Thames Television. In the aftermath of the *Curry and Chips* broadcast on ITV and its subsequent

---

[24] On Haldane, see Jeremy Potter, *Independent Television in Britain*, Vol. 3.
[25] This approach had been in place since 1969 at the ITA; see David Wilsworth, 'Viewers to Judge ITA Items', *The Times*, 1 January 1969, 3.

abandonment, Speight also did not find his star much dimmed at the BBC. On the contrary, in June 1970 a *Till Death Us Do Part* general election special penned by Speight was aired on BBC, and in September 1972, *Till Death Us Do Part* returned in a weekly format.

Seven years after *Till Death Us Do Part* debuted on BBC and three years after the *Curry and Chips* study at ITV, Brian Emmett was tasked by the BBC's Board of Governors to investigate, as he put it, 'the possibility that the "*Till Death Us Do Part*" series might be "backfiring" by strengthening prejudices'.[26] This concern of the Board of Governors arose in part from ongoing criticisms by civil rights campaigners about the BBC's treatment of racism more broadly. The special audience research report on the show was commissioned in March 1973 after the 1972 Uxbridge by-election, which saw gains for the National Front but before their relative success in the local elections in April and the West Bromwich by-election of May.[27] Ignoring this political context the Audience Research Department proved its ongoing fidelity to both the concept of the racially innocent British audience and notions of British tolerance with Emmett clearly laying out to staff what he expected the study to find and optimistically titling the report based on this thesis, '*Till Death Us Do Part* as Anti-Prejudice Propaganda'.[28] Emmett indicated: 'The only sort of change that seems at all likely is a shift in the point of view of some who were formerly opposed to certain prejudices but at the same time had a sneaking feeling that there might be something in them, to a more positively antagonistic feeling that the prejudices in question are risible.'[29]

In keeping with the logic of the racial innocence of British audiences, Emmett anticipated that the racial stereotypes *Till Death Us Do Part* deployed could have little negative impact on viewers but could bring about a slightly positive impact in terms of racial prejudice. He imagined that racial prejudice, which he characterised quite benignly as that 'sneaking feeling' of some white viewers, would melt away when made manifest on the television screen. This was Audience

---

[26] Audience Research Department, Till Death Us Do Part *as Anti-Prejudice Propaganda: A Study of the Relationships Between Viewing the Series, Perceptions of the Garnett Family and Attitudes Such as Authoritarianism and Racial Prejudice*, March 1973, p. 1, *Till Death Us Do Part*, Part I/R78/2.811/1, WAC.

[27] Matthew Worley and Nigel Copsey, *Tomorrow Belongs to Us: The British Far Right Since 1967* (London: Routledge, 2017); Nigel Copsey and John E. Richardson, *Cultures of Post-War British Fascism* (London: Routledge, 2015); Evan Smith, *British Communism and the Politics of Race* (Leiden: Brill, 2017).

[28] Audience Research Department, Till Death Us Do Part *as Anti-Prejudice Propaganda*, ii.

[29] Brian Emmett, 'A Proposal for Studying the Impact of *Till Death Us Do Part*', undated, *Till Death Us Do Part*, Part I, R78/2.811/1, WAC.

Research's version of Speight's long-running argument in favour of the show's racist content.[30]

The special audience research report on *Till Death Us Do Part* possessed all the hallmarks of the reports that had come prior to it. This one ran to 61 pages in length with 23 pages of analysis and 38 pages of data in appendices but was again identified by its authors as 'hastily mounted research' based on the responses of the study's 772 interviewees.[31] This was nevertheless a more robust and geographically diverse data set than that provided in either the *Rainbow City* report at the BBC or the *Curry and Chips* one at the IBA having been drawn from interviews conducted in ten UK cities where respondents 'completed lengthy questionnaires in local halls hired for the purpose'.[32] The report's authors included, as usual, an introduction that began by noting the difficulty in trying to establish cause and effect between the programme's impact on the pre-existing views of its audiences. This was described as: 'Attempting to disentangle the complex web or relationship between past experiences (e.g. of foreigners), present social environment (e.g. non-British workmates, neighbours, etc), viewing or not viewing of the series, and present attitudes towards foreigners, Unions, etc.'.[33]

The report's authors concluded that their aim was 'the exploration of the significance of the series for viewers rather than its effects on them'.[34] It noted that the sheer popularity of *Till Death Us Do Part* made it difficult to obtain the usual matching of non-viewers with viewers leading to a spread of 382 self-described regular viewers, 235 occasional viewers and 156 non-viewers. The demographic balance of those interviewed was also weighted towards younger viewers as poor weather impeded turnout, leaving viewers over the age of 55 under-represented in the study.[35] All respondents were guaranteed anonymity and were given 50p for participating.

What resulted was a potential indictment of the existing logic of racial innocence that had animated BBC programming up to this point. The 'sneaking feeling' of racism that the BBC's Audience Research Department was eager to imagine was quickly dispatched in favour of a blunter adherence to racialised thinking as both viewers and non-viewers largely endorsed the character Garnett's more extreme statements on race such as, 'All these immigrants shouldn't have been let in in the first place' (21 per cent agreed strongly, 22 per cent agreed and an

---

[30] Schaffer, '*Till Death Us Do Part* and the BBC: Racial Politics and the British Working Classes 1965–75', *Journal of Contemporary History* 45, no. 2 (2010): 454–477.
[31] *Till Death Us Do Part as Anti-Prejudice Propaganda*, 2.   [32] Ibid. ii.   [33] Ibid., 2.
[34] Ibid.   [35] Ibid., 4.

uncommonly large 24 per cent were undecided).[36] Viewers were asked to consider whether the following statements best described Alf:

- A foul-mouthed ignorant fool unfortunately typical of too many people in this country.
- People as stupid and ignorant as him make progress impossible.
- So extreme in his views that he's just a joke.
- Unimportant and insignificant.
- Misguided but harmless.
- Although his views are too extreme most of the time, some of the things he says are true.
- Right more often than he's wrong.[37]

What is striking is the study's initial positioning of the programme and its characters within the framework of harmlessness. Three of the questions invoked the terms 'harmless', 'unimportant' or 'joke' for interpreting the relative power of Alf's impact and views. Viewers, however, were notably reluctant to characterise Alf as an unimportant and insignificant character with 50 per cent of regular viewers refusing to characterise him as such, a result that may also intersect with the relatively scarce representations of the working classes on television at the time. Most telling of all, however, were the responses to the statement, 'Although his views are too extreme most of the time, some of the things he says are true.' Of regular viewers, 84 per cent endorsed this statement; of occasional viewers, 74 per cent did; non-viewers registered 50 per cent agreement. Staff in the Audience Research Department noted this strong response. Concerns over immigration and a desire to curb it were also expressed by viewers and non-viewers alike: 47 per cent 'agreed strongly' and 29 per cent 'agreed' with the statement 'The laws on immigration should be much stricter.' This statement also raised an uncommonly low number of 'undecided' responses at 7 per cent and another 12 per cent of respondents disagreeing with it and only another 5 per cent disagreeing strongly. Immigration was clearly a potent issue for the majority of both viewers and non-viewers of the programme.[38] There was, however, less hostility towards interracial marriage than what was registered in the 1968 Special Audience Research Report on *Rainbow City* with 52 per cent of respondents now agreeing with the statement 'Marriages between

---

[36] Ibid., 36.    [37] Ibid., 8.
[38] Ibid., 36–37. It is worth noting the anti-union and anti-'women's lib' sentiment evident in this survey. Florence Sutcliffe-Braithwaite, *Class, Politics, and the Decline of Deference in England, 1968–2000* (Oxford: Oxford University Press, 2018); Florence Sutcliffe-Braithwaite and Natalie Thomlinson, 'Vernacular Discourses of Gender Equality in the Post-War British Working Class', *Past & Present* 254, no. 1 (2022): 217–233.

persons of different races should be socially acceptable' and a further 24 per cent agreeing strongly. Racial attitudes were not, on this basis, set in stone among viewers, although the report made no explicit reference to the *Rainbow City* study.

Aside from the positive development of audiences exhibiting some acceptance of interracial relationships, the evidence of audience prejudice unearthed amongst viewers in the 1973 report found the Audience Research Department again attempting to analyse discomforting data about the racial prejudice of white Britons and audiences. The department tried to adhere to Emmett's initial thesis and worked to minimise the report's findings in its written summary by acknowledging some of the more disturbing data evident within it but noting that these results may have been a fault of the study's own methodology: 'All in all, this hastily mounted research confirms the expectations with which it was begun, i.e. That there has been little or no attitude change as a direct result of viewing the latest *Till Death* series, but probably some reinforcement of existing views, both liberal and illiberal.'[39]

The programme and the racist attitudes expressed within it were again presented as harmless for British viewers. Emmett's initial guess that the show was likely to have a small impact towards increasing tolerance was recast instead as a slightly sharper assessment that the programme simply firmed up existing attitudes. British audiences were left constructed as racially innocent within the analysis, if not the data, and hasty arrangements, it was implied, largely bore the fault of any outcome that pointed to audience responses rooted in anti-immigrant sentiments in Britain in the year 1973.

As the report circulated through the halls of the BBC, however, some readers drew different conclusions from the *Till Death Us Do Part* study than those presented by the Audience Research Department in its analysis. What followed was a type of uncomfortable dance when it came to talking about racism. We see this play out in the minutes of the archive. The BBC first defended the study, then hastily moved away from the study and then partially decried the Audience Research Department itself as the difficult and indeed institutionally challenging nature of the findings became clear. Support for the study's veracity was initially articulated by Tom Morgan, Controller for Information within the BBC, who warmly thanked Emmett's department stating 'In my opinion, it is a useful and commendable piece of research which I am delighted was undertaken by your department', before asking that it be circulated

---

[39] Till Death Us Do Part *as Anti-Prejudice Propaganda*, ii.

'according to normal procedures' after the Board of Management's General Advisory Council (GAC) and the Board of Governors had received copies to examine.[40] It was at the GAC that a critical interpretation of the report's findings was voiced. In a minuted meeting on 18 July 1973, members of the GAC commenced a brief discussion of the report without much comment initially from the BBC's Director-General Charles Curran (1969–1977).[41] Curran's own shift away from Hugh Greene's investment in the BBC as anti-racist in its stance and towards a concept of neutrality for the BBC in the 1970s is well documented by Gavin Schaffer. Curran was increasingly intent for issues of racism to be debated by BBC coverage as a means of demonstrating that the BBC was not, as Schaffer notes, 'choosing sides'.[42]

In the GAC's discussion oversights in the report were politely aired. Mrs Peggy Joy first noted that an 'accidental omission' in the survey's instructions had obviously and regrettably led to an absence in the study of questions about the programme's female characters. The protagonists consistent habit of referring to his wife as a silly cow was perhaps at the forefront of Mrs Joy's thinking. Miss Noira Shearer followed this up by noting that 'trivial grounds for complaint' and swearing preoccupied public responses to the programme. Yet it was the comments of Professor Richard Aaron, a professor of philosophy at the University of Aberystwyth, that provoked a direct response from the Director General.[43] 'Professor Aaron said that one interesting point in the Report was that it had shown that a programme which had started as "anti-prejudiced propaganda" had in fact had the reverse effect, of increasing prejudice.'[44]

This was a much sharper interpretation of the report's data than had been put forth by the Audience Research Department. Indeed, the very aim of the report and its carefully passive language deliberately abandoned the notion that such a firm relationship between racist content on screen and audience prejudice could even exist. Professor Aaron's interpretation overlooked this obfuscation and had the weight of an academic's analysis of the sometimes baffling data put forth by the Audience Research Department. None of the members of the GAC responded

---

[40] Confidential memo from Tom Morgan to BBC General Advisory Council, 4 July 1973, *Till Death Us Do Part*, Part I, R78/2.811/1, WAC.
[41] General Advisory Council, Extract from the minutes of a meeting held on 18 July 1973, *Till Death Us Do Part*, Part I, R78/2.811/1, WAC.
[42] Schaffer, *The Vision of a Nation*, 82–85.
[43] Aaron's background is described in Asa Briggs, *The History of Broadcasting in the United Kingdom*, Vol. 5 (Oxford: Oxford University Press, 1995), 460.
[44] General Advisory Council, Extract from the minutes of a meeting held on 18 July 1973.

until Curran himself weighed in to offer his own rather softer interpretation:

> The Director-General said that the Report presented certain difficulties in interpretation. It showed conclusively that the programme had been considered entertaining, and it had, for him, diminished his confidence in the argument that it was possible to make anti-prejudicial comedy, while reinforcing the feeling that what mostly happened was that prejudice was reinforced by references to them of any kind.[45]

This was the perspective of a Director General with a hit on his hand but who also expressed frank doubts about the approach of 'anti-prejudicial comedy'. Curran noted immediately the flexibility that had always been inherent in audience research at the BBC – the 'certain difficulties in interpretation' meant data could be interpreted to a variety of ends and this was, in fact, its well-established institutional function by the 1970s. He also noted that the show was a hit. Yet Curran seemed somewhat ready to abandon presentations of racism at all on screen arguing that racial prejudice should simply not be presented at all. In some ways, Curran seemed ready to acknowledge the concept of the racially innocent, white British audience was not a sound foundation upon which to build programming on 'race', however broadly conceived. Curran, thinking in line with that logic, mused out loud that to 'reference' bad behaviour, in this case racial prejudice, was to prompt its imitation by the audience.

What followed the Director-General's statement in the meeting was a pattern of uncomfortable reactions that critical race theorists have repeatedly identified in discussions of race and racism among majority-white groups. White fragility was clearly on display. The topic of audience racism was avoided after Aaron and Curran's exchange, in favour of a critique of the methods that unearthed it which helpfully invalidated the findings of racism among the white audience. We see a neat alignment of the sleights of hand that racially discomforted white executives could mount to evade discussions of racism within an institution. Audience Research's own slippery role within the BBC proved useful in discounting the very thing it unearthed. Tom Morgan had already done early work in this regard noting in the Business Committee's discussion on 6 June 1973 that 'while the study did not purport to provide final or definite conclusions, the Committee felt that it did achieve the purpose of providing useful information on a number of points'.[46] Nothing 'final' or

---

[45] Ibid.
[46] Confidential Memo from Tom Jones, Controller of Information, to the General Advisory Council, 4 July 1973, *Till Death Us Do Part*, Part I, R78/2.811/1, WAC.

'definite' could be drawn from such a study, and this was made before Professor Aaron made his point. Morgan also felt compelled to highlight immediately in his cover letter for the report to the GAC that the Business Committee 'regretted that, as pointed out in the report, a separate sample of coloured people could not be included'.[47] Audiences of colour, crucially, had not been interviewed in this expansive new study on the anti-prejudicial aspect of a show renowned for its racist jokes and did not form part of the regular viewing panels. The report was thus shown to be flawed on two counts: firstly for demonstrating that white audiences were prejudiced and secondly for focussing only on a white audience. The Chairman of the GAC further contributed to doubts abouts the report's methodology and findings when he commented that 'some member of the Council would no doubt consider that only the most thorough research had any value' before carefully noting that he 'personally did not share that opinion of the report, and he felt that the Council might well express its gratitude to the BBC for having a followed up a line of thought developed out of earlier discussion'. Audience Research had been a good servant again and done what it had been asked to do. Professor Aaron also did not press his point. However, most damningly for the Audience Research Department's credibility, the Chairman was then recorded as noting 'even a limited research project had value if its limitations were realised and accepted'.[48] Further points were clearly made but not minuted in the archival evidence. The discussion ended with Sir Michael Swann stating that the BBC had chosen not to publish the report as it was 'vulnerable to attack from experts in the field of sociological research'.

It would have indeed been relatively easy to invalidate elements of the report's methodologies if the study had been subject to peer review. The report cited as foundational to its approach a study from 1947 on responses to a newspaper cartoon series referred to as 'the Mr Biggott cartoons'. The use of a 26-year-old article by Eunice Cooper and Maria Jahoda, 'How prejudiced people respond to anti-prejudice propaganda' in the *Journal of Psychology*,[49] as the basis of an approach to examining the media's impact on race-relations in 1973, would likely have formed part of the criticism of the report's methodologies. Instead the ground was laid for the report to be swept away and limited to the dusty and rather irrelevant confines of the Audience Research Department. No news of

---

[47] Ibid.
[48] General Advisory Council, extract from the minutes of a meeting held 18 July 1973.
[49] Eunice Cooper and Maria Jahoda, 'How Prejudiced People Respond to Anti-prejudice Propaganda', *Journal of Psychology* 23 (1947): 15–25.

the report's findings ever reached the press in the summer of 1973. Ever attentive to the work that Audience Research did and both unwilling and unable to abandon what was by then a well-established and flexible arm of the BBC, Swann went on to state of the report that 'they had recognised its value and he hoped that it might be possible to strengthen the audience research team so that they could undertake more penetrating studies in the future'.[50] Once again Audience Research at the BBC seemed poised to expand based on criticisms of its murky but vital data production. More importantly the crucial issue of the pleasures of audience racism that attended some BBC programming was studiously avoided through a quiet dismissal of the report; it was much easier to discuss faulty methodologies and to dismiss outcomes than it was to discuss what was by then an emergent pattern within audience research at the BBC, four years on from the report on *Rainbow City* that documented audience racism in Britain. White fragility and the inability to acknowledge and discuss racism within the institution of the BBC led to silence and inaction. *Till Death Us Do Part* continued on the BBC with no evident restraint in the racist sentiments of the character of Alf Garnett. Less than a year after the Audience Research special report was discussed at the BBC's General Advisory Council in July, *Till Death Us Do Part* broadcast an episode in February 1974 in its fifth series titled 'Paki-Paddy', reviving a blacked-up Spike Milligan in his *Curry and Chips* role as Kevin O'Grady as a new neighbour to the Garnetts.[51] The logic of the racially innocent audience seemed firmly in place.

## 6.2 Audiences of Colour in the BBC's and IBA's Audience Research

It was not until 1975 at the IBA and 1978 at the BBC that audiences of colour were present within audience research studies. This presence was also highly circumscribed by the racialised assumptions of both audience research departments and those engaged in content production. The long absence of Black and south Asian audiences from the institutional environments of audience research shaped subsequent engagement in important ways that favoured an emphasis upon continuity rather than change when it came to depictions of racialised people on screen and the framing of an uncomfortable subject such as racism. The pathways and methods of audience research at the BBC and the IBA, as we have seen,

---

[50] General Advisory Council, extract from the minutes of a meeting held 18 July 1973.
[51] 'Paki-Paddy' was broadcast on BBC1 on 28 February 1974. Dick Fiddy, *Till Death Us Do Part* Series Guide, DVD (London: Network BBC, 2016), 31.

hinged on two seemingly contradictory central beliefs by the audience research departments; firstly, that audience research was thoroughly measuring Britain's television audience and doing this well even while expecting the audience panels to consist solely of white people; secondly, that the racism that both organisations had encountered when measuring the attitudes of white audiences might possibly be explained away by the departments' own methodological inferiorities, which presented as largely unrelated to the racial composition of the panels, but linked to the external pressures that the BBC placed upon them through hasty requests and plans. It was in the realm of audience racism that the audience research departments seemed particularly willing to abandon their own expertise on audiences. The presence of Black and south Asian audiences thus posed a provocation to audience research's claim to comprehensiveness, ultimately leading to more marginalisation and a pronounced disengagement with these communities in Britain. For audiences of colour, a late invitation into the powerful institutions of television at the end of the 1970s set a scene that hinted at the potentially fleeting and contingent nature of their presence. Audience research's overdue engagement with audiences of colour clearly favoured and signalled to the latter the fruitfulness of a collaboration with the racism of audiences, rather than invitations for education or reproach. White fragility, in other words, became the unacknowledged actor in these encounters and a presence obvious to most Black and south Asian participants yet painfully less so to white staff in these institutions.

The first invitation for Black British audiences to comment on programming of the 1970s was made through ITV. In May 1975, seven months before the Race Relations Board made its formal entreaty to the Annan Committee that 'more races should be represented in viewing and listening panels' and a month before the nation would vote to stay in the European Common Market, IBA's Audience Research Department produced a survey of responses to their own hit racial sitcom *Love Thy Neighbour* but with a new and novel approach of surveying 'coloured immigrants'.[52] *Love Thy Neighbour* was very much in the tradition of *Till Death Us Do Part* with a bigoted lead, Eddie Booth and his long-suffering wife Joan Booth, but with one significant change in that it included two Black actors as central characters in the programme, Bill and Barbie Reynolds as the new neighbours to the Booths. They show did not rely on blackface and the two Black actors, played by Rudolph Walker and Nina Baden-Semper were substantial roles as they played a

---

[52] J.M. Goose, 26 November 1975, Race Relations Board's Evidence to the Committee on the Future of Broadcasting/HO 245/1568, TNA.

comparatively hip and fashionable young couple next to the more staid Booths. In 1972 when the show debuted, this counted as progress within British television as two Black actors took prominent roles on the small screen.[53] Yet the show itself was still rooted in a formula that saw the racist thinkings of the protagonist as a central animating force in its weekly episodes and the show was, as a result, not without its critics in the period, prompting the creation of this new and novel survey of what Black viewers thought of the programme.

What resulted was a unique report in terms of methodology which drew on only 21 interviews with immigrants, making for a brief, double-spaced report of only nine pages that strikes one as immediately materially different from the longer, denser Special Audience Research Reports that had been previously conducted for the IBA.[54] Media Studies scholar Sally Shaw has examined this report and *Love Thy Neighbour*'s approach to racial comedy more broadly but divorced from the broader activities of audience research in the period.[55] The report's premise was like the others we have already examined, rooted in assumptions about the racial innocence of white viewers as its introduction noted. It cited the long-standing argument by both Johnny Speight and Vince Powell that *Love They Neighbour* 'allows, so the argument goes, the racial bigot to see, and laugh at, a reflection of his own prejudices and thereby encourages him to modify them'.[56] Yet the authors of the report also admitted that this premise resulted in 'anti-coloured abuse directed (albeit in the framework of comedy) towards the Black neighbour Bill' on screen and acknowledged the protagonist Eddie Booth's 'racialist outpourings'. The show's consistent use of the term 'nig nog' by Eddie Booth and his often racist outbursts towards his Black neighbours were thus gently framed. The authors commented that this intent and these 'outpourings' may well prompt different outcomes among Black audiences, who were presented as sensitive and potentially fiery: 'Overtly these are seen to be so inane and outmoded that they are not to be taken seriously. But with race – and more particularly coloured immigrants – the tinder-box issue

---

[53] For a discussion of another vital aspect of 1970s television programming, see, Chelsea Saxby, 'Making Love on British Telly: Watching Sex, Bodies, and Intimate Lives in the Long 1970s', (PhD diss., University of Birmingham, 2021).

[54] It is also worth noting that the report is printed in landscape, rather than portrait, format. A portrait format would have highlighted its slimness even further; IBA Special Report, *Love Thy Neighbour – What Coloured Immigrants Think*, 1975, IBA/00416, ITA/ITB Collection, University of Bournemouth.

[55] Sally Shaw, 'Light Entertainment as Contested Socio-Political Space: Audience and Institutional Responses to *Love Thy Neighbour* (1972–76)', *Critical Studies in Television* 7, no. 1 (2012): 64–78.

[56] IBA Special Report, *Love Thy Neighbour*, 1.

that it is, doubt has been expressed as to just what the programme is achieving in terms of race relations.'[57]

Where this 'doubt' originated from is not specified, but ITV clearly felt compelled to respond with this study. At the outset of the report, discussion of *Love Thy Neighbour*'s popularity with eighteen million viewers gave way to a consideration of the programme's effect, 'if only in an exploratory manner'.[58] The study decided against a formal approach of the usual panel of 600 people or more, which it had pursued for white viewers of *Curry and Chips* in 1970, in favour of 'loosely guided taped interviews' with 21 'mainly adult coloured immigrants' later identified as 'all West Indians' in a variety of locations in London that included Brixton, Shepherds Bush, Edmonton and Swiss Cottage. The survey took place in 'locations varying from sittings rooms to railway stations'. The interviews were also conducted by 'an experienced coloured interviewer to help allay any doubts, suspicion or hesitations that the respondents may feel if confronted about race by a white interviewer'.[59] No record or transcription of the interviews accompanied the report although the existence of a tape was noted; nor was any statistical analysis incorporated beyond a rudimentary summation. Instead quotes from responses were included which sided with the report's central findings that 'of the twenty-one people interviewed sixteen said they enjoyed watching *Love Thy Neighbour* and took not offence from its racial motif' and that 'anyone listening to the tape searching for an underlying yet widespread anxiety among coloured immigrants about the programme would find themselves unrewarded'.[60] In this case the views of Black audiences were offered as an authority on whether the show was racist or not racist and the resulting, largely anecdotal data from a methodology unlike any previously pursued in audience research supported this.

The singular nature of IBA's brief report on 'What coloured Immigrant Viewers Think' of *Love Thy Neighbour* spoke to a broader issue at both broadcasters about their consistent reluctance to engage with Black and south Asian audiences. The 1975 *Love Thy Neighbour* report exemplified this when it effectively abandoned the usual methods of Audience Reaction Assessment (AURA) that had been in place since 1974. The decision at IBA to pursue a study of Black audiences of *Love Thy Neighbour* outside of AURA signalled the discomfort the study raised within the workings of the institution. Such as study indicated just how marginal this audience was to ITV's programming decisions and underlined the institutional whiteness of the IBA. The IBA instead introduced

[57] Ibid.  [58] Ibid., 2.  [59] Ibid., 3.  [60] Ibid., 4.

a degree of separation between the white IBA Audience Research Department and audiences of colour as a central component of the study. A relationship between audiences of colour and the white-oriented programming of ITV for the purpose of the report was instead mediated by an interviewer of colour, ostensibly in order to fend off what the department imagined would be 'doubts, suspicion or hesitation' on the part of Black audiences but which also likely encompassed and served the racial fragility of white interviewers from AURA who did not necessarily want to discuss this sitcom and its 'racialist outpourings' with Black viewers.

Locating Black viewers of *Love Thy Neighbour* necessitated a different approach to sample size. Audience Research was thus content with a small, informal sample and one that the report deemed 'the most practical approach'. The relative size of the Black population in the UK was not pointed to in the report as justification for such a small sample size and nor was the white composition of the existing television panels mentioned. No explanation for the unique methodology was offered. From the historian's perspective the informal approach, the very limited size of the study and its departure from existing norms in the field raises the possibility that the survey may have resulted from someone at ITV knowing a West Indian man who liked the programme and subsequently asking him to produce a study to that end to mollify criticisms of the programme. Certainly the reference to interviews in drawing rooms meant that the unnamed interviewer who crucially was never claimed as part of the Audience Research Department at IBA but was nevertheless identified as 'experienced' spoke to the possibility of a small discreet network of the Black interviewer himself. Regardless the interviews seemed to provide on first glance the answers that ITV wanted. Most enjoyed the show the report concluded confidently: 'Whilst a small number mentioned that they enjoyed the comedy but would prefer to see the race jokes moderated, a roughly comparable number specifically mentioned the racial humour as one of the programme's main attractions.'[61]

No numeric qualification was provided in the report to further define what a 'roughly comparable' or a 'small number' translated into. The report pointed out that the majority of respondents who were not bothered by the racialising language of the series 'followed the escapist line by talking about getting home from work, putting their feet up, and wanting simply good entertainment'.[62] This was a powerful argument in

---

[61] Ibid., 4.  [62] Ibid.

favour of a type of universalising, racially innocent category of 'simply good entertainment' that echoed the 'traditional' British pleasures on screen talked about in Chapter 4. Such an argument could and no doubt did encompass Black audiences as well as white audiences, but crucially this argument favoured existing structures of racialising narratives on screen and necessitated no change to ITV's hit series, nor did it point to the need to further incorporate Black audiences into its audience research practices.

A closer examination of the responses given by the West Indian interviewees gives us a much fuller discussion of the experiences and expectations of Black audiences than what the white authors compiling the report were able or willing to acknowledge. The report itself documents an impressive act by the white authors of not knowing or recognising expressions of racial discomfort by the Black interviewees in their frank discussions of the limited opportunities for West Indian audiences to see Black actors and actresses on screen at the time. The white authors in the Audience Research Department cheerfully summarised the positive response of one male interviewee who stated he enjoyed *Love Thy Neighbour* 'because it was the only British programme which regularly featured black artists in the leading roles – this alone was enough to please him'.[63] This on-screen scarcity informed the acceptance of the programme for this Black audience member in a period when *The Black and White Minstrel Show* was also still being broadcast on television. The report further noted the main grounds for objection to the programme among the 'the few who found cause for criticism' centred on the argument that 'the gibes should not be there at all, that they are offensive to black people and that they are likely to be picked up by suggestible viewers'. No comment was made about this by the report's authors but two sentences were spent on the suggestions by 'two or three' interviewees, including a 12-year-old school boy that Bill's character could be 'hitting back a little harder' at Eddie's digs. The 12-year-old school boy was also quoted as commenting that 'kids at school pick up names from the programme but that doesn't worry me too much'.[64] The racist language Eddie used in the series, referring constantly to West Indian immigrants as 'nig nogs' was thus cast as 'gibes' by the report's authors.

The report further noted with approval 'on the credit side' that 'one of those interviewed said he thought the programme positively showed people how to take taunts and not feel hurt when called racial names'. The IBA Audience Research Department's perspective on the

---

[63] Ibid., 6.   [64] Ibid., 8.

contributions of the racial sitcoms to the lived experiences of Black audiences in 1975 came into view, and the programme's normalisation of racial slurs for Black viewers was written up at the IBA as a positive outcome at the time. The back of the report included selected quotes as 'illustrative excerpts' from the participants including one 'social worker, male 16–34', who was quoted as saying, 'The insults may seem offensive on "the surface" but beneath you can see clearly that they're not – they're just jokes. Years ago people used the word "nigger" and meant it – nowadays you can be called nig-nog and no-one is offended – it's taking the edge off things.'[65]

This assessment of *Love Thy Neighbour* reveals the racialised everyday of this Black viewer in 1970s Britain which involved the evaluation of racialised encounters as endangering or not but which also fell short of exonerating *Love Thy Neighbour* of racist language and stereotyping. Out of the eleven 'illustrative excerpts' from the interviews included in the report, eight qualified whatever praise they offered *Love Thy Neighbour* by pointing out the racial context in which the series operated with two respondents recounting that 'I get called far worse things at work by my mates but I don't mind [Painter]' and 'there are far worse things on television – violence and swear words – for people to pick up: that worries me far more [Retired Male]'. The report's white authors, analysing the data provided by the un-named West Indian interviewer, did attempt in the last paragraph of the report to consider the perspective of Black audiences of the programme: 'Even taking into account that the sample size was very small and that the nature of the exercise was such that only the barest motive and attitudes would be revealed, it still seems unlikely that the coloured immigrant population as a whole is offended by Love Thy Neighbour.'[66]

The summary went so far as to suggest that a 'coloured AI' (appreciation index) of the programme, placing this in quotations to signal the relative novelty of such a thing, would probably be high. Yet the report did sound a note of doubt as it examined the responses of the statistically irrelevant sample it featured when it reflected on its findings:

'How significant is it that of the twenty-one interviewed, not one claimed he enjoyed the programme because in it the white man for a change was made to look stupid and primitive whereas the black man was portrayed as handsome and clean living?'[67] The answer to this, no doubt, lay in the unremarkability of such a representation in both the lives and imaginations of Black audiences.

---

[65] Ibid.    [66] Ibid., 6.    [67] Ibid.

Such a premise was not a novelty or a stretch of one's imagination for a Black viewer. White men could be 'stupid' and 'primitive' but also powerful in the Black everyday, just as Black men and women were also likely to be 'handsome and clean living' as a matter of course. The report ended its analysis on a speculative note that simultaneously raised the prospect of a modern form of racial representation in post-war Britain and a white audience that might not have an appetite for it, when it mused: 'It could well be that "Love Thy Neighbour" less the racial abuse (i.e. with Eddie as clown rather than racialist clown) would be just as popular with coloured viewers as it is at present. Quite what affect such a move would have on the white audience though is a different matter.'[68]

The report hinted at what had been found when shows that explicitly relied upon racist treatments such as *The Black and White Minstrel Show* altered their format. It touched ever so briefly on the possibility of the pleasures of racism for white audiences of *Love Thy Neighbour* in 1975. Regardless, *Love Thy Neighbour* continued on as it had until 1976 unchanged and with no discernible moderation of Eddie's racial abuse. No 'coloured AI' manifested at IBA even as the Children's and Teenagers AURAs emerged in 1977 and as Britain's audiences of colour grew. West Indian and also south Asian audiences remained at a distance.

The inability of both broadcasters to effectively reach out to and measure Black and south Asian audience response was by the end of the 1970s a well-entrenched but also slightly defensive aspect of both audience research branches. At the BBC, in lieu of meaningful work in the Audience Research Department, references were frequently made as late as 1978 to the two one-day 'Conferences of Immigrants' held under General Director Hugh Greene fifteen years earlier in 1965 as evidence of the BBC's engagement with audiences of colour. These two days of discussion did significant institutional work regarding 'race' at the BBC, so much so that the existence of these replaced any need for further engagement with the Audience Research department in the subsequent years. Into the latter half of the 1970s Audience Research continued to argue that connections with south Asian or Black immigrants was all but impossible in terms of data gathering and measurement. Records at the BBC indicate that even those Units tasked with producing 'minority programming' for both Britain's south Asian and 'West Indian' audiences did so without evidence from Audience Research on minority audiences. A report in 1977 titled 'A report on the contribution made by broadcasting to meeting the educational needs of immigrant workers

[68] Ibid.

and their families in Great Britain' by Dan Cook and John Robottom included an extended section on the work of the BBC's Asian Programme Unit.[69] The history of the unit included repeated reference to the conferences of 1965 when 'the BBC engaged in a process of consultation with representatives of immigrant groups.[70]' This 'process of consultation,' in reality a one-day meeting with selected representatives of the community, was referenced again and again and was credited a prompting swift action at the BBC and its establishment of radio broadcasting for south Asian audiences. The 1977 report noted that the Black representatives felt different and that 'the consensus of opinion from organisations representing immigrants from the Caribbean was that they did not wish to be treated as separate or different from the bulk of the British population, though they did ask for greater participation in the BBC's general programmes'.[71] Black audiences were consequently left largely uncatered to in the BBC's structure by their own request at a one-day conference in 1965 according to Cook and Robottom's report, which was certainly a creative interpretation of the frustration of West Indian delegates at that conference with existing representations on screen. South Asian audiences were, the report noted, catered to through 'one hour of television and half hour of radio per week'.[72]

Even this small amount of radio programming for south Asian audiences was largely conducted, however, without benefit of Audience Research. South Asian audiences were instead described in intimidating terms by the unit as numerous and whose very diversity was reason for the unit's lack of engagement with them:

'To appreciate the unit's task, one must first consider the audience. It numbers more than 700,000 and is much less homogenous [sic] than the indigenous British population in its tastes, attitudes, social classes, religious beliefs, language, and general way of life.'[73] The report included the sub-heading 'Are we getting through?' asking the key question, 'What proportion of the target audience see or hear the BBC's programmes for immigrants?' The report admitted, 'To date there has been no formal survey by BBC Audience Research in this area. The potential audience is small for sampling purposes and the difficulties, linguistic and other, of communicating effectively with its members are considerable.'[74]

---

[69] For a more contemporary view of this unit, see Aujla-Sidhu, Gurvinder. *The BBC Asian Network: The Cultural Production of Diversity* (London: Palgrave, 2021).
[70] Dan Cook and John Robottom, 'A Report on the Contribution Made by Broadcasting to Meeting the Educational Needs of Immigrant Workers and Their Families in Great Britain', November 1977, 1–2, Programming for Racial Minorities-General Part 1, R78/2.538/1, WAC.
[71] Ibid., 1.   [72] Ibid., 3.   [73] Ibid.   [74] Ibid., 8.

Asian audiences were both too large at 'more than 700,000' on page three of the report and then too 'small for sampling purposes' on page eight of the report.[75] South Asian audiences were also imagined and characterised in November 1977 as not only diverse in terms of language but also as unable to speak English. Second or third generation south Asian people growing up and attending British schools were not acknowledged in this, those who were the descendants of participants at the 1965 conferences, and instead the emphasis seemingly lay on the immigration of south Asian people from Uganda into cities such as Leicester and elsewhere in the UK five years prior.[76] As south Asian communities were cast as beyond the abilities of the Audience Research Department to engage with, the Asian Programme Unit described what it did rely upon:

'From the evidence of correspondence, from contacts with the Advisory Committee and from its own researches [sic], the Asian Programme Unit has reason to believe that it is getting through, occasionally if not always regularly, to a very large proportion of that audience and that its efforts are greatly valued.'[77] This report created by the Asian Programme Unit about its own success made the construction of a particularly elusive Asian audience a useful foil through which to claim its own effectiveness and silenced the need for an approach that would potentially move the Unit into systematic engagement with the minority audiences it was meant to serve.[78]

The BBC's Audience Research Department did not undertake a consultation with television audiences of colour until 1979 when a visiting

---

[75] Ibid., 3, 8.
[76] Frances Eames, 'ITV and the 1972 Ugandan Migration', *Media History* 15, no. 4 (2009): 453–469; Joanna Herbert, *Negotiating Boundaries in the City: Migration, Ethnicity, and Gender in Britain* (London: Routledge, 2016).
[77] Dan Cook and John Robottom, Report on the Contribution, 8.
[78] Of the three television series that the Asian Programme Unit took credit for producing between 1965 and 1977, two had audience figures produced through the Audience Research Department. The first television series from 1968 to 1969, *In Our Midst*, was five 30-minute programmes broadcast in February and March 1969 at 9.30am on Sundays and 4.10pm on Mondays, aimed at white British teachers, on south Asian and West Indian children immigrating into Britain. It only gained 300,000 viewers or 0.6 per cent of the population, which the unit nevertheless praised 'for the kind of programme it was and the type of transmission which it had'. The unit's second programme, broadcast in 1974, was 'Black Man in Britain 1550–1950' and was meant to give a history of black people in British society. The report noted that 'although it was thought that the programme would be of particular interest to black people arriving in Britain, it also sought to give a much wider perspective on the settlement of black people in Britain to the host community'. The series had an average of 250,000 viewers or 0.5 per cent of the population, peaking at 500,000 viewers or 1 per cent of the population. This was enough to justify the programme being broadcast twice more in 1975; Cook and Robottom, Report on the Contribution, 14.

academic and social psychologist from the US, Professor Percy H. Tannenbaum from the University of California-Berkeley, mounted another speculative pre-broadcasting study how Black and white viewers might respond to what was called in pre-production 'The Multi-Racial Britain Programme'.[79] This study was conducted after the department had already measured the success of the American television series *Roots* – based on Alex Hale's novel about a multigenerational African-American family grappling with the legacies of slavery – with white British audiences.[80] The report on *Roots* was conducted in February 1978, almost a year after the programme was broadcast on BBC1 in April 1977, and showed enthusiasm for what was clearly identified by the audiences as an American story of slavery, but it was in March 1979 when Tannenbaum on sabbatical from Berkeley conducted the pre-broadcasting study for 'The Multi-Racial Britain Programme' with support from the Audience Research Department.[81] Tannenbaum worked in conjunction with another staff member at the Audience Research department, Irene Shaw, with Brian Emmett as then Head of the department and put at the centre of his study the question as to whether white or Black audiences would react differently to material conveyed by Black or white narrators or speakers on television. The report opened with the hypothesis, 'Does the racial identity of the voice-over reporter make a difference to audience reaction?'[82] Tannenbaum's introduction to the report described the usual practice of broadcasting on race relations and posed further questions for the study:

The conventional practice hitherto has been to have a typical white BBC announcer read the commentary prepared by a white BBC non-West Indian – and, indeed, that is how 'Black Roots' was originally prepared. What would happen if a clearly West Indian voice read the same commentary? What would be the difference, if any, if the commentary itself was written by a West Indian?[83]

The study pointed to an established practice within the documentary tradition under John Grierson when white middle-class narrators were

---

[79] 'Race: The Multi-Racial Britain Programme,' VR/79/86 Audience Research, R9/795/1, WAC.
[80] Audience Research Report: A Study of British Viewers' Reactions to the 'Roots' Series, February 1978, WAC; Martin Stollery, 'The Same, but a Step Removed: Aspects of British Reception of *Roots*', in Erica L. Ball and Kellie Carter Jackson, eds., *Reconsidering Roots: Race, Politics, and Memory* (Athens, GA: University of Georgia Press, 2017), 147–164.
[81] The outlines of this study and Tannenbaum's team are noted in the appendix of the report; Percy H. Tannenbaum, 'Research Related to Production: The Multi-Racial Britain Programme', VR/79/86 Audience Research, R9/795/1, WAC.
[82] Ibid., 2. [83] Ibid.

used in empire films to offer white audiences a guide through the strangeness they were encountering, as we have seen. In 1979 Tennenbaum sought to overturn this practice and see whether West Indian voices could act as that guide for both white and Black audiences. The study, however, downplayed the potential impact of such a shift within the landscape of broadcasting stating, 'these may not be the most profound questions involved in the race relations issue in the United Kingdom or in the production of a television series' before noting that it was of 'immediate concern to the series in question' from a production point of view and that it was also of a 'theoretical interest' in terms of 'cognitive consistency' where 'verbal and visual content was consistent'.[84] Buried within this academic study was the novel and previously untested concept at the BBC that perhaps it should be Black people who should be seen to speak on Black experiences. Tennenbaum further introduced a new methodology to the BBC in order to answer these questions by engaging not just with the well-established white television panels but also engaging with what the survey termed 'special interest groups' including 'professionals in the race industry' from the Runnymede Trust and the Commission for Racial Equality who it must be pointed out were not necessarily and indeed quite likely were not Black and another group involving 'West Indians active in community organisation in Tooting'.[85] The incorporation of these two groups was much more systematic than the scattershot approach taken by the IBA when surveying West Indian attitudes to *Love Thy Neighbour* in 1975.

The survey included at its outset a justification for examining a broader audience response than in previous studies based on the topic of the programme: 'The current research focussed on a series dealing with Britain as a multi-racial society, intended for a broader audience and involving, as any politically loaded issue must, a variety of interested constituencies.'[86] The section of the report outlining the incorporation of 'special interest' audiences into the study made a careful outline of the BBC's relationship to audiences of colour, again using similar phrasing:

As we noted at the outset of this report, one of the factors motivating the inclusion of the Multi-Racial Britain series in our current research programme was that it involved a number of different constituencies in a rather charged, if not volatile political environment. In such instances, the broadcaster, faced with the central mass communications dilemma of delivering essentially the same message to a vast but diversified audience, can rarely please all of them all the time, even some of them some of the time.[87]

[84] Ibid.   [85] Ibid., 9.   [86] Ibid., 1.   [87] Ibid., 9.

'A Sneaking Feeling' 223

A 'charged, if not volatile' political environment and 'different constituencies' signalled the challenges of diversity within the department. The two groups of race relations professionals and community organisers 'with particular vested interests in the topic of hand' were only included because, 'It was accordingly deemed worthwhile to obtain reaction from some of these, both for their own value as input to the producers, and for comparisons with the main experimental groups which were more representative of the ostensible target-audience for the multi-racial series.'[88]

The findings stemming from the two groups of race relations professionals and West Indian community organisers who presumably knew something different about 'race' were immediately situated as secondary to those from the main audience that the BBC and Audience Research department were interested in. A survey of the thoughts and responses of the 'professionals' and the 'West Indians' was presented as mere information gathering for the producers of the programme and as a point of comparison to the main event of the targeted audience's response to it and not something likely to influence programming decisions. What resulted from the survey in regards to its stated goal was a rather mixed response. There was a slight tendency among all the audience groups to view the footage with a voice-over from the white BBC commentator, using the script penned by the white BBC producer as most favourable; however, the West Indian commentary with the West Indian script was also seen as fairly positive by all sets of viewers. What was pointed to was an affirmation of a thesis floated in the report, that the voice-over and script should 'match' in order to establish continuity in terms of the authenticity of the report with audiences. No discernible negative response to the sounds of a West Indian speaker was registered by any group, which made a welcome change from some of the data previously collected by the Audience Research Department as we have seen.

What did come through in this survey of the 'special interest groups' was also a broad consensus on the mediocre content of the sample programme itself that was shown to the groups called 'Black Roots' and irrespective of which commentator offered the voice-over or script. The programme had distinct sections listed as 'Street Carnival, Slave Trade, Immigration, Unemployment, Rastafarians',[89] topics already familiar fodder when it came to representations of racialised groups on screen in Britain in 1979. News reporting covered these topics again and again as both Malik and Schaffer have noted.[90] The 'Professional Group' found the programme they saw which was the one with the 'BBC

---

[88] Ibid.  [89] Ibid., 3.
[90] Malik, *Representing Black Britain*; Schaffer, *The Vision of a Nation*.

commentary with West Indian commentator' as 'superficial, predictable, and disturbing' and noted in the discussion after the survey itself that a section showing 'the Street Carnival was considered a predictable if not a trite way of representing West Indians in the media'.[91] The response of the West Indian group who were shown the all-white programme penned by the white BBC producer and voiced by a white BBC commentator was granted an entire paragraph of discussion. The group was not enthusiastic about 'Black Roots' as a whole. At the heart of the lukewarm responses to the 'Black Roots' was a criticism by the West Indian audience of the rut that British television found itself in when it came to both presenting Black stories on television and to catering to white audiences and white audiences only:

> In the discussion which followed the viewing, there was a considerable amount of criticism of what was labelled a platitudinous and stereotyped portrayal of West Indians and the failure of the programme to tell the 'real' or 'full' West Indian community story. These reactions were not universally shared but they were frequent enough to deserve note. Several of the participants did make the point that such programmes were aimed not at a West Indian but at a 'white' audience who were apt to be relatively uninformed about West Indian community life, aspirations, hopes, and fears.[92]

The West Indian group invoked their own history as a Black audience in Britain and argued that programmes about multiracial Britain were imagined as for majority white viewers with critical Black audiences on the margins left pointing out the failures of such programming to move beyond stereotypes. Indeed, the Audience Research Department evidenced a discomfort with acknowledging even the racial identity of its majority audience placing quotation marks around the West Indian group's use of the term 'white audience'. This was an expressed unwillingness to see or know race, manifesting in a reluctance to even identify the audience as 'white' in institutional settings where the very methodologies of the Audience Research Department were rooted in its own problematic colour-blindness.

The audiences of colour who participated in the second component of the experiment called 'The West Indian Interview' viewed eight minutes of a white or Black reporter interviewing a West Indian community leader who highlighted the issues that West Indian students faced in the school. The responses of the 'professionals' and the 'West Indian group' were collected right after they were shown the 'Black Roots' footage with its commentary and presumably on the same day at

---

[91] Tannenbaum, 'Research Related to Production', 9–10.   [92] Ibid., 11.

Broadcasting House. This approach departed from the methodology of the rest of the experiment which saw new predominantly white respondents located and interviewed for the two separate programmes. Yet the two racialised groups were visited twice for their opinions, rather than placing the Audience Research Department and Tennenbaum in the position of locating more Black and 'professional' audiences. This amendment to the methodology limited the institution's exposure to audiences of colour. From the department's perspective this was undoubtedly for the sake of convenience, and it is difficult to know whether the West Indian and professional groups were aware of this exceptional treatment. Regardless, what resulted was a limited engagement by the BBC and the Audience Research Department with audiences of colour. This group spoke twice, not for the empowerment of the group but with the result that the institution did not encounter more non-white opinions and perspectives. Both groups were, however, more positive about the footage they were shown with the second part of the experiment and 'The West Indian Interview' as the report stated: 'It may be worthy to note that, in general, the West Indian group responded more favourably to this selection than they did to the "Black Roots" programme.' The poor quality and content of the 'Black Roots' programme primed the two racialised groups for a positive response to what they were given, which was a 'black interviewer asking white questions' as the study termed it. The West Indian group found this interview to be '*more* interesting, worthwhile, believable, truthful, fair and thorough'.

The final analysis in the report noted that when the white viewing groups each viewed a version of the interview that was either a white interview or Black interviewer asking questions originally posed by the white interviewers, or a third option that saw the 'Black interviewer asking his own questions', when comparing the white and Black reporter asking the 'white' questions 'on the whole the reaction to the Black interviewer version of the film is *less* favourable': '[White] [r]espondents found this version concerned them less closely and judged it as being *less* thorough, harmless, thought-provoking, inoffensive, and believable than was the case with the white interviewer version.'[93]

Further into the discussion of the 'Judgement of the interviewer' as ranked by the audience response, 'the *black* interviewer (group 2) does emerge as somewhat *more* sincere, warm and informative but at the same time *less* fair and emotionally detached'.[94] Just as Chapter 5 noted, the emotional frameworks of racialisation that white audiences applied to

[93] Ibid., 12.   [94] Ibid., 13.

Black audiences, within the pages of the glossies, pointed to this process at work within television viewing. The anticipated emotionality of Black people extended to positive attributes of 'warmth' amongst white viewers but also an expected bias and emotional investment that the white audience found less fair, less thought-provoking, and less believable.

Tennenbaum as the architect of the report ended it by noting the he could 'not fully resist adding some additional, though not necessarily novel, observations' and ultimately argued that given the overall picture of the data which did not draw any strong reactions from the audiences as a whole, particularly in the first component of the experiment, that 'departing from the hitherto standard BBC commentary-reporter format is a low risk proposition'. He further noted that 'both the Professional and West Indian pressure groups urged more use of black television personnel'; that 'at times, there may be other reasons to employ a racially identified, non-white reporter'; and that 'the data would recommend that the commentary match the individual'.[95] This was Tenenbaum's intervention as an academic from the US, accustomed to a different viewing experience of American television. He aligned himself, albeit in a rather distanced way, with the arguments of the West Indian and professional group who pointed to a lack of representation on screen and rewarded through their responses and manufacturing of data in the study any Black presence they encountered in the experiment. The data produced from them demonstrably pointed to their existence as an audience out of step with the racialising preferences of the BBC's usual white subjects of research. Tenenbaum's intervention on the side of greater Black representation on screen was a cautious encouragement to the BBC bound within the confines and discomforts of white fragility to desegregate both audience research and television content in Britain. This was in keeping with the earlier points of the Race Relations Board in its evidence to the Annan Committee in 1975 that pointed to the lack of Black or south Asian audiences in audience research. Yet Tenenbaum's experiment and his recommendation were also divorced from the Audience Research Department's own knowledge, however resisted or ignored, of a pattern of audience racism among white television viewers.

## Conclusion

Audience Research departments in the 1970s at both of Britain's major broadcasters amassed evidence of white British audiences expectant of

[95] Ibid., 15.

and immersed in the racialising pleasures of post-war television. Audience research demonstrated that the racism that was broadcast in *Curry and Chips*, *Till Death Us Do Part* and *Love Thy Neighbour* marked out a racialising world view that white audiences largely did not see as satire but instead as confirmation and even an extension of existing attitudes towards Black and south Asian people. Far from being racially innocent and only possessing 'a sneaking feeling' of racism, most British audiences seemed willing to believe the worst of immigrants in terms of social, intellectual and economic capabilities all rooted in notions of white supremacy. These were forms of racism that did not necessarily translate in the racial violence that audiences of the 1970s were still broadly defining as racism but rather a type of casual everyday racialisation that was visualised and spoken on the screen as humour, as authentic 'true to life', and as relatable. When Humphrey Barclay, Head of Comedy at London Weekend Television, responded to accusations in 1978 about the potentially negative impact on viewers of the comedy series *Mind Your Language* and its stereotypes of south Asian and European people, he struck a note of uncertainty that echoed Glencross's earlier misgivings when he said, 'I don't think that series is socially damaging. I hope it isn't. Otherwise, we really ought not to be doing it.'[96]

The damning data and evidence of this widespread racism among white viewers and amounted to a slow, uncomfortable and ultimately ignored discovery of audience racism in the halls of the BBC's and ITV's affiliates. Racism circulated in the way that Sara Ahmed notes that diversity work, policy or documents move within institutions that are either not serious about this work or have not done this work previously.[97] Instead, as Ahmed has noted often happens to diversity work, this knowledge and this tangible evidence became blocked or stagnant in some element of the institution, necessitating what Ahmed calls 'institutional plumbers' who can move forward new messages and practices through such blockages.[98] Audience research at the BBC and ITV acted as a unique site of knowledge about the racism of viewers within these organisations but which lacked personnel within or adjacent to it who were willing to engage with these patterns and conclusions. Information about audience racism was gathered and disseminated among people through the usual means in the institution and then silenced and rarely

---

[96] Q&A footage at the festival broadcast in *It Ain't Half Racist Mum*, 1979, CARM, Open Door, BBC2.
[97] Sara Ahmed, *Living a Feminist Life* (Durham, NC: Duke University Press, 2017), 94–97.
[98] Ibid., 96.

acted upon. This was particularly easy to do with audience research which was known for its flexibility. The existence of audience racism among white viewers as a measured phenomenon became in some ways the dirty secret of British broadcasting that could not be acted upon nor easily spoken of. The lack of innovation when it came to representing racialised people on screen was partly tied to the inability of the BBC and ITV to fully acknowledge that their approach throughout the 1960s and 1970s to racial satire as *the* primary aid to race relations in Britain had been misguided at the very least but also potentially damaging. A more powerful instinct to preserve white executives and white audiences from an uncomfortable acknowledgement of systemically racist content on British television and the deep, popular appeal of these racist pleasures to audiences ultimately prevailed.

This instinct to preserve spheres, institutions, and screen content that was wedded to the racialising pleasures that white audiences enjoyed also meant that both the BBC and ITV found it exceedingly difficult to engage with Black and south Asian audiences in any meaningful way in the 1970s. In order to ignore or move past data on audience racism and institutional culpability for fostering this and to maintain what Curran and Seaton aptly call the 'power without responsibility' of both broadcasters, both organisations needed to limit their engagement with Black and south Asian viewers. The discomfort of the audience research departments and their own roles as branches within the institutions to be drawn on or ignored made this a relatively easy proposition. It was racialised viewers who could point to, as they certainly did when granted the opportunity, their ongoing knowledge and experience of the harmful effects of an unreconstructed media environment that traded in racism as a humorous and persistent pleasure for many white audiences. The limited means by which Black and south Asian audiences were invited into audience research, in 1975 in a methodologically suspect survey for ITV on *Love Thy Neighbour* and again in 1979 when a white American academic made it his focus to investigate white British audience responses to Black reporters and voices on screen, highlighted this.

## 7 'Black Magic'
### Racially Comfortable Viewing on British Television in the 1980s and 1990s

When the affluent Black families of the Huxtables and then the Bankses emerged on British television in the 1980s and 1990s, a young Black British viewer, Reni Eddo-Lodge, took note: 'The first black family I saw on television was on *The Fresh Prince of Bel-Air*. For many late-eighties and early-nineties babies, the Banks were the archetypal black family that all black people were aiming to be. They were affluent and upper middle-class, well-dressed, and incredibly well-educated. They even came complete with Geoffrey, the (black) British butler.'[1]

Eddo-Lodge understood the Banks as a model and one that had historical precedent on television, writing 'As well as *The Fresh Prince*, I was peripherally aware of the Huxtable family on *The Cosby Show* (see Figure 7.1), although it was a little bit before my time. As far as I can tell, the set-up was essentially the same'.[2] These two families were 'the archetypal black family that all black people were aiming to be' according to the author of *Why I Am No Longer Talking to White People About Race*.[3] Eddo-Lodge, born in 1989 in London, would have seen *The Fresh Prince of Bel-Air* on BBC2 where it was broadcast from 1991, a year after its debut in America, until 2004 and building upon the previous success of *The Cosby Show* (Channel 4, 1985–1992) with British television viewers. The Bankses and the Huxtables offered Black models of aspiration that stood out as singular to Eddo-Lodge in a television environment primarily featuring and catering to white people. When it was first broadcast in 1985 *The Cosby Show* was described by Mary Kenny, a *Daily Mail* television critic, as a 'relaxing addition to Friday night viewing' that the average viewer could watch 'in comfort with your family without feeling you are going to be offended or assaulted with bad language'.[4] It seemed

---

[1] Reni Eddo-Lodge, 'Forming Blackness Through a Screen', in Nikesh Shukla, ed., *The Good Immigrant* (London: Unbound, 2016), 79–80.
[2] Ibid.
[3] Reni Eddo-Lodge, *Why I'm No Longer Talking to White People about Race* (London: Bloomsbury, 2017).
[4] Mary Kenny, 'This New Black Magic...', *Daily Mail*, 16 February 1985, 22.

7.1. The cast portrait of the Huxtables as played in *The Cosby Show* during the 1984 to 1985 season one. (Front row l–r) Lisa Bonet, Keshia Knight Pulliam, Bill Cosby, Sabrina Le Beauf. (Back row l–r) Tempestt Bledsoe, Malcolm-Jamal Warner, Phylicia Ayers-Allen. Photo taken 13 September 1985. Photo by Michael Ochs Archives/Getty Images. Source: Michael Ochs Archives, https://www.gettyimages.co.uk/detail/news-photo/cast-portrait-of-cosby-show-for-the-1984-85-season-lisa-news-photo/73907276?adppopup=true.

that for white television critics who were ostensibly representing the views of white television viewers reading their newspapers that the key to the popularity of *The Cosby Show* was that it was 'comfortable' and 'relaxing' and free from the offence and 'bad language' that Kenny inferred accompanied other representations of Blackness on screen at the time. The comedy series did not present an image of the 'welfare queens' and Black gangs that so preoccupied 1980s British coverage of Black men and women in the US.[5] Nor did it offer the searing portrayal

---

[5] Amy Ansell, *New Right, New Racism: Race and Reaction in the United States and Britain* (London: Palgrave Macmillan, 1997), 180; E. James West, 'Roil Britannia! Al Sharpton,

of historic Black experiences that the American miniseries *Roots* had brought to British viewers in 1977 with its story of multigenerational experiences of slavery. When a British all-Black sitcom *Desmond's* (Channel 4, 1989–1994) began broadcasting in the UK four years later it was immediately labelled by the *Daily Mail* as 'Britain's answer to The Cosby Show', full of 'lots of loveable scallywags'.[6] *Desmond's* was also, in other words, comfortable viewing. When the *Fresh Prince of Bel-Air* debuted not long afterwards in 1991 it offered a point of continuity with British critics and audiences who were by now well used to this type of sitcom. The American images of Black affluence that the Huxtables and the Bankses embodied were joined by the Guyanese Ambrose family featured in *Desmond's* with the character of Desmond Ambrose, played by Norman Beaton, and his successful barber shop.

In the audience consensus that emerged around and drove the success of all three of these hit programmes in Britain it was clear that the screen culture of the 1980s and 1990s offered a rather broader lens through which audiences could know about the lives of Black men and women than previous decades had. The racial sitcom was slowly falling out of favour if certainly not altogether absent. *Love Thy Neighbour* had finished broadcasting in 1976; *Mind Your Language* stopped broadcasting in 1979 barring a brief resurgence in 1985; and *It Ain't Half Hot Mum* came to an end in 1981. *Till Death Us Do Part* had finished its first run in 1975 but was resurrected ten years later as a new series, *In Sickness and in Health* (BBC 1985–1987, 1989–1990, 1992), also starring Alf Garnett. Yet in 1985, Garnett's return was met with largely negative reactions from critics with even Mary Kenny willing to acknowledge that 'Garnett's bitterness' was 'going sour' and Herbert Kretzmer arguing in the same paper that 'Garnett in full Speight isn't funny any more'.[7] The old ways of talking about race on screen where racism and white bigots were treated as jokes were becoming seen by television critics as ill-suited to a decade which saw a surge in white nationalism.[8] As Kretzmer wrote about Garnett in 1985 for the *Daily Mail*, '[he] no longer invites our mockery of the lunatic bigotries of the far right, but appears now to represent them without apology' and just as 'racial attitudes in Britain

---

the British Press, and the 1991 Murder of Rolan Adams', *Immigrants & Minorities* 37, no. 3 (2019): 184–210.

[6] Gerald Hobson, 'Desmond's', *Daily Mail*, 9 October 1989, 28.

[7] Mary Kenny, 'Is Garnett's Bitterness Going Sour?', *Daily Mail*, 5 September 1986, 23; Herbert Kretzmer, 'Garnett in Full Speight Isn't Funny Any More', *Daily Mail*, 16 September 1985, 21.

[8] E. James West, 'Hunt the Wizard! Race, Immigration, and British Tabloid Coverage of David Duke's 1978 Tour', *Contemporary British History* 35, no. 1 (2021): 100–124.

have hardened and turned nastier since the original series'.[9] The presence of white nationalism could no longer be easily dismissed as the paranoia of Black and south Asian people seeing racism everywhere with Kretzmer also noting the string of arson attacks against south Asian homes in London in the summer of 1985.[10] The old approach now looked, indeed, old and outdated. As the decades marched on, Eddo-Lodge and other Black television viewers in 1980s and early 1990s Britain grew up with more and more Black and south Asian actors on the screen and with blacked-up actors a relative rarity. After *The Black and White Minstrel Show* ended in 1978, the racist content of it and other television programmes were rarely spoken of as broader understandings of what constituted racism seemingly took hold in parts of the UK among some producers, critics and audiences albeit in rather uneven ways.

The three central broadcasters that now existed in the UK, the BBC, ITV and its affiliates, and Channel 4, experimented with new shows in terms of both news reporting and original programming. The introduction of Channel 4 in 1982 brought a sizeable commitment by a British broadcaster to producing programming for Britain's ethnic minorities, a direction that would have significant implications for ITV's broadcasters and the BBC, which scrambled to catch up. For news reporting and in the face of the new Channel 4's directive to serve what were classed as overlooked 'minority viewpoints', regional broadcasters were encouraged to mount programming for Black and south Asian audiences and for white audiences on Black and south Asian subjects. ITV's Midlands broadcaster, for instance, broadcast a programme called *Here and Now* (Central News, 1980–1990) highlighting dance, cuisine and customs from multicultural Britain and featuring Black and south Asian reporters on the street and in the studio.[11] In terms of original programming primarily Black or south Asian shows were seen on the small screen. These included *Empire Road* (BBC 1978–1979), *Mixed Blessings* (ITV LWT, 1978–1980), *Tandoori Nights* (Channel 4, 1985–1987), *No Problem!* (Channel 4, 1983–1985) and the variety show, *The Lenny Henry Show* (BBC1, 1984–1985, 1987–1988). A small number of Black and south Asian men and to a much lesser extent women were also bringing their experiences and expertise to television and film scripts if not yet in the production sphere. As media historian Sarita Malik has

---

[9] Kretzmer, 'Garnett in Full Speight Isn't Funny Any More'.
[10] Pat Healy, 'Asian Leaders Want Police Race Unit', *The Times*, 15 August 1985, 3.
[11] Rachel Yemm, chapter on *Here and Now* in 'Immigration, Race and Local Media in the Midlands, 1960–1985' (PhD diss., University of Lincoln, 2018).

argued about the incorporation of talent of colour at the end of the twentieth century, 'for the first time in television history, these were programmes that really were "ours" to criticize, and furthermore, they had emphatically produced disparate readings and opinion'.[12] Television shows such as *Tandoori Nights*, *No Problem!*, *Desmond's* and *The Lenny Henry Show* were written by Black and south Asian writers *for* Black and south Asian viewers alongside white viewers.

It was in this context that *The Cosby Show* (Channel 4, 1985–1992), *Desmond's* (Channel 4, 1989–1994) and *The Fresh Prince of Bel-Air* (BBC2, 1991–2004), all featuring primarily Black casts, became hit programmes in Britain and meriting a close examination in this chapter. All three shows seemingly gave audience what they wanted and avoided the two-season curse that the Black actor and comedian Lenny Henry has highlighted as a well-established pattern for series that featured primarily Black or south Asian writing teams and casts: 'The thing about shows with black writers is that there's a one- or two-season jinx. What I've noticed is things such as *Dad's Army* and *Only Fools and Horses* get sixteen years to get the content right, while people of colour have one or two goes.'[13] Avoiding the trend that *Rainbow City*, *The Fosters*, *Empire Road* and *No Problem!* had all succumbed to, these three successful sitcoms instead ran into multiple seasons. In the process they offered a sustained view of prosperous, intelligent and witty Black families who were not characterised primarily as a problem on the screen for British viewers. These shows provided viewers the opportunity to see Black people at relative ease and not just constantly grappling with or speaking at length of the everyday racism they experienced with white people. Racism, in other words, was not their animating plot point. While discussions of explicitly Black experiences were evident in these programmes to varying degrees, the Blackness of the families and friends was not signalled as the primary reason for the programme to exist on screen. For Carmen Munroe, the legendary Black stage actress who also starred in almost every production on British television that purported to address 'race' in post-war Britain including *Fable*, *Rainbow City*, *The Fosters* and then opposite Norman Beaton in *Desmond's*, the success of the latter hinged on the series being able to show regular Black everyday life for a family and extended community:

---

[12] Sarita Malik, *Representing Black Britain: Black and Asian Images on Television* (London: Sage Publishing, 2002), 99.
[13] Lenny Henry Q&A Royal Television Society, *Television Magazine*, October 2019; https://rts.org.uk/article/sir-lenny-henry-diversity-makes-tv-better.

We are now able to do what other series are trying to do, and that is to be about real people. We don't have to constantly be begging for acceptance, begging to be understood – that's gone, that's past. We now must live the way we really do live, and we can represent that.[14]

For Munroe the ability to be at ease on screen signalled a new direction in representations of people of colour on screen. Such a presentation was understandably deeply appealing to an actress such as Munroe who had played a variety of limited roles in productions by white writers that often mounted painfully awkward discussions of race relations on screen. Crucially all three series were popular and well received in both Black and white households. It is tempting, therefore, to situate these shows as sites of a new sort of racial consensus in the period and as evidence of white British audiences willing to see and know about the experiences of Black people. Yet this chapter highlights evidence that white and Black audiences embraced these programmes for very different reasons in 1980s and 1990s Britain. This was what Derek Bell has called 'interest convergence', where he argued that Black people in the United States saw moments of advancement in the civil rights movement only when these dovetailed, or converged, with a benefit to white people.[15] While Bell postulated 'interest convergence' in a very different time period and place, we can also see map such a convergence onto a story of racial progress on screen in 1980s and 1990s Britain.

For Black audiences, actors and writers, a move away from racism as the primarily lens through which Black representation occurred on screen in Britain offered relief from what had previously been shown to audiences. This type of presentation came somewhat closer to real life for Black viewers: Black characters did not always have to be shown experiencing, speaking of, and responding to racism on screen but living their lives instead. The Black man, woman and family at ease and in comfort on screen was almost radical at the time, compared to what suffused the screen through the social problem films produced in both Britain and the US. Images of Black racial comfort also offered a welcome change from negative representations in the British tabloid press that centred on the poverty and hardships of Black communities, stereotypical associations with crime and an obsession with gangs and gangsters. These programmes showcased Black life outside of that 'mundane extreme environment' of everyday racism described by Pierce in Chapter 5 and devoid

---

[14] Carmen Munroe, 'Interview', in Jim Pine, ed., *Black and White in Colour: Black People in British Television since 1936*. (London: BFI Publishing, 1992), 64.

[15] Derrick A Bell, '*Brown v. Board of Education* and the Interest-Convergence Dilemma', *Harvard Law Review* (1980): 518–533.

of the 'racial battle fatigue' that Black people can experience while living in historically white spaces.[16] Instead, Black men, women, children and teenagers were living 'the way we really do live' as Munroe pointed out. When Munroe argued about Black people's representation on screen that 'anyway, we're all grown up and I don't think the public wants to be told any more how difficult life is. We all know how difficult life is, black and white', she was speaking to white audience fatigue and also Black viewers' fatigue with social problem narratives. As she contended in 1991, 'with *Desmond's* we have successfully created a space for ourselves, where we can just be a real, honest, loving family, with problems like lots of people, and we can present that with some degree of truth and still not lose comedy'.[17] This was a space for Black people in the everyday that also, we shall see, conveniently intersected with the emphasis on affluence that was a hallmark of 1980s and 1990s Britain.

A type of racial comfort was also at play for white audiences who enthusiastically embraced these Black television comedies for rather different reasons. This chapter focuses on the response to these programmes by white television critics writing in the national daily press in Britain as they erected racialised language such as 'comfortable' and without 'pressure' around the programmes that signalled a colour-blind comfort for white audiences. Television critics at a range of newspapers including *The Times*, the *Daily Mail* and the *Guardian* all deployed strikingly similar language when speaking of these programmes and in the absence of audience research on this topic (as audience research at both ITV and the BBC migrated into BARB from 1981), the presumed ability of these critics to persuade audiences to view television programme is front and centre here.[18] Alongside these are further audience responses drawn from the Mass Observation Project of 1981 to 2009 as well as varied recollections of Black viewers looking back at their historic viewing habits. We shall see that to the relief of many white television

---

[16] Chester M. Pierce, 'Psychiatric Problems of the Black Minority', in S. Arieti, ed., *American Handbook of Psychiatry* (New York: Basic Books, 1974), 512–523; William A. Smith, et al., '"You Make Me Wanna Holler and Throw Up Both My Hands!" Campus Culture, Black Misandric Microaggressions, and Racial Battle Fatigue', *International Journal of Qualitative Studies in Education* 29, no. 9 (2016): 1189–1209; Nicola Rollock, '"I Would Have Become Wallpaper Had Racism Had Its Way": Black Female Professors, Racial Battle Fatigue, and Strategies for Surviving Higher Education', *Peabody Journal of Education* 96, no. 2 (2021): 206–217.
[17] Munroe, 'Interview', 64.
[18] Here, I am giving credence to the television critic as a member of the audience, but also as one of the rare voices to discuss individual responses to media and culture; See my discussion in Christine Grandy, 'Cultural History's Absent Audience', *Cultural and Social History* 16, no. 5 (2019): 643–663.

critics these shows were not 'all about race' and rarely put discussions of anti-Black racism at their heart. The first two programmes, debuting in 1985 and 1989, were explicitly praised by white television critics for not making Blackness an issue. Instead the domestic comedy they provided was seen as a welcome departure from the persistently negative depictions of contemporary Black communities in the press in the 1980s and 1990s which highlighted uncomfortable racialised inequalities and related experiences. For white audiences this 'comfortable' viewing allowed them to embrace a colour-blind ethos that claimed that racism was less of a problem than it was in both the US and Britain. These programmes were seemingly post-racial in their presentation of comedy, ignoring race altogether and allowing audiences to celebrate this as colour-blind progress, itself a framework built on ignoring the racism that still dominated Black experiences. The emphasis on social mobility and Black affluence in these sitcoms almost perfectly dovetailed in Britain with a move towards a type of colour-blind enterprise culture under Thatcher's Conservative party. The successful Conversative political campaign in 1983 to identify and hail Black voters as businessmen first rather than just Black highlighted the appeal of colour-blindness for Black and also south Asian British men and women.

A convergence of interests thus occurred in the period hinged on a mutual desire for racially comfortable viewing but stemming from the different experiences and expectations of Black and white audiences when it came to screen culture. White audiences, including critics, wanted to avoid the discomfort of confronting representations of structural racism linked to white privilege and historic injustices while Black audiences wanted to see Black people at ease on screen. Hence I argue here that the colour-blind racism of white British audiences was still evident in the successes of Black television in the 1980s and 1990s and circumscribed the success of these representations as the capacity of white viewers to tolerate racial discomfort narrowly limited representations of Black experiences. The arrival in 1985, in the same year as protests by Black unemployed youth in Handsworth and elsewhere, of the American import *The Cosby Show* offered white British producers, audiences and critics the appearance of racial acceptance while also catering to the reality of ongoing adherence to notions of racial innocence and colour-blind viewing. The success of these shows effectively recast ideas of a silent, racially innocent audience enjoying traditional forms of entertainment into a new post-racial vision of British audiences consuming these programmes in 'racial comfort' and tolerant of multiculturalism on the crucial condition that race was not spoken of. Black representation was briefly expanded by the existence of these three shows but was ultimately circumscribed by a new dogma of colour-blindness on television that left Black writers, producers and actors circling a small range of formats, genres and roles. The frustrations of Black and south Asian writers and producers with the limits of white audiences were palpable by the start of the twenty-first century as the heritage film and television industry shaped opportunity and expectation. What this chapter demonstrates is that the old ways of not knowing about race were left safely intact for white British viewers of television in the 1980s and 1990s.

## 7.1 Viewing in Comfort: *The Cosby Show* and Colour-blindness in 1980s Britain

In the 1980s and 1990s, the cosy duopoly of the 1960s and 1970s gave way to the arrival of Channel 4 in 1982, Channel 5 in 1997, MTV Europe from 1987 and MTV UK commencing in 1997 alongside other pay-television or cable television options as television moved firmly into the realm of 24-hours-a-day broadcasting. The writing was on the wall for ITV and the BBC in 1977 when the Annan Report, published in March of that year, recommended a new fourth channel in the UK that would serve 'minority interests'. Just what this meant, as Gavin Schaffer notes, was subject to wide-ranging interpretation by television producers but often centred on an assumption that Black and south Asian viewers would need to be brought in as largely untapped audiences for both the BBC and ITV.[19] The discussions that had happened at the 1978 International Edinburgh Television Festival on 'race' and 'stereotyping' indicated that the old approach of either playing racism for laughs or offering earnest leaden discussions of racism on screen was being reconsidered. A showing of *Mixed Blessings*, the latest London Weekend Television comedy centring on an interracial couple and fated to run for only two seasons, was met there with 'stony silence' by an audience of media professionals; Sue Woodford, producer at Granada, even noted out loud that the programme made a joke of West Indian communities.[20] Carmen Munroe, who starred in the show, later commented on the *Mixed Blessings'* somewhat preachy tone: 'I don't think we were really versed in the art of marking social comment without it becoming just that, and without it losing the comedy of the situation.'[21]

---

[19] Gavin Schaffer, *The Vision of a Nation: Making Multiculturalism on British Television, 1960–80* (London: Palgrave Macmillan, 2014), 231–272.
[20] 'RACE Broadcast', *Entertainment Industry Magazine Archive*, 11 September 1978, 20.
[21] Munroe, 'Interview', 63.

With the arrival of Channel 4 imminent, efforts were clearly being made to think anew about what was represented on screen when it came to Black and south Asian communities. Channel 4 quickly emerged in 1982 as a notable host of Black and south Asian television even if that trajectory was not entirely smooth. In 1983, the broadcaster featured a primarily Black sitcom with actors from Black Theatre Co-operative, *No Problem!* (Channel 4, 1983–1985). The show's premise of Black teenagers left to their own devices after their parents returned to Jamaica did not sit well with either Black or white viewers and when the series ended, Channel 4 invested in securing American content and the rights to *The Cosby Show* in 1985. *Desmond's*, set in south London, would follow in 1989 and only after Channel 4 made a specific effort to court local Black and south Asian British writing talent through its Debut'84 competition.[22]

The BBC, for its part, was sufficiently spooked by the presence of Channel 4 that it undertook more definitive steps in the 1980s towards featuring Black talent on screen than it had throughout most of the 1970s. These efforts translated into support for the Black comedian Lenny Henry and his sketch programme *The Lenny Henry Show* (BBC1 1984–1985, 1987–1988) before BBC2 then committed to airing *The Fresh Prince of Bel-Air* in 1991. By 1991 it was increasingly clear that importing American television was the primary means of addressing issues around 'race' or diversity on the small screen for British television broadcasters. *The Cosby Show* was a huge hit with audiences in Britain when it arrived on Channel 4 in 1985 and steadily remained in the top ten shows on UK television throughout its eight seasons, proving that an all-Black sitcom could sustain an audience in the UK. American network television had a much more established track record of producing successful situation comedies with primarily Black casts prior to *The Cosby Show*. *The Jeffersons* (CBS, 1975–1985) and *Good Times* (CBS, 1974–1979) had both been ratings successes in America although neither was broadcast in the UK. Scripts for *Good Times*, however, had been purchased and adapted for the short-lived *The Fosters* on ITV's LWT. That show, which featured an all-Black cast, did not land with audiences again ceasing after two seasons. The *Guardian* wrote in 1976 that 'it's all very well writing in references to North Sea Oil and Guyana – but it's not British humour: neither black nor white'.[23] In the US however, *Good Times* had been a moderate success to build upon. The US had also in its more diverse cable television programmes seen a new network launch in

---

[22] Channel 4, *Guardian*, 21 March 1985, 28.
[23] 'Black Comedy', *Guardian*, 9 April 1976, 10.

1980, Black Entertainment Television (BET), that emphasised Black talent and was aimed explicitly at Black audiences. Black actors and scriptwriters were able to find more opportunities in American television and the onset of cable television with its myriad channels further broadened these opportunities. In Britain with a much more rigid and limited broadcasting structure, it was Channel 4 that cemented its position as offering racially diverse content for 'minority audiences' by securing the broadcasting rights to *The Cosby Show*.

In the 1980s, Bill Cosby, the now disgraced actor and comedian, was already a hugely successful figure in the US. His stand-up comedy had won him the Grammy for Best Comedy Album six years in a row starting in 1965 and he also won an Emmy in 1966, the first awarded to a Black actor, for his co-starring role in the spy series *I Spy*, an action-adventure drama with comedic touches, on NBC. A short-lived programme, *The Bill Cosby Show*, saw Cosby develop a programme for NBC from 1969 to 1971 yet he had a continued Saturday morning cartoon success with the animated series *Fat Albert* from 1972 to 1985. Cosby had broad commercial and critically acclaimed success. As Malcolm Frierson notes, Cosby's relationship to the politics and actions of the civil rights movement was highly strategic, anchored in part in his belief in appealing to white audiences with his performances.[24] Cosby's own politics became increasingly apparent as the decades wore on; he did not hesitate to place the onus for Black improvement on the failures of Black American communities and was often dismissive of systemic racism. In 1985, however, his talent had already been enthusiastically embraced in America and the new show bearing his name, *The Cosby Show*, was an instant hit with audiences. The programme's popularity paved the way for two other primarily Black-led half-hour comedy shows popular with British audiences, *Desmond's* and *The Fresh Prince of Bel-Air*.

The embrace of *The Cosby Show* by British audiences on its debut in 1985 was very much tied to existing white audience expectations of Black men and women on screen and the programme's ability to upend these. American film, television and the press in the early 1980s was heavily influenced by and producing stereotypes of 'welfare queens' and 'gangsters' running wild, in keeping with President Ronald Reagan's focus on reducing access to social care by Black Americans. James West and Kieran Connell have demonstrated that the daily press in Britain were equally well versed in narratives of Black welfare scroungers in the US and were also willing to draw such comparisons with Black people

---

[24] Malcolm Frierson, *Freedom in Laughter: Dick Gregory, Bill Cosby, and the Civil Rights Movement* (Albany, NY: SUNY Press, 2020).

experiencing unemployment in Britain.²⁵ This built upon a practice in the local and national press that was more than willing to appeal to audience racism as a means of dramatising narratives of peril for white readers as Benjamin Bland has noted.²⁶ Anna Marie Smith has further argued that the 1980s revival of 'Powellism' under Margaret Thatcher replaced the threat of the Black immigrant with the Black criminal in the public's imagination.²⁷ Thinkers such as Stuart Hall despaired at the time about Britain's own 'great moving right show' that accompanied Thatcher's emphasis on British enterprise at all costs.²⁸ The decade was fraught with racial tensions surrounding areas like Handsworth as Tory policies on unemployment, policing and housing bit deeply into Black neighbourhoods in particular and while multiplying expressions of white nationalism went largely unchecked.

Yet even as racial tensions remained throughout the decade, Black and south Asian voters were also a subject of concern for political parties. The 1983 election saw the Conservative Party explicitly attempt to appeal to Black and south Asian voters by deploying a new campaign. As Matthew Francis has written, the Conservatives had been steadily increasing their attempts to woo ethnic minority votes from the middle of the 1970s led, in part, by the grassroots enthusiasm of organisations like the Anglo-Asian Conservative Society and the National Anglo-West Indian Conservative Society.²⁹ Organisations like these saw a natural pairing between the interests of immigrant groups in hard work, family and tradition with the Conservative Party agenda. In 1983, this convergence of interests took a step forward in a direct campaign steeped in notions of a colour-blind Conservative Party during the general election. At the heart of this campaign were two full-page advertisements, one featuring a south Asian man and one a Black man, both smartly dressed in business suits with the headline, 'Labour says he's black. Tories say he's British.' Using the language of political Blackness of the day, the

---

[25] E. James West, 'Roil Britannia! Al Sharpton, the British Press, and the 1991 Murder of Rolan Adams', *Immigrants & Minorities* 37, no. 3 (2019): 184–210; Kieran Connell, *Black Handsworth: Race in 1980s Britain* (Berkeley: University of California Press, 2019).

[26] Benjamin Bland, '"Publish and Be Damned?" Race, Crisis, and the Press in England during the Long, Hot Summer of 1976', *Immigrants & Minorities* 37, no. 3 (2019): 163–183.

[27] Anna Marie Smith, *New Right Discourse: Britain 1968–1990* (Cambridge: Cambridge University Press, 1994): 129–182.

[28] Stuart Hall, 'The Great Moving Right Show, 1979', in *Selected Political Writings: The Great Moving Right Show and Other Essays* (Durham, NC: Duke University Press, 2017).

[29] Matthew Francis, 'Mrs Thatcher's Peacock Blue Sari: Ethnic Minorities, Electoral Politics and the Conservative Party, c. 1974–86', *Contemporary British History* 31, no. 2 (2017): 274–293.

first line of the pitch declared: 'With the Conservatives, there are no "blacks," no "whites," just people.' The rest of the ad laid out the Conservative record on voting for more 'coloured policemen' and in tackling inflation ending with the lines, 'To the Labour Party, you're a black person. To the Conservative Party, you're a British citizen. Vote Conservative and you vote for a more equal, more prosperous Britain.' A central message of unity based in aspiration and work rather than racial identity, became a key plank of the Conservatives' efforts to win over voters of colour and offers us yet another window into the ability of Thatcher's Conservative party to shift the language and thinking of the period.[30]

The colour-blindness of this campaign in 1983 was not entirely uncontroversial. Two weeks before the election a *Times* article noted that the advertisements were not particularly well received by some Black readers with a headline 'Advertisement Banned by Black Editor'.[31] The article pointed out that the existing controversy over the ad had only increased when editors of several Black press publications refused to run it without qualifications or at all. Editors for the *Caribbean Times*, described by *The Times* as 'the most radical, controversial, and combative of the black press', refused to print it while the editor of *The West Indian World*, David Gordon, chose to print it but with a leader describing the advertisement as 'insensitive and offensive'. *The Times* article ended, however, by reporting that some editors of the Black press thought 'the Conservatives might win votes' based on the appeal. The concept of colour-blindness was indeed attractive to some south Asian and Black business owners. This type of appeal was wide-ranging and even Pakistani-British writer Hanif Kureshi included a nod to this in his script for the 1985 independent film *My Beautiful Laundrette*; one central character, a wealthy south Asian businessman and landlord played by British-Indian actor Saeed Jaffrey, stated bluntly 'I'm a professional businessman, not a professional Pakistani' while physically removing a Black man squatting in one of his properties.[32] Certainly Thatcher's Tories were able to return to power in 1983, and the diversity of the

---

[30] Much attention has been paid to the language of ordinariness that Thatcher cloaked middle-class aspiration in, but very little has been written, beyond Matthew Francis' work, on the deep appeal of colour-blindness to Conservative voters – white, Black and south Asian. Jon Lawrence and Florence Sutcliffe-Braithwaite, 'Margaret Thatcher and the Decline of Class Politics', in Ben Jackson and Robert Saunders, eds., *Making Thatcher's Britain* (Cambridge: Cambridge University Press, 2012), 132–147.

[31] Nicholas Timmins, 'Advertisement Banned by Black Editor', *The Times*, 24 May 1983, 1.

[32] *My Beautiful Laundrette*, Stephen Frears, director, Working Title and Channel Four Films (1985).

party outpaced Labour's claim to this as financial aspiration became a primary mode of identity and belonging in late twentieth and early twenty-first-century Britain.[33]

*The Cosby Show* tapped into a trans-Atlantic longing among white people for colour-blind aspiration that ignored existing stereotypes of Blackness on screen and ignored the conditions in which anti-Black racism continued to persist in both countries. *The Cosby Show's* particular emphasis on family sat well with both American and British audiences. Cosby himself lamented about how Black people were typically represented on screen: 'I got tired of seeing shows that consist of a car crash, a gunman, and a hooker talking to a black pimp. It was cheaper to do a series than to throw out my family's six TV sets.'[34] British television critics also initially encountered *The Cosby Show* through this prism of audience expectations. By pointing out what was new, fresh and different about *The Cosby Show* these critics brought the racialised expectations of white British audiences into view. The first of these expectations was articulated in *The Times* review of the programme indicating that a show about a Black family might only appeal to Black audiences and that an audience cross-over was not likely. Celia Brayfield, writing in 1985, stated: 'A new comedy for black actors – and presumably also for a black audience – began its first screening on Channel 4 last night.' Brayfield invoked that audience again when she argued that the show's 'entire raison d'etre is obviously to present educated, affluent role models to the black audience in America'.[35] Brayfield was left initially unimpressed by the programme, and what she saw as its overt upending of the usual presentation of Black people on screen. Kenny, writing for the *Daily Mail*, also made the connection between THE *Cosby Show* and its presumed Black audience while skewering existing television programming featuring Black people: 'What have been the main flaws about TV comedy featuring blacks? First, such comedies have tended to be self-conscious. And second, they have tended to assume that most black folk want to identify with radical outsiders, alienated Rastafarians, or ghetto poverty.'[36]

To Kenny's delight, *The Cosby Show* brought the tastes of Black audiences newly into view, as she proclaimed: 'Most black people

---

[33] Amy Edwards, *Are We Rich Yet? The Rise of Mass Investment Culture in Contemporary Britain* (Berkely: University of California Press, 2022).

[34] Ian Markham-Smith, 'Meet the Real First Family of America', *Daily Mail*, 15 March 1986, 18. Cosby would increasingly refer to this representation as an accurate account of Black experiences in America and was unwilling to acknowledge systemic racism as a factor in this experience.

[35] Celia Brayfield, 'Television', *The Times*, 16 February 1985, 7.

[36] Mary Kenny, 'This New Black Magic'.

themselves, meanwhile, would prefer to watch *Dallas*. Like many white people, they would rather focus their fantasies on beautiful, sleek, rich individuals riding around in fast cars than on deprived and misunderstood youngsters on welfare.'[37]

This union of Black and white audience preferences resulted in a show that Kenny labelled 'corny' but 'utterly inoffensive', 'harmless' and 'very sweet, very endearing, and manages to raise quite a few sympathetic laughs'.[38] Kenny was also particularly interested in the wealthy polish of the Huxtables labelling them 'well groomed and sophisticated', 'attractive' and 'well-heeled'. Kenny ended her enthusiastic review by noting that there was a spot of social good in the show even though efforts to do good was the original sin of TV comedy featuring Black people according to her: 'And perhaps it has social significance, too. For it conceivably represents black middle-class aspirations towards upward mobility – and away from alienated resentment.' The *Guardian*, on the other hand, was quick to note that the show was essentially white but in the process the paper's own racialised expectations of what a Black show would look like came to the fore: 'If it is white humour played by black actors, does that count as unethnic or just racist' and noting of the family that 'it is not, on the face of it, a typical ghetto household'.[39] The Huxtables, by not being 'typical' or 'ghetto', pleasantly surprised British critics.

The colour-blindness that white television critics attributed to *The Cosby Show* was one that was explicitly stated and celebrated as a type of progress for representations of Black people on the screen and one linked to the positive, happy tone of the show. This was not just a Black family who seldom discussed race, this was a Black family that was both not talking about race and was happy. The Huxtables' positive outlooks were repeatedly remarked upon in the press and often in conflict with what Kenny had described as the 'alienated resentment' that white Britons easily ascribed to Black grievances about racial inequality. The industry paper, *The Stage and Television Today*, wrote about the show's success in 1987: 'On the surface the overwhelming popularity [of *The Cosby Show*] could be considered a surprise. But colour is never mentioned and all the show is in essence is one more Happy Families sit-com.' It also possessed a 'leisurely pace and you are not under pressure while watching'.[40] The potential success of this all-Black programme with British viewers was thus linked to the lack of 'pressure'

---

[37] Ibid.  [38] Ibid.
[39] Hugh Hebert, 'The Cosby Show', *Guardian*, 16 February 1985, 12.
[40] James Green, 'Television Review: Putting the Family into Entertainment', *The Stage and Television Today*, 3 December 1987, 5564.

it placed on British audiences who it was heavily implied were white. The 'leisurely pace', the 'Happy Families' element and, crucially, the lack of discussion of race made the programme racially comfortable for white audiences who did not have to contemplate racial inequalities or Black emotions while viewing it. Elizabeth Cowley, writing for the *Daily Mail*, repeatedly praised the show for not talking about race. On its debut in 1985, she called the show 'likeable and refreshing, not least because nobody ever makes a joke or even a mention that they're black'.[41] On its second series debut she again praised this feature: 'As I said when this larky, beautifully scripted, American award-winner first surfaced here, one of the nicest things about it is that although it concerns a black family nobody ever makes any fuss or even refers to the fact.'[42]

When the third series premiered, Cowley again praised the show's lack of attention to being Black in the *Daily Mail's* television 'Pick of the Day': 'The middle-class family sitcom which tops the ratings in America and, happily, never makes any particular point about being black ... Welcome back!'[43] Cowley repeated her praise using the positive language of happiness that both ascribes that state of being to the family who does not make 'any fuss' over its blackness and also by inference to the typical white viewer who can also 'happily' enjoy it as 'refreshing' and 'likeable'. For Cowley, the lack of discussion of race seemingly buttressed the happy emotional state of the Black people on the screen and the white viewer watching them. Not talking about race and being both colour-blind and positive in tone were deeply appealing parts of the programme for white British critics. In the evidence of audience response that we can glean from the Mass Observation Project, British viewers were likewise charmed by the cheerfulness of the show using not dissimilar language from the critics. One viewer, identified as born in the 1940s and living in southeast England, wrote on 1 November 1988 about her and her husband's viewing of the programme which they used a video recorder to record:

Finally my husband and I watched *The Cosby Show*. I am far more selective in my viewing habits than he is and so we make a point of watching together those programmes which we both enjoy. We always laugh together during *The Cosby Show*, the humour in it is so innocent and appeals to me, whereas so many situation comedies tend to be smutty and I don't watch them at all.[44]

---

[41] Elizabeth Cowley, 'The Cosby Show', *Daily Mail*, 15 February 1985, 26.
[42] Elizabeth Cowley, 'The Cosby Show', *Daily Mail*, 21 March 1986, 22.
[43] Elizabeth Cowley, 'The Cosby Show', *Daily Mail*, 20 November 1987, 30.
[44] H1766's response to 1988 Autumn directive part 2. SxMOA2/1/27/2/1/204, Mass Observation Project, 1981–2009, University of Sussex Special Collections.

For this viewer, the show was an innocent counterpoint to smutty sitcoms otherwise on television. No mention is made of the Huxtables being Black. Another Mass Observation respondent, male, older, born in the 1920s and living in Yorkshire and Humber, recorded his viewing habits on the same date. This man said of the show, which he watched while eating dinner and after the football: 'Still on Channel Four, *The Cosby Show*, which I enjoy immensely. I find it to be good wholesome fun and I recommend it to all my friends.'[45] This viewer, like the one previous, also did not mention race but instead concentrated on the wholesomeness of the programme. This was what made for relaxed, appreciative viewing.

Much like Kenny's early assessment of *The Cosby Show* for the *Daily Mail* which spoke both of the 'comfortable viewing', it offered Britons and the show's images of Black affluence as a positive move away from racial hostility the programme itself very rarely addressed experiences of racism in America. Black life at ease was presented instead. Some critics found the lack of discussion of racism unconvincing. Hugh Hebert, a white critic for the left-leaning *Guardian* in the 1980s and towards the end of his career, repeatedly downplayed the show's popularity and found the lack of discussion of race perplexing and even offensive, rather than comforting. He wrote that 'puzzled liberals can discuss whether or not this is a family of uncle, aunt, and cousin Toms'.[46] He went on to argue that 'the alternative is to see it as an honourably colour-blind series that treats a black family exactly as though it were a white family ...' albeit a wealthy one. Hebert had earlier referred to the Huxtables as 'not, on the face of it, a typical ghetto household' and he saw the 'ghetto' household as having an element of a truth of Black experiences that should be seen and discussed.[47] Herbert did not easily see the Huxtables as experiencing all that a white family did. His frustration with the show's approach extended to the spin-off *A Different World* which was broadcast to a much more muted response from critics on Channel 4 from 1988 to 1994. Hebert derisively dismissed its first season: 'Though it is much the same world as the parent series in that almost everyone is black, and no-one, therefore, ever mentions, let alone worries, about the fact. Never mind, there's always Lenny Henry.'[48] Herbert's frustration with the colour-blindness of the Cosby worlds, although never particularly well

---

[45] P1643's response to 1988 Autumn directive part 2, SxMOA2/1/27/2/1/321, Mass Observation Project, 1981–2009, University of Sussex Special Collections.
[46] Hugh Hebert, 'Poll-Axed and Poorly', *Guardian*, 23 September 1988, 34.
[47] Hebert, 'The Cosby Show'.   [48] Hebert, 'Poll-Axed and Poorly'.

articulated, came through in his repeated dismissal of the programme and later the first and certainly tamest season of its spin-off.

Representations of Black experiences were, of course, present in *The Cosby Show* although experiences of racism were very rarely touched upon. Instead, positive Black experiences of community, music, Black institutions and culture were emphasised. In the first series the family all paused to watch in silence a broadcast of one of Martin Luther King Jr's historic speeches, imagery that was itself seldom shown on prime time television. Black leadership could be displayed even if racism was not. For the most part the show was happy to present an affluent Black experience on the screen as a counter to representations of experienced racism or broad stereotypes.[49] This was not an entirely colour-blind approach but it was seen as such by white critics. This viewing experience allowed white viewers to embrace a type of complacency about Black experiences and anti-Black racism, and this tendency was increasingly acknowledged by some critics, academics and audiences – and even Cosby himself. *The Stage and Television Today* reported in 1992 on an audience study commissioned in the US by Cosby on *The Cosby Show's* appeal to audiences. The study was conducted by academics at the University of Massachusetts with 'no strings attached', causing the reporter, Jane Garner, to note, 'I bet he's regretting it now.'[50] Garner recounted that the study drew 'some rather disturbing conclusions about [the show's] overall impact on attitudes towards race relations'. Quoting the study's authors, she reported, 'white people see the success of the Huxtable family as, as well as its many imitators, as proof that racial inequality is a thing of the past' and that for white audiences, the family's affluence only allowed racist ideas about inferiority among most Black people to proliferate. The successful example of the Huxtables, fictional as they were, allowed white audiences to project assumptions regarding a failure of effort by those Black people who did not reach such lofty heights. White audiences 'believe that the vast majority of black people who have not made it only have themselves to blame'. Recounting the study's central argument: 'So, they claim, white viewers appear liberal and enlightened because they watch and enjoy the programme, yet at the same time they embrace the insidious logic of racism that sees most blacks, rather than all, as inferior.'[51] *The Stage and Television Today* had

---

[49] Robin R. Means Coleman and Andre M. Cavalcante, 'Two Different Worlds', in Beretta E. Smith-Shomade, ed., *Watching While Black: Centring the Television of Black Audiences* (New Brunswick: Rutgers University Press, 2012).
[50] 'Television Diary: Study Paints a Black Picture ...', *The Stage and Television Today* 27, 1992, 20.
[51] Ibid.

little to say about these central findings beyond recounting them, and the study was not examined in other British papers.

The audience study was undertaken by two American professors of communication studies, Sut Jhally and Justin Lewis, who were engaged in a type of audience research in the early 1990s that had largely eluded the BBC and ITV in the previous decades. The study was entitled *Enlightened Racism: The Cosby Show, Audiences, and the Myth of the American Dream* and published in monograph form.[52] This in-depth research project acknowledged the generous funding of Bill and Camille Cosby in its introduction, noting that 'as the reader will realize from our conclusions, this funding came with no strings attached'.[53] Jhally and Lewis thanked the Cosbys 'for their open-mindedness and their commitment to scholarship and education'.[54] The audience research presented tells us what the academic field of media studies looked like in the US of 1991. The study involved 52 groups of two to six people and included Black, white and what were called Hispanic participants; 23 Black groups, 26 white groups and three Hispanic groups.[55] This was a much more diverse audience panel than had been pursued in audience research at the BBC and ITV in previous decades. The resulting study demonstrated that for white viewers the exceptional nature of the Huxtables' life of affluence and success in white America actually deepened existing racial prejudice about the abilities of the broader Black American population to succeed because systemic racism was largely absent from the show. Without a framework on the programme for discussing and acknowledging racism more broadly in the lives of the Huxtables and other Black people, white viewers were content to think that racism was no longer a factor for those Black men and women in America who had simply worked hard enough. This study was rooted in a particularly American context, and a British survey would have undoubtedly raised different outcomes. Yet the willingness of white audiences to find emotional pleasure in considering a world without anti-Black racism cut across the Atlantic. The emotional language that British television critics used when talking about the programme as 'comfortable', without 'pressure', 'relaxing', 'happy' and 'refreshing' all pointed to the racial discomfort that white viewers in Britain experienced when faced with the prospect of examining anti-Black racism on the screen.

---

[52] Sut Jhally and Justin Lewis, *Enlightened Racism: The Cosby Show, Audiences, and the Myth of the American Dream* (New York: Routledge, 1992).
[53] Ibid.   [54] Ibid, xvii.   [55] Ibid, 3.

## 7.2  *Desmond's*

The relief that a colour-blind Black comedy like *The Cosby Show* brought to white television critics in Britain carried over into the enthusiastic response of the British press to the premiere of *Desmond's* on Channel 4 in 1989. This was a show that was in many ways quite different from *The Cosby Show*: it was set in a barber shop in south London; it did not have the luxurious domestic setting of the Huxtables' comfortable brownstone in Brooklyn; and it featured a range of West Indian, African, south Asian and white British voices that reflected the legacy of colonialism in the British metropole. Yet *Desmond's* also occupied a similar space for white critics as *The Cosby Show* as it too largely avoided discomforting representations of racism. The British press embraced *Desmond's* because it spoke this same language of colour-blindness but within a British produced and staffed programme. The show was immediately heralded as 'Britain's answer to *The Cosby Show*'.[56] Similarities between the shows were repeatedly stressed, and there was indeed a recognisable affluence on display in the successful barber shop that Desmond ran and in his role as father of the family. In front of the neatly placed hair products lining the shelves of the shop was the image of men and women partaking in the leisurely activity of paying to have their hair done.

Elizabeth Cowley emphasised the small business aspect of *Desmond's* in the *Daily Mail*, describing the premise as 'a harassed dad and owner of Desmond's Barber Shop in South London'.[57] The *Guardian* said the premise 'revolves round the south London barber's shop cum social centre run by Desmond (Norman Beaton) who dreams of going back to the old country to retire. Carmen Munroe is his much more enterprising, culturally-adjusted wife'.[58] Desmond and Shirley's college-educated, immaculately-suited, London-born son Michael (matching his father's neat tie and waistcoat under a barber's jacket) has his own plans to expand the business and was featured heavily in the first season and mentioned in early reviews of the programme. Michael was the face of enterprising Black Britain. The rest of the changing cast of characters who visited the barber shop included African students, first-generation and second-generation West Indian immigrants, white friends and girlfriends and others, while the focus on the family unit offered further

---

[56] Jeannette Kupfermann, 'Wives Who Won't Stay on the Shelf', *Daily Mail*, 6 January 1989, 23.
[57] Elizabeth Cowley, 'Desmond's', *Daily Mail*, 5 January 1989, 24.
[58] 'Television and Radio: Watching Brief', *Guardian*, 5 January 1989, 34.

grounding. The show's setting of a successful business owned by an immigrant mirrored the premise of another programme on Channel 4, *Tandoori Nights*, about an Indian restaurant in London that finished in 1987 after two seasons. *Desmond's*, however, had a staying power that can be directly attributed to the new audience framework of expectations for Black sitcoms that had been erected by *The Cosby Show*.

Similarities between the two shows were acknowledged by *Desmond's* creator, Trix Worrell, even as he denied a colour-blind approach to writing the series. Worrell was born in St. Lucia and was a winner of Channel 4's 'Debut '84' competition to find new writing talent among Black and south Asian writers, a fact that was often raised when introducing the new comedy.[59] Like Cosby, Worrell shared a similar approach in telling positive stories of Black life outside of racist interactions with white people. It was on the way to the offices of Channel 4 and a discussion with television producer Humphrey Barclay that Worrell passed by a local barber shop and came up with the idea of it as a setting for a situation comedy: 'We wanted to say something positive about black families and, more importantly, about migrant families within this country and what it is to be black in England.'[60] Worrell was also explicitly motivated by a desire to educate white audiences about Black life. He was particularly focused on trying 'to highlight that there are a number of different islands in the Caribbean, and that we're not all Jamaican!'[61] In a retrospective discussion of the show Worrell largely rejected Carmen Munroe's claim that he wrote the show primarily for a Black audience arguing, 'I never wrote *Desmond's* for Black people because we know who we are. I wrote it for white people so you knew, so you get to know who we are, and ultimately see that there is no difference really.'[62] For Worrell the show's expected audience was white but with the hope that a greater knowledge of Black experiences would collapse imagined differences between the two. Like Cosby he was also motivated by what he called the front page of *The Sun* showing negative depictions of Black people in Britain.[63] *Desmond's* positive portrayal of Black Britain was one that Cosby himself admired, and he invited Norman Beaton to guest star

---

[59] 'Channel 4', *Guardian*, 21 March 1985, 28. See also Worrell's discussion of the award in 'Just Like Mohicans writer Trix Worrell', BFI Q&A, 8 February 2019: www.youtube.com/watch?v=crmZntaJR0M&ab_channel=BFIThe.
[60] 'Trix Worrell', *Black and White in Colour*, 184.   [61] Ibid., 185.
[62] BFI panel with Ashley Clark, 'Desmond's Creator Trix Worrell: "Desmond's is a Migrant Story"'; BFI, 21 December 2016: www.youtube.com/watch?v=yKX7u3srcxk&ab_channel=BFI.
[63] Ibid.

on an episode of *The Cosby Show*.⁶⁴ Beaton made a brief appearance in 1991, and Worrell accompanied him to the set in the US. Inspired by a full writer's room with dedicated writing teams for individual characters and the Black talent evident there, Worrell worked to introduce a similar approach on his return to Britain.⁶⁵

The connections between the production teams of the two shows were not, however, well known among the British press, and it was again the similarly happy and cheerful tone of a primarily Black show that was most often remarked upon in reviews of both programmes. Critics used *The Cosby Show* as shorthand to indicate the lack of challenge posed to white audiences. Gerald Hobson of the *Daily Mail* wrote as *Desmond's* success began to be apparent: 'Britain's answer to *The Cosby Show* gets another airing, paving the way for a new series transmission next year. And judging from the rapturous reception accorded by the studio audience, it would do equally well as a stage show.'⁶⁶ Cowley, also for the *Daily Mail*, introduced the show as 'a happy, rapping all-black sitcom which radiates goodwill very much in the manner of Bill Cosby and company'.⁶⁷ The *Guardian* described it less enthusiastically as 'Trix Worrell's cheerful sitcom which seems aimed to be a down-market *Cosby*, set in the black community of south London'.⁶⁸ Jeannette Kupfermann, a guest critic for the *Daily Mail*, referred to *Desmond's* as an 'upbeat … C4 sitcom about a black family and their barber shop. Desmond's – Britain's answer to *The Cosby Show* perhaps.'⁶⁹ Kupfermann summed up the series: 'The overall feel was affectionate and amusing, if not wildly funny.'⁷⁰ Philip Purser referred to the show as 'an attractive and companionable comedy of manners, man, among the Caribbean – or specifically Guyanian – community … It's cosy, safe, and just a little stereotyped'.⁷¹ Upbeat, companionable, cosy and cheerful were all terms that could easily have been extended and sometimes were to *The Cosby Show* when it preceded *Desmond's*. Even the *Guardian*, which continued to be rather cantankerous about *Desmond's*, admitted in 1990 that its second season was the 'return of Trix Worrell's likeable black London sitcom'. Such an emphasis on the show's cheerfulness rather belied what Worrell himself described as the source of such

---

⁶⁴ 'Television Diary: Cosby's a Big Fan of Our Norm', *The Stage and Television Today*, 19 November 1992, 5823.
⁶⁵ 'Desmond's Creator Trix Worrell'.
⁶⁶ Gerald Hobson, 'Desmond's', *Daily Mail*, 9 October 1989, 28.
⁶⁷ Elizabeth Cowley, 'Desmond's', *Daily Mail*, 5 January 1989, 24.
⁶⁸ Hugh Hebert, 'The Good Get Going', *Guardian*, 6 January 1989, 28.
⁶⁹ Kupfermann, 'Wives Who Won't Stay on the Shelf', 23.    ⁷⁰ Ibid.
⁷¹ Philip Purser, 'Mary's Got the Midas Touch, Too', *Daily Mail*, 20 January 1989, 27.

humour: 'Being Black, we're funny. Being Black in a minority situation in a dominant culture, you have to laugh, otherwise you're going to cry.'[72] The emotional landscape of a Black scriptwriter and show developer was a rather more complicated one than what was being projected by white television critics.

*Desmond's* was also praised by the newspaper press for its adherence to the colour-blindness that *The Cosby Show* had proved was so successful in appealing to white audiences. *The Times* on *Desmond's* debut treated it to a feature in its television page and used similar language to the other dailies, referring to it as 'a likeable new situation comedy'. Peter Waymark described the show's colour-blindness in positive terms:

Ostensibly a portrait of contemporary Black Britain, *Desmond's* has few racial points to make. On the contrary, it derives most of its jokes from such traditional sources as generation gaps (Desmond cannot understand his son's computer), marital misunderstandings (Desmond suspects that Shirley's French lessons are an excuse for an affair with the teacher) and blind dates. As a comment on our multi-racial society, it is comfortably reassuring.[73]

The 'few racial points' that *Desmond's* might be interested in were lost instead to the 'traditional' sources of jokes that the sitcom mined. This was the 'comment on our multi-racial society' that *The Times*, very much embodying a white television viewership, found 'reassuring' and comfortable to view. This reassuring vision was further compounded by the fact that these immigrants were settled in England although in a highly circumscribed way: 'Desmond and family may be restricted to their own cultural world (only one white character appears, at least in the opening episode) but they have been in Peckham for 30 years and appear contented with their lot.' The family that did not move beyond their own world was seemingly content in their isolated Blackness and *The Times* ended its review with a reference to the alternative negative visions of multi-racial Britain that were on the large screen at the time: 'We are miles away from the bitter polemics of *Sammy and Rosie Get Laid.*'[74] That film was a follow-up to *My Beautiful Laundrette*, again directed by the white director Stephen Frears and based on a script by Hanif Kureishi. Released in 1987 and set in a Britain seized by racial tension and riots, the film showed a strained interracial marriage and a society riven by conflict with no easy resolution in sight and was met with a stinging response by critics. The particular path of *Desmond's* was one that other television writers saw as already tied to the quickly established

---

[72] 'Desmond's Creator Trix Worrell'.
[73] Peter Dear and Peter Waymark, 'A Barber Shop Quintet', *The Times*, 5 January 1989, 7.
[74] Ibid.

traditions of the Black sitcom. For Hugh Hebert, writing for the *Guardian* and still cynical about *The Cosby Show*, 'Like *Cosby*, this looks like a show intended to take race out of the sitcom.'[75] He went on to compare the series' spotlight on a Black diaspora to the regional differences in the United Kingdom: 'It distinguishes between the Caribbean background of the parents and the African or French/African backgrounds of some of their friends and visitors, so they become like Scots, Welsh, and Irish in an all-white sitcom.'[76] Hebert's willingness to map white ethno-cultural differences onto the show's comedy demonstrated the extent to which *Guardian* readers were likely themselves able to grasp the complexities of the Black and imperial diaspora on screen. Such false equivalencies were nevertheless eagerly mapped out in press coverage of the Black diaspora born of empire in confused efforts to relate comedic slurs to each other.

As *Desmond's* continued, its steps outside of a colour-blind presentation were occasionally policed by television critics. Peter Paterson, writing for the *Daily Mail*, was particularly quick to note when the show strayed into discussions of racism which were consistently viewed as unwelcome. Reviewing the last episode of the second season, Paterson remarked that the episode 'tempted one to think that the ethnic minority is just as capable of the white community of producing really bad comedy' and 'perhaps because this was the last of the series, Desmond's also went in for a little preachifying'.[77] In what was described by Paterson as 'an attack on the advertising community' the Gambian character Matthew was quoted as saying: 'When was the last time you saw a black family in an advert? ... As far as advertisers are concerned, we do not use credit cards, we do not smoke cigars, and according to them, only Jewish people use telephones. Did you ever see a black man in a car commercial?'[78]

Paterson then countered with a comment on the number of Black people already on television: 'The point is fair enough, although Lenny Henry and Frank Bruno are hardly under-used by advertisers, and dusky maidens often make their appearance in ads for chocolates and various alcoholic beverages.' Paterson went on to point out that the Black consumer was hardly a lucrative audience for advertisers, using the language of progress to explain this to readers, and presumably the writers of *Desmond's*: 'The hope must obviously be that minorities make sufficient progress in society to constitute a more obvious economic attraction to

---

[75] Hebert, 'The Good Get Going'. [76] Ibid.
[77] Peter Paterson, 'Of Mice, Men and Mincemeat', *Daily Mail*, 17 April 1990, 23.
[78] Ibid.

advertisers. But whether the case is best argued by a comedy programme is quite another question.'[79]

For Paterson, the show had strayed out of its remit to tackle something that Paterson felt it hardly qualified to address – the lack of recognition of Black men and women as consumers and not just faces on the advertisements of chocolates and drinks. The Black perspective and experience that was outlined in the show was thus dismissed. Paterson's dislike of the programme only sharpened as the series went on, and in its third season he made his opinion clear by also using *The Cosby Show* as a point of comparison and finding the British show distinctly lacking: '*Desmond's* is a sitcom which is sometimes outrageously flattered by being described as our home-grown version of *The Cosby Show*. It is, of course, nothing of the kind.'[80] Noting that *The Cosby Show* had been criticised for showing the Huxtables living in a luxury not easily afforded by most Black Americans, Paterson wrote that 'the same charge cannot be levelled at *Desmond's* which depicts a black family living in near-squalor behind, or above, a barbershop in south London'. Going on to observe that the show at least employed Black actors 'burning in Equity at the moment', Paterson offered his scathing final assessment: 'What it lacks, however, which *The Cosby Show* has in abundance, is pride and self-confidence. It is, after all, set among a group which desperately needs to cultivate a greater sense of respect and esteem, both towards itself and the wider community.'[81]

What had so irked Paterson about the show was unclear, but his words unsettled the middle-classness of these programmes which so upheld the racial comfort of white audiences watching them. Paterson's accusation that *Desmond's* showed a family in 'near squalor' and his passing remark that the show at least did something to address Black unemployment in the acting industry all pointed to an audience member whose notions of Black economic inferiority were deeply entrenched.

Other viewers also rejected the programme and were increasingly willing to invoke the novel term 'political correctness' as reason for *Desmond's* success. One, Simon Lewis, felt compelled to write into *The Stage and Television Today* in 1994 as the final season of the show debuted to counter the praise that the publication had recently placed upon it. A previous article had called *Desmond's* 'quality mainstream comedy with universal appeal' and so offended Lewis that it prompted him to write a

---

[79] Ibid.
[80] Peter Paterson, 'A Barber's in Need of Some Style', *Daily Mail*, 3 December 1991, 24.
[81] Ibid.

rebuttal.[82] Lewis's letter was featured prominently in the letters page where he argued that the show was only a success due to its primarily Black cast and political correctness, a relatively new term in Britain primarily imported from American media outlets. Lewis opened by stating baldly: 'The trouble is that this series is criticism-proof because of the political correctness lobby. It stars and is made by black people so it must be brilliant.'[83] While criticising the show for its lack of humour, its 'Am dram' theatrics and for mobilising stereotypes about Black people, the writer concluded that critics were too afraid of being called racist to speak truthfully about the show's quality. He also argued that the show's mediocre existence prevented better-quality programmes featuring Black casts from being produced: 'It is neither fair nor right to turn a blind eye to a show just because of the colour of its cast or production team. *Desmond's* is not very good, and that is the truth.'[84] Here the uses and abuses of colour-blindness increasingly come into play as this 'truth' from a white, unbiased viewer was positioned against the un-truth of 'political correctness' with the potential consequence of limiting the presence of a Black show on the screen. Lewis laid out this 'truth' of the invisible structures of affirmative action that he imagined as unfairly buttressing *Desmond's* relatively rare success in the history of British television. Yet the untimely death of Norman Beaton, *Desmond's* star, in 1994 did indeed change the shape of offerings in Britain as the show ceased broadcasting that year.

### 7.3   *The Fresh Prince of Bel-Air*

What remained on British television in the 1990s was the show that a young Reni Eddo-Lodge watched while growing up, *The Fresh Prince of Bel-Air*. The *Guardian*, discussing the arrival of the *Fresh Prince* in the UK in 1991, described it as 'a new imported comedy with a culture-clash theme' about 'a streetwise city kid sent to polish up his act with the California home of his grand relatives'.[85] As Eddo-Lodge remembered, the aptly named Banks family were 'affluent and upper middle-class, well-dressed, and incredibly well-educated'.[86] The Bankses left the Huxtables' comfortable middle-classness behind and instead had tennis courts and a British butler, Geoffrey, taking the juxtaposition of ghetto

---

[82] James Towler, 'Barber of Civility has the Cutting Edge', *The Stage and Television Today*, 6 October 1994, 24.
[83] Simon Lewis, 'Barber Tells a Different Story', *The Stage and Television Today*, 13 October 1994, 5922.
[84] Ibid.   [85] 'BBC2', *Guardian*, 14 January 1991, 40.
[86] Eddo-Lodge, 'Forming Blackness Through a Screen', 79–80.

and affluence to its extreme. *The Fresh Prince* is an interesting example of a programme that both built upon the clear success with white and Black audiences of *The Cosby Show* in ways that its spin-off, *A Different World*, did not quite claim but also continued to air in a decade that saw significant changes to how television was broadcast in the UK. BBC2 aired *The Fresh Prince* in an effort to keep pace with Channel 4's successful programming. Even the *Daily Mail* had noted by 1991 that Channel 4 'seems to be the only station where communities of black people are allowed to be funny. It has had a huge hit with *Desmond's* and *The Cosby Show* which it imports from the States'.[87] The entirety of the *Fresh Prince's* six seasons were shown on BBC2 in the prime weekday slot of 6.20pm, a year after the show had proved itself with American audiences before then moving into syndication and repeated episodes for another further seven years on the channel. It was in this period that the existing five channels of British television (Channel 5 launched in March 1997) were joined by new offerings for British viewers in the form of cable or digital television. New listings in the television pages from 11 December 1998 onwards entitled 'Satellite, Cable, and Digital' provided readers complete coverage of what was available to watch and distinguished these channels from the traditional television broadcasters.[88] A suite of Sky channels (Sky Cinema, Sky Sports, etc.) were available alongside the Disney channel, TNT, the History Channel, Eurosport and others. American content dominated the world of cable, satellite and digital television, making the decision to keep broadcasting the *Fresh Prince* an easy one.

The duration of the *Fresh Prince's* run on British televisions was notable but so was the relatively quiet arrival of the programme, its enduring popularity and the ways in which it did not quite conform to racially comfortable viewing for white audiences. Very little was said in the press about the show's debut, unlike the flurry of coverage that had accompanied both *The Cosby Show* and *Desmond's*. The novelty of an affluent Black family had largely worn off by 1991; instead the show joined what was something close to a genre, and the strictures of comedy programming were being commented on in Black publications. The same year saw the debut of the sketch comedy show *The Real McCoy*, also on BBC2, which featured a primarily Black and south Asian cast and ran for five seasons on the channel. *The Voice*, which proclaimed itself as 'Britain's Best Black Newspaper' in 1994, ran an article called 'The Jokes on Us' that bemoaned the lack of programming outside of comedy for

[87] Jaci Stephen, 'Sickening Slaughter at the Fiesta', *Daily Mail*, 13 September 1991, 42.
[88] 'Pay TV: Satellite, Cable and Digital', *The Times*, 11 December 1998, 55.

Black programmes in Britain. The article quoted Paulette Randell, a Black Associate Producer on *Desmond's* saying 'There is only one Black British sketch show and that is *The Real McCoy*, yet everyone lumps it together with *Desmond's* and tries to compare them. They are not the same.'[89] *The Fresh Prince* was part of a small increase in the presence of Black and south Asian faces on television in the 1990s, but it too was rooted in comedy and was an American import. The show was also rooted in the already substantial star power of the Black American actor and singer Will Smith who was primarily known for his music career at the time. Smith would also become a movie star during the *Fresh Prince's* broadcast in Britain, starring in the hit action film *Independence Day* in 1996.

*The Fresh Prince of Bel-Air* certainly followed in the footsteps of *The Cosby Show* in its adherence to a vision of Black success and a wealthy domestic setting for the comedy. It played with stereotypes about inner-city America, where its protagonist Will was from, and often mobilised these while consistently bringing the perspective of a working-class Black teenager into the lives of the affluent Bankses. The show, while still rooted in a focus on the family, was however much more explicitly political in its representation of Black experiences than *The Cosby Show* had been. The first episode alone showed Smith's character Will code-switching, or altering his speech and intonations, as he moves between the affluent, comparatively white world of the Bankses who he accuses directly of being Uncle Toms and his reflections on his own experience growing up in 'West Philly', a primarily Black neighbourhood in Philadelphia. The first season also addressed police intimidation of Black men as well as class and race prejudice more widely, things *The Cosby Show* largely shied away from. Consequently the show did not quite offer the same sort of happy, cosy and comfortable viewing experience that *The Cosby Show* and *Desmond's* did, even if it did provide plenty of comedy. The British press made relatively little comment for the good or bad on the show but instead consistently highlighted the work of Joseph Marcell, the British actor best known in Britain for being best known in Britain for playing Othello on the stage in the West End in 1984, as the Bankses' icy British butler Geoffrey (Marcell also had a small part on *Desmond's* and a more substantial one on *Empire Road* in the late 1970s.).

For Black audiences, however, the show was a vital link to explicit discussions of Blackness. The Nigerian-Scottish writer, Saidat Giwa-Osagie, wrote that when watching *The Fresh Prince* in the highlands of

---

[89] Allister Harry, 'The Jokes on Us', *The Voice*, 22 November 1994, 4 &5/BCA.

Scotland 'I finally saw people who looked like me, who lived like me – as rare black faces in a predominantly white place' and that 'The Fresh Prince powerfully showed me how to embrace my blackness, irrespective of situation or location'.[90] Giwa-Osagie outlined the show's arrival among what she experienced as a dearth of shows featuring Black people on television: 'In the '90s, only the barbershop-family sitcom *Desmond's* and the BBC sketch show *The Real McCoy* offered a tiny, comedic glimpse into black British life.' *The Fresh Prince* was a means by which Giwa-Osagie could navigate her blackness: the character of Carlton, who was consistently shown as largely divorced from his Blackness through his affluence, was a particularly fascinating one for her alongside the youngest Banks daughter, Ashley, as she came of age as a Black teenage girl. The show offered mainstream and crucially repeated images of posh Blackness on television to viewers. The relative quiet around the show's run in the British press points to one of two possibilities in terms of white viewers: first, that much of the epistemological work necessary for white viewers to accept representations of Black experiences on screen had occurred during the broadcast of *The Cosby Show* and *Desmond's*, or conversely, that type of knowing of Black experiences could more easily be avoided in a television climate that had a channel for almost every audience. As cable, digital and satellite television revolved around a model of chasing comparatively small, fragmented audiences who were nevertheless watching throughout a 24-hour cycle, audiences who did not want to encounter Blackness on screen certainly did not have to.

What also emerged in the 1990s in Britain, it must be acknowledged, was a genre of television and film that would not be kind to either Black actors or UK viewers – so-called heritage film and television content. Instigated by the success of feature films produced by Ishmael Merchant and James Ivory, including *A Room with a View* (1985) and *Howards End* (1992), the new emphasis on nineteenth-century period dramas and comedies produced countless imitators and leapt onto television with several BBC and ITV mini-series based on Jane Austen's and E. M. Forster's historic novels. The *Sharpe* series (ITV, 1993–1997) offered a long-running example of heritage television set during the Napoleonic wars for viewers to immerse themselves in. The heritage film genre has been extensively discussed by Andrew Higson who has argued that this genre perfectly encapsulated 1980s and 1990s Britain with its attention

---

[90] Saidat Giwa-Osagie, 'Finding My Identity Via The Fresh Prince of Bel-Air', *The Atlantic*, 24 May 2016, www.theatlantic.com/entertainment/archive/2016/05/the-enduring-freshness-of-the-fresh-prince-of-bel-air/484082.

to opulence, grand spaces and its celebration of middle-classness in keeping with a Thatcherite and then Blairite ideal after 1997.[91] The trend continued into the twenty-first century. The merits of this argument can be debated but the turn towards historical settings for British television is hard to argue against.[92] The implication of the 'heritage turn' on British screens was quite profound for racialised actors in Britain. Black British actor Thandiwe Newton said in an interview in 2017 with the *Sunday Times*: 'I love being here, but I can't work, because I can't do *Downton Abbey*, can't be in *Victoria*, can't be in *Call The Midwife* – well, I could, but I don't want to play someone who's being racially abused.'[93] Newton went on to say that 'there just seems to be a desire for stuff about the Royal Family, stuff from the past, which is understandable, but it just makes it slim pickings for people of colour'. Actor David Oyelowo also commented on period films in Britain to *Radio Times*, saying: 'We make period dramas here, but there are almost never black people in them, even though we've been on these shores for hundreds of years.' Oyelowo went on:

There's a string of black British actors passing through where I live now in LA. We don't have [casting opportunities in] *Downton Abbey*, or *Call the Midwife*, or *Peaky Blinders*, or the 50th iteration of *Pride and Prejudice*. We're not in those. And it's frustrating, because it doesn't have to be that way. I shouldn't have to feel like I have to move to America to have a notable career.[94]

The turn in British screen culture since the mid-1980s towards period films and their rich depiction of a primarily white Britain left relatively little room for Black British history or Black actors on the large or small screen. Instead, the past began to be imagined on both film and television screens as primarily white for British audiences. In the process the contemporary television landscape again remained largely white. Nostalgia for a British history that was imagined as primarily white offered its own deeply appealing, comfortable viewing pleasures for British audiences.

---

[91] Andrew Higson, 'Re-Presenting the National Past: Nostalgia and Pastiche in the Heritage Film', in Lester Friedman, ed., *Fires were Started: British Cinema and Thatcherism*, 2nd ed (London: Wallflower Press, 2006), 91–109.
[92] This genre extended into the twenty-first century, when the writer Julian Fellowes would have success with *Downton Abbey*, which ran for six seasons on ITV from 2010.
[93] Thandie Newton, 'The Interview: Thandie Newton, Actor', *Sunday Times*, 19 March 2017, www.thetimes.co.uk/article/the-interview-thandie-newton-actor-2pr3v0lgf. The actor now goes by 'Thandiwe', her birth name.
[94] David Oyelowo, 'I Had to Leave Britain to Have an Acting Career', *Radio Times*, 2 February 2015; www.radiotimes.com/movies/selma-star-david-oyelowo-i-had-to-leave-britain-to-have-an-acting-career.

Sarita Malik, a doctoral student of Stuart Hall in the mid-1990s and now professor of Media Studies, remembers how a belief in meritocracy began to shape the future of Black cinema production in that decade.[95] Whereas the 1980s felt like a period of diverse and disruptive work in support of anti-racist initiatives to Malik, with help from diverse bodies such as the Institute of Contemporary Arts (which would host the Black Film British Cinema conference in 1988), the GLC, BFI and Channel 4, the decade that followed saw a dismantling of much of this in the name of a 'post-multicultural society' under both the Conservatives and Labour. As Malik has written, 'Post-multiculturalism was underpinned by an assumption of cultural meritocracy and assimilation' which saw new priorities for funding when it came to supporting Black cinema. The colour-blindness that the Conservative Party had tapped into in its 1983 general election campaign and which was taken up, in part, by the Black sitcoms of the 1980s would ultimately translate into a post-multiculturalism that offered less support for still-disadvantaged Black film-makers and producers. Multiculturalism became the new colour-blindness while heritage film and television and its own emphasis on white traditions continued to find its audience in the UK.

## Conclusion

It is always tempting when talking about representations of Black and south Asian people on the big or small screen to talk in terms of progress. The last two decades of the twentieth century in Britain saw a move largely away from the racial sitcoms of the 1960s and 1970s which continually deployed racist language and phrases because, the argument went, this was a means of making these less powerful. *Till Death Do Us Part's* 1980s spin-off on the BBC, *In Sickness and In Health*, was met with a sceptical response from television critics in 1985 even if audience enthusiasm was enough to keep it on the air for five seasons. When the show came to an end in 1992 it was met with something akin to relief.[96] *The Black and White Minstrel Show*, which had placed blacking up at the heart of British television and the BBC, also finally came to a quiet end in Britain in 1978. What the audience wanted seemed to have shifted. The

---

[95] Sarita Malik, 'Reflections on Representing Black Britain', *Journal of Cultural Economy* (October 2022 online). www.tandfonline.com/doi/full/10.1080/17530350.2022 .2138502; Sarita Malik, 'Black Film British Cinema: In Three Acts', in Clive James Nwonka and Anamik Saha, eds., *Black Film British Cinema II* (London: Goldsmiths Press, 2021), 29.

[96] Rebecca Hardy, 'You've Gone Too Far This Time, Alf Garnett is Told', *Daily Mail*, 17 July 1992, 39.

last two decades of the twentieth century offered audiences a new approach to racialised people and racism on screen by decoupling the two. Through two imported series and one British, Black communities were shown on screen not always for the purpose of visualising racism but rather to show a Black everydayness, however extraordinary in the case of the Huxtables and the Bankses, that was not always defined by race relations with white people. This was the primary approach of writers such as Bill Cosby and Trix Worrell in those last two decades. It seemingly worked with white British critics and audiences who embraced all three shows.

Yet we are far enough into the twenty-first century and the age of the internet to be sceptical of the promises of racial progress and any related idea of a post-racial and post-racist audience. Indeed critical race theory with its attention to the multiple ways in which racialised thinking informs and persists in the structures of institutions and the everyday points us towards the many techniques that white people, and in this case white audiences, deploy to avoid confronting racism. The progress of the three Black sitcoms I have examined here was still limited by the constraints of racialised thinking in Britain at the time. The decoupling of images of people of colour from experiences of racism on the screen did little to alter the ways of thinking about Black people for British television critics and the audiences they represented but instead seemingly prolonged a confrontation with British racism itself by assuring British audiences that Black people need not always talk about race. These shows allowed many white viewers to retreat to a world where the anti-Black racism of white audiences did not have to be known, confronted, or addressed. Comfortable Black families could own businesses, own wonderful homes, and dress like they were in *Dynasty* on the small screen; white viewers could passively watch this while sheltered from the discomforts and realities of anti-Black racism. This was a novel pleasure that delighted many critics and viewers alike and added yet another racialised dimension to what the audience wanted, even at the end of the twentieth century.

# Conclusion
'Of the Time'

It is a common occurrence in the current age when discussing the racist sentiments of a historic person or programme for these to be described and defended as being 'of the time' or 'of their time'. This defence is a solid, seemingly impenetrable and certainly not an irrational one often mobilised in favour of keeping monuments to certain individuals in place or keeping the names unchanged of music venues, universities or sports teams. As I have worked on this book, these debates have occurred about the durability of such things and whether they should remain in our time. The argument that these are just 'of the time' is quite often an argument for inaction in the present, accepting what was and moving on into a future where such views have less purchase. 'Of the time' is thus a powerful and appealing umbrella cast over all manner of sins as the past acts as a vast and uneasy shelter for views that cannot easily be spoken of in today's society. That time might have produced uncomfortable beliefs or behaviour, the thinking goes, but oh well that was then and this is now and it is all a part of history. We can be thankful that things have changed and no further intervention is needed.

For the historian tasked with knowing the past, this 'of the time' defence is frustrating for several reasons. This line of argument is inevitably a vast simplification of a period housing divergent experiences and perspectives of people that have often been overlooked for reasons related to race, gender, sexuality, region and class. Oftentimes proponents of the 'of the time' argument simply do not know that other people living in the period thought differently from the majority. When it comes to racist thinking in the past, they are ignorant of the counterpoints or protests at the time by people of colour who possessed different experiences, points of view and language on racism. This information and these people's voices have been lost or forgotten in the overwhelming white voice that writes the narratives of the past and present in archives, institutions and the arena of public history. Illuminating the other voices of the past who were often silenced by the dominant, whiggish narrative has been a central albeit uneven project of social history since the 1960s. It is this endeavour that has perhaps strained, if not broken, the alliance of history and politics that existed previously and which has been documented by writers such as David Armitage, Jo Guldi and numerous other historians.[1] Certainly, this historiographic turn to history from below has offered us a vision of the past with far more voices in it than had existed previously.

This book has spotlighted the overlooked audiences watching television and film in twentieth-century Britain who were consistently pointing out that this material was racist. These were the counter-protests and counter-storytelling by Black, south Asian and occasionally white viewers who were also part 'of the time'. I have admittedly succumbed to the temptation that Walter Johnson cautions us against to champion those Black and south Asian audiences who were treading against the dominant thinking, and I have sought those records of protest and alternative ways of seeing and knowing race and racism.[2] These voices are some of the more striking in this book. As we have seen, Clive West the Trinidadian stoker who organised the petition against the BBC's *The Black and White Minstrel Show* in May 1967, argued in the face of great controversy that a show that hinged on the practices of blacking up was, in fact, racist. For West the show offered audiences 'a laugh at the expense of a minority and it causes distress to coloured people by showing them as a race that cannot be taken as serious-minded citizens', providing both an eloquent analysis of what was happening on the screen and an account of its emotional impact on Black audiences.[3] That white audiences at the time were resoundingly unwilling to give up the distinct pleasures of viewing blacking up on screen, arguing that the show was 'not about race', indicates the collective effort by audiences and producers of television to deny the existence of anti-Black racism in modern Britain while ultimately fostering its continued existence.[4] When the BBC's white accountant Barrie Thorne, on the same day Clive West's interview with the *Daily Mirror* was published, pleaded in a memo with BBC executives for the programme to be shown to members of the NAACP in the US and other big broadcasters there, he was wanting a type of response and education that would upend this wilful ignorance about racism among BBC executives.[5] He was hoping for a shift in the

---

[1] Jo Guldi and David Armitage, *The History Manifesto* (Cambridge: Cambridge University Press, 2014).
[2] Walter Johnson, 'On Agency', *Journal of Social History* (Fall 2003): 113–124.
[3] 'Race Rumpus Over the Black and White Minstrels', *Daily Mirror*, 19 May 1967, 3.
[4] Brian Dean, 'The White-and-White Minstrel Show', *Daily Mail*, 19 September 1968, 3
[5] Barrie Thorne to C.A. to Director General, 19 May 1967, R78/1,921/1 'Black and White Minstrel Show' WAC.

very epistemologies that underpinned the production of the programme for white, racially innocent British audiences. Thorne wrote:

'Many regard the show as Uncle Tom from start to finish, as such it is underlyingly offensive to many, no matter what the outward gloss and the size of audience prove to the contrary. Those of us who think this way may be entirely wrong. But so might the BBC.'[6] Thorne outlined a group of people seeing things rather differently than the BBC and *The Black and White Minstrel's* sizeable white audience in Britain were. These statements against the show by both Black and white viewers were part of the time as well but were effectively shouted down in that moment.

Other voices have come to the fore in this account to point out the problems with white audiences consuming racist screen content. The first Nigerian High Commissioner in 1957, Matthew T. Mbu, questioned why an empire film such as *Sanders of the River* with its infantile and violent depiction of Nigerians was being shown on television in the post-war period.[7] The writings of Buddy Bradley and Edward Scobie in the post-war glossy magazines, *Bronze, Checkers, Tropic* and *Flamingo* pointed out the same tired historic stereotypes alongside blacking up that informed contemporary films. Even the laughter and jeers of colonial audiences of colour, both in the interwar period and during World War II, demonstrated the existence of audiences of colour bringing a different framework of seeing and knowing to their encounters with screen content. Likewise the small group of 21 West Indian respondents asked to absolve the racial sitcom *Love Thy Neighbour* of racism in 1975 through a dubious audience research exercise for ITV were equivocal in their endorsement and pointed to both the tremendously white landscape of British television and their existence as Black people encountering discomforting racism in Britain on an often daily basis. These voices I am tempted to say represent Black and south Asian agency in the white *habitus* of British film and television. As Johnson himself notes, it is difficult to entirely abandon that concept, particularly when these voices spoke out in an environment of everyday racism in a supposedly non-racist Britain. Stuart Hall and the Campaign Against Racism in the Media (CARM) and their broadcast on the BBC's 'Open Door' programme *It Ain't Half Racist Mum* in 1979 further worked to spectacularly point out the racism of the times on one of the only two broadcasters in the country that they could push their way onto. These voices are the ones that are overlooked when the familiar 'of the times' defence is

---

[6] Ibid.   [7] 'Film "Damaging to Nigeria"', *The Times*, 22 November 1957, 6.

paraded and left without interrogation or supplementary work. That train of thought does not see the persistent labour that was being done by ordinary and occasionally extraordinary racialised people to name racism as racism and who were dismissed, marginalised or shouted down for it. The archive still notes that action of speaking out primarily through the white press and white institutions either recording and working against these protests or commenting on them as ridiculous or amusing. Speaking out in those times was no easy thing.

It is the enveloping racist thinking of the past that has been the focus of this book and which is also referred to in the 'of the time' argument. Perhaps the most frustrating thing about the 'of the time' defence is that it is absolutely correct but in ways that the public and even many historians have not much grappled with.[8] Racist content and viewpoints were widely held by an astonishing number of people in both halves of twentieth-century Britain as this book has shown. As the BBC Audience Research Department relayed in 1968 following the questions it posed to ordinary Britons about immigrants and immigration:

'The startling, but inescapable, impression left by these results is that *most* of these people showed anti-colour/immigrant attitudes in at least some degree and that what can only be described as racial prejudice proved to be alarmingly common.'[9] Racism or racial prejudice was 'alarmingly common' according to the people tasked with knowing what audiences thought and felt when they watched television. It was not limited to a small group, but in this period and in this audience research exercise it was manifest in a fairly young group of white Londoners at the end tail of the permissive sixties and as London was imagined as the epicentre of generational change. Racialised thinking even among that group and that time and that city was firmly in place. Perhaps common racial prejudice forms a more central part of modern British identity than we have allowed as historians. How central is whiteness to British identity outside of empire as Marc Matera and others have noted?[10] Does a focus on empire and decolonisation detract from the work of whiteness across these, within these and occasionally against political framings of these as projects of empire?

---

[8] Camilla Schofield's piece offers an excellent example of what can be done; Camilla Schofield, 'In Defence of White Freedom: Working Men's Clubs and the Politics of Sociability in Late Industrial England', *Twentieth Century British History* 34, no. 3 (2023): 515-551.

[9] 'Race Relations and *Rainbow City*', An Audience Research Report, 4 March 1968, BBC Audience Research Special Reports Television, R9/10/15, p. 2, WAC.

[10] This begins to be circled in Erik Linstrum, 'Decolonizing Britain: An Exchange', *Twentieth Century British History* 33, no. 2 (2022): 274-303, and is addressed more directly in Marc Matera, Radkhika Natarajan, Kennetta Hammond Perry et al, 'Introduction: Marking Race in Twentieth Century British History', *Twentieth Century British History* 34, no. 3 (2023): 407-414.

That work of not knowing about, not seeing and actively avoiding racism was manifold, complex and almost impressively collective in its effort to paint twentieth-century Britain as racially tolerant even while upholding screen culture that manifestly was not. The words of numerous white people involved in thinking about and imagining audience preferences in twentieth-century Britain, such as Johnny Speight, Stephen Tallents and William Sellers, wove an immensely strong and opaque fabric that informed what white audiences were able to see, imagine and enjoy when it came to Black and south Asian people on screen. The work of emergent experts on the audience and the media producers that they engaged with offers valuable insight into how powerful assumptions about the audience would continue to shape this content: John Grierson's academic treatise, 'On the Psychology of Popular Appeal', amended for the Empire Marketing Board in 1927, built an approach to documentary film centred on a belief that white people were not particularly interested in and were only curious about racialised people; Grace Wyndham Goldie's question to the BBC's Audience Research Department in September 1952 about whether white people would object to seeing Black people 'expressing their own point of view' on screen demonstrated a canny understanding of the willingness of an institution like the BBC to know and act upon such information. The many overtly racist comments that white BBC audiences were willing to endorse about Black people in Britain when they were asked about a television show showing or discussing them in 1968 and also in the 1973 study on *Till Death Us Do Part* showed us this audience again.[11] The seemingly casual agreement of 78 per cent of respondents in 1968 with statements such as 'it was a mistake to allow so many coloured people to settle here', which were just as casually put to them by staff in the Audience Research Department, shone a spotlight on the racialised thinking of the time.[12] The story of how the BBC and ITV worked around this racism, with it at times and too rarely against it is I think an important and overlooked story about the will to not know about racism in twentieth Britain.

My frustration with the fuzzy defences of past racist thinking is how poorly mapped and poorly considered the bridge between then and now

---

[11] Grace Wyndham Goldie to Audience Research Department, 15 September 1952, T/32/209, WAC.

[12] 'Race Relations and Rainbow City', An Audience Research Report, 1, 4 March 1968, Audience Research Special Reports Television, 1968, R9/10/15, WAC.

is. What does it really mean that the relatively recent past was littered with widespread racist thinking? What are the implications of that for British society and its politics and economics? And above all *when* did thinking, behaviour, language and attitudes change or did they at all? Did the steady creation of interracial families reaching all parts of the country, as David Holland has shown, offer new experiences and new thinking about race?[13] Did new thinking occur in some places faster than in others? The racist thinking of ordinary Britons has not been, I would argue, sufficiently examined by historians of modern Britain, and the sheer level of uninterest in the topic by historians in Britain who are not working explicitly on Black British history or history of empire is a subject of its own. Perhaps this is because the dissection of class and gender has preoccupied us more in this country that what is, or was, racist. Or perhaps it is because, as Johnson has argued, historians who tend to be white look for the Thompsonian heroes and the exceptional actors overcoming such an environment instead of examining the common, distasteful ground below them.[14] Customs in common indeed. Regardless, we do not know enough about the racist thinking of the past in Britain, which leaves us uniquely ill-equipped to study it as we march into the history of twenty-first-century Britain. This book has traced some of the more rigid and enduring thinking in the twentieth century on what white film and television audiences knew or thought they knew about 'race'. It has uncovered the highly racist screen environment of the period and noted the assumptions about white audiences and what they wanted when it came to 'race' on screen that underpinned this. It has started to show the varied types of work and workers involved in maintaining racialised thinking and content. It has, I hoped, started an excavation of racist thinking and imagining among white British audiences and media shapers in both the pre- and post-war periods that allows us to see where and when things shifted and when they did not.

The book does not, by any means, give a huge amount of comfort in that regard, and it is the sheer cynic in me, and perhaps my own contemporary experiences as a white woman from an 'acceptable' country like Canada, that has come to notions of racial progress in twentieth-century Britain with scepticism. The story of what looks like progress in television in 1980s and 1990s Britain, upon closer inspection, is not simply one of times changing towards greater racial tolerance; rather, it is the outsourcing of British television and film's inability to address its

---

[13] David Holland, *Imperial Heartland: Immigration, Working-Class Culture and Everyday Tolerance, 1917–1947* (Cambridge: Cambridge University Press, 2023).
[14] Walter Johnson, 'On Agency', *Journal of Social History* (Fall 2003): 113–124.

own 'race problem' with white British audiences and a related lack of knowledge or engagement with audiences of colour to another English-speaking country. America was both the much-acknowledged site of racial intolerance on British television in the 1950s and 1960s in the minds of many British people but also ultimately the solution to Britain's inability to convincingly present the lives of Black people on the small or big screen. That an American television programme like *The Cosby Show* was what allowed many white Britons to think that they could feel 'comfortable' watching a primarily Black-cast programme on screen and even enjoy it is a rather damning comment on the state of the British small screen at the end of the twentieth century. That segue between the quiet end of the television behemoth *The Black and White Minstrel Show* in 1978 and the arrival of *The Bill Cosby Show* in 1985 did not, as I have shown, herald any great progress in Thatcher's Britain but rather a willingness of white audiences to trade one type of show that was 'not about race' for another. This was yet another plank in the defence of Britain as not racist and as racially tolerant.

Alongside this audience embrace of three successful Black sitcoms of the 1980s and 1990s lies the enduring presence of Alf Garnett on British television as he returned in 1985. The character of Alf Garnett, much like *The Black and White Minstrel Show*, is a spectre across this book; he could be in every chapter. It is he who I most often return to when I think about racism in Britain as being 'of the time' forty-odd years ago. The premiere of *Till Death Us Do Part* in 1965 was heralded as bringing an innovative working-class voice to the BBC alongside a refreshing discussion of taboo topics such as immigration and politics to the screen. The Audience Research Department repeatedly documented it as ringing 'true to life' for audiences in the 1960s. By 1992 when the last incarnation of the character in the spin-off *In Sickness and in Health* (BBC1) would finally depart the screen, Alf Garnett spanned three decades of British television. The invocation of the name Alf Garnett became a type of shorthand for a particular viewpoint and particular type of Briton that was ultimately beloved by audiences. The show itself is a shocking watch nowadays as a recent attempt at a one-off version of it demonstrated but standard audience research reports in the 1960s showed a steady enthusiasm for it.[15] The troublesome 1973 Audience Research study which demonstrated that already racist audiences were becoming even more

---

[15] *Till Death Us Do Part: A Woman's Place Is in the Home* (2016). This was a recreation of a 1965 script, starring Simon Day as Alf Garnett and part of the BBC's sitcom season. *Are You Being Served?* had a similar treatment; Alf Garnett back as part of BBC sitcom revival, 10 March 2016, www.bbc.co.uk/news/entertainment-arts-35774053.

racist by watching it was quickly shunted to one side. Television critics, who we spent the last chapter with, showed real concern when the character returned in *In Sickness and in Health*. As Herbert Kretzmer mused, Alf was untouched by the changing times and had 'not grown or developed'.[16] Critics in the right-leaning *Daily Mail* such as Mary Kenny even directly quoted Alf's shocking words in 1985 as if convincing themselves and audiences that this was what was allowed on television:

> 'It goes without saying that he's a chauvinist, and screams hysterics at women, given half the chance. "You bloody silly old faggot! You stupid old witch!" – and should any man seem pleasant and cultivated he will be dismissed as a "pooftah"'.[17] The old argument regarding racial sitcoms, that they lambasted racists and improved race relations as a result, no longer held water with the critics at least.

Yet audiences beyond the critics continued to love the character of Alf Garnett perhaps because of his views and not in spite of them as even television writers at the *Daily Mail* began to suspect. This was a case of the audience's love going beyond the critics and showing a comfort with all things extreme that may have foreshadowed what was to come in terms of political events in the twenty-first century. As Paul Donovan at the *Daily Mail* wrote in an article titled 'That Bigot Is Back...and We Still Love Him': 'With the passing years, Alf has become bloated into an enduring folk hero. He is conceivably almost as much a celebration of those attitudes as condemnation of them. What we tend to feel about him is that he is a revolting foul-mouthed old volcano, and faintly loveable with it.'[18]

Something akin to a faint if queasy acknowledgement of both the death of the racially innocent audience and the existence of an outsized and vaguely incomprehensible audience is evident in Donovan's assessment and that of Kretzmer and Kenny. Indignant letters to the *Daily Mail* followed, lambasting those critics who had voiced their new scepticism. This response translated into a type of apology from one offender at least; Kretzmer felt compelled to state in a subsequent issue that he was aware of the ire he had caused readers with his criticisms and he was 'happy to reaffirm here my awestruck admiration of writer Johnny Speight for creating in Alf Garnett so vivid an emblem of ill-tempered times'.[19]

---

[16] Herbert Kretzmer, 'Garnett in Full Speight Isn't Funny Any More', *Daily Mail*, 16 September 1985, 21.
[17] Mary Kenny, 'Is Garnett's Bitterness Going Sour?', *Daily Mail*, 5 September 1986, 23.
[18] Paul Donovan, 'That Bigot Is Back... and We Still Love Him', *Daily Mail*, 2 September 1985, 21.
[19] Herbert Kretzmer, 'Goodbye to the Immortal Alf!', *Daily Mail*, 14 October 1985, p. 25.

*In Sickness and in Health* would have a healthy five seasons on the BBC before finally retiring in 1992 a year after *The Fresh Prince of Bel-Air* debuted on BBC2. It seems a miracle that Garnett did not make it into the age of satellite television considering his enduring popularity with British audiences. Audience discomfort with the content of Alf's racist tirades was patchy at best and did not quite mirror the growing albeit ultimately inert unease in the halls of the BBC or in the tabloid press with the enduring appeal of the character.

The varied responses to *In Sickness and in Health* also capture some of the methodological challenges I wrote about in my article 'Cultural History's Absent Audience'.[20] That article, written at the outset of this project, discussed the difficulties cultural and media historians have in locating an historic audience that spoke of the culture or media it was consuming. This book has continued to wrestle with that with mixed results. On the one hand, it is clear that the audience was a figment or a construct of many people's imaginations who collectively pulled together some sense of what might please this nebulous blob. This book has chased the audience through academic treatises, through memos among producers, through the dubious graphs of audience research, through pieces of audience response recorded in indignant letters or complaints and finally through attendance at and popular endorsement of what made it to the screens. If the audience has been hard to pin down among all the people busy imagining its wants and preferences, certain common contours of this imagining emerged and stayed surprisingly static in the century. If the people doing the imagining were white then the audience was also imagined as white and with the particular preferences of white people. This book has traced those imaginings in their various homes and in the finished on-screen products of producers, writers, film and television executives, and censors. As these groups thought aloud about what the audience wanted, what it loved and feared, what it was uninterested in, I have attempted to trace the outline of the audience they invoked with attention to the racial boundary-making that was involved in producing audiences that mattered and audiences that did not.

There is also, as I have inferred, a 'real' audience at work in here captured through the imperfect efforts of people hired to interview and survey what ordinary Britons thought when they watched television in particular. That audience, which has emerged in the book through an examination of audience research's activities in the twentieth century, is still rendered somewhat voiceless through the methodologies of the field

---

[20] Christine Grandy, 'Cultural History's Absent Audience', *Cultural and Social History* 16, no. 5 (2019): 643–663.

that turned records of opinions or endorsements of statements into quantifiable data and which only selectively quoted this data. However even through the quantitative data this audience spoke quite bluntly, awkwardly and clearly at times against what those in power imagined them to want, an experience that sometimes confounded the rather genteel staff working at the BBC and ITV in the post-war period. They also spoke with their television dials, tuned in week after week, and their seats in cinema theatres, or not as they turned away from the screen. This audience that claimed and agreed with racialised thinking as a type of common sense is seemingly the one that upheld the return of Alf Garnett for another five series of his racist imaginings from 1985 to 1992 and which supported *The Black and White Minstrel Show* in its remarkable 20 years on the BBC and in its post-broadcasting life as a touring show until the 1990s and the similarly impressive run of the empire films in the interwar period and beyond. This audience of ordinary Britons with its blunt, racist ideas is one that has also come through in this work.

Audience research as a field and practice, it turns out, knew a fair bit about this tendency of British audiences to be quite comfortable with racist thinking and language even if the staff conducting the surveys and writing the reports were not. Audience research, as this book has demonstrated, was very much a twentieth-century field and preoccupation. As a pseudo-discipline caught between notions of public good and private gain, it captures all the traits of an aggressive, changeable period in British history and the march into neoliberalism discussed by James Vernon.[21] Audience research was both full of tremendous early opportunity and then decline, in quick succession. Certainly audience research as an endeavour has persisted well into the twenty-first century even if the mode of research developed first at the BBC under Robert Silvey has been largely abandoned in favour of technical and now digital solutions that are jealously guarded by corporations. It seems remarkable now to conceive of something as old-fashioned as phoning people and asking them what they thought of a television programme or mailing out hundreds and often thousands of questionnaires to people who would, just as remarkably, duly fill them in. Audience research's own myopic interests in the audience, tied always to its own inability to see the audience as different from itself, and the uneasy relationship of audience research within British media institutions marked it out as a site of impressive flexibility as it served the institution first and foremost. It certainly offers us an early lesson in the uses and abuses of such data within institutions.

---

[21] James Vernon, 'Heathrow and the Making of Neoliberal Britain', *Past & Present* 252, no. 1 (2021): 213–247.

The field built from the ruminations of white middle-class men reflects all of the perspectives of this group. Audience research's almost complete lack of engagement with Black and south Asian audiences even as it amassed with little comment or connection a series of reports speaking to the racism of white audiences in Britain is one of the more scandalous elements of the account I have laid out here.

The story of screen culture, audience racism and twentieth-century Britain is thus a story of a desperate chasing of the audience and the associated inventions of racist pleasures on screen to secure that audience. This was ultimately shaped by powerful middle-class men and occasionally women who presumed to know and measure what audiences wanted and also those film and television producers and shapers who likewise pulled the levers to get things onto the screen. These white men and women imagined what the audience wanted when it came to 'race' on screen and also what they adamantly did not want, which was a discussion of the racism of white people. Black and south Asian audiences knew this and stated it repeatedly in their critiques of film and television content and in their limited interactions with these shapers of the screen. The resulting televisual archive is the logical outcome of such a convergence. It is full of the 'difficult heritage' that Sharon Macdonald defines as material that is 'contested and awkward for public reconciliation with a positive self-affirming contemporary identity' or as John Grierson might have said, it doesn't make one feel good.[22] This historic screen culture raises profound nostalgia among white people remembering the simpler times of the past while for audiences of colour and white audiences with different perspectives on race it is more likely to raise the myriad emotions associated with witnessing the casually racist viewpoints and practices of film and television of the past. These two quite different frameworks of knowledge, memory and viewing brought to the televisual archive by the audiences who encounter this material now make it a site of shame and nostalgia, and one hell of a puzzle for the companies that manage their back catalogues. I only hope this puzzle does not translate into a lack of access for the researcher to this difficult archive.

What is clear, however, is it will be both harder and easier to chase audiences in the digital age. Audience research departments, with their mystifying graphs, prosaic reports and large panels of audiences have given way to more precise, technologically driven, digitally enabled ways of knowing the audience, and these archives of behaviour are not open yet. Behaviour when watching a film or series on Netflix can be measured

---

[22] Sharon Macdonald, 'Is "Difficult Heritage" Still "Difficult?"', *Museum International* 67, no. 1–4 (2015): 6–22.

by the time spent on a programme or the moments when audiences collectively abandoned it. It can be measured through the 'watchlists' that people compile themselves sometimes in a fit of virtue and the perhaps quite different screen material they actually watch. Views and engagement can be measured and quantified now in ways that they simply were not in the twentieth century even if elements of what audience research is doing and certainly the drive behind it are the same. New understandings of the assumptions underpinning the production of code and algorithms point to the same issues of a tech industry looking for users who look and act like themselves.[23] This process and material, however, resides in closed rooms behind company copyright and in proprietary software and code. Audience research is still very much present but is so present as to be practically invisible in our new digital and AI age. The screen and the viewer have been liberated to live and watch everywhere and anywhere. The audience can consume material in huge quantities on whatever device they wish and at any time of the day. Crucially, audiences are themselves able to produce screen content in ways that were impossible to imagine in Britain with the advent of relevantly affordable home-movie making after 1965.[24] Black and south Asian audiences can now speak back to the material of film and television through visual or text-based commentaries over a number of digital platforms. The audience does not seem so absent any longer but abundantly there and vocal all the time. The challenge now is the scale of that abundance for historians and access.[25] Whether the twenty-first century has truly empowered and unleashed the voice of the audience through the digital or actually fundamentally shaped and changed that voice is a subject for critical digital studies and related fields and also for us emergent historians of the early twenty-first century.

As for audience racism in the twenty-first century, the story is one of continuity with what I laid out as existing in the twentieth century but also with some shifts in these first few decades. The contemporary racism and sexism of audiences and production environments has been laid bare in the production of film and television material in the age of social

---

[23] Mar Hicks, *Programming Inequality: How Britain Discarded Women Technologists and Lost its Edge in Computing* (Cambridge, MA: MIT Press, 2018); Daniel Meyerend, 'The Algorithm Knows I'm Black: From Users to Subjects', *Media, Culture & Society* 45, no. 3 (2023): 629–645; Thomas Mullaney, Mar Hicks and Benjamin Peters, eds., *Your Computer is on Fire* (Cambridge, MA: MIT Press, 2021).

[24] Heather Norris Nicholson, *Amateur Film: Meaning and Practice, 1927–1977* (Manchester: Manchester University Press, 2012).

[25] Daniel J. Story et al., 'History's Future in the Age of the Internet', *The American Historical Review* 125, no. 4 (2020): 1337–1346, https://doi.org/10.1093/ahr/rhaa477.

media, but likewise it has been newly scrutinised in those spheres. The tools of critical race theory that have helped me, as a white academic, to write this book, are tools that are being attacked and pilloried in the US, the United Kingdom and Canada. Critical race theory is misunderstood, misrepresented and creating a growing reluctance to claim its contributions by those disturbed by its seemingly new ways of seeing and the liberal birth of 'wokeness'. This knowledge, it is argued, must be prevented from spreading even as it most obviously has. These are tools and ways of seeing that my students now arrive at university already knowing as simply part of what one knows about race and prejudice nowadays. My students came to discussions of the various disparate events of 2020, which included the murder of an American Black man George Floyd by a white police officer captured on screen in the US and the exit of a Black duchess and her white royal husband from the UK, with much more knowledge and language around the concepts of white privilege, white fragility and the structural and emotional weight of Blackness than they did even two or three years prior. That is something. These are the students who I have to prepare to introduce something like *The Black and White Minstrel Show* and for whom this particular past represents a truly different, alien country. David Edgerton contends in his sweeping survey of, and attempt to disrupt, twentieth-century narratives of Britain that twentieth-century Britain is a familiar place to most with known villains and heroes.[26] The existence of *The Black and White Minstrel Show* is not such a known space for the youth coming into our classrooms. This aspect of the country and the twentieth-century past is alien to them. Their times are different than those times and I cannot help but feel that is a very good thing.

---

[26] David Edgerton, *The Rise and Fall of the British Nation: A Twentieth-Century History* (London: Penguin, 2018), 1.

# Bibliography

### Archives and Manuscripts

BBC Written Archive Centre (WAC)
Black Cultural Archive (BCA)
British Board of Film Censors (BBFC)
British Film Institute (BFI)
British Library
Churchill Archives
Institute of Race Relations
ITA/ITB special collections
Margaret Herrick Library (USA)
Mass Observation Online
Mass Observation Project, 1981–2009
Media Archive for Central England (MACE)
National Archives
Scottish National Archive
UK Parliamentary Papers
Yorkshire Film Archive (YFA)

### Newspapers and Periodicals

*Bronze*
*Checker's*
*Cinema Quarterly*
*Colonial Cinema*
*Daily Express*
*Daily Mail*
*Daily Mirror*
*Daily Telegraph*
*Entertainment Industry Magazine*
*Evening Standard*
*Flamingo*
*Guardian*
*The Listener*
*Spectator*
*Stage and Television Today*

*Sunday Mail*
*Sunday Times*
*The Times*
*Tropic*
*The Voice*
*West Indian Gazette*

## Government Inquiries

Davies, Gavyn, *The Future Funding of the BBC: Report of the Independent Review Panel* (London, DCMS, 1999).
*The Future of the BBC: A Consultation Document*, Command Paper 2098 (London, HMSO, 1992).
*The Future of the BBC: Serving the Nation, Competing Worldwide*, Command Paper 2621 (London, HMSO, 1994).
*Report of the Broadcasting Committee* (aka the Beveridge Committee, formed in 1949), Command Paper 8116, *Report of the Broadcasting Committee, 1949* (Vol. I) (London, HMSO, 1951).
*Report of the Broadcasting Committee* (aka the Crawford Committee, formed in 1925), Command Paper 2599, *Report of the Broadcasting Committee* (London, HMSO, 1925).
*Report of the Broadcasting Committee* (aka the Sykes Committee, formed in 1923), Command Paper 1951, *Broadcasting Committee Report* (London, HMSO, 1923).
*Report of the Broadcasting Committee* (aka the Ullswater Committee, formed in 1935), Command Paper 5091, *Report of the Broadcasting Committee* (London, HMSO, 1936).
*Report of the Committee on Broadcasting* (aka the Pilkington Committee, formed in 1960), Command Paper 1753, *Report of the Committee on Broadcasting, 1960* (London, HMSO, 1962).
*Report of the Committee on Financing the BBC*, Command Paper 9824 (London, HMSO, 1986).
*Report of the Committee on the Future of Broadcasting* (aka the Annan Committee, formed in 1974), Command Paper 6753, *Report of the Committee on the Future of Broadcasting* (London, HMSO, 1977).
*Report of the Television Committee* (aka the Selsdon Committee, formed in 1935), Command Paper 4793, *Report of the Television Committee,* (London, HMSO, 1935).

## Published Primary Sources and Pamphlets

*Annual Review of BBC Broadcasting Research Findings*, no. 1–17, 1973–1991 (London: BBC).
Baldwin, James et al., 'The Negro in American Culture', *CrossCurrents* 11, no. 3 (Summer 1961), 205.
Constantine, Learie, *Colour Bar* (London: Stanley Paul and Co, 1954).

Fanon, Franz, *Black Skin, White Masks* (New York: Grove Press, 2007).
*The Film in National Life: Being the Report of an Enquiry Conducted by the Commission on Educational and Cultural Films into the Service Which the Cinematograph May Render to Education and Social Progress* (London: George Allen & Unwin, 1932).
*Grierson on Documentary*, edited and compiled by Forsyth Hardy (London: Faber and Faber, 1966).
Jhally, Sut, and Justin Lewis, *Enlightened Racism: The Cosby Show, Audiences, and the Myth of the American Dream* (New York: Routledge, 1992).
Little, Kenneth, *Negroes in Britain: A Study of Racial Relations in English Society*, revised (London: Routledge and Kegan Paul, 1972).
National Council of Public Morals, *The Cinema: Its Present Position and Future Possibilities. Being the Report and Chief Evidence Taken by the Cinema Commission of Inquiry Instituted by the National Council of Public Morals* (London: Williams and Norgate, 1917).
Paulu, Burton, *British Broadcasting in Transition* (Minneapolis: University of Minnesota Press, 1961).
Pierce, Chester M., 'Psychiatric Problems of the Black Minority', in S. Arieti, ed., *American Handbook of Psychiatry* (New York: Basic Books, 1974): 512–523.
Rotha, Paul, *Documentary Film* (London: Faber and Faber, 1936).
Silvey, Robert, *Who's Listening: The Story of BBC Audience Research* (London: George Allen & Unwin, 1974).
Tallents, Stephen G., *The Projection of England* (London: Faber and Faber, 1932).
Wyndham Goldie, Grace, *Facing the Nation: Television and Politics, 1936–76* (London: The Bodley Head, 1977).

## Secondary Literature

Ahmed, Sara, 'Affective Economies', *Social Text* 22, no. 2 (2004): 117–139.
  *On Being Included: Racism and Diversity in Institutional Life* (Durham, NC: Duke University Press, 2012).
  *Living a Feminist Life* (Durham, NC: Duke University Press, 2017).
Amsterdam, Anthony G., and Jerome S. Bruner, *Minding the Law: How Courts Rely on Storytelling* (Cambridge, MA: Harvard University Press, 2009).
Anthony, Scott, *Public Relations and the Making of Modern Britain: Stephen Tallents and the Birth of a Progressive Media Profession* (Manchester: Manchester University Press, 2012).
Aujla-Sidhu, Gurvinder, *The BBC Asian Network: The Cultural Production of Diversity* (London: Palgrave, 2021).
Bailkin, Jordanna, *The Afterlife of Empire* (Berkeley, CA: University of California Press, 2012).
Baldwin Clark, LaToya, 'The Critical Racialization of Parents' Rights', *Yale Law Journal* 113 (2023): 2139, 2160.
Barber, Sian, *Censoring the 1970s: The BBFC and the Decade That Taste Forgot* (Newcastle: Cambridge Scholars Press, 2011).

Bebber, Brett, 'The Short Life of *Curry and Chips:* Racial Comedy on British Television in the 1960s', *Journal of British Cinema and Television* 11, no. 2–3 (2014): 213–235.
'*Till Death Us Do Part*: Political Satire and Social Realism in the 1960s and 1970s', *Historical Journal of Film, Radio and Television* 34, no. 2 (2014): 253–274.
Beckles, Colin A., '"We Shall Not Be Terrorized Out of Existence": The Political Legacy of England's Black Bookshops', *Journal of Black Studies* 29, no. 1 (1998): 51–72.
Bell, Derrick A., *Race, Racism, and American Law* (Cambridge, MA: Harvard Law School, 1970).
'*Brown v. Board of Education* and the Interest-Convergence Dilemma', *Harvard Law Review* (1980): 518–533.
Bernal, Dolores, 'Critical Race Theory, Latino Critical Theory, and Critical Raced-Gendered Epistemologies: Recognizing Students of Color as Holders and Creators of Knowledge', *Qualitative Inquiry* 8, no. 1 (2002): 105–126.
Bernstein, Robin, *Racial Innocence: Performing American Childhood from Slavery to Civil Rights* (New York: New York University Press, 2011).
Bhambra, Gurminder K., *Rethinking Modernity: Postcolonialism and the Sociological Imagination* (London: Palgrave, 2007).
Bhambra, Gurminder K., and John Holmwood, *Colonialism and Modern Social Theory* (London: Polity, 2021).
Bidnall, Amanda, *The West Indian Generation: Remaking British Culture in London, 1945–1965* (Liverpool: Liverpool University Press, 2017).
Bivins, Roberta, 'Picturing Race in the British National Health Service, 1948–1988', *Twentieth Century British History* 28, no. 1 (2017): 83–109.
Black, Lawrence, 'Whose Finger on the Button? British Television and the Politics of Cultural Control', *Historical Journal of Film, Radio and Television* 25, no. 4 (2006): 547–575.
'There Was Something About Mary: The National Viewers' and Listeners' Association and Social Movement History', in J. McKay, M. Hilton, and N. Crowson, eds., *NGOs in Contemporary Britain: Non-State Actors in Society and Politics since 1945* (London: Palgrave Macmillan, 2009): 182–200.
Black, Lawrence, Hugh Pemberton, and Pat Thane, eds., *Reassessing the 1970s Britain* (Manchester: Manchester University Press, 2013).
Bland, Benjamin, '"Publish and Be Damned?" Race, Crisis, and the Press in England during the Long, Hot Summer of 1976', *Immigrants & Minorities* 37, no. 3 (2019): 163–183.
Bland, Lucy, *Britain's Brown Babies: The Stories of Children Born to Black GIs and White Women in the Second World War* (Manchester: Manchester University Press, 2019).
Bonilla-Silva, Eduardo, *Racism without Racists: Color-Blind Racism and the Persistence of Racial Inequality in the United States*, 3rd ed. (Lanham, MD: Rowman & Littlefield, 2010).
'Feeling Race: Theorizing the Racial Economy of Emotions', *American Sociological Review* 84, no. 1 (2019): 1–25.

Bourdieu, Pierre. *Outline of a Theory of Practice* (Cambridge: Cambridge University Press, 1977).
Bourne, Stephen, *Black in the British Frame: The Black Experience in British Film and Television* (London: Bloomsbury, 2005).
Briggs, Asa, *The History of Broadcasting in the United Kingdom*, Vol. 5 (Oxford: Oxford University Press, 1995).
Brooke, Stephen, *Sexual Politics: Sexuality, Family Planning, and the British Left from the 1880s to the Present Day* (Oxford: Oxford University Press, 2011).
  'Space, Emotions and the Everyday: The Affective Ecology of 1980s London', *Twentieth Century British History* 28, no 1. (2017): 110–142.
Brown, Callum, *The Battle for Christian Britain: Sex, Humanists and Secularisation, 1945–1980* (Cambridge: Cambridge University Press, 2019).
Butler, Lise, 'The Social Scientific Turn in Modern British History', *Twentieth Century British History* 33, no. 3 (2022): 445–450.
Carby, Hazel V., 'White Woman Listen! Black Feminism and the Boundaries of Sisterhood', in Heidi Safia Mirza, ed., *Black British Feminism: A Reader* (London: Routledge, 1997): 45–53.
Cohen, Deborah, *Family Secrets: Shame and Privacy in Modern Britain* (Oxford: Oxford University Press, 2013).
Connell, Kieran, *Black Handsworth: Race in 1980s Britain* (Berkeley, CA: University of California Press, 2019).
Corbould, Clare, 'Race, Photography, Labor, and Entrepreneurship in the Life of Maurice Hunter, Harlem's "Man of 1,000 Faces"', *Radical History Review*, no. 132 (2018): 144–171.
Crenshaw, Kimberlé, 'Race, Reform and Retrenchment: Transformation and Legitimation in Anti-Discrimination Law', *Harvard Law Review* 101, no. 7 (1988): 1331–1387.
Curran, James, and Jean Seaton, *Power Without Responsibility: Press, Broadcasting, and the Internet in Britain* 8th ed. (London: Routledge, 2018).
Davies, Aled, Ben Jackson, and Florence Sutcliffe-Braithwaite, eds., *The Neoliberal Age: Britain since the 1970s* (London: UCL Press, 2021).
Delap, Lucy, 'Agency and Domestic Workers', in Nitin Sinha and Nitin Varma, eds., *Servants' Pasts: Late Eighteenth to Twentieth-Century South Asia*, Vol. 2 (Hyderabad: Orient BlackSwan, 2019): 265–278.
Delgado, Richard, 'Storytelling for Oppositionists and Others: A Plea for Narrative', *Michigan Law Review* 87, no. 8 (1989): 2411–2441.
Delgado, Richard, and Jean Stefancic, 'Critical Race Theory: Past, Present, and Future', *Current Legal Problems* 51, no. 1 (1998): 467–491.
  *Critical Race Theory: An Introduction* (New York: New York University Press, 2012).
DiAngelo, Robin, 'White Fragility', *International Journal of Critical Pedagogy*, 3, no. 3 (2011): 54–70.
  *White Fragility: Why It's So Hard for White People to Talk about Racism* (London: Allen Lane, 2018).
Dixon, Thomas. *Weeping Britannia: Portrait of a Nation in Tears* (Oxford: Oxford University Press, 2015).

Dixson, A. D. et al., eds., *Critical Race Theory in Education* (London: Routledge, 2018).
DuBois, W. E. B., *Black Reconstruction in America 1860–1880* (London: Free Press, 1998).
Durgnat, Raymond, 'Two "Social Problem" Films: *Sapphire* and *Victim*', in Alan Burton, Tim O'Sullivan, and Paul Wells, eds., *Liberal Directions: Basil Dearden and Postwar British Film Culture* (Wiltshire: Flicks Books, 1997): 59–83.
Dyer, Richard, *White: Essays on Race and Culture* (London: Routledge, 1997).
Eddo-Lodge, Reni, 'Forming Blackness Through a Screen', in Nikesh Shukla, ed., *The Good Immigrant* (London: Unbound, 2016): 79–80.
*Why I'm No Longer Talking to White People about Race* (London: Bloomsbury, 2017).
Edgerton, David, *The Warfare State: Britain, 1920–1970* (Cambridge: Cambridge University Press, 2006).
*The Rise and Fall of the British Nation: A Twentieth-Century History* (London: Penguin, 2018).
Edwards, Amy, *Are We Rich Yet? The Rise of Mass Investment Culture in Contemporary Britain* (Berkeley: University of California Press, 2022).
Ellis, John, 'Scheduling: The Last Creative Act in Television?', *Media, Culture, and Society* 22, no. 1 (2000): 25–38.
El-Enany, Nadine, *(B)ordering Britain: Law, Race and Empire* (Manchester: Manchester University Press, 2020).
Faragher, Megan, *Public Opinion Polling in Mid-Century British Literature: The Psychographic Turn* (Oxford: Oxford University Press, 2021).
Francis, Matthew, 'Mrs Thatcher's Peacock Blue Sari: Ethnic Minorities, Electoral Politics and the Conservative Party, c. 1974–86', *Contemporary British History* 31, no. 2 (2017): 274–293.
Friedman, Lester, ed., *Fires Were Started: British Cinema and Thatcherism*, 2nd ed. (London: Wallflower Press, 2006).
Fuentes, Marisa J. *Dispossessed Lives: Enslaved Women, Violence, and the Archive* (Philadelphia, PA: University of Pennsylvania Press, 2016).
Gilroy, Paul, *There Ain't No Black in the Union Jack* (London: Routledge, 1992).
*Post-Colonial Melancholia* (New York: Columbia University Press, 2005).
Gilroy, Paul, and Ruth Wilson Gilmore, eds., *Stuart Hall: Selected Writings on Race and Difference* (Durham, NC: Duke University Press, 2021).
Goldthorpe, John, 'Historians' Uses of Archived Material from Sociological Research: A Response to the Commentaries on My Paper', *Twentieth Century British History* 33, no. 3 (2022): 451–459.
Gopal, Priyamvada, *Insurgent Empire: Anticolonial Resistance and British Dissent* (London: Verso, 2019).
'On Decolonisation and the University', *Textual Practice* 35, no. 6 (2021): 873–899.
Grandy, Christine, 'The Empire and "Human Interest": Popular Empire Films, the Colonial Villain, and the British Documentary Movement 1926–39', *Twentieth Century British History* 25, no. 4 (2014): 509–532.
*Heroes and Happy Endings: Class, Gender, and Nation in Popular Fiction in Interwar Britain* (Manchester: Manchester University Press, 2014).

'Cultural History's Absent Audience', *Cultural and Social History* 16, no. 5 (2019): 643–663.
Grieveson, Lee, *Cinema and the Wealth of Nations: Media, Capital, and the Liberal World System* (Oakland, CA: University of California Press, 2017).
Grist, John, *Grace Wyndham Goldie: First Lady of Television* (London: New Generation Publishing, 2006).
Hall, Stuart, *Selected Political Writings: The Great Moving Right Show and Other Essays* (Durham, NC: Duke University Press, 2017).
'Race and Moral Panics in Post-war Britain', in Paul Gilroy and Ruth Wilson Gilmore, eds., *Stuart Hall: Selected Writings on Race and Difference* (Durham, NC: Duke University Press, 2021): 56–70.
Hall, Stuart, and Tony Jefferson, eds., *Resistance Through Rituals: Youth Subcultures in Post-War Britain* (Birmingham, Centre for Contemporary Cultural Studies, 1976).
Hall, Stuart, with Bill Schwartz, *Familiar Stranger: A Life Between Two Islands* (Durham, NC: Duke University Press, 2017).
Hall, Stuart, et al., eds., *Policing the Crisis: Mugging, the State and Law and Order* (London: Macmillan, 1978).
Hammond Perry, Kennetta, '"Little Rock" in Britain: Jim Crow's Transatlantic Topographies', *Journal of British Studies* 51 (2012): 155–177.
*London is the Place for Me: Black Britons, Citizenship, and the Politics of Race* (Oxford: Oxford University Press, 2015).
Haney Lopez, Ian, *Racism on Trial: The Chicano Fight for Justice* (Cambridge, MA: Harvard University Press, 2003).
Harper, Sue, 'A Lower-Middle-Class Taste Community: Admission Figures at the Regent Cinema, Portsmouth, UK', *The Historical Journal of Film, Radio, and Television* 24, no. 4 (2004): 565–587.
Hartman, Saidiya V., *Scenes of Subjection: Terror, Slavery, and Self-making in Nineteenth-century America* (Oxford: Oxford University Press, 1997).
Hebdige, Dick. *Subculture: The Meaning of Style* (London: Methuen & Co ltd, 1979).
Hendy, David, 'Bad Language and BBC Radio Four in the 1960s and 1970s', *Twentieth Century British History* 17, no. 1 (2006): 74–102.
*The BBC: A People's History* (London: Profile, 2022).
Hilton, Matthew, *Consumerism in Twentieth-Century Britain: The Search for a Historical Movement* (Cambridge: Cambridge University Press, 2003).
Hilton, Matthew et al., *The Politics of Expertise: How NGOs Shaped Modern Britain* (Oxford: Oxford University Press, 2013).
'History and Humanitarianism: A Conversation', *Past & Present* 241 (2018): 1–38.
Hinds, Donald, 'The West Indian Gazette: Claudia Jones and the Black Press in Britain', *Race & Class: A Journal on Racism, Empire and Globalisation* 50, no. 1 (2008): 88–97.
Hirsch, Shirin, *In the Shadow of Enoch Powell: Race, Locality, and Resistance* (Manchester: Manchester University Press, 2018).
Holland, David, *Imperial Heartland: Immigration, Working-class Culture and Everyday Tolerance, 1917–1947* (Cambridge: Cambridge University Press, 2023).

Hubble, Nick, *Mass Observation and Everyday Life: Culture, History, Theory* (London: Palgrave Macmillan, 2006).
Irwin, Mary, 'Grace Wyndham Goldie at the BBC: Reappraising the "First Lady of Television"', *Critical Studies in Television* 17, no. 3 (2022): 284–296.
Jackson, Ben, and Robert Saunders, eds., *Making Thatcher's Britain* (Cambridge: Cambridge University Press, 2012).
Jeppesen, Chris, '"Sanders of the River, Still the Best Job for a British Boy", Colonial Administrative Service Recruitment at the End of Empire', *The Historical Journal* 59, no. 2 (2016): 469–508.
Johnson, Catherine, and Rob Turnock, *ITV Cultures: Independent Television Over Fifty Years* (London: Open University Press, 2005).
Johnson, Walter, 'On Agency', *Journal of Social History* 37, no. 1 (Fall 2003): 113–124.
Jones, Max, '"National Hero and Very Queer Fish": Empire, Sexuality and the British Remembrance of General Gordon, 1918–72', *Twentieth Century British History* 26, no. 2 (2015): 175–202.
Jung, Moon-Kie, João Helion Costa Vargas, and Eduardo Bonilla-Silva, eds., *State of White Supremacy: Racism, Governance, and the United States* (Stanford, CA: Stanford University Press, 2011).
Kassimeris, George, and Leonie Jackson, 'Negotiating Race and Religion in the West Midlands: Narratives of Inclusion and Exclusion during the 1967–69 Wolverhampton Bus Workers' Turban Dispute', *Contemporary British History* 31, no. 3 (2017): 343–365.
Kendi, Ibram X., *Stamped from the Beginning: The Definitive History of Racist Ideas in America* (New York: Random House, 2017).
Ladson-Billings, Gloria, 'Just What Is Critical Race Theory and What's It Doing in a Nice Field Like Education?' *International Journal of Qualitative Studies in Education* 11, no. 1 (1998): 7–24.
Lawrence, Jon, *Me, Me, Me? The Search for Community in Post-war England* (Oxford: Oxford University Press, 2019).
   'On Historians' Re-Use of Social-Science Archives', *Twentieth Century British History* 33, no. 3 (2022): 432–444.
Lentin, Alana, *Why Race Still Matters* (London: Polity Press, 2020).
Linstrum, Erik, 'Decolonizing Britain: An Exchange', *Twentieth Century British History* 33, no. 2 (2022): 274–303.
   *Age of Emergency: Living with Violence at the End of the Empire* (Oxford: Oxford University Press, 2023).
Linstrum, Erik, Peter Clarke, Adrian Bingham et al., 'Forum: The Past, Present, and Futures of Modern British History', *Modern British History* 35, no. 1 (2024): 7–29.
Long, Max. 'The Ciné-biologists: Natural History Film and the Co-production of Knowledge in Interwar Britain', *British Journal for the History of Science* 53 (2020): 527–551.
MacCabe, Colin, and Lee Grieveson, eds., *Empire and Film* (London: Bloomsbury Press, 2019).
Macdonald, Sharon, 'Is "Difficult Heritage" Still "Difficult"?', *Museum International* 67, no. 1–4 (2015): 6–22.

Malik, Sarita, *Representing Black Britain: Black and Asian Images on Television* (Sage Publications: London, 2002).
  'Black Film British Cinema: In Three Acts', in Clive James Nwonka and Anamik Saha, eds., *Black Film British Cinema II* (London: Goldsmiths Press, 2021): 21–40.
  'Reflections on *Representing Black Britain*', *Journal of Cultural Economy* (October 2022, online). www.tandfonline.com/doi/full/10.1080/17530350.2022.2138502
Malik, Sarita, and Darrel M. Newton, eds., *Adjusting the Contrast: British Television and Constructs of Race* (Manchester: Manchester University Press, 2017).
Mandler, Peter, 'The Problem with Cultural History', *Cultural and Social History* 1, no. 1 (2004): 94–117.
  *The Crisis of the Meritocracy: Britain's Transition to Mass Education Since the Second World War* (Oxford: Oxford University Press, 2020).
Matera, Marc, 'An Empire of Development: Africa and the Caribbean in *God's Chillun,*' *Twentieth Century British History* 23 (2012): 12–37.
  *Black London: The Imperial Metropolis and Decolonization in the Twentieth Century* (Durham, NC: University of North Carolina Press, 2015).
Matera, Marc, Radkhika Natarajan, Kennetta Hammond Perry, et al., 'Introduction: Marking Race in Twentieth Century British History', *Twentieth Century British History* 34, no. 3 (2023): 407–414.
Mayes, Sean, and Sarah K. Whitfield, *An Inconvenient Black History of British Musical Theatre 1900 – 1950* (London: Bloomsbury, 2021).
McClintock, Anne, *Imperial Leather: Race, Gender, and Sexuality in the Colonial Conquest* (London: Routledge, 1995).
McKenzie, John, ed., *Popular Culture and Imperialism* (Manchester: Manchester University Press, 1986).
Mills, Charles W., *The Racial Contract* (Ithaca, NY: Cornell University Press, 1997).
  'White Ignorance', in Shannon Sullivan and Nancy Tuana, eds., *Race and Epistemologies of Ignorance* (Albany, NY: SUNY Press 2007).
Moran, Joe, *Armchair Nation: An Intimate History of Britain in Front of the TV* (London: Profile Books, 2013).
Morgan, D. L., 'Robert Merton and the History of Focus Groups: Standing on the Shoulders of a Giant?' *American Sociologist* 53, no. 3 (2022): 364–373.
Newton, Darrel M., *Paving the Empire Road: BBC Television and Black Britons* (Manchester: Manchester University Press, 2011).
Nixon, Sean, *Hard Sell: Advertising, Affluence and Transatlantic Relations, c.1951–69* (Manchester: Manchester University Press, 2013).
Norris Nicholson, Heather, *Amateur Film: Meaning and Practice, 1927–1977* (Manchester: Manchester University Press, 2012).
Nwonka, Clive James, 'Love Knows No Colour Bar: Windrush, Racism and *Flame in the Streets*', *Ethnic and Racial Studies* 43, no. 12 (2020): 2199–2216.
Nwonka, Clive James, and Anamik Saha, *Black Film British Cinema II* (London: Goldsmiths Press, 2021).

Oppenheim, Naomi. 'Popular History in the Black British Press: Edward Scobie's *Tropic* and *Flamingo*, 1960–64', *Immigrants & Minorities* 37, no. 3 (2019): 136–162.

O'Sullivan, Tim, 'Researching the Viewing Culture: Television and the Home, 1946–1960', in Helen Wheatley, ed., *Reviewing Television History: Critical Issues in Television Historiography* (London: IB Tauris, 2007): 159–170.

Owen, Nicholas, '"Facts are Sacred": The *Manchester Guardian* and Colonial Violence, 1930–1932', *The Journal of Modern History* 84, no. 3 (2012): 643–678.

Paul, Kathleen, *Whitewashing Britain: Race and Citizenship in the Postwar Era* (Ithica: Cornell University Press, 1997).

Peplow, Simon, 'The "Linchpin for Success"? The Problematic Establishment of the 1965 Race Relations Act and Its Conciliation Board', *Contemporary British History* 31, no. 3 (2017): 430–451.

*Race and Riots in Thatcher's Britain* (Manchester: Manchester University Press, 2019).

Pickering, Michael, *Blackface Minstrelsy in Britain* (London: Aldershot, 2008).

Rice, Tom, *Films for the Colonies: Cinema and the Preservation of the British Empire* (Berkeley, CA: University of California Press, 2019).

Richards, Jeffrey, 'The British Board of Film Censors and Content Control in the 1930s: Images of Britain', *Historical Journal of Film Radio, and Television* 1, no. 2 (1981): 95–116.

*The Age of the Dream Palace: Cinema and Society in 1930s Britain* (London: IB Tauris, 2009).

Richards, Jeffrey, and Dorothy Sheridan, eds., *Mass-Observation at the Movies* (London: Routledge, 1987).

Roediger, David, *The Wages of Whiteness: Race and the Making of the American Working Class* (New York: Verso, 2007).

Rollock, Nicola, '"I Would Have Become Wallpaper Had Racism Had Its Way": Black Female Professors, Racial Battle Fatigue, and Strategies for Surviving Higher Education', *Peabody Journal of Education* 96, no. 2 (2021): 206–217.

Rollock, Nicola, et al., *The Colour of Class: The Educational Strategies of the Black Middle Classes* (London: Routledge, 2015).

Royal Historical Society, *Race, Ethnicity & Equality in UK History: A Report and Resource for Change* (Royal Historical Society, October 2018).

Saha, Anamik. 'Scheduling Race', in Sarita Malik, and Darrell M. Newton, eds., *Adjusting the Contrast: British Television and Constructs of Race* (Manchester: Manchester University Press, 2017): 50–70.

Sands-O'Connor, Karen, *Children's Publishing and Black Britain, 1965-2015* (London: Palgrave, 2017).

Satia, Priya, *Spies in Arabia: The Great War and the Cultural Foundations of Britain's Covert Empire in the Middle East* (Oxford: Oxford University Press, 2008).

'Inter-war Agnotology: Empire, Democracy and the Production of Ignorance', in Laura Beers and Geraint Thomas, eds., *Brave New World: Imperial and Democratic Nation-Building in Britain between the Wars* (London: Institute of Historical Research, 2012): 209–226.

*Empire of Guns: The Violent Making of the Industrial Revolution* (London: Duckworth Books, 2018).
Saunders, Robert, *Yes to Europe! The 1975 Referendum and Seventies Britain* (Cambridge: Cambridge University Press, 2018).
Schaffer, Gavin, 'Till Death Us Do Part and the BBC: Racial Politics and the British Working Classes 1965–75', *Journal of Contemporary History* 45, no. 2 (2010): 454–477.
  *The Vision of a Nation: Making Multiculturalism on British Television, 1960–80* (London: Palgrave Macmillan, 2014).
Schofield, Camilla, *Enoch Powell and the Making of Postcolonial Britain* (Cambridge: Cambridge University Press, 2013).
  'In Defence of White Freedom: Working Men's Clubs and the Politics of Sociability in Late Industrial England', *Twentieth Century British History*, 34, no. 3 (2023): 515–551.
Schwarz, Bill, '"The Only White Man in There": The Re-Racialisation of England, 1956–1968', *Race and Class* 38 (1996): 65–78.
  'Claudia Jones and the West Indian Gazette: Reflections on the Emergence of Post-colonial Britain', *Twentieth Century British History* 14, no. 3 (2003): 264–285.
  *The White Man's World* (Oxford: Oxford University Press, 2011).
Scriven, Tom, 'The Jim Crow Craze in London's Press and Streets, 1836–39', *Journal of Victorian Culture* 19, no. 1 (2014): 93–109.
Sedgwick, John, *Popular Filmgoing in 1930s Britain: A Choice of Pleasures* (Exeter: University of Exeter Press, 2000).
Shaw, Sally, '"Light Entertainment" as Contested Socio-Political Space: Audience and Institutional Responses to *Love Thy Neighbour* (1972–76)', *Critical Studies in Television* 7, no. 1 (2012): 64–78.
Shepherd, Ben, 'Showbiz Imperialism', in John McKenzie ed., *Popular Culture and Imperialism* (Manchester: Manchester University Press, 1986): 94–112.
Sherwood, Marika, *Claudia Jones: A Life in Exile* (London: Lawrence and Wishart, 2000).
Shukla, Nikesh, ed. *The Good Immigrant* (London: Unbound, 2016).
Smart, Billy, 'The BBC Television Audience Research Reports, 1957–1979: Recorded Opinions and Invisible Expectations', *Historical Journal of Film, Radio and Television*, 34 no. 3 (2014): 452–462.
Smith, Anna Marie, *New Right Discourse: Britain 1968–1990* (Cambridge: Cambridge University Press, 1994).
Smith, Evan, *British Communism and the Politics of Race* (Leiden: Brill, 2017).
Smith, Sarah J., *Children, Cinema, & Censorship: From Dracula to the Dead End Kids* (London: IB Tauris, 2005).
Smith, William A. et al., '"You Make Me Wanna Holler and Throw Up Both My Hands!": Campus Culture, Black Misandric Microaggressions, and Racial Battle Fatigue', *International Journal of Qualitative Studies in Education* 29, no. 9 (2016) 1189–1209.
Smith-Shomade, Beretta E. ed., *Watching While Black: Centring the Television of Black Audiences* (New Brunswick, NJ: Rutgers University Press, 2012).
Solórzano, Daniel, and Tara Yosso, 'Critical race methodology: Counter-storytelling as an analytical framework for research', *Qualitative Inquiry* 8,

no. 1 (2002): 23–44.

Steinmetz, George, *The Colonial Origins of Modern Social Thought: French Sociology and the Overseas Empire* (Princeton, NJ: Princeton University Press, 2023).

Stephens, Daniel, *The Empire of Progress: West Africans, Indians, and Britons at the British Empire Exhibition 1924–25* (London: Palgrave Macmillan, 2013).

Stokes, M., *D.W. Griffith's The Birth of a Nation: A History of the Most Controversial Motion Picture of All Time* (Oxford: Oxford University Press, 2007).

Stollery, Martin, 'The Same, but a Step Removed: Aspects of British Reception of *Roots*', in Erica L. Ball and Kellie Carter Jackson, eds., *Reconsidering Roots: Race, Politics, and Memory* (Athens, GA: University of Georgia Press, 2017): 147–164.

Sutcliffe-Braithwaite, Florence, *Class, Politics, and the Decline of Deference in England, 1968–2000* (Oxford: Oxford University Press, 2018).

Swann, Paul, *The British Documentary Film Movement, 1926–1946* (Cambridge: Cambridge University Press, 1989).

Tabili, Laura, *Global Migrants, Local Culture: Natives and Newcomers in Provincial England, 1841–1939* (London: Palgrave, 2011).

Thomas, Martin, *Violence and Colonial Order: Police, Workers, and Protest in the European Colonial Empires, 1918–1940* (Cambridge: Cambridge University Press, 2012).

Thomlinson, Natalie, *Race and Ethnicity in the Women's Movement in England, 1968– 1993* (London: Palgrave Macmillan, 2016).

'"Second-Wave" Black Feminist Periodicals in Britain', *Women: A Cultural Review* 27, no. 4 (2016): 432–445.

Trouillot, Michel-Rolph, *Silencing the Past: Power and the Production of History* (Boston, MA: Beacon Press, 1995).

Tuck, Eve, and K. Wayne Yang. 'Decolonization Is Not a Metaphor', *Decolonization: Indigeneity, Education, & Society* 1, no. 1 (2012): 1–40.

Vernon, James, *Distant Strangers: How Britain Became Modern* (Berkeley, CA: University of California Press, 2014).

'The History of Britain is Dead; Long Live a Global History of Britain', *History Australia* 13 (2016): 19–34.

'Heathrow and the Making of Neoliberal Britain', *Past & Present*, 252, no. 1 (2021): 213–247.

Ware, Vron, *Beyond the Pale: White Women, Racism, and History* (London: Verso, 2015).

Waters, Chris, '"Dark Strangers" in Our Midst: Discourses of Race and Nation in Britain, 1947–1963', *Journal of British Studies* 36, no. 2 (1997): 207–238.

Waters, Hazel, *Racism on the Victorian Stage: Representation of Slavery and the Black Character* (Cambridge: Cambridge University Press, 2007).

Waters, Rob, 'Black Power on the Telly: America, Television, and Race in 1960s and 1970s Britain', *Journal of British Studies* 54, no. 4 (2015): 947–970.

*Thinking Black: Britain, 1964–1985* (Berkeley, CA: University of California Press, 2018).

*Colonized by Humanity: Caribbean London and the Politics of Integration at the End of Empire* (Oxford: Oxford University Press, 2023).

Webster, Wendy, *Englishness and Empire, 1939–1965* (Oxford: Oxford University Press, 2007).
  *Mixing It: Diversity in World War Two Britain* (Oxford: Oxford University Press, 2018).
Weinberger, Stephen, 'The Birth of a Nation and the Making of the NAACP', *Journal of American Studies* 45, no. 1 (2011): 77–93.
Wekker, Gloria, *White Innocence: Paradoxes of Colonialism and Race* (Durham, NC: Duke University Press, 2016).
West, E. James, 'Roil Britannia! Al Sharpton, the British Press, and the 1991 Murder of Rolan Adams', *Immigrants & Minorities* 37, no. 3 (2019): 184–210.
  'Hunt the Wizard! Race, Immigration, and British Tabloid Coverage of David Duke's 1978 Tour', *Contemporary British History* 35, no. 1 (2021): 100–124.
Wheatley, Helen. ed., *Reviewing Television History: Critical Issues in Television Historiography* (London: IB Tauris, 2007).
Whipple, Amy, 'Revisiting the "Rivers of Blood" Controversy: Letters to Enoch Powell', *Journal of British Studies* 48, no. 3 (2009): 717–735.
Womack, Autumn, *The Matter of Black Living: The Aesthetic Experiment of Racial Data, 1880–1930* (Chicago: University of Chicago Press, 2022).
Wood, Helen, 'Television – the Housewife's Choice? The 1949 Mass Observation Television Directive, Reluctance and Revision', *Media History* 21, no. 3 (2015): 342–359.
Worley, Matthew, *No Future: Punk, Politics and British Youth Culture, 1976–1984* (Cambridge: Cambridge University Press, 2017).
Worley, Matthew, and Nigel Copsey, *Tomorrow Belongs to Us: The British Far Right Since 1967* (London: Routledge, 2017).
Wu, Tim, *The Attention Merchants: The Epic Scramble to Get Inside Our Heads* (New York: Knopf, 2016).
Yemm, Rachel, 'Immigration, Race and Local Media: Smethwick and the 1964 General Election', *Contemporary British History* 33, no. 1 (2019): 98–122.

# Index

Aaron, Richard, 208, 210
Abrams, Mark, 44, 46–50, 53
Actors of colour, 132, 159, 212, 233
Adam, Kenneth, 130, 146
Adorno, Theodor, 106
*Africa's Fighting Men*, 90, 92
African audiences, 88–89
　laughter, 89
Ahmed, Sara, 68, 126, 198, 227
Ali Khan, Mirza, 75
*All Quiet on the Western Front*, 74
*Amateur Cine World*, 78
Amateur film, 26–27, *see* Home movies
Annan Committee, 37–38, 43, 57, 60, 195
Annan Report, 31–33, 37, 43–44, 58, 198, 212, 237
Annual Review of BBC Audience Research Findings, 58
Ansorge, Peter, 160
*Arabian Nights*, 139
*Armchair Theatre*, 141
Association of Technical and Managerial Staffs (ASTMS), 202
Atwell, Winifred, 190
Audience Reaction Assessment (AURA), 214, *see* ITV audience research
Audiences of colour, 34–35, 43–44, 60–61, 68–69, 86–88, 199, 271
　audience research, 211–226
　*Love Thy Neighbour*, 212–218
　'Multi-Racial Britain Programme' BBC, 220–226

Baden Powell, Robert, 39
Baden-Semper, Nina, 212
Baird, Harry, 115
Baker, Roy, 141
Baldwin, James, 184
Barclay, Humphrey, 227, 249
Barnes, George, 52
BBC
　and extremism, 113

BBC Asian Programme Unit, 219–220
BBC Audience Research Department, 32–33, 53, 57–58, 96, 264
　group surveys, 96, 106, 205
　*Handbook for Interviewers*, 61
　phone surveys, 54–55
　reaction index, 112–113, 120, 123
BBC General Advisory Council (GAC), 208
BBC Listener Research, 44, 50
BBC 'Multi-Racial Britain Programme', 220–226
BBC Written Archive Centre (WAC), 23–25, 129, 133, 135
Beaton, Norman, 115, 231, 233, 248–249, 254
Belafonte, Harry, 173
Bell, Derek, 234
Beveridge Committee, 18, 37, 57
Beveridge Report on Broadcasting, 42
Beveridge, William, 18, 37, 42, 54, 57–58
*Bill Cosby Show, The*, 239
Birkenhead Vigilance Committee, 47
Birmingham Cinema Enquiry Committee, 47
Birmingham's Centre for Contemporary Cultural Studies, 12
*Birth of a Nation, The*, 76, 85
Black agency, 167–168, 192
Black Entertainment Television (BET), 239
*Black Magic*, 102–103, 109
Black Power movement, 137, 170
*Black Voice*, 171
*Black and White Minstrel Show, The*, 1–3, 6, 24, 26, 28, 128–131, 182, 187, 232, 259, 262, 267
　Campaign Against Racial Discrimination (CARD), 128–130, 143–144
　*Flamingo*, 130
　newspaper press, 146–149
　*1957 Television Minstrels*, 142
　viewership figures, 142, 157

287

## Index

Black, Peter, 121–122
Blackface, 72–73, 76–78, 128–155
   emotional response, 187–188
   history, 131–132
   home movies, 155–157
Boer Wars, 72
Bogle Books, 171, 176
Bonilla-Silva, Eduardo, 14, 184, 277
Booth, Eddie, 22
Bradley, Buddy, 165, 173, 189, 191, 263
Brayfield, Celia, 242
Brecht, Bertol, 63–64, 66
*Bridge on the River Kwai*, 140
British Board of Film Censors (BBFC), 20–23, 39–41, 78, 140, 150, 162
Broadcast listings
   blackface, 137–142
Broadcasters Audience Research Board (BARB), 33, 56, 235
*Bronze*, 144, 164, 172–173, 177–178, 186–187, 191, 263
Bruno, Frank, 252

*Call the Midwife*, 258
*Camels are Coming*, 74
Cameron, Earl, 115, 136, 140–141, 173, 189
Campaign Against Racial Discrimination (CARD), 4, 143–144, 148
   *Black and White Minstrel Show, The*, 128–130
Campaign Against Racism in the Media (CARM), 5, 263
Canada, 45, 121, 266, 273
Capra, Frank, 92
*Cargo from Jamaica*, 82
*Caribbean Times*, 241
*Carmen Jones*, 173, 189
Carnegie Trust, 40
Carnival, 223
Channel 4, 29, 32–33, 38, 56, 229, 232–233, 237–239, 242, 245, 248–249, 255, 259
Channel 5, 255
*Checkers*, 144, 164, 172, 176–178, 183, 185–186, 190, 263
Chisholm, George, 142
Cinematograph Exhibitors' Association, 39
*Clive of India*, 73, 137
Cochrane, Kelso, 2, 175
Collins, Norman, 102–103
*Colonial Cinema*, 89
Colonial Film Unit, 88–91
Colonial Office, 86–87
Colour Bar
   Constantine, Learie, 86

Commission on Educational and Cultural Films (CECF), 40
Commission for Racial Equality, 222
Commonwealth Immigrants Act (1962), 115, 132
Commonwealth Immigrants Act (1968), 115, 132
Commonwealth Immigrants Acts, 98
Conferences of Immigrants, BBC, 218–219
Connor, Pearl, 181
Conservative Party, 240
Constantine, Learie, 86, 147
Corbett, Ronnie, 134
Cosby, Bill, 260
*Cosby Show, The*, 29, 229–231, 233, 236, 238–239, 242–250, 252–253, 267
   audience research study, 246–247
Cotton, Tim, 161
Cowley, Elizabeth, 244, 248
Crawford Committee, 37
Critical race theory, 8–17, 273
   Black success, 188–192
   code-switching, 256
   colour-blindness, 7–8, 11–14, 22–23, 99–100, 108, 130–131, 216, 235–237
   counter-storytelling, 65–66, 84, 165–166, 168–169, 188–192
   emotions, 114, 167, 170, 182–188, 225
   interest convergence, 234, 236, 240
   tone-policing, 14, 167, 181–184
   white discomfort, 178, 209, 211–212
Crowther, Leslie, 142
Cultural history, 18, 269
Curran, Charles, 208–209
*Curry and Chips*, 117, 154, 201–204

*Dad's Army*, 233
*Dance of the Harvest*, 83
Dandridge, Dorothy, 173
Dawbarn, Bob, 145, 151
Dean, Brian, 120, 153–154
Dearden, Basil, 140
*Desmond's*, 29, 231, 233, 235, 238, 256
*Different World, A*, 245, 255
Digital broadcasting, 255
Dilland, Harrison, 176
Disney Channel, 255
Dixon of Dock Green, 158
*Downton Abbey*, 258
*Drum*, 70, 74, 76–77, 82
*Dynasty*, 260
Dyrenforth, James, 186

Eddo-Lodge, Reni, 229, 232, 254
Edinburgh Television Festival, 237

# Index

Edinburgh University, 60
Educational film, 81
*Elephant Boy*, 74, 139
Elliott, John, 96, 120–121
Emmett, Brian, 53, 101, 200, 204, 207, 221
Empire, 122
  Africa, 110–111
  slave trade, 223
Empire Marketing Board (EMB), 70–72, 78, 80–82, 103
*Empire Road*, 232–233, 256
European Community, 212
European Economic Community (EEC), 195
Eurosport, 255

*Fable*, 233
Family viewing, 136
  blackface, 137–139
Fanon, Franz, 85–86, 185
Faqir of Ipi, *see* Ali Khan, Mirza
*Fat Albert*, 239
*Fawlty Towers*, 25
*Film in National Life*, 40
Flaherty, Robert, 79
*Flame in the Streets*, 110, 141
*Flamingo*, 3, 144, 164–166, 171–172, 174–175, 178, 181–184, 187, 191, 263
  *Black and White Minstrel Show, The*, 130
Floyd, George, 25, 273
*Fosters, The*, 233, 238
*Four Feathers*, 78, 138, 152
*Fresh Prince of Bel-Air, The*, 29, 229–231, 233, 238, 254–257, 269
Geoffrey, 254
Future of the BBC
  A Consultation Document (1992), 38
  Serving the Nation, Competing Worldwide (1994), 38
Future Funding of the BBC
  Report of the Independent Review Panel (1999), 38

Garnett, Alf, 22, 99, 116, 267
General election (1983), 236
  colour-blindness, 240
Giwa-Osagie, Saidat, 256
Glencross, David, 194–197
Go Into your Dance, 138
*God's Chillun*, 82–83
Goldie, Grace Wyndham, 105, 109, 112, 265
*Good Times*, 238
*Goon Show, The*, 141, 154
Gordon, David, 241

GPO Film Unit, 78
Grassroots Bookshop, 176
*Green Goddess*, 73, 87
Greenberg, Bradley S., 162
Grierson, John, 44, 46, 68, 70–72, 78–81, 93, 103, 221, 265, 271
*Gunga Din*, 63–64, 74
*Guns at Batasi*, 140

Haldane, Ian, 56, 202
Haley, William, 58
Hall, Stuart, 1, 4–6, 240, 259, 263
Handsworth, 236, 240
Hebert, Hugh, 245, 252
*Hello! West Indies*, 92
Henry, Lenny, 134–135, 143, 233, 238, 245, 252
*Here and Now*, 232
Heritage film and television, 257–259
Hinds, Donald, 171–172
Hines, Gerry, 160
History Channel, 255
History of emotions, 11, 114, 170
Home movies, 26–27, 72–73, 135
  blackface, 155–157
*Hot Summer Night*, 189
  *Flame in the Streets*, 141
*Howard's End*, 257
Hugh Greene, 21, 208, 218
Human interest, 70, 79
Huxtables, 229, 243, 245

Immigrants Programme Unit, 60
*In Sickness and in Health*, 231, 259, 267, 269
*Independence Day*, 256
Independent Broadcasting Authority (IBA), 194
Indian Workers' Association, 154
Inns, George, 128, 130, 148
International Commentary, 112
Interracial marriage, 109–110, 120–121, 266
Iraqi audiences, 87
*It Ain't Half Hot Mum*, 155, 197
'It Ain't Half Racist Mum', 263
  Hall, Stuart, 161
ITV archives, 23
ITV audience research, 33, 54–56, 198–201
  *Curry and Chips*, 201
  group surveys, 214
  Independent Broadcasting Authority (IBA), 58

Jaffrey, Saeed, 241
James, Horace, 96, 121

*Jazz Singer, The*, 136
*Jeffersons, The*, 238
Jennings, Humphrey, 78
*Jericho*, 67
Jhally, Sut, 247
John, Errol, 95, 115, 136, 189
Johnson, Walter, 168, 262, 266
Joint Industry Committee for Television Advertising Research (JICTAR), 157
Jolson, Al, 136, 139, 142, 148
*Jolson Story, The*, 136
Jones, Claudia, 164, 171
Jones, Gemma, 120
Joshi, Jagmohan, 154
Joy, Peggy, 208

Kaas, Erling, 176
Kenny, Mary, 231, 242–243, 268
Kentucky Minstrels, 142
Kenya, 75, 87, 103, 113, 175
Kenyan audiences, 87
*Keys*, 171
*Khartoum*, 138, 141
*King Solomon's Mines*, 67, 73–74
Komey, Ellis, 130
Korda, Alexander, 137
Korda, Zoltan, 64, 66, 152
Kretzmer, Herbert, 231, 268
Ku Klux Klan, 175
Kureishi, Hanif, 241, 251

Labour Party, 241
Lamb, Kenneth, 128–130, 135
Lambert, R.S., 51
*Lawrence of Arabia*, 140
Learie Constantine
  Lady Constantine, 147
*Lenny Henry Show, The*, 232, 238
Leontovich, Eugenie, 138
Lewis, Justin, 247
*Link*, 171
*Lives of a Bengal Lancer*, 69, 73, 75–77, 139, 154
London bookshops, 175
London Press Exchange (LPE), 44, 48, 50–51
London Public Morality Council (LPMC), 21
*Love Thy Neighbour*, 22, 28–29, 130, 197, 200–201, 228, 231
  methodology, 214–215
  Special audience research report, 212–218, 263
Lovegreen, J. Y., 172, 185
Lynch, Kenny, 201

*Magnet*, 171
Malik, Sarita, 259
*Man From the Sun, A*, 115
Manley, Carmen, 188
Marcell, Joseph, 256
Markle, Meghan (Duchess of Sussex), 273
Martin Luther King Jr, 246
*Masquerade*, 153
Mass Observation, 47, 69, 235, 244–245
Mau Mau, 173, 175
Mayhew, Christopher, 98, 103, 112–113
Mbu, Matthew T., 139–140, 263
McKinney, Nina Mae, 77
McLean, William, 91
McNish, Althea, 190
'Men of Africa', 91
Milligan, Spike, 154, 201–202, 211
*Millionnairess*, 141
*Mind Your Language*, 197, 231
Minstrelsy, see Blackface
Mitchell, George, 142, 158
Mitchell, Warren, 117
*Mixed Blessings*, 232, 237
*Monsoon Island*, 83
Morgan, Tom, 207, 209
'Multi-Racial Britain', 201
Munroe, Carmen, 115, 136, 233–235, 237, 248–249
Murphy, Stephen, 129, 146
*Mutiny on the Bounty*, 74
*My Beautiful Laundrette*, 241, 251

NAACP (National Association for the Advancement of Colored People), 85, 262
*Nanook of the North*, 79
National Committee for Commonwealth Immigrants (NCCI), 129
National Council of Public Morals (NCPM), 39–40
National Front, 194–195, 204
National Viewers' and Listeners' Association (NVLA), 21, 31, 42–43
*Negombo Coast*, 83
*Negro Soldier*, 92
Netflix, 271
Neutrality, 17–18, 113, 208
New Beacon Books, 171
Newbould, A. E., 39
Newton, Thandiwe (Thandie), 258
NHS, 133
Nielsen ratings, 54
*Night Mail*, 82
*No Problem!*, 232–233, 238
'Non-Whites on British Television', 162, 201

# Index

O. J. Whitley, 21
O'Connor, T. P., 39, 41
Okuri, P., 130
*Old Bones of the River*, 74
Olivier, Laurence, 140
*One Family*, 80
*Only Fools and Horses*, 233
Oyelowo, David, 258

*Palaver*, 73
*Party, The*, 154
Paulu, Burton, 53
Peace Ballot, 47
Peacock Committee (1986), 38
*Peaky Blinders*, 258
Pierce, Chester M., 169
Pilkington Committee, 37, 42, 57, 150
Pilkington Report, 42–43, 58
Pitt, David, 128, 144, 149
Poitier, Sidney, 7, 133
Police intimidation, 256
*Pool of London*, 140
Porter, David, 96
Powell, Enoch, 98, 194, 196, 240
Powell, Vince, 213
*Projection of England*, 31, 39, 45
*Proud Valley*, 67

Race Relations Act, 98, 126, 150, 202
'Race Relations in Africa', 98–99, 101–114
Race Relations Board, 157, 195, 197, 202, 212
Racial battle fatigue, 166, 235
Racial slurs, 201, 213, 216–217
Racial violence, 122, 227
  in the United States, 7
*Rainbow City*, 28, 35, 99, 107, 116–117, 120–125, 197, 199, 202, 233
  BBC Special Audience Research Report, 95–98, 124–125
*Rains of Ranchipur, The*, 138
Randell, Paulette, 256
Rastafarians, 223, 242
Reagan, Ronald, 239
*Real McCoy, The*, 255, 257
Reilf, Robert, 194
Reith, John, 17, 46, 50–51
Relph, Michael, 140
Report of the Committee on the Future of Broadcasting, *see* Annan Report
*Rhodes of Africa*, 69, 73
Rice, Thomas Dartmouth, 182
Robeson, Paul, 63–67, 77, 85, 93, 169
Rockefeller Foundation, 46, 70
Romero, Cesar, 138

*Room with a View, A*, 257
*Roots*, 159, 201, 221
*Rose of Washington Square*, 136
Rose, E. J. B., 129
Rotha, Paul, 78, 81, 103
Royal Historical Society, 16
  *Race, Ethnicity & Equality in UK History: A Report and Resource for Change*, 17
Royal Statistical Society, 101
Runnymede Trust, 222
Ryan, Pat, 51

*Sammy and Rosie Get Laid*, 251
*Sanders of the River*, 64–67, 74–77, 84, 93, 138, 143
*Sapphire*, 110, 140, 187
Scobie, Edward, 130, 144, 164, 173, 178, 182, 185, 192, 263
Sekka, Johnny, 115, 141, 189
Sellers, Peter, 141, 154
Sellers, William, 88–89, 93, 265
Selsdon Committee, 37, 50
Sharma, Mardav, 160
*Sharpe*, 257
Shearer, Noira, 208
*Sheik, The*, 73
Silvey, Robert, 33, 44, 50–58, 101, 106, 200, 270
*Simba*, 173
Simms, Hilda, 176
Sims, Sylvia, 141
Sloane, Tom, 134
Smethwick, 98, 119
Smith, Will, 256
Smith, William, 166
Sociology, 100, 210
*Son of the Sheik*, 73
*Song of Ceylon*, 82
Speight, Johnny, 19, 117, 154, 202, 265, 268
Squires, Lloyd, 145
Stopes, Marie, 39
*Storm over the Nile*, 152
*Swanee River*, 138
Swann, Michael, 210
Sykes Committee, 37

*Tales of Manhattan*, 67
Tallents, Stephen, 19, 30–31, 33, 39, 44–46, 265
TAM (Television Audience Measurement), 53–56
Tam-O-Meter, 200
*Tandoori Nights*, 232, 249
Tannenbaum, Percy, 221

*Tarzan the Ape Man*, 74
Television Act of 1954, 18
*Tell England*, 86
Tennenbaum, Percy, 222, 226
Thackeray, William, 187
*That Was the Week That Was*, 21, 146
Thatcher, Margaret, 194, 240
The Commission on Educational and
    Cultural Films (CECF), 40
*Thief of Baghdad, The*, 138
Thorne, Barrie, 134, 146, 152, 262
*Till Death Us Do Part*, 22, 29, 35, 99–100,
    114, 116–120, 130, 142, 154, 197,
    200–201, 204, 212, 227, 231, 265,
    267
  'Alf's Dilemma, or Cleaning Up TV',
    118–120
  blackface, 155, 211
  Special Audience Research Report,
    204–211
TNT (US cable channel), 255
*Tropic*, 144, 164, 173, 177–178, 181, 187,
    189–190, 263
  Attack on offices, 174

Ullswater Committee, 18, 37, 50
  Ullswater Report, 37

Unity Bookshop, 175
University of Leicester, Centre for Mass
    Communications Research, 31, 60

*Villages of Lanka*, 83
*Voice*, 255

Walker, Rudolph, 212
Ward, Roy, 140
*West Indian Gazette*, 164, 171–172
*West Indian World*, 241
*West Indies Calling*, 92, 101
*West Indies Observer*, 171
West, Clive, 4, 143–144, 150, 262
Whitehouse, Mary, 31, 43, 119
Whitley, O. J. (Oliver), 149–150
Williams, Patrick, 173
*Windmill in Barbados*, 82
Winston, Brian, 160
World War II, 88–93
  documentary film, 88
Worrell, Trix, 249–250, 260
Wright, Basil, 78–79, 82, 91–92, 103
Wright, Lorenzo, 176
Wyndham Goldie, Grace, 104–106

*Z-Cars*, 115, 158

For EU product safety concerns, contact us at Calle de José Abascal, 56–1°, 28003 Madrid, Spain or eugpsr@cambridge.org.